# THE SOLDIER'S GUIDE

# THE SOLDIER'S GUIDE

## THE COMPLETE GUIDE TO U.S. ARMY TRADITIONS, TRAINING, DUTIES, AND RESPONSIBILITIES

### DEPARTMENT OF THE ARMY

Skyhorse Publishing

www.skyhorsepublishing.com

Library of Congress Cataloging-in-Publication Data

The soldier's guide.
    p. cm.
 ISBN-13: 978-1-60239-164-2 (alk. paper)
 ISBN-10: 1-60239-164-5 (alk. paper)
 1. United States. Army—Handbooks, manuals, etc.

U113.S57 2007
355.00973—dc22

                                    2007020056


10 9 8 7 6 5 4 3 2 1

Printed in the United States of America

# FOREWORD

The Soldier is the ultimate guardian of America's freedom. In over 120 countries around the world, Soldiers like you are protecting our Nation's freedom and working to provide a better life for oppressed or impoverished peoples. It is no accident our Army succeeds everywhere we are called to serve—the loyalty and selfless service of the American Soldier guarantee it.

Today our Army is fighting directly for the American people. This global war on terrorism is about our future. It's about ensuring our children and grandchildren enjoy the same liberties we cherish. While difficult tasks remain, victory is certain. The efforts and sacrifices of the American Soldier will assure it.

Although our technology has changed, the core of our success remains the American Soldier. Whether equipped with a bayonet or an Apache helicopter, the American Soldier is the most lethal weapon in the world. Regardless of MOS or location on the battlefield, the American Soldier will accomplish the mission—and will destroy any enemy interference with that mission.

This Soldier's Guide applies to every soldier in the Army—active, reserve, and National Guard—in every rank and MOS. It condenses important information from a number of Army Regulations, Field Manuals, DA Pamphlets and other publications. This manual describes your role in the Army, your obligations, and what you can expect from your leaders. Other subject areas are Army history, training, and professional development. This manual also describes standards in appearance and conduct and selected individual combat tasks that are important for every Soldier to master.

This manual gives you a good reference to find answers for many questions. It helps clarify and reinforce standards and helps prepare you to assume leadership positions. Read it thoroughly and continue to do the great work American Soldiers have done for almost 230 years.

JACK L. TILLEY
Sergeant Major of the Army

PETER J. SCHOOMAKER
General, US Army
Chief of Staff

# Tables

---

Field Manual
No. 7-21.13

**FM 7-21.13**
Headquarters
Department of the Army
Washington, DC, 2 February 2004

# The Soldier's Guide

## Contents

This publication supersedes FM 7-21.13, 15 October 2003.

# Figures

# Vignettes

# Illustrations

# Preface

This Field Manual is dedicated to the men and women of the United States Army in the active component, the Army National Guard and the US Army Reserve—altogether America's finest fighting machine. You are the soldiers that fight and win the Nation's wars. Be proud.

FM 7-21.13, *The Soldier's Guide*, is a pocket reference for subjects in which all soldiers must maintain proficiency, regardless of rank, component or military occupational specialty (MOS). It condenses information from other field manuals, training circulars, soldier training publications, Army regulations, and other sources. It addresses both general subjects and selected combat tasks. While not all-inclusive or intended as a stand-alone document, the guide offers soldiers a ready reference in many subjects.

FM 7-21.13 is divided into seven chapters. Chapter 1 describes the importance of Army Values and the obligations of every soldier. Chapter 2 provides a short history of the Army and examines the environment in which it operates. Chapter 3 addresses the duties, responsibilities and authority of the soldier, how to present a military appearance, and an introduction to the Uniform Code of Military Justice. The importance of customs, courtesies, and traditions is in Chapter 4. The soldier's role in training and a brief description of training management are in Chapter 5. Chapter 6 discusses the importance of counseling and professional development. The benefits of serving in the Army are described in Chapter 7. The appendices contain specific combat tasks that are important to every soldier and information on programs the Army offers to assist soldiers and their family members.

*The Soldier's Guide* provides information critical to the success of soldiers in the operational environment. Reading this manual will help prepare soldiers for full spectrum operations and is a tool in building the Future Force soldier. This book will be useful to every soldier who reads it.

The proponent for the publication is Headquarters, US Army Training and Doctrine Command (TRADOC). Send comments and recommendations on DA Form 2028 (Recommended Changes to Publications and Blank Forms) to Commandant, US Army Sergeants Major Academy, ATTN: ATSS-D, Fort Bliss, TX 79918-8002 or through the Sergeants Major Academy website at usasma.bliss.army.mil.

Unless stated otherwise, masculine nouns or pronouns do not refer exclusively to men.

This publication contains copyrighted material.

# ACKNOWLEDGMENTS

The copyright owners listed here have granted permission to reproduce material from their works. The Source Notes lists other sources of quotations, vignettes, and examples.

*Top Sergeant: The Life and Times of Sergeant Major of the Army William G. Bainbridge,* by William G. Bainbridge, © William G. Bainbridge, New York: Ballantine, 1995.

"To Relieve Bastogne," by Don Stivers, © Don Stivers, Stivers Publishing, 1990.

Dale E. Wilson, "American Armor in the First World War," *A Weekend With the Great War: Proceedings of the Fourth Annual Great War Interconference Seminar,* ed. by Steven Weingarten, © Cantigny First Division Foundation, 1996.

"Captain Nathan Hale (1755-1776)," by Mary J. Ortner, Ph.D., © Mary J. Ortner, 2001, Connecticut Society of the Sons of the American Revolution.

Stephen Hardin, "The Battle of the Alamo," Handbook of Texas Online, www.tsha.utexas.edu/handbook/online, © Texas State Historical Association, 2003. Used with permission.

Don Rivers, "William Pittenger, Medal of Honor Recipient," *Village News* (13 Aug 1998) © Fallbrook Historical Society, Fallbrook, CA, 1998-1999.

*We Were Soldiers Once... and Young,* LTG Harold G. Moore, US Army (Retired) and Joseph L. Galloway, © LTG H. G. Moore and Joseph L. Galloway, Random House, Incorporated, 1992.

*War as I Knew It* by General George S. Patton. Copyright © 1947 by Beatrice Patton Walters, Ruth Patton Totten, and George Smith Totten. Copyright © renewed 1975 by MG George Patton, Ruth Patton Totten, John K. Waters, Jr., and George P. Waters. Reprinted by permission of Houghton Mifflin Company. All rights reserved.

*The Greenhill Dictionary of Military Quotations,* edited by Peter G. Tsouras. Copyright © Peter G. Tsouras, London: Greenhill Books and Mechanicsburg, PA: Stackpole Books, 2000.

Carl von Clausewitz, *On War,* edited by Michael Howard and Peter Paret. Copyright © 1976 by Princeton University Press. Reprinted by permission of Princeton University Press.

# Introduction

Since the events of 11 September 2001, it is more evident than ever that every American has the duty to contribute to the well being of our Nation and its people; military service is one form of contribution. It is a privilege to bear arms as a soldier in the defense of a free people. This privilege is afforded only to individuals of good standing and of good reputation. What you do with this opportunity is up to you. You took an oath that binds you to this organization called the Army. Taking that oath meant that you would defend our Constitution and comply with all the orders, regulations and directions given by superiors. Always remember this commitment.

Although being a soldier is a dangerous profession, it can be the greatest and most rewarding adventure of your life. The friends you make while in the service will be your friends for life. This is especially true if you serve with them in combat. If you stay in the Army you may serve with them again in various jobs and locations. Where the Army takes you depends on your personal and professional goals. When I was drafted in May of 1966, I planned to serve only two years, but given all the opportunities the Army afforded me, I spent a total of 24 years in the service. Many of those opportunities are available to you; it is up to you to place yourself in the position to take advantage of them.

This manual is a general guide that gives you a wealth of information about the United States Army. Throughout your military service you have many questions. Even if this guide does not have every answer you need, it should give you the source to find the answer. I remember reading my Soldier's Guide (the 1961 version) during basic training and advanced individual training as a medical corpsman. While it answered some questions and was helpful in refreshing my memory, its main purpose was to help us adjust to Army life because the more we knew about the Army, the quicker the adjustment would be. This manual you have today applies to every soldier in the Army. Still, it's a guide. You may have to look in other Army publications for more detailed answers. Form the habit of using it whenever a question about the Army comes to mind or in discussion with your fellow soldiers.

Chapter 1 describes the individual soldier's obligations to the Army and leaders' obligations to soldiers. You will find a discussion of Army values, those qualities that make the Army the elite organization it has become. Although you already know Army values, this chapter will help explain why they are important. This chapter tells you about team building and its importance in the successful completion of the mission. Some day you will be ready to assume a leadership position. When you demonstrate the qualities highlighted in this chapter, you will have to accept the responsibility to lead. In 1968, I was a staff sergeant responsible for 100 soldiers going through medical training. My leaders saw something in me and I also thought I could contribute even more to the Army, and so I applied for a direct commission. The teaching, coaching, and mentoring of my leaders and my own assessment of my leadership skills allowed me to assume positions of greater responsibility. It is the nature of military service for soldiers to become leaders.

Chapter 2 contains a short history of the Army and it describes the environment in which the Army operates. You can also refresh your knowledge of how our government is organized and the Army's place within the government. The history of our Army goes back over 300 years, and you are part of a page in that history. I didn't imagine when I came in the Army that I would receive the Medal of Honor, much less among a group that, for the first time ever, was composed of all four branches of the service. As you are reading do your very best to understand where you fit in the larger picture. As a member of the military you might serve in any number of locations so be prepared to meet an ever widening set of situations. You are a soldier but you could perform a variety of duties in the completion of your service. Because you support and defend the Constitution, it is important to understand how the government works and how it affects you.

Chapter 3 details the duties, responsibilities, and authority of soldiers. You will learn the sources of military authority and the reasons why authority exists. This chapter also provides a guide on appearance and uniform standards of the Army and answers most questions you may have about the Uniform Code of Military Justice and the Army's standards of conduct. These are basic requirements of all soldiers.

Chapter 4 addresses the customs, courtesies, and traditions of the Army. Any organization that has been in existence as long as the Army has many customs and traditions. They help make the Army and each unit unique. It may be the motto or greeting that sets you apart as a member of a specific unit, or it can even be the simple act of standing at parade rest, but our customs and traditions are important to the spirit and morale of soldiers. Take the time to learn these customs and traditions and what they mean, always remembering that someone like you may have been the one that started that tradition.

Chapter 5 contains information on training and how it will impact you. For a person to be proficient in any skill, they must first have a good understanding of what is to be accomplished. The knowledge needed may come from classroom instruction, demonstrations, or field exercises. Keep in mind that your training teaches you to shoot, move, communicate, and survive so your unit can succeed in combat. The more you know the better your chances for success. As a combat medic with an infantry company during the Vietnam War, I trained on a number of skills that were not normally expected of a medic. Our company required each soldier to be able to adjust artillery, operate a radio, and many other tasks that, at the time, I did not consider necessary. But a short time later I had to perform all those tasks together, along with my basic medical training, and it made a difference. During your training you must trust the knowledge and experience of your leaders and learn all that is asked of you. Skills that you consider unnecessary now may turn out to be important later.

Chapter 6 is about counseling and professional development. Here is how the Army lets you know how you are doing and what you need to improve. The service has a set path along which you can advance but you are responsible for achieving your full potential. Your self-improvement program is up to you. My experience over a period of 24 years shows how a person can plan and advance in the service. Even though I had planned to serve only two years when I was drafted, I discovered that I enjoyed soldiering and wanted to continue being a soldier. I took advantage of opportunities the Army offers every soldier who has the ability, discipline, and desire to succeed and improve. I was able to have what was a rewarding and successful career.

In Chapter 7 you'll find detailed information on the benefits of serving in the Army and in the appendices, the various programs the Army has to help soldiers and their families. It is good information that will answer many of the questions you have throughout your career.

I wish I could give you the secret of success, but I don't have it. All I can say is that your success in the Army is a direct reflection of your effort. Work each day to improve yourself. Make a commitment to make your unit better by being a productive, proactive member of that unit. Try to learn something new each day because the Army is a fast moving organization and you must never stop learning. Treat your fellow soldiers as if they were part of your family. They are. In all things, do your best; what you make of yourself is your responsibility. And one last thing—be proud of being a soldier. You are defending our Nation, our people, and our way of life. There is no more honorable profession. Even after you leave the service you can be proud to say, "I am a soldier."

Charles C. Hagemeister
LTC, US Army (Retired), MOH
1 September 2003

## Biography of LTC Charles C. Hagemeister, US Army (Retired), MOH

Lieutenant Colonel Charles Chris Hagemeister (US Army, Retired) has served the Nation in both the enlisted and commissioned ranks. He has been both a reserve and regular Army officer. His assignments include tactical and training units, in peacetime and in combat.

He was drafted into the United States Army in March 1966 and entered service in May 1966 at Lincoln, Nebraska. He went through basic training at Fort Polk, Louisiana, and completed advanced individual training as a combat medic at Fort Sam Houston, Texas, in November 1966.

LTC Hagemeister was assigned to the 1st Battalion, 5th Cavalry of the 1st Cavalry Division in the Republic of Vietnam. He was a Specialist 4 (SPC) at the time, supporting a platoon in A Company in Binh Dinh Province on 20 March 1967 during the Vietnam War. SPC Hagemeister's platoon suddenly came under heavy attack from three sides by an enemy force occupying well concealed, fortified positions and supported by machineguns and mortars.

After SPC Hagemeister saw two of his comrades seriously wounded in the initial action, he unhesitatingly and with total disregard for his safety raced through the deadly hail of enemy fire to provide them medical aid. SPC Hagemeister learned that the platoon leader and several other soldiers also had been wounded. He continued to brave the withering enemy fire and crawled forward to render lifesaving treatment and to offer words of encouragement. While attempting to evacuate the seriously wounded soldiers, SPC Hagemeister was taken under fire at close range by an enemy sniper. Realizing that the lives of his fellow soldiers depended on his actions, SPC Hagemeister seized a rifle from a fallen comrade and killed the sniper and three other enemy soldiers who were attempting to encircle his position. He then silenced an enemy machinegun that covered the area with deadly fire.

Unable to remove the wounded to a less exposed location and aware of the enemy's efforts to isolate his unit, he dashed through the heavy fire to secure help from a nearby platoon. Returning with help, he placed men in positions to cover his advance as he moved to evacuate the wounded forward of his location. These efforts successfully completed, he then moved to the other flank and evacuated additional wounded men, despite the fact that his every move drew fire from the enemy. SPC Hagemeister's repeated heroic and selfless actions at the risk of his life saved the lives of many of his comrades and inspired their actions in repelling the enemy assault. SPC Hagemeister received the Medal of Honor on 14 May 1968.

After his service in Vietnam, LTC Hagemeister (then Specialist 5) served at McDonald Army Hospital in Fort Eustis, Virginia, and then as a medical platoon sergeant in C Company, 1st Battalion, US Army Medical Training Center at Fort Sam Houston, Texas.

LTC Hagemeister received a direct commission in the US Army Reserve as an armor officer. After training at Fort Knox, Kentucky he was assigned to Fort Hood, Texas where he served as a platoon leader, cavalry troop executive officer, and squadron liaison officer. In 1970 LTC Hagemeister went to Schweinfurt, Germany where he commanded Headquarters and Headquarters Troop, 3d Squadron, 7th Cavalry of the 3d Infantry Division where he was also the Squadron Intelligence Officer.

After attending the Armor Officer Advanced Course and the Data Processing Course LTC Hagemeister went back to Fort Hood in September 1977. There he served in the Communications Research and Development Command as the Tactical Operations System Controller. In 1980 he returned to Fort Knox and served as the Chief of Armor Test Development branch and later became the Chief of Platoon, Company, and Troop Training. LTC Hagemeister became a Regular Army officer on 15 December 1981 and was later promoted to Major. Following this promotion, LTC Hagemeister became the executive officer for the 1st Battalion, 1st Training Brigade at Fort Knox. He then attended the US Army Command and General Staff College at Fort Leavenworth, Kansas. He remained at Fort Leavenworth as the Director of the Division Commander's Course and then as the Author/Instructor for Corps Operations, Center for Army Tactics in the Command and General Staff College.

LTC Hagemeister retired from the Army in June 1990 but continued to serve the Nation as a contractor supporting the Battle Command Training Program (BCTP) as a Maneuver and Fire Support Workstation Controller with the World Class Opposing Forces (WCOPFOR).

**Chapter 1**

# The Individual Soldier's Role in the Army

Soldiers are the Army's most important resource. Trained, fit, and determined soldiers, strengthened by the warrior ethos, win America's wars. This chapter describes the importance of the Army values in developing and maintaining the warrior ethos—the will to win. The importance of the team and the soldier's role in it is in this chapter, too. Here also are some of the basics of leadership—decision making, ethical reasoning and what leaders must BE, KNOW, and DO.

For more information on Army values, teambuilding, leadership, and ethical reasoning, see FM 6-22 (22-100), *Army Leadership* and the Army Leadership website at www.leadership.army.mil.

## SECTION I - THE WARRIOR ETHOS AND ARMY VALUES

1-1.    The profession of arms involves the disciplined use of legally sanctioned force. It imposes many demands but imparts lasting rewards upon those who enter it. While the professional calling of the soldier is to support and defend the Constitution, the challenge is to learn the profession well enough to accomplish any mission effectively while protecting the force. The soldiers of the United States Army serve around the world in a multitude of different missions and roles. We are all volunteers. Although there are many reasons why each soldier joins the service, at some level one of them is the desire to serve our Nation.

1-2.    Soldiers serve America, our fellow citizens, and protect our way of life. That is a tough job and a great responsibility considering the dangerous state of the world. But soldiers—and marines, sailors, airmen, and coastguardsmen—throughout America's history have stepped forward and pledged their lives, their fortunes, and their sacred honor to do precisely that. It is no different today.

> *The most impressive thing about any Army is the individual Soldier. He will always be the one responsible for taking and holding the ground in support of our foreign policy, mission, goals, and objectives. Even with sophisticated technology and advanced equipment, an Army cannot fight, sustain, and win a war without individual, quality Soldiers.*
>
> **SMA Glen E. Morrell**

1-3.    In the oaths of enlistment and commissioning, every soldier promises to support and defend the Constitution from all enemies and to be faithful to it. Enlisted soldiers also promise to obey the orders of the President and the officers appointed over them. Every team has a leader, and that leader is responsible for what the team does or fails to do. That is why obeying orders is necessary; your leader is responsible for all your military actions. When you take this oath you put into words your belief in the United States, our form of government, and our way of life. It is a formal statement supporting our freedoms that you will, if necessary, fight any enemy who tries to take those freedoms from us. In taking the oath, you became subject to military law as well as civilian law. You became a soldier. Because you are a soldier, you will bear arms in defense of our country until released by lawful authority. These are the fundamental obligations of every soldier in the US Army.

1-4.    Human nature and inalienable rights are the same now as when the writers of the Declaration of Independence put those immortal words to paper: "We hold these truths to be self-evident..." The dangers our Nation and people face now are as real and daunting as then. We have a common bond with those soldiers who first won our freedom and with those who paid in blood to maintain it. We today have their example to inspire and educate us. We all stand a little taller because we share the title, soldier.

1-5.    The soldier, with comrades in arms from other services, is the Nation's ultimate guarantor of our way of life. Where America sends her soldiers is where America makes the commitment to free the oppressed, relieve suffering or protect freedom. The newly recruited Private and the General who has served 35 years in multiple wars each have made the same promise: to support and defend the Constitution of the United States. We live by the same Army values and exhibit the same warrior ethos.

## THE WARRIOR ETHOS

1-6.    Your adherence to Army values and your commitment to doing your best is the basis of the warrior ethos. The warrior ethos is an individual and collective quality of all soldiers. It is that frame of mind whereby soldiers will not quit until they have accomplished their mission. It compels soldiers to fight through all conditions to victory, no matter how long it takes and no matter how much effort is required. It is the professional attitude that inspires every soldier to fulfill his obligations, regardless of the obstacles.

> *Yours is the profession of arms, the will to win, the sure knowledge that in war there is no substitute for victory, that if you lose, the nation will be destroyed, that the very obsession of your public service must be Duty, Honor, Country...*

**General of the Army Douglas MacArthur**

1-7.    At its core, the warrior ethos is the refusal to accept failure and instead overcome all obstacles with honor. It begins as the soldier's selfless commitment to the Nation, mission, unit and fellow soldiers. It is developed and sustained through discipline, realistic training, commitment to Army values, and pride in the Army's heritage. This demands continual development, learning new skills and preparing to lead soldiers. Take another look at the Introduction to this FM. When (then) SPC Hagemeister, a medic, saw that he would have to fight in order to do his job, he did it without hesitation. He was trained and confident in his ability to provide medical care for his fellow soldiers and in his ability to fight to get it done.

1-8.    The Army has forged the warrior ethos on training grounds from Valley Forge to the Combat Training Centers and sharpened it in combat from Bunker Hill to Baghdad. It echoes through the precepts in the Code of Conduct. The warrior ethos produces the will to win. Will and a winning spirit apply in more situations than just those requiring physical courage. Sometimes you'll have to carry on for long periods in very difficult situations. The difficulties soldiers face may not always be ones of physical danger, but of great physical, emotional, and mental stress, as can occur in support operations. Will empowers you to drive on during extended deployments, under appalling conditions, and without basic necessities.

1-9.    Confidence enhances both physical courage and will. That confidence in the ability of leaders, fellow soldiers, and the justness of the mission strengthen the soldier's resolve to fulfill his duty to the best of his ability. He knows that if he is wounded, his buddies and the Army medical system will do everything in their power to save his life. He knows that if he is captured or missing, the Nation will spare no resource in returning him to US control. And he knows that if he is killed in battle, he died fighting for his fellow soldiers and protecting our people in a just cause.

1-10.    Self-confidence is the faith that you'll act correctly and ethically in any situation, even one in which you're under stress and don't have all the information you want. Self-confidence comes from competence. It's based on mastering skills, which takes hard work, realistic training and dedication. Soldiers who know their own capabilities and believe in themselves are self-confident. Don't mistake loudmouthed bragging or self-promotion for self-confidence. Self-confident soldiers don't need to advertise because their actions say it all. Self-confidence is important for leaders, soldiers, and teams. Self-confident leaders instill confidence in their people. In combat, self-confidence helps soldiers control doubt and reduce anxiety. Together with will and self-discipline, self-confidence helps leaders act—do what must be done in circumstances where it would be easier to do nothing—and to convince their people to act as well.

> *No mission too difficult, no sacrifice too great—Duty First!*
> **Motto of the 1st Infantry Division**

1-11.    The effect of the warrior ethos is that all soldiers understand they must be prepared, and are confident in their ability, to accomplish their assigned tasks—even in the face of enemy resistance—anytime, anywhere on the battlefield. The clear message is this: regardless of where adversaries encounter you, the American soldier, you will not hesitate to destroy them if they attempt to interfere with your mission, whatever it may be. Don't overlook the importance of this. Many other soldiers depend on what you do, so you cannot allow any obstacle or enemy action to prevent you from accomplishing your assigned task.

1-12.    America has a proud tradition of winning. The ability to forge victory out of the chaos of battle includes overcoming fear, hunger, deprivation, and fatigue. The Army wins because it fights hard; it fights hard because it trains hard; and it trains hard because that's the way to *win*. The warrior ethos fuels the fire to fight through the worst of conditions to victory no matter how long it takes, no matter how much effort is required. It sustains the will to win when the situation looks hopeless and doesn't show any indications of getting better, when being away from home and family is a profound hardship. The soldier who jumps on a grenade to save his comrades is courageous, without question. That action requires great physical courage, and pursuing victory over time also requires a deep moral courage to persevere and concentrate on the mission.

1-13.    Actions that safeguard the nation occur everywhere that you find soldiers. The warrior ethos spurs the lead tank driver across a line of departure into uncertainty. It causes the bone-tired medic continually to put others first. It pushes the sweat-soaked military police soldier to remain vigilant regardless of the extreme temperature. It drives the infantry soldier steadily toward the objective despite heavy enemy fire. It presses the signaler to provide communications in a blinding sandstorm. And the warrior ethos urges the truck driver along roads bounded by minefields because fellow soldiers at an isolated outpost need supplies. Such tireless motivation comes in part from the comradeship that springs from the warrior ethos. Soldiers fight for each other; they would rather die than let their buddies down. Such loyalty runs front to rear as well as left to right: mutual support marks Army culture regardless of who you are, where you are, or what you are doing.

*We will always complete the Mission to the Best of our Ability.*

*We will Never Surrender.*

*We will Never leave a Soldier behind.*

*An attack on any one of us is an attack on us all.*

*Where goes one so goes us all.*

**Creed of the 272nd Chemical Company, Massachusetts ARNG**

1-14.    Each soldier has an important job to do, necessary to the overall unit mission. Soldiers throughout the Army, for example, perform the duties of medics, infantrymen, cooks, truck drivers, mechanics, legal clerks, and aviators. We bring fuel to the tanks, we scout for the enemy, we listen to the enemy's signals, and we teach young Americans what it takes to be a soldier. We defend against air attacks, ensure soldiers are properly paid, and process awards to recognize soldiers' accomplishments. We know that these efforts and more support a team and that the whole is greater than the sum of its parts. That realization, coupled with the warrior ethos, cause us to complete our task successfully. If the enemy tries to interfere with our ability to accomplish an assigned task, the warrior ethos causes us to defeat that interference.

1-15.    The warrior ethos concerns character, shaping who you are and what you do. It is linked to Army values such as personal courage, loyalty to comrades, and dedication to duty. Both loyalty and duty involve putting your life on the line, even when there's little chance of survival, for the good of a cause larger than yourself. That's the clearest example of selfless service. Soldiers never give up on their comrades and they never compromise on doing their duty. Integrity underlies the character of the Army as well. The warrior ethos requires unrelenting and consistent determination to do what is right and to do it with pride, both in war and military operations other than war. Understanding what is right requires respect for both your comrades and other people involved in complex arenas like peace operations and nation assistance. In such situations, decisions to use lethal or nonlethal force severely test judgment and discipline. In every circumstance, soldiers turn the personal warrior ethos into a collective commitment to win with honor.

**A soldier provides security during Operation Iraqi Freedom.**

## THE ARMY VALUES

1-16.  Our individual effectiveness as part of the Army team comes from within, from our upbringing, our character, and our values. The Army is an organization that is guided by values. Army values are the basic building blocks that enable us to see what is right or wrong in any situation. They build the warrior ethos and they are mutually dependent—you can't fully follow one while ignoring another.

1-17.  The Army's core values are loyalty, duty, respect, selfless service, honor, integrity and personal courage. They form the acronym LDRSHIP. Fulfilling your obligations as an American soldier is possible by accepting and living these values. These values tell you what you need to be, every day, in every action you take and remind us and the world who we are and what we stand for.

### LOYALTY

1-18.  Bear true faith and allegiance to the US Constitution, the Army, your unit, and other soldiers.

> *To be a good leader and a good soldier, you must be loyal. Stand by your organization and the officers, non-commissioned officers, and fellow soldiers in it.*
>
> **FM 21-13, *The Soldier's Guide*, 1961**

1-19.  Bearing true faith and allegiance is a matter of believing in and devoting yourself to something or someone. You began your Army career by promising to support and defend the Constitution. Your loyalty to the Constitution also means obedience to the orders of the President and higher ranking officers and NCOs. Since before the founding of the republic,

America's Army has respected its subordination to the President—a civilian. A loyal soldier is one who supports the leadership and stands up for fellow soldiers. You show your loyalty to your unit by doing your share, without complaint and to the best of your ability. The Army's service ethic is fundamental in building loyalty.

1-20. As a soldier who displays loyalty do the following:

- Put obligations in correct order: the Constitution, the Army, the unit, and finally, self.

- Show faithfulness to unit and comrades by finishing all tasks with them.

- Carry out tough orders without expressing personal criticism.

- Defend soldiers against unfair treatment from outside or above.

1-21. Loyalty to fellow soldiers is critical for generating confidence and trust. Loyalty to one's leaders and fellow soldiers is the most vital resource a unit has. It is this commitment that causes units and soldiers to risk everything to succeed and to bring everyone back. You will find that after enduring a difficult experience the bond between the soldiers of your unit will be even stronger.

---

### The Loyalty of Private First Class Ernest E. West

Private First Class West, was a soldier assigned to L Company, 14th Infantry Regiment in the 25th Infantry Division. On 12 October 1952, near Sataeri, Korea, PFC West voluntarily accompanied a contingent to locate and destroy a reported enemy outpost. Nearing the objective, the patrol was ambushed and suffered numerous casualties. Observing his wounded leader lying in an exposed position, Private First Class West ordered the troops to withdraw and then braved intense fire to reach and assist him.

While attempting evacuation, he was attacked by three hostile soldiers employing grenades and small-arms fire. Quickly shifting his body to shelter the officer, he killed the assailants with his rifle and then carried the helpless man to safety. He was critically wounded, losing an eye in this action, but courageously returned through withering fire and bursting shells to assist other wounded soldiers. While evacuating two comrades, he closed with and killed three more enemy soldiers. Private First Class West's loyalty to his fellow soldiers and intrepid actions inspired all who observed him. He received the Medal of Honor.

---

## DUTY

1-22. Fulfill your obligations.

*I just wanted to serve my country. So here I am.*

PV2 Jeremiah Arnold

1-23. Duty is the sum total of all laws, rules and expectations that make up our organizational, civic, and moral obligations. We expect all members of the Army to fulfill their obligations, and we often expect individuals to exceed their duty, especially in ethical matters. Duty also means being able to do your job as part of a team. We each have a part to play in accomplishing the unit's mission. Some parts may be more visible, as in the leader's role, but every task is important. Recognition and willingness to do your duty is what protects all Americans' liberty.

1-24. Expressing the value of duty means, at a minimum, doing the following:

- Carry out the requirements of the position to the best of your ability.
- Fulfill legal, civic, and moral obligations.
- Sacrifice personal time in pursuit of excellence.

1-25. Duty begins with everything required of you by law, regulation, and orders; but it includes much more than that. Professionals do their work not just to the minimum standard, but to the very best of their ability and then try to improve on their performance. Commit to excellence in all aspects of your professional responsibility so that when the job is done you can look back and say, "I could not have given any more."

---

### Private First Class Clarence Eugene Sasser and Duty

While still a private first class, Sasser displayed devotion to duty while assigned to Headquarters and Headquarters Company, 3d Battalion, 60th Infantry, 9th Infantry Division in Ding Tuong Province of the Republic of Vietnam on 10 January 1968. He was serving as a medical aidman with Company A, 3d Battalion, on a reconnaissance in force operation. His company was making an air assault when suddenly it was taken under heavy small arms, recoilless rifle, machinegun and rocket fire from well fortified enemy positions on three sides of the landing zone. The company sustained over 30 casualties in the first few minutes. Without hesitation, PFC Sasser ran across an open rice paddy through a hail of fire to assist the wounded. After helping one soldier to safety, PFC Sasser was painfully wounded in the left shoulder by fragments of an exploding rocket. Refusing medical attention, he ran through a barrage of rocket and automatic weapons fire to aid casualties of the initial attack and, after giving them urgently needed treatment, continued to search for other wounded.

Despite two additional wounds immobilizing his legs, he dragged himself through the mud toward another soldier 100 meters away. Although in agonizing pain and faint from loss of blood, PFC Sasser reached the man, treated him and proceeded on to encourage another group of soldiers to crawl 200 meters to relative safety. There he attended their wounds for five hours until they were evacuated. PFC Sasser later received the Medal of Honor.

## RESPECT

1-26.    Treat people as they should be treated.

*Regardless of age or grade, soldiers should be treated as mature individuals. They are engaged in an honorable profession and deserve to be treated as such.*

**GEN Bruce C. Clarke**

1-27.    In the Soldier's Creed (on the back cover of this FM), we pledge to "treat others with dignity and respect and expect others to do the same." The Army is one huge team, made up of hundreds of component parts. There must be connections—ground rules—so that when one soldier approaches, works with, or talks to another, it is with immediate and unquestioned cooperation and respect. Respect is what allows us to expect and appreciate the best in other people instead of distrusting what is different. Respect is trusting fellow soldiers to do their duty, even while checking the quality of their work, if you are in a leadership position. Respect for others also means avoiding the use of profanity or obscene gestures.

1-28.    To consistently demonstrate respect, do the following:

* Have genuine concern for the safety and well being of others.

* Be discreet and tactful when correcting or questioning others.

* Be courteous and polite.

* Take care of yourself physically to show your self-respect.

1-29.    Respect is an essential component for the development of disciplined, cohesive, and effective war fighting teams. Discrimination or harassment on any basis eats away at trust and erodes unit cohesion. The Army has no tolerance for it. But respect also includes the broader issue of civility, the way people treat each other and those they come in contact with. Tact and courtesy demonstrate respect for others. Are there occasions when someone needs to raise his voice? Of course. When a soldier sees a safety problem, for example, he may have to get someone's attention right away, and it may be in a way that someone else may take offense to. But most soldiers realize such occurrence results from the desire to keep fellow soldiers free of unnecessary risk. Soldiers and DA civilians, like their leaders, treat everyone with dignity and respect. The soldiers who stand watch over the Tomb of the Unknown Soldier protect, for all of us, the respect we have for those who gave their lives in the defense of freedom.

---

## The Sentinel's Creed

My dedication to this sacred duty is total and wholehearted.

In the responsibility bestowed on me never will I falter.

And with dignity and perseverance my standard will remain perfection.

Through the years of diligence and praise and the discomfort of the elements, I will walk my tour in humble reverence to the best of my ability.

It is he who commands the respect I protect.

His bravery that made us so proud.

Surrounded by well meaning crowds by day, alone in the thoughtful peace of night, this soldier will in honored glory rest under my eternal vigilance.

(Creed of the Sentinel of the Tomb of the Unknown Soldier)

---

## SELFLESS SERVICE

1-30.  Put the welfare of the Nation, the Army, and your soldiers before your own.

> ... If a man hasn't discovered something that he will die for, he isn't fit to live.
>
> Dr. Martin Luther King, Jr.

1-31.  In serving your country, you are doing your duty loyally, without thought of recognition or gain. Your fellow soldiers and the mission come before your personal comfort or safety. Selfless service is your commitment as a team member to go a little further, endure a little longer, and look a little closer to see how you can add to the effort of the unit, platoon, or company. Selfless service is larger than just one person. With dedication to the value of selfless service, each and every soldier can rightfully look back and say, "I am proud to have served my country as a soldier."

1-32.  To demonstrate the value of selfless service, do the following:

- Focus your priorities on service to the Nation.
- Place the needs of the Army, your unit and your fellow soldiers above your personal gain.
- Balance the mission, your family, and your personal needs.
- Accept personal responsibility for your own performance.

1-33.  Selfless-service signifies the proper ordering of priorities. An old saying from horse cavalry days is "the horse, the saddle, the man." What it means is to fulfill your duty before thinking of your own comfort. Think of it as service before self. The welfare of the Nation and the organization come before the individual. You can easily see how closely related selfless service is with loyalty and duty. This only illustrates the importance of accepting all the Army values and ignoring none.

## SPC Michael John Fitzmaurice at Khe Sanh

SPC Fitzmaurice, 3d Platoon, Troop D, 2d Squadron, 17th Cavalry displayed selfless service at Khe Sanh in the Republic of Vietnam on 23 March 1971. SPC Fitzmaurice and three fellow soldiers were occupying a bunker when a company of North Vietnamese sappers infiltrated the area. At the onset of the attack SPC Fitzmaurice observed three explosive charges which had been thrown into the bunker by the enemy. Realizing the imminent danger to his comrades, and with complete disregard for his personal safety, he hurled two of the charges out of the bunker. He then threw his flak vest and himself over the remaining charge. By this courageous act he absorbed the blast and shielded his fellow-soldiers.

Although suffering from serious multiple wounds and partial loss of sight, he charged out of the bunker, and engaged the enemy until his rifle was damaged by the blast of an enemy hand grenade. While in search of another weapon, SPC Fitzmaurice encountered and overcame an enemy sapper in hand-to-hand combat. Having obtained another weapon, he returned to his original fighting position and inflicted additional casualties on the attacking enemy. Although seriously wounded, SPC Fitzmaurice refused to be medically evacuated, preferring to remain at his post. SPC Fitzmaurice's heroism in action at the risk of his life contributed significantly to the successful defense of the position and resulted in saving the lives of a number of his fellow soldiers. SPC Fitzmaurice received the Medal of Honor.

## HONOR

1-34.    Live up to all the Army values.

*Soldiers don't leave their buddies behind.*

**SSG David Santos**

1-35.    When we talk about "living up to" something, we mean being worthy of it. We must make choices, decisions, and actions based on the Army core values. Nowhere in our values training does it become more important to emphasize the difference between "knowing" the values and "living" them than when we discuss the value of honor. Honor is a matter of carrying out, acting, and living the values of respect, duty, loyalty, selfless service, integrity, and personal courage in everything you do.

**The Army Medal of Honor**

1-36. As an individual with honor do the following:

- Develop and maintain a keen sense of ethical conduct.

- Adhere to a public code of professional Army values.

- Identify with the ideals embodied in the Army values.

- Realize that your actions reflect on the unit and soldiers around you and act accordingly.

1-37. Noticing a problem and deciding to take action involves respect, duty, and honor. It was a matter of honor that soldiers, at great risk to themselves, distributed food in Somalia and kept the peace in Bosnia, while managing to protect the communities within their unit areas of responsibility. There are thousands of examples of soldiers who have distinguished themselves with honorable actions and service. It is significant that the Nation's highest military award is named The Medal of Honor.

---

### Private First Class Silvestre Santana Herrera in France

The day the draft notice came, Silvestre S. Herrera learned for the first time that he was not a US citizen. Even more shocking, the man he thought was his father wasn't. Herrera was born in Camargo, Mexico. After his parents died, his uncle brought the infant Silvestre to El Paso, Texas and raised him as his own son. Because he was a citizen of Mexico, he didn't owe service to the United States. Besides, he was 27, married with three kids, and another on the way. But he went anyway because, in his words, "I didn't want anybody to die in my place."

He joined the 36th Infantry Division of the Texas National Guard. Months later, on 15 March 1945, Private First Class Herrera was with his unit, E Company, 142d Infantry Regiment, near Mertzwiller, France. As his platoon was moving down a road, they came under heavy enemy fire from the woods, forcing most of the men to seek cover. But PFC Herrera charged the enemy alone and neutralized the position, capturing eight enemy soldiers.

With that threat ended, the platoon continued down the road. They soon came under enemy fire again from a second stronghold, pinning down the platoon. This time a minefield stood between the soldiers and the enemy gun emplacement. Disregarding the danger, Herrera rose to his feet and entered the minefield to attack the enemy. Mines exploded around him, but he continued to attack the enemy and draw their fire away from his comrades. Then a mine exploded under him, severing his leg below the knee. Still determined to stop the threat to his fellow soldiers, he struggled back up on his good leg to continue the attack.

Another mine exploded, this one severing his other leg below the knee. Despite intense pain and the unchecked bleeding of his wounds he lay in the minefield, firing to suppress the enemy while others of his platoon skirted the minefield to flank the enemy position.

His courage and fighting spirit reflected honor upon his adopted nation and that of his birth. Private First Class Silvestre S. Herrera received the Medal of Honor.

## INTEGRITY

1-38.   Do what's right, legally and morally.

> *I hope I shall possess firmness and virtue enough to maintain what I consider the most enviable of all titles, the character of an honest man.*

George Washington

1-39.   When we say that someone has integrity, we mean that person respects the rules of an organization, the country, and life. Such persons can be counted on to do the right thing, live honestly, and relate to others without playing games or having false agendas. Integrity is a quality you develop by adhering to moral principles every day, 24/7. As your integrity develops, so does the trust others place in you.

1-40. Display integrity by the following actions:

- Act according to what you know to be right even at personal cost.

- Be truthful and show consistency between your words and deeds.

- Use the authority and power that comes with your rank or position for mission accomplishment or for soldiers' benefit.

1-41. Integrity requires us to pay our debts on time, return items that someone else has lost, and follow rules and regulations. Integrity is essential in self-discipline.

## PERSONAL COURAGE

1-42. Face fear, danger, or adversity.

*I knew when I signed up the job would bring risk. It's a risk I'm willing to take.*

**PFC Trent James David**

1-43. Personal courage includes the notion of taking responsibility for your decisions and actions. Additionally, courage involves the ability to perform critical self-assessment, to confront new ideas, and to change. Leaders must make decisions that involve risk and often must take a stand with incomplete information during times of great stress. Personal courage has long been associated with our Army. Accounts of the dangers and hardships that soldiers have successfully faced are legendary. Personal courage is not the absence of fear; it is taking positive action in spite of the fear. It takes two forms: physical and moral.

1-44. Physical courage means overcoming fears of bodily harm and still being able to do your duty. It's the bravery that allows a soldier to operate in combat in spite of the fear of wounds or death. It is what gets the soldier at airborne school out the aircraft door. It's what allows an infantryman to assault a bunker to save his buddies or a medic to treat the wounded while under fire. With physical courage, it is a matter of enduring physical duress and, at times, risking personal safety.

*Fear is a natural reaction to the unknown; it is not necessarily a negative. A positive from fear is the heightened awareness that comes from being afraid. Harnessed, this heightened awareness is an asset.*

**CSM Michael T. Hall**

1-45. Moral courage is the willingness to stand firm on your values, principles, and convictions, even when threatened. Moral courage is sometimes overlooked, both in discussions of personal courage and in routine, daily activities. Moral courage often expresses itself as candor. Candor means being frank, honest, and sincere with others while keeping your words free from bias, prejudice, or malice.

1-46.   Your courage will allow you to do the following:

- Control your fear in physical and moral contexts.
- Take responsibility for your actions, mistakes, and decisions.
- Confront problems and do what you believe is right.
- Report successes and failures with equal candor.

1-47.   When considering personal courage, physical or moral, there is one important point to be made. Nowhere does the value say that fear must disappear—that you should not feel fear. Nor does it imply that courage is only required in combat. Many soldiers who have never seen a battlefield have carried out acts of great courage. Demonstrate personal courage by daily standing up for and acting upon the things that you know are right.

---

### Private First Class Parker F. Dunn in the Argonne Forest

Private First Class Dunn displayed personal courage while assigned to the 1$^{st}$ Battalion, 312$^{th}$ Infantry Regiment of the 78$^{th}$ Division. On 23 October 1918, near Grand-Pre, France, PFC Dunn's battalion commander needed to send a message to a company in the advanced lines of an attack. Because of the extreme danger due to heavy enemy fire and limited prospect for survival, he hesitated to order a runner to make the trip. But PFC Dunn, a member of the intelligence section, volunteered for the mission.

After advancing only a short distance across a field swept by artillery and machinegun fire, he was wounded but continued on. He was wounded a second time and fell to the ground. Despite his painful wounds he got up again and persistently attempted to carry out his mission until enemy machinegun fire killed him before reaching the advance line. PFC Dunn received the Medal of Honor posthumously.

---

## DISCIPLINE

1-48.   Many civilians—and maybe a few soldiers—misunderstand what discipline really is. Discipline is the glue that holds units together in order to accomplish assigned missions. It is the culmination of the genuine acceptance of the Army values. This acceptance results in self-discipline, without which there cannot be military discipline. Discipline, then is an individual quality that allows the soldier to see that despite his own preferences, he must accomplish assigned jobs well to ensure the team can do its tasks. Discipline is an essential part of the warrior ethos.

**An NCO inspects his soldiers prior to assuming guard duty.**

1-49. Discipline isn't blindly following orders or just imposing punishment for infractions but is something leaders and soldiers build together. It is the desire to do what is right even if it is difficult or dangerous. It doesn't matter if the "boss" isn't watching; the task will be done and done properly. It is the desire to accomplish the task well, not because of fear of punishment, but because of pride in one's unit and oneself. Discipline means putting the task of the unit—the team—ahead of personal desires.

1-50. Your duties require you to accomplish tasks with your equipment under the most difficult conditions: uncertainty, confusion, stress and fear of battle. In those challenging circumstances your courage and that of your fellow soldiers will be tested to the limit. You can expect fear to complicate duty performance in crisis situations. Fear is a natural reaction to combat and unknown situations. With the Army value of personal courage and the discipline developed in training you will get the job done despite the presence of fear. That discipline enhances the confidence that you'll act correctly and properly even under stressful conditions.

*Discipline must be a habit so ingrained that it is stronger than the excitement of battle or the fear of death.*

GEN George S. Patton, Jr.

1-51.    Discipline in the Army is important because of the stakes involved. In civilian life a lack of discipline may cause some discomfort or maybe problems with the law. In the Army poor discipline could result in the unnecessary loss of soldiers' lives—a cost too high to pay. As a disciplined soldier you place the unit's mission above your personal welfare. It means understanding your task and obeying orders promptly and cheerfully because your fellow soldiers and leaders depend on you to do so. This is military discipline; the kind of discipline that wins battles and saves lives.

1-52.    The purpose of discipline is to make soldiers so well trained that they carry out orders quickly and intelligently under the most difficult conditions. Insistence on performing tasks properly enhances military discipline. For example, ensuring soldiers wear their uniforms properly, march well or repeat tasks until they do them correctly are part of military discipline. This is not harassment or punishment. Proper and prompt execution of orders will save lives in combat. This in no way means you should not exercise initiative to solve a problem or to ensure the job gets done. American soldiers have a long tradition of displaying initiative and disciplined soldiers focus their efforts toward the success of the team.

1-53.    Discipline is essential when we receive urgent orders. There are times when success or failure depends on the immediate, correct execution of tasks that may result in the deaths of the soldiers carrying them out. But these successes are made possible through good training that breeds confidence within units. Confidence in yourself, your fellow soldiers, and your leaders all reinforce the discipline to finish the job, regardless of the difficulty of the task.

> *Discipline is a measure of what a soldier does when the commander is not there...*
>
> FM 22-100, *Army Leadership*, 1983

1-54.    Discipline in routine things like saluting, police call and physical training leads to discipline in the difficult things like advancing under fire, disposing of unexploded ordnance, and safeguarding enemy prisoners of war. That is why the Army insists on training to standard. It starts with self-discipline but grows with pride in the unit and confidence in the leaders' and other soldiers' abilities. A disciplined unit is made up of well-trained soldiers who trust each other and know they can accomplish any mission they are given. Those soldiers will not let each other down nor even consider failure.

## SECTION II - THE TEAM

1-55.    The Army is made up of hundreds of thousands of men and women from different backgrounds, with different views of the world, who look different and may even have been born outside the US. But they all have one thing in common: they are soldiers and Department of the Army Civilians (DAC) who promised to support and defend the Constitution to keep our Nation free. This commitment is as it should be—free men and women who have declared that, if necessary, they will fight to maintain the right to live in our own American way and continue to enjoy the privileges and benefits which are granted to no other nation.

*The Army...mirrors the nation.*

SGT Jack F. Holden

1-56.    You are one of those great soldiers. You may be a US Army reservist in Iraq, a national guardsman in Alaska, or an active component soldier in Texas. Your unit and the soldiers you serve with are part of a team that can only operate effectively when each of its parts works well together. This great team also works with the other services—the Marine Corps, Navy, Air Force, and Coast Guard—as well as allied nations. Our Army assists non-Department of Defense (DoD) governmental agencies and even non-governmental organizations in disaster relief or support operations. But the common factors remain the necessity, and the ability and willingness to operate and succeed as a team.

1-57.    Throughout your life, you have and will continue to perform as a part of a team. It is true many people admire great leaders, sports stars or celebrities. But it is equally true that when soldiers work together to achieve a common goal the world sees the enormous strength of the people of the United States. Teamwork has been a defining quality of our Army. It overcomes individual shortcomings, builds confidence in the unit and among soldiers, enhances each person's courage, and magnifies the commitment to succeed.

## TYPES OF TEAMS

1-58.    A team is a group of individuals banded together along organizational lines for the purpose of accomplishing a certain goal. While you are in the Army you will be a member of many teams and groups, often many at the same time. To be a good soldier you must be a good team member. We organize teams in different ways. The following shows types of groups or teams:

- A functional team is organized to accomplish a particular task and is one of long standing in the organization. Squads, platoons and companies are examples of functional teams.

- Task groups are formed when two or more functional teams contribute team members for a specific period of time to accomplish a specific task. This is like task organization. Task groups are disbanded after their mission is completed.

- Cliques are small informal groups held together by common interests and friendship outside recognized organizational lines.

- Primary groups are closely knit and deeply committed to each other. Your immediate family is an example of a primary group. In the

Army, tank crews, two-person buddy teams, squads, and platoons should be primary groups.

- Secondary groups are impersonal but in which members often interact. Secondary groups could be private or professional organizations or the larger Army organizations of which your unit is a part (e.g. division and corps).

- Membership groups require little if any involvement of their members. An example of this is an affiliated regiment.

- Reference groups influence our attitudes, values, and behavior. Examples of reference groups are church or chapel groups, political parties, or unit sports teams.

1-59.   Most soldiers will be members of more than one, even many teams or groups. Your family, your unit, your friends, and other associations form some of those groups. Sometimes these different groups may have conflicting values, priorities, or goals. If conflicts occur, solve them with the problem solving steps or the ethical reasoning process found later in this chapter.

*Nothing wrong with having a clique, so long as everybody's in it.*

SMA William G. Bainbridge

1-60.   Teamwork thrives when the soldiers on the team are closely associated with each other both on and off duty. Relationships, friendships, and teamwork should spill over into the post housing area, the barracks, the bowling alley, the chapel, the club system, the recreation center, and other organizations. Such camaraderie increases esprit de corps and improves the team's performance.

1-61.   Most of us have the ability and desire to be a part of a winning team and to help it succeed. Once part of a team we can stay the course despite obstacles. The Army's service ethic is a soldier's commitment to place the Nation, the Army, its soldiers, and their families above self. This commitment is expressed by the willingness to perform one's duty at all times and to subordinate personal welfare for the welfare of others, without expecting reward or recognition.

1-62.   Productive members of a team do their duty as well as they know how and actively seek to improve their performance. They also cooperate with other members of the team and help them willingly. The members of a team are more interested in the success of the team than in personal gain. Finally, the team knows that the leader has authority over the team because he is responsible for the team's performance.

*The one question that always presents itself on the battle field every minute of the time to every person, whether he be a general or a private, is "What play has my team captain ordered, and how best may I act so as to work in conjunction with the other players to bring about the desired result?"... A poor play in which every player enters with his whole heart (teamwork) will often win, while, on the other hand, the best play in which some of the players are skulkers and shirkers will probably fail.*

*Manual for Noncommissioned Officers and Privates of Infantry of the Army of the United States, 1917*

1-63. Leaders and soldiers all contribute to teambuilding. In all training, operations, and routine daily duties, the potential to further build the team exists. Teambuilding also occurs in athletics, social activities, and unit functions like a Dining-In or Dining-Out. Leaders are the primary teambuilders, but every soldier properly motivated and trained can help in teambuilding. Stay informed of what is going on. If you don't know, ask. You can't help your fellow soldiers accomplish the unit's mission if you don't know what the mission is or the commander's intent for the operation. Every soldier brings previous training and experience to benefit the team. As long as you share that experience and accomplish your duties as best you are able, you make a valuable contribution.

## LEADERS, SOLDIERS

1-64. One of the great aspects of our Army is that we develop future leaders from within the force. As soldiers gain training and experience, they also develop the skills necessary to lead other soldiers of junior rank and experience. Every soldier is a leader in the making. Leadership is learned, and it takes time. It takes more than 20 years to develop a brigade commander or command sergeant major. Today's lieutenants and captains will command tomorrow's Future Force brigades and divisions. The enlisted soldiers entering service today will be the 1SGs and CSMs of the Future Force. Still, the necessities of combat may place soldiers into leadership positions sooner than they expected. So even junior enlisted soldiers should begin learning about leadership early in their careers.

1-65. Perhaps you are a junior enlisted soldier now, responsible for performing the duties of your MOS. But some day, probably sooner than you think, you will lead other soldiers. Even if you are already in a leadership position as an NCO or officer, the following paragraphs should help you in leading well. And this will help you understand how the Army values can be put into action. You can find detailed information on direct leadership—face-to-face, first-line leadership—in FM 6-22 (22-100) *Army Leadership*. It is the Army's key publication on the subject and provides all the nuts and bolts you need to know in Chapters 1-5.

## Leaders' Obligations to Soldiers

1-66. The first obligation of the leader of every organization is to accomplish his assigned missions. In doing this, leaders must be proficient in both individual and collective tasks. Leaders ensure soldiers are well trained, informed, and capable of accomplishing the assigned mission. Leaders create a disciplined environment where soldiers can learn and grow both personally and professionally. It means holding their soldiers to high standards, training them to do their jobs effectively in peace and win in war. Leaders take care of soldiers by being fair, refusing to cut corners, sharing their hardships, and setting the example.

1-67. Taking care of soldiers includes everything from enforcing training standards, to making sure a soldier has time for an annual dental exam, to ensuring soldiers' housing is adequate. Leaders have an obligation to ensure soldiers and their families are living in safe and healthy environments. Leaders set up the systems to prepare families so soldiers know their families will be taken care of, whether the soldier is home or deployed. Family readiness also means ensuring there's a support group in place, that even the most junior soldier and most inexperienced family members know where to turn for help when their soldier is deployed.

---

### The Deployment

Preparations were almost complete. Equipment was loaded, the soldiers' gear was ready, and their families knew what was going on. SFC Lamb thought his soldiers were as ready to deploy as any, except for one. SPC Garrett is probably the best junior enlisted soldier in the platoon, a real workhorse. But Mrs. Garrett is expecting their first child, due three days after the unit deploys. SPC Garrett hasn't asked for any favors and he wants to be with the unit when it goes. He had arranged for his mother to stay with his wife after the baby is born to help while he is away. But SFC Lamb thought that SPC Garrett should not be deprived of such an important experience as the birth of his child.

"I've spoken to the 1SG and he agrees with me and the Commander okayed it. You're going to stay and see your baby born. We're coordinating transportation for you with another unit leaving a week after us." Before SPC Garrett could protest, SFC Lamb went on, "It's already decided. I know you want to deploy with us, but we'll make it without you for a little while. Anyway, this is one of those things where the family can and will come first. Sometimes that's the way it has to be."

SPC Garrett knew his platoon sergeant was right, but he also knew the mission had to come first. He was a little surprised that didn't seem to be the case, this time. Or was it?

---

1-68. Taking care of soldiers also means demanding that soldiers do their duty, even at the risk of their lives. It doesn't mean coddling them or making training easy or comfortable. In fact, that kind of training gets soldiers killed unnecessarily. Training must be rigorous and as much like combat as is possible while avoiding undue risk. Hard training is the best way to prepare soldiers for the rigors of combat. No training, no matter how realistic, can prepare a soldier completely for combat. But leaders must provide the best available training, equipment, and support to give soldiers the best chance of survival while accomplishing the mission.

### The Enduring Competencies: Self-Awareness and Adaptability

1-69.    Effective Army leaders consistently demonstrate self-awareness and adaptability. Self-awareness is the ability to understand how to assess your abilities, know your strengths and weaknesses in the operational environment and learn how to correct those weaknesses. For example, the First Sergeant gave CPL Lawson a mission and three soldiers to accomplish it. CPL Lawson was to lead the three soldiers from other platoons on a detail to set up Target Reference Points (TRP) for training use that night. CPL Lawson knew he had to refresh himself on the company's SOP for setting up TRPs so he allotted some time to review the SOP. He also knew that heavy rain was expected by late afternoon so he wanted to get to work with his soldiers quickly to put the TRPs in place before the rain. Nonetheless, he prepared his soldiers for the environmental effects by ensuring they brought appropriate rain gear. He knew one of the soldiers had a HMMWV license and tasked him with requesting and preparing a vehicle for use. CPL Lawson's ability to recognize his own weaknesses caused him to seek the knowledge he needed and he prepared himself and his soldiers to adapt to foreseen environment changes.

1-70.    Adaptability is the ability to recognize and react effectively to changes in the environment. Let's say that once out on the range and executing his mission, CPL Lawson sees that it has gotten significantly colder and instead of rain, it has started to snow. The cold and reduced visibility were two of the variables he had not foreseen. Still CPL Lawson adapted by having the soldiers warm up in the HMMWV periodically, telling his driver to go slower due to the more slippery driving surface, and calling the First Sergeant on the radio to inform him of the conditions.

1-71.    Your unit will receive varied missions in varied environments and you will have to adapt to the environment while training to perform many different tasks. Infantry could be supporting relief operations after a natural disaster or a quartermaster unit could be defending its perimeter against a terrorist attack. But because of the speed that information travels now and in the future, one soldier can have an impact far beyond his unit's actual area of operations. One soldier's actions could determine the success or failure of an operation. And that soldier could be you.

### Be-Know-Do

1-72.    With the competencies of self-awareness and adaptability, Army leadership begins with what the leader must BE—the Army values and attributes that shape a leader's character. Interpersonal, conceptual, technical, and tactical skills compose what a leader must KNOW. Leadership demands competence in a range of human activities that become more complex with positions of greater responsibility.

1-73.    But character and knowledge—while absolutely necessary—are not enough. Leadership demands application—action to DO what is needed— often in complex and dangerous conditions. Action is the essence of leadership. The Army Leadership Framework (Figure 1-1) shows the relationship of values, attributes, skills and actions to Be, Know, and Do. It isn't important to memorize these as much as to understand what they mean in your circumstances to best demonstrate and act upon them.

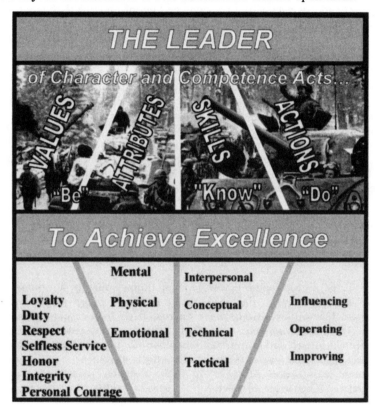

**Figure 1-1. The Army Leadership Framework**

1-74.    Be a person of character by living the Army values. Adhering to Army values further develops character in a soldier. Remember that character is an inner strength that helps you know what is right and what is wrong. It is what gives you the desire and fortitude to do what is right even in the toughest situations and it gives you the courage to keep doing what is right regardless of the consequences. That desire and fortitude is the warrior ethos. Your qualities and characteristics—attributes—are both inherited (eye and hair color, for example) and learned (self-discipline and military bearing, for example). Experience has shown that the Army values and leader attributes make for better leaders. These are attributes worth aspiring to even for a soldier not in a leadership position.

1-75. One of the most obvious ways to demonstrate character is to be honest. Tell it like it is, not how you think someone wants to hear it. The Army and your fellow soldiers want, need and deserve the truth. If you make a mistake, admit it. If something is wrong, you must be willing to say so, even to higher-ranking NCOs and officers. Tell them in an objective, straightforward and tactful manner and present the facts. This often takes moral courage. What you have to say may not be easy or even welcomed, but your candor is necessary to develop and maintain trust. Soldiers need to know whether they have met the standard and leaders need to know the true status of units. A mark of loyalty is a burning desire to help the team improve its performance. That demands honesty. Make it a habit to be candid because in battle, lives will depend on it.

1-76. Spiritual fitness can help develop the attributes of leaders. Often (but not necessarily) religious in nature, spiritual fitness reflects a sense of self-worth and the value of human lives. Many soldiers find solace and draw moral strength from their religious beliefs that support the acceptance of Army values. Other soldiers who do not practice a religion may draw that same moral strength from other sources. Soldiers may freely practice their religion or none at all as they desire. However expressed or sought, spiritual fitness is an individual concern that can be enhanced.

> *There are only two powers in the world, the sword and the spirit. In the long run the sword will always be conquered by the spirit.*
>
> Napoleon Bonaparte

1-77. To be a good leader, **know** your job, know yourself, and know your fellow soldiers. Every day the Army becomes more technologically advanced. Our fellow citizens have entrusted us to use complex tools to protect the Nation and our way of life. This requires each soldier to be proficient in his job and to work as a member of a team. Know how to think and plan ahead and learn to visualize the effects of your actions. Know your equipment and tactics and how to make decisions based on available information. Knowledge is reflected in a soldier's skills. As you continue in the Army, you will develop or improve these skills. Even the most senior leaders work to improve certain skills. Knowledge is never complete; we keep learning all our lives.

1-78. Being an expert in fieldcraft reduces the likelihood you will become a casualty. The requirement to do one's job in a field environment is one of the differences between soldiering and most civilian occupations. Likewise, the requirement that Army leaders make sure their soldiers take care of themselves and provide them with the means to do so is unique. *The Soldier's Manual of Common Tasks* (STP 21-1-SMCT) lists individual skills soldiers must master to operate effectively in the field. The field manual *Combat Skills of the Soldier* (FM 3-21.75) is another good source. Those skills include everything from how to keep your feet dry in the field to tracking. Most MOSs require other skills and you can find them in unique soldier training publications (STPs). If you see or know of a better way to perform a task, speak up. You may save your fellow soldiers' time and effort and perhaps even their lives!

---

**A Better Way**

In World War I, then Colonel George S. Patton was in France, training American tankers and preparing to lead them in combat. "Given the propensity of the tanks for breaking down, maintenance was one of Patton's chief concerns. He was constantly after his men to keep their tanks in good running condition, a difficult task greatly hampered by a shortage of spare parts and the absence of repair facilities close to the battlefield.

As it happened, it was neither Patton nor one of his officers, but rather a... private who came up with a solution to the problem. The private, whose name has long been forgotten, suggested that one tank in each company be converted into a sort of roving repair shop loaded with various spare parts (particularly fan belts) and equipped with towing apparatus to retrieve damaged, mired, or broken-down vehicles from the battlefield. Patton thought this an excellent idea and immediately saw to its implementation.

This led to the creation of the first tank company maintenance team, which consisted of mechanics from battalion headquarters who were assigned to each tank company to operate the company's recovery vehicle. It was the beginning of a system that is still in use today in American armored units. And it is worth remembering that it was the brainchild of a private, which just goes to show how much Patton encouraged initiative in the ranks of the AEF Tank Corps."

---

1-79. Know the rules of engagement (ROE) and, if applicable, rules on the use of force. Conditions in every area of operations differ, and they will change within those areas, as well. Knowing the ROE not only saves time in reacting to a potential threat but gives soldiers the confidence that they will react properly. See more on ROE in Chapter 5.

1-80. Know the commander's intent. Included in every operation order, commander's intent is a clear, concise statement of what the unit must do and the conditions the unit must meet to succeed with respect to the enemy, terrain, and the desired end state. While usually specific to a given operation or mission, knowing the commander's intent and your unit's mission will help you accomplish the mission even in the absence of specific orders. This isn't just for leaders—every soldier should know their commander's intent and that of the next higher commander. The comander's intent channels the natural initiative of soldiers to take advantage of opportunities on the battlefield in a disciplined manner. The commander's intent will let you know what is the most important thing the unit has to accomplish and when it must be done.

1-81. Know your own capabilities and believe in yourself and your training. Understand right now that courage is not a substitute for proper training, working equipment or firepower. Putting rounds on target quickly and accurately is the best antidote to fear, but it requires well trained, disciplined soldiers to accomplish.

## Decision-Making

1-82.    Do what is necessary to fulfill your duties and support your fellow soldiers by putting your knowledge into action. Taking action requires making decisions. Everyone makes decisions every day to solve problems. A problem is an existing condition in which what you want to happen is different from what actually is happening. So decision making is knowing whether to decide and then when and what to decide. The Army uses a method known as the problem solving steps to help choose the best course of action. The seven problem solving steps are in Figure 1-2.

---

### The Problem Solving Steps

**Problem definition**. Don't be distracted by the symptoms or effects of the problem, get at its root cause. For example, if you get called down to the motor pool on Saturday because there is a lot of oil under your truck, the problem is not the oil or the loss of free time. The problem is the worn seal that is allowing the oil to leak out.

**Information gathering**. In the time you have available, gather facts about the situation. You may also make assumptions to help in the next step. Assumptions are statements of what you believe about the situation but don't have the facts to support them. Make only those assumptions you believe are true and are necessary to come up with alternatives.

**Course of action (COA) development**. Courses of action are ways to solve the problem. Develop as many different COAs as time permits. Don't be satisfied with the first thing that comes into your mind. The third or fourth or tenth COA you come up with might be the best one.

**COA analysis**. Identify what is likely to occur from each COA and any resource or other constraints. Determine what are the advantages and disadvantages of each COA, without favoring any COA over the others.

**COA comparison**. Evaluate each COA as to its probability of solving the problem. Consider the cost of each COA, also. For example, replacing the engine in your leaky truck might solve the problem, but so will replacing the bad seal at far less cost.

**Decision**. Select the best COA that solves the problem.

**Execution and Assessment**. Once you've decided, make it happen! Plan how to accomplish the tasks required to solve the problem so you can get it done in an organized, efficient manner. Then assess the results. Does the truck run properly? Is there any oil leaking?

---

**Figure 1-2. The Problem Solving Steps**

1-83.    This process is the basis for all decision making and includes understanding the consequences of your actions. Apply the problem solving steps even when time is short. You can reduce the length of the process by developing fewer COAs or gathering less information.  Even when time is constrained, the steps will help you decide on the best available solution. You may find that sometimes you need to take into account your knowledge, your intuition, and your best judgment. Intuition comes from accumulated experience and is often referred to as "gut feeling." But don't rely only on intuition, even if it has worked in the past. Use your experience, listen to your instincts, but do your research as well.

**Convoy Briefing during Operation Iraqi Freedom.**

1-84.   Another tool that small unit leaders use is called the troop leading procedures (TLP). The TLP, shown in Figure 1-3, elaborates on the problem solving steps to support tactical decision-making. The TLP is a series of eight inter-related steps that may be accomplished concurrently. The TLP enables a leader to use available time effectively and efficiently in the planning, preparing, executing, and assessing of missions. Collectively, the TLP is a tool to assist leaders in making, issuing, and supervising operation orders. While the TLP does not necessarily follow a rigid sequence, it is important to accomplish every step to ensure planning is thorough and all soldiers know their required tasks.

1-85.   The TLP is the best tool for planning at the small unit level to be sure every important detail is considered. Using the TLP keeps all soldiers fully informed on future operations. But its usefulness is not limited to tactical field conditions. You can use it even in garrison situations in everyday tasks.

## The Troop Leading Procedures

**Receive the mission**. Once you receive your mission, analyze to determine what exactly has to be done and what other factors will affect your ability to do it.

**Issue warning order**. As soon as you understand the mission, let subordinates know so they can begin planning.

**Make a tentative plan**. After analyzing the mission, develop some different ways (courses of action – COA) to get it done. Then compare these COAs to determine which one is best.

**Initiate movement**. Begin soldiers' and equipment movement to where they will be needed or where they will rehearse the operation.

**Conduct reconnaissance**. Survey, as much as possible, the ground on which you will operate. At a minimum, conduct a map reconnaissance.

**Complete the plan**. Based on the reconnaissance and any changes in the situation complete the plan of action.

**Issue the order**. Fully brief soldiers on what has to get done, the commander's intent, and how you are going to accomplish the task.

**Supervise and assess**. Supervise preparation for the mission through rehearsals and inspections.

**Figure 1-3. The Troop Leading Procedures**

### Reverse Planning

1-86.    The reverse planning process is a time management technique. You develop your time schedule by starting at "mission time" and working backward to the time it is now. For example, let's say that you have a Class A uniform inspection on Friday at 0900 and it is now Monday 1630. You could list the tasks you have to do to prepare for the inspection, how much time each will take, and when they should start, such as in Table 1-1.

**Table 1-1. Reverse Planning Example**

| Action | Time | Start time |
|---|---|---|
| Class A uniform inspection | - | Friday, 0900 |
| Final uniform check by your squad leader | 10 minutes | Friday, 0850 |
| Place awards, insignia, etc., on your uniform | 20 minutes | Thursday, 1900 |
| Clean and shine insignia and brass | 30 minutes | Thursday, 1830 |
| Get new ribbon mount from clothing sales | 30 minutes | Thursday. 1800 |
| Pick up uniform from the dry cleaner | 30 minutes | Thursday, 1730 |
| Drop off uniform with the dry cleaner | 3 days | Monday, 1730 |

1-87.    The reverse planning process helps you accomplish important tasks without wasting time. By the example you can see that you would have to turn in your uniform Monday night for cleaning and pick it up on Thursday. Then you would pick up a new ribbon mount (you didn't have a chance since getting that new ARCOM) Thursday afternoon before the PX closes. Finally you'll probably want to set up your uniform Thursday night for your squad leader to check the next morning before the inspection. Reverse planning is a tool to see if there is enough time to accomplish all required tasks.

### Ethical Reasoning

1-88. Our nation places a premium on our professional values, and entrusts the success of its defense to our actions. Ethics is the process of putting our professional values into action. In making decisions we all come across situations where more than one solution appears to be correct. As a soldier who accepts and lives the Army values, the various COAs you develop for any given problem will most likely be legal, appropriate and can solve the problem. How then, do we select the right COA if they all appear to be equally effective? In these situations we decide on a COA not only because it can solve the problem, but because it can do so ethically, in a way that is most consistent with Army values, rules and the situation.

1-89. The values themselves may, in certain situations, conflict with each other or some other valid factor such as rules, orders or the situation itself. An ethical dilemma is a situation where two or more factors conflict in deciding the "right" course of action. These are dilemmas in which there are two apparent "right" answers. So how do we decide which "right" is "_right?_"

---

### Ethical Dilemma—The Checkpoint

Two days after a suicide car-bombing killed four soldiers at a checkpoint, another unit is operating a similar checkpoint some distance away. The unit was recently involved in offensive operations but was beginning the transition to stability operations. Unit training has emphasized the importance of helping the citizens return to a "normal" lifestyle. Nonetheless, the events of the previous day demonstrate that the enemy is still active, and will use civilian vehicles loaded with explosives to kill themselves in an attempt to also kill US soldiers.

At this time, soldiers at the checkpoint notice a large civilian passenger vehicle approaching at a high rate of speed.

---

1-90. In the example above we know that the rules, in this case the rules of engagement (ROE), say that the US soldiers may anticipate an attack and take action to prevent it—if an approaching vehicle appears to be a suicide bomber, soldiers may use deadly force to stop it. The soldiers also know that their mission is part of stability operation to maintain public order and protect innocent civilians. Analysis of METT-TC for this type of mission, the Law of Land Warfare, and both personal and Army values tells soldiers to protect noncombatants. Yet those same values, orders, training, and the mission also place a high value on protecting our fellow soldiers. Innocent civilians could possibly be the occupants of the approaching vehicle. What is the right thing to do?

1-91. This dilemma illustrates that we cannot, in some situations, simultaneously honor two or more values and follow given rules while accomplishing the mission. In these situations we have an ethical dilemma. When this happens the ethical reasoning process can help us decide the correct course of action. This thinking must be done as part of mission preparation—prior to the moment of decision. The ethical reasoning process is outlined in Figure 1-4.

---

### The Ethical Reasoning Process

Step 1. Problem definition. Same as the problem solving steps.

Step 2. Know the relevant rules and values at stake. Laws, ARs, ROE, command policies, Army values, etc.

Step 3. Develop possible courses of action (COA) and evaluate them using these criteria:

a. Rules—Does the COA violate rules, laws, regulations, etc.? For example, torturing a prisoner might get him to reveal useful information that will save lives, but the law of war prohibits torture under any circumstances. Such a COA violates an absolute prohibition.

b. Effects—After visualizing the effects of the COA, do you foresee bad effects that outweigh the good effects? For example, you are driving along a railroad and you see a train on the tracks. If you speed up to beat the train to the crossing, you might save a little time getting to your destination. But the potential bad effects outweigh the time you might save.

c. Circumstances—Do the circumstances of the situation favor one of the values or rules in conflict? For example, your battle-buddy was at PT formation this morning but now is absent at work call formation. Do you cover for him? Your honor and loyalty to the unit outweigh your friendship and loyalty to your buddy, so the ethical COA would be to report the truth rather than lie about his whereabouts.

d. "Gut check"—Does the COA "feel" like it is the right thing to do? Does it uphold Army values and develop your character or virtue? For example, you come upon a traffic accident and a number of vehicles have stopped, apparently to render aid, but you aren't sure. Stopping may cause further congestion in the area, but ensuring injured are cared for and that emergency services are on the way further strengthens the values of duty and honor.

Step 4. Now you should have at least one COA that has passed Step 3. If there is more than one COA, choose the course of action that is best aligned with the criteria in Step 3.

---

**Figure 1-4. Ethical Reasoning Process**

1-92.   Ethical reasoning is patterned after the problem solving steps. Ethical reasoning helps soldiers and DA civilians decide the best course of action for ethical dilemmas. As explained in FM 6-22 (22-100), *Army Leadership*, Chapter 4, ethical reasoning isn't a separate process used only when you have discovered an ethical problem. It is a part of making any decision. Admittedly, most decisions don't involve ethical dilemmas. But ethical reasoning will help you select the best COA from among those in which there is no obvious best solution (because they all appear to be right).

1-93.   In applying ethical reasoning to the (Checkpoint) example, the problem is that a possible suicide bomber in a large civilian passender vehicle is approaching at a high rate of speed. The ethical dilemma is the risk involved in civilian protection vs. force protection The relevant rules include Army values, the ROE, the current mission, and the Law of Land Warfare. So what should be done? There may be more, but let's say there are four possible Courses of Action (COA):

- COA a) do nothing.
- COA b) call higher for instructions.
- COA c) disable or destroy the vehicle.
- COA d) block the vehicle with a Bradley.

1-94.   The first COA (a) reduces the risk of harming any noncombatants in the approaching vehicle but it probably does not fulfill the unit's mission at the checkpoint. The second COA (b) offers a way to seek advice or higher guidance on what to do but will probably take time, during which the soldiers at the checkpoint could suffer casualties if the vehicle is carrying explosives. The third COA (c) complies with the ROE and should stop the vehicle but could harm any noncombatants in it. The fourth COA (d) puts soldiers and equipment at risk but it might stop the vehicle without harming any noncombatants in it.

---

**Ethical Dilemma – The Checkpoint (continued)**

The commander ordered the platoon manning the checkpoint to fire a warning shot at the vehicle to signal the occupants to stop the vehicle. When the vehicle continued to approach, he ordered the platoon to fire into the vehicle's radiator. When he saw nothing happening he ordered the platoon to stop the vehicle, immediately followed by a number of loud reports from the 25 mm guns of the Bradley Fighting Vehicles of the platoon.

The commander ordered the platoon to cease firing. In the now destroyed vehicle were a number of civilians, many killed or wounded by the fire of the Bradleys. The vehicle contained no explosives or weapons.

---

1-95.   Nobody has a crystal ball to see all the future results of our actions. However, ethical action requires us to live out our values in a way that considers the future. The soldiers at the checkpoint, not realizing the approaching vehicle carried noncombatants, made a decision to prevent an anticipated attack against fellow soldiers. It demonstrates the serious consequences of putting our values into action and their effect upon our Nation, the Army, our fellow soldiers, and those whom we protect. Not all ethical dilemmas have life or death consequences, but nevertheless they affect our professional identity in the way we place our values into action.

---

### Ethical Dilemma—Guard Duty

PFC Rust was conducting a patrol of the motor pool while on guard duty one night. He saw two figures about 20 meters away climbing over the fence into the motor pool. He ordered them to halt and when he got closer recognized them as two friends from his own company. They explained they were on the way to the club on the other side of the Motor Pool and were cutting across so they didn't have to walk all the way around. There didn't seem to be any damage to the fence and it was a long way around the motor pool to the club.

Should PFC Rust bring them to the sergeant of the guard (SOG) or let them go their way?

---

1-96.    In the guard duty ethical dilemma there is apparently more than one right answer. Referring back to the ethical reasoning process, what are the factors?

- Rules—the unit SOP requires soldiers to report in to the SOG if going to the motor pool after duty hours.

- Effects—PFC Rust doesn't want his buddies to get into trouble, but he knows the effect on unit discipline by letting them go would be worse.

- Circumstances—duty and honor cause PFC Rust to bring his friends to the SOG because while they said they were just going to the club, he isn't completely sure of their intentions.

- "Gut check"—even though his friends might resent him for it, PFC Rust feels best about taking the two soldiers to the SOG as it seems to be the more professional COA.

1-97.    The warrior ethos is defined by our professional values, and it is lived out as we put those values into action. The ethical actions of a soldier require both a self-understanding of these values and the determination to apply them in all situations. But ethical reasoning is not a science, despite the crisp procedure laid out in this manual. It is an art that improves as your character grows stronger and as you gain experience. Even senior leaders continue to learn and also work through ethical dilemmas.

1-98.    Whenever time permits, seek advice from more experienced soldiers to help you solve such problems. You will gradually gain the ability to solve even complex dilemmas. Just like playing a sport where with enough practice you begin to develop better coordination and "muscle memory," so too will it be as you develop character, gain experience, and find that you can make decisions more quickly because of "ethical memory."

### TRANSITION TO A LEADERSHIP POSITION

1-99.    Nearly every soldier, at some point in his service, will have to supervise other soldiers of junior rank and experience. It may even happen before promotion to the NCO ranks for enlisted soldiers. At that point, the leader is no longer "one of the guys" but accountable for accomplishing a task and for the welfare of the soldiers he leads.

**A junior NCO decides his team's next move along the Administrative Boundary Line in Kosovo.**

1-100. The transition to a leadership position is from one that was cared for to one who cares for others and from one who was taught to one that teaches, prepares for, and supervises tasks. You might stay in the same section or perhaps you will move to a different organization entirely. Either way, you will do the job you have been selected to do; lead soldiers.

> *When [a corporal] first receives his appointment, his caliber meets with the severest tests. Soldiers, for a time, will be apt to try the material he is made of, which they do in many ways, and by progressive steps, and, if not checked, will increase to a complete disregard, and terminate in an entire inefficiency of the corporal.*
>
> *Customs of Service for Noncommissioned Officers and Soldiers, 1865*

1-101. The transition to a leadership position may be difficult but is important to make. Identify exactly whom you report to. You should learn what your responsibilities are and what is expected of you. Right away, ask what is the standard of performance so there won't be any confusion later. Once you know these things, look to the soldiers you will lead. What are their strengths and weaknesses? Make sure the soldiers you lead and the resources you have access to are sufficient to complete the mission. Determine if additional preparation or training is necessary. Even if you are a PFC and in charge of two PV2s on police call, these steps will help you complete the mission.

*We should be shaping today's soldiers to be tomorrow's leaders. The things we learned in basic training were taught for a reason.*

**SGT Kerensa Hardy**

1-102. Your experience helps prepare you for assuming a leadership position. But you also have to make an effort to learn about leading through study, reflection and observing leaders. Our Army's history and the leaders of your own unit are good places to start. The Army expects total commitment from those who are selected to lead, train, and care for its soldiers. It is an honor and a privilege to lead America's finest men and women during peacetime and at war. To learn more about the transition to a leadership position take a look at FM 7-22.7, *The Army Noncommissioned Officer Guide*, Chapter 2.

## SOLDIER RECOGNITION

1-103. Leaders of effective teams recognize the good work of their soldiers. The Army has a number of ways to recognize outstanding performance in soldiers. The most obvious is through promotion. You receive promotions because you have demonstrated the potential to succeed in the next higher rank. Your leaders observe that potential in the daily performance of your duties (a brief description of the Army's promotion system is in Chapter 6). Another way to recognize achievement or service is through awards, decorations, and badges. Medals, ribbons, certificates, qualification badges, patches and coins provide various degrees of recognition for a soldier's hard work. See AR 600-8-22, *Military Awards*, for a full description.

1-104. The Medal of Honor is the Nation's highest military award. The Medal of Honor may be given to a member of the Armed Forces of the United States who in "action involving actual conflict with an enemy, distinguish himself conspicuously by gallantry and intrepidity at the risk of his life above and beyond the call of duty." Many of the recipients of the Medal of Honor were killed during the action for which they received it.

1-105. Other awards, below the Medal of Honor in the order of precedence, recognize extraordinary bravery in combat. These are the Distinguished Service Cross and the Silver Star. The Bronze Star may be awarded for valor in action or for other meritorious service in a combat zone. The Purple Heart is recognition of injuries received in combat or a terrorist attack. But soldiers also do outstanding work in noncombat areas and for that they may receive the Meritorious Service Medal, the Army Commendation Medal, or the Army Achievement Medal. Soldiers performing noncombat heroic acts may be recognized with the Soldier's Medal.

1-106. Service ribbons and qualification badges are other visible means of soldier recognition. By looking at the ribbons, badges, and insignia a soldier wears, you can really discover a lot about him. For example, suppose you have just met your new platoon sergeant and she was wearing her Class A uniform. You can deduce her name (SSG Jordan), that she is a quartermaster soldier who has been in the Army over six years, and is both airborne qualified and a parachute rigger. She has completed Basic Noncommissioned Officer Course (BNCOC) and been on two overseas tours as well as a humanitarian relief mission. You can also see that her service has been exemplary by noting a Meritorious Service Medal as well as both the Army Commendation Medal and an Army Achievement Medal each with three oak leaf clusters. You would probably conclude that your new platoon sergeant is squared away. You would probably be correct.

1-107. Commanders and command sergeants major or first sergeants often give certificates of achievement or the highly prized unit coin to recognize the impact a hardworking soldier has on his unit. All in all, awards and decorations serve to recognize soldiers for their accomplishments and tend to both motivate fellow soldiers and build the team. When you receive an award for a noteworthy accomplishment you should be proud. When your leaders receive awards, be equally proud because your efforts are reflected in those awards. As you progress in rank and assume supervisory roles, remember that the awards you receive are the results of your soldiers' work as much as your own efforts.

1-108. Other means of recognition are in the form of competitions such as Soldier of the Month or Year boards. These boards are held at the unit, installation, and even Department of the Army Level. They challenge soldiers' knowledge and skill and often the winners receive awards and prizes. NCOs also may compete in monthly, quarterly or yearly NCO boards at the various levels. NCOs of outstanding ability may also compete for membership in the prestigious Sergeant Audie Murphy or Sergeant Morales clubs. Company grade officers may compete for the MacArthur Leadership Award.

1-109. No form of recognition detracts from the Army value of selfless service. As long as your priorities are straight, awards and decorations add to the pride of a unit and to the confidence of individual soldiers.

1-110. Few professions in this world are more satisfying, rewarding and challenging than that of the soldier. It isn't easy and isn't meant to be. We have a serious job to do in protecting our freedom and our way of life. Do your duty, treat people the way you wish to be treated, learn to lead and prepare for the day when it is you in front of soldiers and they look to you to make the right decisions. Look forward to it!

## Chapter 2

# The Army and the Nation

The Army serves the Nation and defends the Constitution, as it has done for nearly 230 years. The Army has had enormous impact on the course of events throughout that time. This chapter provides a brief description of the Army's role in our Nation's history and of the environment the Army operates in today. This chapter also shows the Army's place as a department of the Executive Branch of the federal government.

For more information on Army history, see the Center of Military History (CMH) homepage at www.army.mil/cmh-pg.

Much of Section I can also be found in CMH's *225 Years of Service: The US Army 1775-2000* and *American Military History* from the Center of Military History's Army Historical Series.

For more information on the operational environment, see FM 3-0, *Operations*. For more information on Army Transformation see the Army homepage at www.army.mil or Army Knowledge Online.

For more information on the US Constitution and our American system of government, see Ben's Guide to the US Government at bensguide.gpo.gov, the House of Representatives homepage at www.house.gov, or the Federal Government information website at www.firstgov.gov.

For more information on the Department of the Army organization and missions, see FM 1, *The Army*, AR 10-5, *Headquarters, Department of the Army*, and DA PAM 10-1, *Organization of the United States Army* and the Army Homepage.

## SECTION I – A SHORT HISTORY OF THE US ARMY

2-1.    The Army's institutional culture is fundamentally historical in nature. The Army cherishes its past, especially its combat history, and nourishes its institutional memory through ceremony and custom. Our formations preserve their unit histories and proudly display them in unit crests, unit patches, and regimental mottoes. Such traditions reinforce esprit de corps and the distinctiveness of the profession. Our history of past battles bonds and sustains units and soldiers. History reminds soldiers of who they are, of the cause they serve, and of their ties to soldiers who have gone before them. An understanding of what has happened in the past can, in many cases, help a soldier solve problems in the present.

> *Those who do not remember the past are condemned to repeat it.*
>
> George Santayana

## COLONIAL TIMES TO THE CIVIL WAR

2-2.    The oldest part of our Army, the Army National Guard, traces its heritage to the early European colonists in America. In December 1636, the Massachusetts Bay Colony organized America's first militia regiments, some of which still serve today in the Army National Guard. Those first colonists and the regiments they formed were primarily made up from colonists who came from England, who brought with them many traditions, including the distrust of a standing army inherited from the English Civil War of the 17th century.

2-3.    The colonists used the militia system of defense, requiring all males of military age (which varied as years went by) to serve when called, to provide their own weapons and to attend periodic musters. Theirs was a reliance on citizen-soldiers who served in time of need to assist in the colony's defense. The various colonies (later states) organized and disbanded units as needed to face emergencies as they arose. Throughout our Nation's history, volunteer citizen-soldiers have stepped forward to fill in the ranks and get the job done.

2-4.    In 1754, George Washington, then 22 years old, led Virginia militiamen in a fight against French regulars at the beginning of the French and Indian War. On one side of the war were the British and American colonists with Indian allies versus the French and their Indian allies. At stake was whether the colonies could continue to expand westward or be limited to the eastern seaboard of the continent. This war would determine who would control North America, the French or the British and American colonists. Such groups as Rogers' Rangers won fame with their abilities and successes. England won the war and assumed control over the area east of the Mississippi—a vast empire in itself.

2-5.   In 1763, the British king decreed that most of the newly acquired territory was off-limits to new colonization and reserved for the use of the native American Indians. The American colonies saw this as complete disregard for what they saw as their right to use the western territories as they saw fit. The following year, Britain imposed the first in a series of taxes designed to pay the cost of British forces stationed in America. The colonists objected to these new taxes. The Billeting Act of 1765 required the Americans to quarter and support British troops. But it was the Stamp Act of that year that most infuriated the colonists. The Stamp Act required that a stamp be affixed to nearly all published materials and official documents in the colonies, as was the case in Great Britain, to produce revenue required for the defense of the colonies.

2-6.   Patrick Henry and the Virginia legislature denounced the Stamp Act as "Taxation without Representation." Americans broke into tax offices and burned the stamps. The level of opposition astonished the British, who thought the Stamp Act was an even, fair way of producing the revenue needed to pay for the defense of the colonies. In the next few years, additional taxes imposed upon other goods further angered Americans. Emotions ran high in Boston where tax officials were occasionally mistreated, causing the British to station two regiments there, which only agitated Americans even more, prompting a number of violent incidents.

---

### Crispus Attucks in the Boston Massacre

On the evening of March 5, 1770, a barber's apprentice chided a British soldier for allegedly walking away without paying for his haircut. The soldier struck him and news of the offense spread quickly. Groups of angry citizens gathered in various places around town.

A group of men, led by the towering figure of Crispus Attucks, went to the customs house and began taunting the lone British guard there. Seven other soldiers soon came to his support. Attucks was a man who had escaped from slavery and became a sailor to maintain his freedom. He also was a man of some leadership ability. He and a growing crowd confronted the soldiers. In some accounts Attucks struck a British soldier but others say there was no such provocation. In any event, the British fired and Attucks lay dead, struck by two bullets. Samuel Gray, James Caldwell, Samuel Maverick and Patrick Carr also died instantly or in the following days and six others were wounded. Citizens immediately demanded the withdrawal of British troops. The deaths of these men "effected in a moment what 17 months of petition and discussion had failed to accomplish."

The town's response was significant. The bodies of the slain men lay in state. For the funeral service, shops closed, bells rang, and thousands of citizens from all walks of life formed a long procession, six people deep, to the Old Granary Burial Ground where the bodies were committed to a common grave. Until the signing of the Declaration of Independence, Boston commemorated their deaths on March 5, "Crispus Attucks Day."

---

## THE REVOLUTIONARY WAR

2-7.     The Declaration of Independence of 4 July 1776 is rightly associated with the birth of our Nation, but the revolution had already been under way for over a year. On 19 April 1775 at Lexington Green, 70 Massachusetts citizen-soldiers stood their ground and refused to allow a British regiment through to destroy a weapons cache in Concord. Without orders, someone on one of the sides fired "the shot heard 'round the world." The British fired and charged, killing eight of the Massachusetts soldiers in what began eight years of war but ended with an independent Nation that one day would become the beacon of freedom for uncounted millions around the world. Those first days of our Army and the Republic it served were difficult times. We lost many battles, but won just enough to hang on and maintain the resolve to continue the fight.

2-8.     The United States Army began 14 June 1775, when the Continental Congress adopted the New England army besieging Boston as an American Army. The next day Congress selected George Washington to command the first Continental Army: "Resolved, that a General be appointed to command all the continental forces, raised, or to be raised, for the defence of American liberty." This resolution of the Second Continental Congress established the beginnings of the United States Army as we know it today. Those early days were tough and the British roughly handled the Army. Yet the Battle of Bunker Hill on 17 June 1775 showed the patriots that they could stand up to British regulars.

**...The Whites of Their Eyes. The Battle of Bunker Hill.**

### New York

2-9.     In one of the first major actions of the war, General Washington defended New York against a far more mobile British force on Long Island, whose evident intent was to seize New York. The patriots were preparing defenses around New York City and expected an attack. But Washington was desperate for information on British intentions and finally resorted to sending a spy to reconnoiter the enemy positions. Captain Nathan Hale volunteered for the mission.

2-10.  After landing on Long Island's northern shore, Captain Hale moved toward New York. He soon discovered that the British had already begun their attack against the Continental Army. Though the immediate purpose of his mission was negated, Hale continued to try and obtain information of value to the patriots' cause. Perhaps betrayed by a kinsman, perhaps just unlucky, Captain Hale was captured on 21 September 1776 with incriminating notes of British dispositions. He was brought before General Howe, the British commander. Captain Hale admitted his spying and without a trial, Howe ordered him to be hanged the following morning. Nathan Hale went bravely to his death, knowing he would be an example to his fellow patriots. His last words were, "I only regret that I have but one life to lose for my country."

2-11.  Despite Captain Hale's bravery, the Americans lost New York to the British and withdrew to New Jersey and then Pennsylvania. General Washington knew that the Nation needed a victory to keep up its spirit and with many soldiers near the end of their enlistment, knew such a victory must come sooner than later. Those were the conditions when Washington decided to attack the Hessian garrison of Trenton, New Jersey. Sailors turned soldiers of Glover's Regiment from Marblehead, Maine ferried the little force of 2,400 across the icy Delaware on Christmas, 1776. After marching nine miles through heavy snowfall, they charged into the town early the next morning, taking the Hessians utterly by surprise. In 90 minutes it was over and the Army had won a victory to keep the fires of liberty alive for awhile longer. Even though more defeats on the field of battle were ahead, our people, our soldiers and our leaders never lost heart.

> *These are the times that try men's souls: The summer soldier and the sunshine patriot will, in this crisis, shrink from the service of their country; but he that stands it NOW deserves the love and thanks of man and woman. Tyranny, like hell, is not easily conquered; yet we have this consolation with us, that the harder the conflict, the more glorious the triumph.*
>
> **Thomas Paine**

## Saratoga

2-12.  Nearly a year later, the Battles of Saratoga again tested the determination of the patriots. The British had intended to seize Albany, New York by simultaneous advances from Canada and New York City along the Hudson River in order to divide the colonies along that vital waterway, with a third axis from Oswego along the Mohawk Valley. The British attack from New York never materialized, instead becoming diverted to Philadelphia. American forces, swelled by many new volunteers from the state militias, were able to mass against the British coming south from Canada. In a series of battles in September and October 1777, America won its first major victory—a pivotal event in the war. It showed the world that America remained unbowed and determined to win and led to active assistance from the French that complicated the war for the British. Ultimately, the British had to contend with America, France, Spain, and the Netherlands.

---

### The Marquis de Lafayette–Patron of Liberty

Gilbert du Motier, Marquis de Lafayette was born into French nobility in 1757. After service in the French army, Lafayette became interested in the cause of American freedom. He desired to provide actual assistance and not only sent money to America but also offered his services to the American Congress in 1776. Since official French policy at the time was to remain neutral, Lafayette went secretly to America. In July 1777, Congress appointed him a major general, though stipulated he would have to serve at his own expense—Lafayette received no pay.

After taking part in several battles in which he demonstrated both his bravery and his skill in combat, Congress appointed Lafayette to command an invasion of Canada. Unknown to him, Lafayette's appointment was wrapped up in a strange conspiracy known as the Conway Cabal. A group of officers had decided that the conquest of Canada was more important than loyalty to America or to General Washington. Lafayette, who was intensely loyal to General Washington, was appointed simply to provide the pretense of legitimacy to the affair. He soon saw the plot for what it was. After determining the mission had insufficient resources, he succeeded in canceling the ill-advised attack entirely. Lafayette continued to lead well in battle elsewhere.

Soon after France allied herself to America, Lafayette decided he could serve the American cause best by returning to France in order to strengthen the relationship and enhance cooperation between the Nations. Lafayette provided a full report on the situation in America and persuasively argued for complete support of the Americans, including ground troops. He returned to America with many French soldiers. The assistance of France was essential to winning the Revolutionary War. With the Marquis de Lafayette, General Washington won the Battle of Yorktown in 1781.

Lafayette continued his support long after the Revolution, though he returned to his native France. He returned to the United States in 1825 for a yearlong visit and was greeted by thunderous applause wherever he went. Americans still remembered his important role in winning freedom. Lafayette died in 1834 and was buried in Paris. An American flag flies over his grave.

---

### Valley Forge

2-13.   Our soldiers endured the harsh winter of 1777-1778 at Valley Forge but learned how to make war under the tutelage of a Prussian drillmaster named Friedrich Wilhelm "Baron" von Steuben. The self-styled "Baron" (he wasn't really a baron, but the soldiers didn't care) took the ragtag remnants of two years of hard campaigning and turned them into a force that could stand against the might of the British empire. Von Steuben carried out the program during the late winter and early spring of 1778. He taught the Continental Army a simplified but effective version of the drill formations and movements of European armies, proper care of equipment, and the use of the bayonet, a weapon in which British superiority had previously been marked. He attempted to consolidate the understrength regiments and companies and organized light infantry companies as the elite force of the Army. He impressed upon officers their responsibility for taking care of the soldiers and taught NCOs how to train and lead those soldiers.

> *I would cherish those dear, ragged Continentals, whose patience will be the admiration of future ages, and glory in bleeding with them.*

> **Colonel John Laurens**

2-14. Von Steuben never lost sight of the difference between the American citizen soldier and the European professional. He realized that American soldiers often had to be told why they did things before they would do them well. He applied this philosophy in his training program. After Valley Forge, Continentals would fight on equal terms with British regulars in the open field. Much of what von Steuben taught our soldiers is still in use today. After his training took effect, the Continental Army became the equal of the British forces. Nonetheless, operations in the northern states degenerated into a stalemate that lasted to the end of the war.

**Von Steuben Instructs Soldiers at Valley Forge, 1778**

## War in the South

2-15. The Revolutionary War after 1777 was mainly fought in the southern states. There it was a war between patriots and Tories—

Americans who remained loyal to the crown and were recruited by the British to fight the rebels. As such, it was more a civil war than not, and neighbors and brothers fought each other in engagements that became increasingly vicious and merciless. They fought as much to protect their homes and families as for the future of the new nation.

2-16. On the patriot side, much of the combat power existed in bands of guerrillas, employing hit and run tactics that helped whittle away British strength and interrupt supplies. Francis Marion, the "Swamp Fox," led one of these partisan groups. What he lacked in numbers he made up for in audacity and thorough knowledge of the terrain, his soldiers, and his enemy. Over the course of three years he harassed the enemy, cut his communications, and caused the British to divert many soldiers to eliminating him.

2-17. The Tories were usually more organized, often led by a British officer, and fought more in line with existing British tactical doctrine. But some of the Tory units took up the practice of burning houses and destroying crops to deny them to the patriots. It had the effect of pushing the southern population, much of whom had been loyal to the Crown, into the American cause. One of these Tory units was under the command of Lieutenant Colonel Banastre Tarleton. Tarleton was the British commander on the field at the American disaster of the Battle of Waxhaws.

2-18. In May 1780, the British captured Charleston, South Carolina and its garrison, leaving the entire south open to attack. The prospects of American victory had never looked worse. But General Washington appointed Nathanael Greene as commander of the Southern Army. Greene began to wear down the British by leading them on a six-month chase through remote areas of the Carolinas and Virginia.

2-19. Greene never won a battle, but maintained constant pressure on the enemy with local guerrilla groups. The British, low on supplies, began stealing from any Americans they encountered, infuriating them. The British recourse to theft and destruction of property turned the local populace against the British. Many had been sympathetic to the Loyalist cause, but no more. The British actions directly resulted in their defeat at the Cowpens on 17 January 1781. Greene's persistence won back the south as the British abandoned post and city to return to the seacoast where they could maintain unhindered communications.

### Cowpens

2-20. Part of Greene's strategy was to split his Army to cause the British to weaken their forces in pursuit. It worked when the British commander detached Tarleton's command, reinforced by two regiments of British regulars, to pursue one of the columns of Continentals and militia, commanded by Brigadier General Daniel Morgan. Though untrained in tactics or strategy, Morgan knew his soldiers' strengths and weaknesses and that of his enemy. He turned to face the British in a field known as Hannah's Cowpens and won a victory that altered the course of the war.

2-21.   Though outnumbered by Tarleton's force, Morgan chose a low, sparsely wooded hill to defend. He would place most of his his militia in the front, instructing them to fire two shots before withdrawing. Behind these militia troops would be his stalwart Continentals and trusty Virginia militia in the main line and a small cavalry force as his reserve. Morgan intended for the first lines of militiamen to fire at close range to strike down enemy leaders and depart the field as if retreating. Then when the British charged after them, they would run into the main line of Continentals and Virginians. He spent much of the evening before the battle ensuring all his soldiers knew the plan and what was expected of them. He knew each soldier would do his duty.

2-22.   Tarleton's aggressiveness was also something Morgan counted on when the battle began the next morning. As expected, after the militia fired and withdrew, the British closed on the main line of patriots. They attempted to outflank the American right, and a misunderstood order caused the Continentals there to move to the rear. Tarleton thought they were retreating and plunged recklessly after them. But Morgan turned the Continentals about and charged the attacking British. While engaged to the front, the American cavalry and the reformed militia surrounded Tarleton's force of 1,100 and killed, wounded, or captured all but 50 who barely escaped, including Tarleton himself. This decisive victory seriously reduced the British strength in the south.

### Yorktown and Victory

2-23.   Soon the British began a withdrawal to Yorktown where they would evacuate part of the force to New York. Instead the French fleet arrived and drove off the outnumbered British vessels that were guarding the Chesapeake Bay. They landed 3,000 more French troops to join the 12,000 Americans and French that had surrounded Yorktown and began a blockade to deny reinforcements or evacuation from Yorktown. The resulting siege ended when the British surrendered on 19 October 1781, the day "the world turned upside down."

2-24.   The victory at Yorktown broke the will of the British to continue the war and ultimately decided it in America's favor. The Revolutionary War officially ended 3 September 1783 with the signing of a peace treaty in Paris. The British recognized the United States as a free and independent nation and that the US boundaries would be the Mississippi River in the west and the Great Lakes in the north. The area west of the Appalachian Mountains was called the Northwest Territory.

### A NEW NATION

2-25.   The United States initially were governed by a document called the Articles of Confederation. After a few years Congress called for a convention simply to mend the document's flaws. But the convention soon decided to write a new instrument, the Constitution. When it was ratified the Constitution left in place a small professional Army supplemented by the militia of all able-bodied males, under strict civilian control. Read more about the Constitution in Section III.

### Fallen Timbers

2-26.    Despite the treaty provisions at the end of the Revolutionary War, the British did not evacuate the Northwest Territory. Even so, American Settlers began moving into the territory. The native American Indians in the area believed the land was theirs because of previous treaties and resisted this encroachment. Americans suspected that the British were arming the Indians and perhaps encouraging their resistance. A confederation of tribes led by Chief Little Turtle of the Miami soundly defeated two major Army expeditions sent to protect the American settlers from Indian raids. This caused a crisis of confidence in the effectiveness of the Federal government and of the Constitution itself. President Washington appointed General Anthony Wayne to prepare a force to remove the Indian threat to the settlers if ongoing negotiations failed.

2-27.    The negotiations did indeed fail. The US would not ban settlers from moving across the Ohio River and the Indian tribes would not allow such intrusion without a fight. On 11 September 1793, President Washington ordered General Wayne to attack. Wayne built forts deeper and deeper into Indian territory and defeated all attacks against them, severely shaking the Indians' confidence in their leaders and in their ability to win the struggle. By August 1794, Wayne had offered the remaining tribes a chance to end to the fighting but received no response.

**The Road to Fallen Timbers**

2-28.    Expecting a battle, Wayne made known the Army would attack on 17 August. Realizing that the Indian warriors habitually did not eat on the day they expected combat, Genereal Wayne waited an additional three days believing many of the Indians would leave to seek food. He attacked on 20 August 1794 near Toledo, Ohio, and fought the remaining 800 Indian warriors in a forest that had suffered severe damage from a recent storm, giving the battle its name "Fallen Timbers." In less than two hours Wayne defeated the Indian force, paving the way for the Treaty of Greenville that secured southern and eastern Ohio and effectively ended British interference in the Northwest Territory.

## LEWIS AND CLARK

2-29. The young Nation more than doubled in size in 1803 when it acquired a huge expanse of territory from France in what became known as the Louisiana Purchase. President Jefferson sent the "Corps of Volunteers for North Western Discovery" to explore and assert American authority over the area. Sergeants John Ordway, Nathaniel Pryor and Charles Floyd (and later Sergeant Patrick Gass when Floyd died along the Missouri River) joined two Army officers, Captains Meriwether Lewis and William Clark.

2-30. With a select group of volunteers from the United States Army and civilian life they ventured west towards the Pacific coast. The skill, teamwork, and courage of each soldier contributed significantly to the success of the expedition. When the soldiers finally returned in September 1806 after traveling almost 8,000 miles in under two and a half years, their journey had already captured the admiration and imagination of the American people.

## WAR OF 1812

2-31. In the early 1800s Britain and France were at war with each other and desperate for men and materiel. Both belligerents seized American ships at sea but Britain was the chief offender because its Navy had greater command of the seas. The British outrages took two distinct forms. The first was the seizure and forced sale of merchant ships and their cargoes for allegedly violating the British blockade of Europe. The second, more insulting type of outrage was the capture of men from American vessels for forced service in the Royal Navy.

2-32. The seat of anti-British sentiment appeared in the Northwest and the lower Ohio Valley, where frontiersmen had no doubt that their troubles with the Indians in the area were the result of British intrigue. Stories circulated after every Indian raid of British Army muskets and equipment being found on the field. By the year 1812 the westerners were convinced that forcing the British out of Canada would best solve their problems. Then on 1 June 1812, President Madison asked Congress to declare war, which it narrowly did by six votes in the Senate.

2-33. American strategy was simple; conquer Canada and drive British commerce from the seas. But in practice, it became clear that public support for an enterprise was critical to the success of American operations. After a few abortive attempts to invade Canada in which many regional militia units were unwilling to take part, the Army quietly went into winter quarters. Repeated attempts throughout the war to make gains in Canada met with similar misfortune.

2-34. In 1813 American forces attempted to take the western panhandle of Florida and southern Mississippi, then territories of Spain. Defending the area were a few tribes of Indians that had long been difficult to control. Initially poor logistics preparation stymied the small American force of volunteers, but after reorganization and additional reinforcements, they drove the remaining tribes into Spanish–held Florida.

2-35.    In 1814 the Army fought its finest engagements of the war. Though strategically the US was frustrated yet again in failing to conquer Canada, time after time the Army fought hard and well against the very best units of the British Empire, many of which were veterans of the war against Napoleon. At Lundy's Lane, where Sergeant Patrick Gass fought with distinction, Baltimore and Plattsburg, well-trained regulars and volunteers acquitted themselves superbly against what was then believed to be the finest infantry in the world.

2-36.    In setbacks like Bladensburg, poor training and poor leadership were the reasons why 5,000 hastily assembled Regulars, militia and naval gunners were swept aside by an inferior British force that then entered and burned Washington. Yet many of these same militia, after two weeks of training, were resolute and inflicted heavy loss on the British in the defense of Baltimore.

2-37.    News of the British defeats at Baltimore and at Plattsburg caused the British government to reevaluate its objectives in North America. As a result it redoubled efforts to reach an agreement in peace negotiations that were already underway, ultimately resulting in peace by the Treaty of Ghent on 24 December 1814, two weeks before what was probably the most famous battle of the war.

### The Battle of New Orleans

2-38.    In late 1814 the British sent 9,000 soldiers to capture New Orleans in order to isolate the Louisiana Territory from the United States. They landed at a shallow lagoon some ten miles east of New Orleans. During an engagement on 23 December 1814, General Andrew Jackson almost succeeded in cutting off an advance detachment of 2,000 British, but after a 3-hour fight in which casualties on both sides were heavy, Jackson was compelled to retire behind fortifications covering New Orleans.

2-39.    Opposite the British and behind a ditch stretching from the Mississippi River to a swamp, Jackson prepared the defense with about 3,500 soldiers and another 1,000 in reserve. It was a varied group, composed of the 7th and 44th Infantry Regiments, Major Beale's New Orleans Sharpshooters, LaCoste and Daquin's battalions of free African-Americans, the Louisiana militia, a band of Choctaw Indians, the Baratorian pirates, and a battalion of volunteers from the New Orleans aristocracy. To support his defenses, Jackson had assembled more than twenty pieces of artillery, including nine heavy guns on the opposite bank of the Mississippi. He was forced to scour New Orleans for a variety of obsolete and rusty small arms to equip his entire force. Knowing many of these dueling pistols and blunderbusses were nearly useless against British muskets, he shaped the battlefield to his advantage by erecting formidable earthworks, high enough to require scaling ladders for an assault.

2-40.    After losing an artillery duel, the British commander decided to launch a frontal assault with 5,400 of his force. On 8 January 1815, waiting patiently behind high banks of earth and cotton bales, the Americans opened a murderous fire, first with artillery and then with small arms. In the area of the main attack the British were decimated and the commanding general killed. The British successor to command, horrified by the losses, ordered a general withdrawal. Over 2,000 British soldiers were killed or wounded as opposed to 13 on the American side.

2-41.   Soon after, word came that a peace treaty had been signed on Christmas Eve—two weeks *before* the battle. The War of 1812 was over, and the Army had kept the Nation free. Although the United States did not conquer Canada (President Jefferson once said it would be "a mere matter of marching"), it did gain new respect abroad and inspired a sense of national pride and confidence. The US Army was recognized as a formidable force.

## 30 YEARS OF PEACE

2-42.   After Wellington's victory at Waterloo in June 1815, Americans feared there would be another war with Britain. Such fears prompted congress to triple the size of the peacetime regular Army (to 10,000), begin an impressive program of building fortifications along the vulnerable eastern seaboard, and improve the facilities at the US Military Academy at West Point. Because of these efforts, America enjoyed 30 years of relative peace, although sharply punctuated by wars with the Creek and Seminole Nations, the Blackhawks, and other Indian tribes.

2-43.   For the first time since von Steuben's Blue Book, the Army developed written regulations to standardize many aspects of Army operations. The Army Regulations of 1821, written by General Winfield Scott, covered every detail of the soldier's life such as the hand salute, how to conduct a march, and even how to make a good stew for the company. General Scott was one of the most prolific writers in the Army of the early 19th century. Based on his combat experience in the War of 1812 and other conflicts, he wrote a manual of infantry tactics that was used with minor modification until the Civil War.

2-44.   Scott believed that the US Army needed a formal system of tactics to enable it to operate effectively. The tactics of the time, based on the line formation, were a result of the small arms technology of that period. Infantry armed with muskets had an effective range of less than one hundred meters. This fact and the extremely slow rate of fire of the weapons meant that to mass fires required massing soldiers. Soldiers had to operate in tightly packed units. But firepower was really a means to an end. The bayonet charge was the decisive movement and the ability to maintain a tightly packed formation simply assured the attacker would be able to outnumber the defender at the point of attack.

2-45.   General Scott also explained the School of the Soldier, providing explicit detail on how a soldier stands, walks and moves, all to most efficiently move large groups of soldiers about the battlefield and to ensure their fire was concentrated where the commander desired it. *Scott's Tactics* provides us a distant echo of how our Army trains today. In the School of the Soldier, School of the Company, and the School of the Battalion, we see familiar traces of individual and collective training. It may be said that Winfield Scott turned the US Army into a professional fighting force with the methodical application of standardized training techniques.

2-46. As America grew, western expansion and exploration brought settlers into more frequent conflict with the Indian nations. Much of the regular Army was stationed on the western frontier to try and maintain peace and order. But the expansion was free of European interference, due to the isolation gained by Britain's naval supremacy that kept the peace at sea. That isolation enforced the Monroe Doctrine and allowed the Army to turn its focus to the west. At times the Army was the buffer between the settlers and the native Americans while at other times it was directed to move the Indian tribes, by force if necessary, from their lands. One such action turned into the Black Hawk War, in which Abraham Lincoln participated as a captain of volunteer infantry.

2-47. From 1821-1830 large numbers of Americans, at the invitation of the Mexican government, moved into the area called Texas. This soon became the focus of a dispute that would lead to war with the United States. The growing numbers of settlers from the United States created suspicion in the Mexican government which then ordered a halt to all immigration and began to reassert its authority in the area. Volunteers from across the United States went to Texas to lend their support.

## The Alamo

2-48. In December 1835 Texians (immigrants from the United States) and Tejanos (Hispanic Texans), fighting for independence, seized the towns of San Antonio de Bexar and Goliad and began preparing them as outposts for an expected Mexican counterattack. The volunteers in San Antonio, under the command of Colonel James C. Neill, expertly strengthened the existing fortifications centered on the old mission of the Alamo. After Neill had to leave to attend an illness in his family, Colonel Jim Bowie and Lieutenant Colonel William B. Travis jointly commanded the garrison at the Alamo, fully expecting Colonel Neill to return in a few weeks.

2-49. The Mexican Army under General Antonio Lopez de Santa Anna would not give them that time. Santa Anna arrived outside the Alamo on 23 February 1836 and immediately demanded the surrender of the garrison, who promptly refused by firing a cannon in reply. General Santa Anna prepared for a siege and began pounding the fort with his artillery.

2-50. Travis took over sole command on 24 February 1836 when Colonel Bowie fell seriously ill. He sent a number of messages calling for reinforcements but only 32 more volunteers had arrived by 1 March 1836. By 5 March 1836 only 189 Texians and Tejanos defended the Alamo. Still, they kept the enemy at their distance, sniping at Mexican work parties and gun crews. But on 5 March, even though the siege and bombardment were having effect on the Alamo's fortifications and defenders, General Santa Anna abruptly decided to assault the fort before dawn the next morning.

2-51.   At 0400 on 6 March 1836, Santa Anna began his assault. About 1,800 Mexican soldiers attacked in four columns, but the rifle and cannon fire of the defenders repelled the first two attempts to scale the outer walls. The vast advantage in numbers allowed the Mexican force to continue its attack and succeeded in breaching and scaling the walls on the third try. The Mexican soldiers poured into the Alamo, killing every defender, but suffered over 600 casualties in doing so. It was a very costly Mexican victory that served to rally Texans in subsequent battles.

2-52.   After Sam Houston's decisive victory at San Jacinto the following month, Mexican forces withdrew from Texas. For the next nine years Texas operated as an independent republic although the Mexican government did not recognize it as such. At the same time, Texas was trying to become part of the United States. Their efforts were frustrated for a time over the issue of slavery, but on 1 March 1845 Congress resolved to admit Texas to the Union. Because Mexico had desired to regain control of Texas for itself, she promptly broke off diplomatic relations with the United States and both countries prepared for war. In addition to regulars, volunteers from Texas and Louisiana joined General Zachary Taylor at the Rio Grande where they built a number of fortified positions to pressure Mexico into accepting that river as the international boundary.

## WAR WITH MEXICO

2-53.   Hostilities began 25 April 1846 near Matamoros and were soon followed by the Battles of Palo Alto and Resaca de la Palma. In these successive battles, the Army fought a defense against a force that was twice as large. The next day, they attacked an entrenched enemy force and drove it from the field. Enlisted soldiers demonstrated their toughness and resiliency, and the officer corps provided skillful leadership, particularly in the use of artillery. Yet these early victories were incomplete because Taylor's force had no means to cross the Rio Grande in pursuit of the defeated Mexican force. By the time Taylor had brought boats from Point Isabel, the enemy had withdrawn into the interior of Mexico.

2-54.   To provide the necessary resources to win the war, Congress authorized an increase of the Regular Army to 15,540 and also authorized the President to call for 50,000 volunteers to serve for one year or the duration of the war. The United States' objective in the war was to seize all Mexican territory north of the Rio Grande and Gila rivers all the way to the Pacific. This area comprised what we know today as New Mexico, Arizona, California, Nevada, Utah and parts of Colorado and Wyoming. To accomplish this huge task the Army would attack to destroy the Mexican Army's offensive capability and occupy key points in northern Mexico to obtain favorable terms. In attacks along three axes in northern Mexico, the US Army never lost a battle. But Mexico continued to resist and American leaders concluded that a direct strike at Mexico City was necessary.

2-55.   The Army under General Winfield Scott made its first ever major amphibious landing at Vera Cruz on 9 March 1847. While heavily fortified, the city fell within the month and soon the Army was moving west. During the next five months, the Army's soldiers again displayed fine fighting qualities at Vera Cruz, Cerro Gordo, Churubusco, and Chapultepec. Army officers distinguished themselves as scouts, engineers, staff officers, military governors, and leaders of combat troops. Many of these officers, including Robert E. Lee, Joseph E. Johnston, Thomas J. Jackson, Ulysses S. Grant, and George B. McClellan, would command the armies that would face each other in the American Civil War fourteen years later.

2-56.    Ultimately, Mexico capitulated and signed the Treaty of Guadalupe Hidalgo on 2 February 1848. After full ratification on both sides, Mexico recognized the Rio Grande as the boundary of Texas and gave control of New Mexico (including the present states of Arizona, California, New Mexico, Nevada, Utah, and part of Wyoming) to the United States in exchange for $15 million. This addition to the United States and the settlement of the Oregon boundary dispute with Great Britain opened a vast area that would occupy the Army's attention until the Civil War.

## THE CIVIL WAR TO WORLD WAR I

2-57.    Slavery had been a bitterly divisive issue among Americans since before the Revolutionary War. By the Presidential election of 1860, a number of political compromises had averted war. Presidential candidate Abraham Lincoln's platform included that he would not support extending slavery into the western territories. Southerners believed this would give political advantage to the northern states. In addition, Congress had imposed a tax on certain imported manufactured goods in order to protect American industries, most of which were in the north. But it was the issue of the expansion of slavery that most directly led to war.

### THE CIVIL WAR

2-58.    After American voters elected Lincoln as President, South Carolina seceded from the Union. Other southern states soon followed, though some took a wait and see approach. Virginia, for example, did not secede until after Fort Sumter fell when the President ordered a partial mobilization to suppress the rebellion. The American Civil War had been avoided for many years but began when South Carolina militia forces fired on Fort Sumter in Charleston Harbor in April 1861.

2-59.    The regular Army at the beginning of the Civil War was tiny in comparison to the task at hand and it was almost totally engaged with peacekeeping on the western frontier. Both the North and the South had to call for volunteers to fight for their respective sides. Initially, many in the North thought it could suppress the rebellion in a short time so the President called for volunteers for a short period of enlistment. The rush to the Colors on both sides following the call for volunteers reflected the country's tradition of a citizenry ready to spring to arms when the Nation was in danger.

2-60.    In overall command at the beginning of the war was General Winfield Scott (the same officer who fought in 1812 and against Mexico and wrote the 1821 regulations). He understood that the defeat of the South would take a long time and the Union would have to attack the Confederacy's economy. His plan was to conduct a naval blockade of the South to prevent imports and exports, split the Confederacy by seizing the length of the Mississippi, and maintain continuous pressure along the entire front while waiting for the Confederacy to either dissolve from internal dissension or seek peace negotiations. But this strategy would take time, so much so that it was initially ridiculed as the "Anaconda Plan" because of the slow effect it would have. War fever was high and politicians, newspaper editors, and the public wanted action. They thought that if the Federal (Union) forces could simply seize the capital of the Confederacy, the South would just give up.

### Early Battles

2-61.   The Union defeat at the First Battle of Bull Run showed the need for more thorough preparation and for more soldiers. That realization allowed professional Army officers like Major General George B. McClellan to begin the hard work of transforming volunteers into soldiers. Within months, the Army increased to almost 500,000 men, and it would grow much larger in the ensuing years. Regular Army personnel, West Pointers returning from civilian life, and self-educated citizen-officers all did their part in transforming raw recruits into an effective fighting force.

2-62.   Ultimately, the North adopted the essential elements of Scott's Anaconda Plan and it did, indeed, take time. The four years of bloody warfare that followed cost nearly as many Americans' lives as in all our other wars combined, before and since. Civil wars, by their nature, are brutal and merciless. Yet, for the common soldier on both sides, there were examples of extraordinary courage, compassion, and fortitude. That they endured is testament to the natural strength of the American soldier.

2-63.   The Confederacy had clear disadvantages in comparison to the Union states. The smaller population of the South and the huge disparity in manufacturing capability were the most obvious of these. But these were partially offset, at least initially, by the great skill of southern commanders and the established trade the Confederacy continued with European nations. The South's greatest advantage was that it simply had to endure to succeed. For the Union to win it would have to conquer the Confederacy or force it to negotiate a truce that included rejoining the Union. This put the northern states on the strategic offensive in order to succeed.

2-64.   In its efforts to restore the Union in 1861 and 1862, the Army achieved mixed results. It secured Washington, DC, and the border states, and provided aid and comfort to Union loyalists in West Virginia. In cooperation with the Union Navy, the Army seized key points along the southern coast, including the port of New Orleans, while the Navy conducted an increasingly stronger blockade of the Confederacy. Under such leaders as Major General Ulysses S. Grant, the Army occupied west and central Tennessee and secured almost all of the Mississippi River.

2-65.   In the most visible theater of the war, however, the Union Army of the Potomac under a series of commanders made little progress against the

Confederate Army of Northern Virginia, commanded by General Robert E. Lee. After victories in the battles of Seven Days and Second Bull Run, Lee invaded Maryland. The Union victory at the Battle of Antietam forced Lee to return to Virginia, although subsequent defeats at Fredericksburg and Chancellorsville brought the Union effort in the East no closer to success than it had been at the start of the war.

---

### Antietam and Emancipation

Lee crossed the Potomac in 1862 for a number of compelling reasons. Primarily he wanted to maintain the initiative in the war. A battle on northern soil would show the people of the Union that it was going to be a long, hard struggle to subdue the Confederacy. Perhaps it would push them to vote more pro-southern politicians into office in the coming election. He also hoped that such an invasion would encourage European support of the Confederacy. Finally, since it was harvest time, he wanted his army to subsist on northern crops.

President Lincoln wanted to prevent any European alliance with the Confederacy. Since the Europeans were opposed to slavery, he thought freeing the slaves would make it politically impossible for European nations to side with the South. Emancipation would also gain the full and continuing support of abolitionists in the North. But issuing an Emancipation Proclamation while Union armies were losing battles might be seen as an act of desperation, rather than one of strength.

The Battle of Antietam on 17 September 1862 was a bloody day on which 6,000 soldiers were killed and 17,000 wounded in a twelve-hour period. In tactical terms, Antietam was a draw. General Lee's army was severely outnumbered at the outset and his enemy, Major General George McClellan, knew his invasion plan, yet the Confederates still held the field at the end of the day. But the terrible losses Lee sustained meant he could not continue operations on Union territory without risk of complete destruction. Lee's resulting withdrawal from Maryland was a strategic victory for the Union and provided Lincoln the opportunity to issue the Emancipation Proclamation.

---

2-66. President Lincoln's Emancipation Proclamation on 22 September 1862 freed the slaves in any areas still under Confederate control as of 1 January 1863. This had no real effect until the Union Army took control of those areas, but it expanded the Army's mission of restoring the Union to include freeing the slaves in the Confederate states. Soon Union armies moving through the South were followed by a fast-growing multitude of African-American refugees, most of them with little means of survival.

2-67. The Army gave food, clothing, and employment to the freedmen, and it provided as many as possible with the means of self-sufficiency, including instruction in reading and writing. African-Americans in the Union Army were among those who achieved literacy. After years of excluding African-Americans, the Army took 180,000 into its ranks. Formed into segregated units under white officers, these free men and former slaves contributed much to the eventual Union victory. One of the notable units was the 54th

Massachusetts Regiment, which led an assault on Battery Wagner at Morris Island on 18 July 1863.

---

### The First Medal of Honor Recipient

Congress authorized the creation of the Medal of Honor on 12 July 1862 and on 25 March 1863, Private Jacob Parrott, Company K, 33d Ohio Volunteer Infantry, received the first Medal of Honor ever awarded.

In April 1862 Private Parrott and 23 other volunteers were part of a raid into Georgia to destroy track and bridges on the railroad line between Atlanta and Chattanooga. They penetrated nearly 200 miles south and boarded a train headed north. During a scheduled stop at Big Shanty, Georgia, the group stayed on the train while the engineer, conductor, and the rest of the passengers went to get breakfast. Then the Union soldiers uncoupled the engine, tender and three boxcars from the rest of the train. Most of the men got into the rear car, while the raid leader boarded the engine with Privates Wilson Brown and William Knight, both engineers, and another soldier who acted as fireman. The group steamed out of the station without incident.

The Union soldiers drove the train north but soon the Confederates began to chase them in another locomotive. The raiders tried to burn bridges, but because they were followed so closely were unable to destroy any. Even dropping off some of the train cars along the way did not slow the pursuers. Eventually, they ran out of fuel north of Ringgold, Georgia and the raiders tried to escape on foot. All were captured, including Private Parrott. He returned to the Union after a prisoner exchange in March 1863. For his part in the undercover mission, Private Jacob Parrott became the first recipient of the Medal of Honor, soon followed by other surviving raiders.

---

### Gettysburg

2-68.   In June 1863 General Lee decided to invade the North again. He intended to draw the Union Army of the Potomac out of its strong defensive positions guarding Washington, DC, and destroy it on ground of his choosing. At the very least, he intended to disrupt the plans of the Army of the Potomac. Lee led his Army of Northern Virginia into Pennsylvania and the Army of the Potomac followed. They met at Gettysburg, Pennsylvania on 1 July 1863, where Union cavalry had occupied favorable defensive positions on Seminary Ridge west of the town. The cavalry held long enough for infantry and artillery of the Army of the Potomac to begin arriving. But then more Confederate units marched in from the north and outflanked the Union positions. They drove the Union soldiers back through Gettysburg onto Cemetery Ridge and Culp's Hill east of the town, where the Union line held.

2-69.   On 2 July 1863 Lee attacked again, on both the Union right and left. Though poorly coordinated and starting late in the day, it nearly succeeded. On the Union left, resolute soldiers from Maine, New York, Pennsylvania, and Minnesota helped prevent the Confederates from flanking the Union

Army. On that day the names Peach Orchard, the Wheatfield, Devil's Den, and Little Round Top were etched into US Army history.

---

## The 1$^{st}$ Minnesota at Gettysburg

On the second day of the Battle of Gettysburg, the Union III Corps moved forward of the Union lines on Cemetery Ridge to occupy a position about 600 meters to its front. While the position was good, the III Corps was too small to secure its flanks and therefore was vulnerable. This became obvious when two Confederate divisions crashed into the III Corps' southern flank.

The fighting in the Peach Orchard and the Wheatfield lasted through the afternoon, but ultimately the III Corps was overwhelmed and began streaming back over Cemetery Ridge with the Confederates in close pursuit. If they succeeded in pushing over the ridge they could outflank the Army of the Potomac and defeat it on northern soil, with disastrous consequences to Union morale. Major General Winfield Hancock, seeing the danger, ordered two brigades to Cemetery Ridge to plug the gap left by the retreating III Corps, but it would take time. The only troops in the area were the soldiers of the 1$^{st}$ Minnesota Infantry. Hancock galloped to its commander, Colonel William Colvill, Jr., and pointing at the enemy closing on the ridge told him, "Colonel! Do you see those colors? Take them!" With no hesitation Colvill and his 262 soldiers moved down the slope toward the 1,600 Confederate soldiers.

The 1$^{st}$ Minnesota drove into the enemy, causing confusion and stopping them in their tracks. Though they suffered terrible casualties, the volunteers from Minnesota bought the five minutes needed to move two brigades into position on Cemetery Ridge and so prevented a rout of the Army of the Potomac. At the end, only 47 of the 262 soldiers on the rolls that morning were left standing. This casualty rate of 82% was the highest of any Union regiment in the war.

---

2-70.   On 3 July 1863, the third day of the Battle of Gettysburg, General Lee thought he could still win with one last attack. After an intense artillery preparation about 13,000 Confederate soldiers advanced across a mile of ground swept by Union artillery and small arms fire into the center of the Union line. With the Confederates was Major General George Pickett's division. The courage of Americans on both sides was never more clearly demonstrated than during Pickett's Charge. Despite the loss of half the attacking force, the Confederate infantry reached the Union line where infantry and artillery turned them back with crippling losses, effectively ending the battle. During the Battle of Gettysburg, a total of 51,000 Union and Confederate soldiers were killed, wounded or became missing but it was unquestionably a Union victory. Though the war would not end for nearly two more years, Gettysburg gave the Union renewed hope in victory.

2-71.   In July 1863 Grant's triumph at Vicksburg gave the North control of the entire Mississippi River. The capture of Chattanooga, Tennessee, in the fall of 1863 opened the way for an invasion of the Confederate heartland. Appointed commander of all the Union armies, Grant planned not only to annihilate the enemy's armies but also to destroy the South's means of supporting them.

*Washington, Nov. 21, 1864.*

*Dear Madam, --*

*I have been shown in the files of the War Department a statement of the Adjutant General of Massachusetts that you are the mother of five sons who have died gloriously on the field of battle.*

*I feel how weak and fruitless must be any words of mine which should attempt to beguile you from the grief of a loss so overwhelming. But I cannot refrain from tendering to you the consolation that may be found in the thanks of the Republic that they died to save.*

*I pray that our Heavenly Father may assuage the anguish of your bereavement, and leave you only the cherished memory of the loved and lost, and the solemn pride that must be yours to have laid so costly a sacrifice upon the altar of freedom.*

*Yours very sincerely and respectfully,*

*A. Lincoln*

**President Lincoln's letter to Mrs. Lydia Bixby of Boston, Massachusetts**

2-72.   Grant wore down Lee's army at the Wilderness, Spotsylvania Court House, and Petersburg during the 1864 and 1865 campaigns. His commander in the West, Major General William T. Sherman, drove through Georgia and the Carolinas, burning crops, tearing up railroads, and otherwise wrecking the economic infrastructure of those regions. "Sherman's March" showed that victory might be hastened by destroying the enemy's economic basis for continued resistance and demoralizing his population.

2-73.   In March and April 1865 Grant pursued Lee and his Army of Northern Virginia to Appomattox Court House, Virginia. General Lee recognized further bloodshed would not alter the outcome of the war and surrendered his army on 9 April 1865. The Confederate formation under General Joseph Johnston surrendered to General Sherman on 26 April 1865, twelve days after the assassination of President Lincoln. The last major Confederate unit west of the Mississippi gave up on 26 May 1865.

2-74.   The bloodiest war in American history was over, slavery was gone, over 600,000 Americans on both sides had died, but the Union was preserved and the South would be rebuilt. The Army's role in reunifying the nation was not finished with the end of the war. The Army had already established military governments in occupied areas, cracking down on Confederate sympathizers while providing food, schools, and improved sanitation to the destitute. This role continued after the collapse of the

Confederacy, when Congress adopted a tough "Reconstruction" policy to restore the Southern states to the Union.

**"The Surrender."**
**General Lee meets General Grant at Appomattox, 9 April 1865.**

2-75.　The Army maintained order in the former Confederate states. Keeping watch over local courts, the Army sought to ensure the rights of African-Americans and Union loyalists, a task that became increasingly difficult as support for Reconstruction waned and the occupation forces declined in numbers. At the same time, military governors expedited the South's physical recovery from the war. Through the Freedmen's Bureau, the Army provided 21 million rations, operated over fifty hospitals, arranged labor for wages in former plantation areas, and established schools for the freedmen. The Army's role in Reconstruction ended when the last federal troops withdrew from occupation duties in 1877.

## THE WESTERN FRONTIER

2-76.　Soon after the Civil War the bulk of the Regular Army returned to its traditional role of frontier constabulary. Early settlers from Europe had been in conflict with native Americans as early as 1622. For over 250 years there were periodic wars and battles as settlers moved west into the wilderness. Conflict often resulted as the Indian nations fought to preserve their way of life while the Army fought to protect settlers, property, and the continued expansion of the United States.

2-77.　Army officers negotiated treaties with the Sioux, Cheyenne, and other western tribes and tried to maintain order between the various tribes and the prospectors, hunters, ranchers, and farmers moving west. Native American tribes were pushed off lands they had inhabited for centuries. They fought against the encroachment, periodically raiding settlements, work parties or wagon trains. When hostilities erupted, the Army was usually ordered to force the Indians onto reservations. Campaigns generally took the form of converging columns invading hostile territory in an attempt to bring the enemy to battle. Most of the time, the tribes lacked the numbers or inclination to challenge an Army unit of any size.

---

### The 7<sup>th</sup> Cavalry at the Little Bighorn

In 1875, the Sioux and Cheyenne left their reservations, infuriated at violations of their sacred lands in the Black Hills. They gathered in Montana with Sitting Bull and vowed to fight. Victories in early 1876 made them confident to continue fighting through the summer. The 7$^{th}$ Cavalry and other units moved to find and destroy hostile encampments and force the Indians back onto their reservations.

On 25 June 1876 Lieutenant Colonel George A. Custer, commanding the 7$^{th}$ Cavalry, learned that a Sioux village was in the valley of the Little Bighorn River in Montana. He expected that the village contained only a few hundred warriors at most and that the Indians would try to slip away from the cavalry as in previous engagments. Custer divided his force of 652 soldiers into four columns to simultaneously attack the northern and southern ends of the village and also block any escape. But the plan did not account for difficult terrain or the fact that the village was much larger than he expected. The village actually contained 1,800 well armed warriors, and they intended to stay and fight.

At about 1500, Major Marcus A. Reno's element of 175 soldiers began their attack on the southern end of the village. Hundreds of Indian warriors spilled out of the village and routed the cavalrymen. By 1630 the Indians had turned their attention to Custer's column of 221 soldiers approaching the village from the east. The Indians pushed them back onto a ridge and encircled them. In an hour all of the soldiers in Custer's group were dead. Though the united Sioux and Cheyenne nations had achieved a great victory, it had aroused the American public who demanded retribution. The boundaries of the reservation were redrawn to exclude the Black Hills and settlers flooded the area. Within a year the Sioux and Cheyenne were defeated.

---

2-78. The Army contributed in other ways to the development of the West. One Army officer, Captain Richard H. Pratt, established the US Indian Training and Industrial School at Carlisle Barracks, Pennsylvania, to teach Native American youth new skills. At the same time, other soldiers conducted explorations to finish the task of mapping the continent. The surveys from 1867 through 1879 completed the work of Lewis and Clark, while discoveries at Yosemite, Yellowstone, and elsewhere led to the establishment of a system of national parks. Army expeditions explored the newly purchased territory of Alaska. For ten years before the formation of a civilian government, the Army governed the Alaska Territory.

## SPANISH-AMERICAN WAR

2-79. As the nineteenth century drew to an end, the Army again served the Nation during the American intervention in Cuba's war of liberation from Spain in 1898. A US Navy battleship, the USS Maine, anchored in the harbor at Havana, Cuba, mysteriously exploded on the night of 15 February 1898 killing 266 American sailors. Public opinion quickly turned hostile toward Spain and Congress declared war on 25 April 1898. The Army once again struggled to organize, equip, instruct, and care for raw recruits flooding into its training camps. By the end of June 1898 the Army had embarked 17,000 soldiers enroute to attack approximately 200,000 Spanish soldiers occupying Cuba.

The 1st Volunteer Cavalry—"The Rough Riders"— at Kettle Hill near Santiago, Cuba on 1 July 1898.

2-80. The expeditionary force that included Lieutenant Colonel Theodore Roosevelt's volunteer cavalry regiment began landing in Cuba on 22 June 1898. The Army drove the Spanish from the San Juan Heights overlooking the port of Santiago, causing the enemy ships in the port to flee into the waiting guns of the United States Navy. Other expeditionary forces landed in the Spanish possessions of Puerto Rico and the Philippines, following Commodore George Dewey's naval victory at the Battle of Manila Bay. With the end of the war and American acquisition of the Philippines, the Army's task of establishing American authority led to a series of arduous counterguerrilla campaigns to suppress the insurrectos—Filipinos who still fought for independence.

---

## Private Augustus Walley in Cuba

On 24 June 1898 during the Battle of Las Guasimas, Cuba, Major Bell of the 1st Cavalry had gone down with a wound to the leg. Another officer attempted to carry him from the field, but his shattered leg bone broke through the skin, causing so much pain that he had to let Bell down. The fire was so intense that in one plot of ground, fifty feet square, sixteen men were killed or wounded. Still, a fellow American soldier was badly hurt and in need of assistance. Private Augustus Walley of the 10th Cavalry, the "Buffalo Soldiers," his compassion overcoming self-preservation, ran to help the wounded soldier. He and the officer together dragged Major Bell to safety.

Conspicuous gallantry under fire was not new to Walley. He had received the Medal of Honor while assigned to the 9th Cavalry for his actions on August 16, 1881 in combat against hostile Apaches at the Cuchillo Mountains, New Mexico. During the fight Private Burton's horse bolted and carried him into enemy fire where Burton fell from his saddle. Assumed dead, the command was given to fall back to another position, but Burton called out for help. Private Walley, under heavy fire went to Private Burton's assistance and brought him to safety.

Walley was recommended for a second Medal of Honor for his role in saving Major Bell at Las Guasimas. Instead he received a Certificate of Merit for his extraordinary exertion in the preservation of human life. In 1918 Congress upgraded Certificates of Merit to the Distinguished Service Medal and in 1934 to the Distinguished Service Cross.

2-81.    The experience of the Spanish-American War, the perception of increased external threats in a shrinking world, and other looming challenges of the new century called for a thorough reform of Army organization, education, and promotion policies. The new Secretary of War, Elihu Root, added an Army War College as the high point of the service's educational system. He also took steps to replace War Department bureaus and a commanding general with a chief of staff and general staff that could engage in long-range war planning. Also, a new militia act laid the foundation for improved cooperation between the Regular Army and the National Guard. These reforms, as well as some first steps toward joint Army-Navy planning, reflected the emphasis on professionalism, specialization, and organization that characterized the Progressive Era and were in accord with Secretary Root's conviction that the "real object of having an Army is to prepare for war." Subsequently, Congress authorized 100,000 as the regular Army strength in 1902.

2-82.    After the turn of the century, the Army began to look into the value of aircraft. Balloons used for artillery spotting had already proven their worth in the Civil War. But new developments, the dirigible and the airplane, caught the interest of President Theodore Roosevelt. On 1 August 1907 Captain Charles D. Chandler became the head of the Aeronautical Division of the Signal Corps, newly established to develop all forms of flying. In 1908 the corps ordered a dirigible balloon of the Zeppelin type, then in use in Germany, and contracted with the Wright brothers for an airplane. Despite a crash that destroyed the first model, the Wright plane was delivered in 1909. The inventors then began to teach a few enthusiastic young officers to fly; Army aviation was born.

## PANCHO VILLA AND THE PUNITIVE EXPEDITION

2-83. Years of injustice and chafing under dictatorial rule caused the Mexican people to revolt in 1910. The United States attempted to stay out of the affair but was reluctantly drawn into the Mexican Revolution. A number of incidents raised tension between the United States and Mexico, and America began to take sides in the conflict. In May 1916 Pancho Villa's Mexican rebels killed eighteen American soldiers and civilians in a raid on Columbus, New Mexico. Part of the 13th Cavalry, then garrisoned in Columbus, drove Villa off and hastily pursued, killing about 100 "Villistas" before returning to Columbus.

2-84. In an attempt to bring Villa to justice or destroy his ability to raid the US, President Woodrow Wilson sent Brigadier General John J. Pershing to lead an expedition south of the border in an unsuccessful pursuit of Villa. The Mexican government threatened war over the violation of its territory, causing Wilson to call up 112,000 National Guardsmen and to send most of the Regular Army to the border. But the two nations avoided a larger conflict and America withdrew the punitive expedition.

# THE WORLD WARS AND CONTAINMENT

2-85. World War I began in August 1914 after a Bosnian separatist murdered the Archduke Francis Ferdinand of Austria-Hungary and his wife during a visit to Sarajevo. Austria-Hungary demanded that Serbia allow them to investigate the crime but under conditions that Serbia would not accept. Because of numerous alliances and agreements, Austria-Hungary's subsequent declaration of war on Serbia soon embroiled most of Europe. For nearly three years the United States remained technically neutral, though its trade favored the Allies who controlled the seas. America, with its large immigrant population, was not eager to go to war against any of the nations in Europe. Even after German submarines sank the passenger ships Lusitania and Sussex, the United States refrained from joining the conflict. The war in Western Europe degenerated into a bloody stalemate, nearly destroying an entire generation of young men. Both the western allies and Germany launched offensive after offensive in the hopes of achieving a breakthrough that would end the war but all in vain.

## THE UNITED STATES ENTERS WORLD WAR I

2-86. On 23 February 1917 the British turned over to the US Government an intercepted note from the German foreign minister to the German ambassador in Mexico. In the note were instructions to offer Mexico an alliance in the event of war with the United States and promising that Mexico could regain Texas, New Mexico and Arizona. Coupled with Germany's recent resumption of unrestricted submarine warfare, this was the last provocation America needed. On 2 April 1917 President Wilson asked Congress to declare war on Germany because "the world must be made safe for democracy."

2-87. A much more professional Army spearheaded American intervention in World War I. After Wilson's war message in April 1917, Army officers worked with business and government counterparts to mobilize the nation's resources. Yet enormous difficulties resulted from the huge size of the effort. To meet the need for a massive ground force capable of fighting on the European battlefield, the Army drew on its Civil War expertise and on popular acceptance of a more activist federal government to develop a more efficient system of manpower allocation through conscription.

> *Lafayette, we are here.*
> **LTC Charles E. Stanton, at the grave of the Marquis de Lafayette**

2-88. The 1st Infantry Division reached Paris in time to participate in a Fourth of July parade, raising French spirits at a low point in the war. Ultimately, 8 regular Army divisions, 17 National Guard divisions, and 17 newly organized National Army divisions served in France. The US divisions were twice the size of Allied and German divisions but American soldiers and marines had a lot to learn about trench warfare. At training centers near the front they practiced and received a hint of what lay ahead.

2-89. Though slower to arrive than France and Britain wished, the sight of fresh, eager, and strong American soldiers in great numbers, with millions more available, raised the allies' spirits and eroded German morale. But the Allies wanted American soldiers sent directly to British and French formations as individual or unit replacements. However, the Commander in Chief of the American Expeditionary Forces (AEF), General John J. Pershing was determined to preserve the independence of the AEF. He would not allow Americans merely to be absorbed into existing British and French units.

2-90. This stance was based not only on national pride but also on President Wilson's vision that the United States would have to take a more active, leading role in the post-war world. Enabling that role would require a significant role in the war as a distinct fighting force. On occasion Pershing did offer the use of American regiments and in a few instances, even smaller units in the British and French sectors. In fact, two US divisions fought as a corps in the British sector. But Pershing resisted all attempts to get American soldiers sent directly to British and French units as individual replacements.

## Harlem Hellfighters

By early 1918 General Pershing relented somewhat in his policy of not sending Americans directly to the Allies. He provided the infantry regiments of one of the African-American infantry divisions, the 93d, (the US Army was still segregated at the time) directly to the French Army. One of these regiments, the 369th Infantry, was formed from the National Guard's 15th New York and was in combat longer than any other American regiment in the war.

In May 1918, Privates Henry Johnson and Needham Roberts of the 369th were part of a five-man patrol on duty in a listening post along the front line. The other three soldiers were off-watch and sleeping in a dugout to the rear when a 24-man German raiding party caught the post by surprise with a grenade attack. Both Johnson and Roberts were seriously wounded but fought off the first attack and crawled to their own supply of grenades. Throwing them one after another like baseballs at batting practice, they fought back with explosives as Johnson shouted, "turn out the guard," over and over. Grabbing his rifle, he shot a German soldier and clubbed another. He then saw three enemy soldiers trying to drag Roberts away.

Out of grenades and with his rifle now jammed and broken, Johnson pulled out his knife and attacked the three Germans, killing one. Roberts broke free and continued fighting. Hit by fire, Johnson fell wounded and dazed, but nonetheless took a grenade off a dead enemy soldier and threw it at his attackers. It devastated the remaining enemy and they withdrew leaving their dead and a number of rifles and automatic weapons. When reinforcements arrived, they found the two soldiers laughing and singing. Privates Johnson and Roberts were both peppered with shrapnel and shot several times, but remained in good humor and reportedly saw the experience as a great adventure.

Later promoted to Sergeant, Johnson was the first American in World War I awarded the Croix de Guerre with Palm, France's highest award for gallantry. On 13 February 2003, Sergeant Henry Johnson received the Distinguished Service Cross posthumously.

2-91.   Germany saw the potential of the United States and resolved to defeat the French and British allies before US power could be fully brought into the war. In July 1918 the Germans launched an offensive that carried it nearly to the outskirts of Paris. In the line east of Chateau-Thierry was the 3d Infantry Division, just arrived to try to stem the German advance at the Marne River.

2-92.   The division's infantry regiments were deployed along the south bank of the Marne River with the French 125th Division on its right. Attached to the French division were four companies of the US 28th Division, National Guardsmen from Pennsylvania. As the German attack reached and began crossing the Marne River, the French units were forced to withdraw but did not inform the American Guardsmen. The Keystone soldiers fought against many times their own number, delaying and inflicting heavy losses on the enemy, but ultimately most of the Americans were killed or captured. Nonetheless, their bravery and sacrifice helped make the historic stand of the 3d Division possible.

2-93.    The 38th Infantry Regiment soon found itself under attack from three sides and the other regiments of the 3d Division under great enemy pressure, as well. Wave after wave of German infantry crossed the Marne and assailed the front and flanks of the 38th, but the resolute Doughboys held on. When asked by a French commander if his division could hold, Major General Joseph Dickman replied, "Nous resterons la"—We shall remain there. They did, helping to break the German attack and entering into Army history. Two months later the US First Army attacked at St. Mihiel. In the Meuse-Argonne campaign, the AEF contributed to the final Allied drive before the Armistice.

---

### Sergeant Edward Greene at the Marne

Sergeant Greene was a cook for the 3d Division's Battery F, 10th Field Artillery in July 1918. He was without a mission when his field kitchens were destroyed in the pre-assault bombardment prior to the German attack across the Marne river. Sergeant Greene, without being ordered, began carrying ammunition forward to his battery's guns.

For several hours while under constant artillery shell fire and enemy observation, he performed his mission until wounded. He had to be ordered to the rear for medical attention. Sergeant Greene received the Distinguished Service Cross.

---

2-94.    World War I was the impetus for many new innovations in weaponry, industry, and medicine. In an attempt to break the stalemate on the Western Front, the Germans used chlorine gas as a weapon in 1915. Not having anticipated the effectiveness of the weapon against unprepared troops, they did not exploit the resulting panic among the Allied soldiers in the affected area. The Allies soon developed defensive measures to mitigate the effects of chemical weapons, though even today they have terrifying potential against unprotected targets.

2-95.    The British first brought the tank to the Western Front in 1916. But while its initial use was poorly exploited, even later, well-prepared attacks using tanks did not always achieve hoped for success because of the poor reliability and maneuverability of the equipment. Nonetheless, the dawn of tank warfare showed many great military thinkers that fixed fortifications and static positions would soon be obsolete. The US Army fielded two tank brigades in Europe, one of which was commanded by Colonel George S. Patton. The tanks were mostly of French manufacture with American crews, and they also suffered from poor mechanical reliability and maneuverability across the moonscape of "no-man's land." But when the AEF was able to break into the open country, tanks were very useful and gave an indication of their future capabilities.

---

## Corporal Harold W. Roberts at Montrebeau Woods

Corporal Harold W. Roberts was a tank driver in A Company, 344<sup>th</sup> Tank Battalion during the St. Mihiel and Meuse-Argonne offensives. His company was advancing under heavy enemy artillery fire in the Montrebeau Woods. After about a mile, the tank commander/gunner, Sergeant Virgil Morgan and Corporal Roberts saw a disabled tank with a soldier crouched by it. As Roberts stopped his tank, the soldier crawled toward them, opened the door and asked for help. They said they could not help at the moment but would return after the battle and render aid and drove off into the heart of the German artillery barrage.

Ahead lay a large mass of bushes that they thought was a machine gun nest and drove the tank into it. In an instant, they found themselves overturned. Recovering from the shock they discovered the tank had fallen into a tank trap with about 10 feet of water in it. The tank had only one hatch and with water rushing in Roberts said to Morgan, "Well, only one of us can get out, and out you go." With this he pushed Sergeant Morgan from the tank. Morgan tried to assist Roberts, but with the heavy gunfire around the area, was unable to do so. After the enemy fire ceased, Sergeant Morgan returned but found Roberts dead.

Corporal Roberts was posthumously awarded the Medal of Honor, the second tanker to receive it. Camp Nacimiento, California, was renamed Camp Roberts in 1941. It was the only Army installation at the time to be named for an enlisted soldier.

---

2-96.    The airplane also demonstrated its potential. The Army first began experimenting with aircraft before the war and, when war came, attempted to build an air component to support its ground forces. Many enthusiastic pilots fought in France, such as Eddie Rickenbacker and Frank Luke. By the end of the war most American pilots were still flying French or British aircraft as American industry had not caught up with the demand. Nonetheless, aircraft and American flyers had proven their worth and that of the US Army Air Service.

2-97.    As a direct result of US entry into the war, Germany realized victory was out of its reach. It still hoped to gain armistice terms allowing it to retain captured territory. But as the American forces helped push the German army back and the naval blockade of Germany made her citizens' lives more miserable, revolutionary elements within Germany began to exert influence. Finally it was clear to the German High Command that it could not continue the war without risking complete destruction of the nation and negotiated for peace.

2-98.    The Armistice ended the fighting at the 11<sup>th</sup> hour of the 11<sup>th</sup> day of the 11<sup>th</sup> month of 1918. Known for many years as Armistice Day, it is now called Veteran's Day in the United States. A final peace treaty was signed at Versailles the following year, although the United States negotiated a separate treaty with Germany in 1921. With the other allies, the US Army began an occupation of Germany west of the Rhine near Cologne on 1 Dec 1918 but had withdrawn all soldiers by 24 January 1923.

---

## The Unknown Soldier

During and after World War I the Graves Registration Service positively identified most of the remains of US servicemen who died in Europe during the war. There were 1,237 who were never identified. Congress resolved to construct a tomb as a final resting-place for one of the unknowns to honor all of them.

On 24 October 1921, four caskets carrying the remains of unidentified American soldiers were brought to a room in the Hotel De Ville in the French town of Chalons-sur-Marne. One American soldier entered, alone. Sergeant Edward F. Younger, Headquarters Company, 2d Battalion, 50th Infantry, from Chicago, Illinois, had fought in the war as a private, corporal and sergeant. He was wounded twice and had received the Distinguished Service Cross for valor in battle. In his hands he carried roses, a gift of Mr. Brasseur Bruffer, a former member of the city council of Chalons, who had lost two sons in the war. As a French band played a hymn outside, Sergeant Younger slowly walked around the caskets several times and finally paused in front of one of them. Gently he laid his roses on the casket, and then came to attention, faced the body, and saluted. He had chosen "The Unknown."

"I went into the room and walked past the caskets," he later explained. "I walked around them three times. Suddenly I stopped. It was as though something had pulled me. A voice seemed to say: *'This is a pal of yours.'"*

The remains were later transported to the French port of Le Havre, put onboard the cruiser *USS Olympia*, and sailed for home, arriving on November 9th. The body lay in state in the Capitol Rotunda for two days as over 90,000 people quietly filed by. On 11 November 1921, this brave soldier, whose true identify will forever be a mystery, was formally interred on native soil. Since then unknown soldiers from World War II, the Korean War and, for a time, the Vietnam War, have joined him. The Unknown Soldier from the Vietnam War was later identified; the space where he once rested remains empty.

## BETWEEN THE WARS

2-99.    Revolutionary turmoil in Soviet Russia induced President Wilson in August 1918 to direct Army participation in allied stability and support operations in European Russia and in Siberia. As a result, about 15,000 soldiers deployed to the Murmansk area and Siberia. These Army contingents guarded supplies and lines of communication but incurred about as many combat casualties as the Army did in Cuba in 1898. After the withdrawal of American occupation forces from Germany and Russia, few Army forces remained stationed on foreign soil. The Marine Corps provided most of the small foreign garrisons and expeditionary forces required after World War I, particularly in the Caribbean area.

2-100.  One result of WWI was the creation of the League of Nations. This international body, roughly similar to the United Nations of today, was envisioned as a forum where disputes could be settled peacefully. If peaceful negotiations failed, the League could collectively force one or more belligerents to comply with League mandates. The United States never joined the League due to a variety of reasons, including George Washington's warning against "entangling alliances" and since a condition of membership was a pledge to provide military forces when and where the League called for them.

### National Defense Act of 1920

2-101. Legislation following the First World War included the new National Defense Act of June 4, 1920, which governed the organization and regulation of the Army until 1950. The Act has been acknowledged as one of the most constructive pieces of military legislation ever adopted in the United States. It established the Army of the United States as an organization of three components: the professional Regular Army, the National Guard, and the Organized Reserves (Officers' and Enlisted Reserve Corps). Each component would contribute its appropriate share of troops in a war emergency. In effect the Act acknowledged the actual practice of the United States throughout its history of maintaining a standing peacetime force too small to meet the needs of a major war and, therefore, depending on a new Army of civilian soldiers for large mobilizations.

2-102. The training of reserve components now became a major peacetime task of the Regular Army. For this reason the Army was authorized a maximum officer strength more than three times that before WWI. The act also directed that officer promotions, except for doctors and chaplains, would be made from a single list, a reform that equalized opportunity for advancement throughout most of the Army. The Regular Army was authorized a maximum enlisted strength of 280,000, but Congress soon reduced that to below 150,000.

2-103. The Act of 1920 contemplated a National Guard of 436,000, but its actual peacetime strength became stabilized at about 180,000. This force relieved the regular Army of any duty in curbing domestic disturbances within the states from 1921 until 1941 and stood ready for immediate induction into the active Army whenever necessary. The War Department, in addition to supplying large quantities of surplus World War I materiel for equipment, applied about one-tenth of its military budget to the support of the Guard in the years between wars. Guardsmen engaged in regular armory drills and 15 days of field training each year. The increasingly federalized Guard was better trained in 1939 than it had been when mobilized for Mexican border duty in 1916. Numerically, the National Guard was the largest component of the Army between 1922 and 1939.

2-104. From 1921 to 1936 Americans thought that the United States could and should avoid future wars with other major powers by maintaining a minimum of defensive military strength, avoiding entangling commitments with Europe, and attempting to promote international peace and arms limits. Subsequently a treaty in 1922 temporarily checked a naval arms race. As long as both the United States and Japan honored treaty provisions, neither side could operate offensively in the Pacific. In effect, these provisions also meant that it would be impossible for the United States to defend the Philippines against a Japanese attack.

## Transformation in the 1920s

After World War I ended, America discovered it had defeated its principle adversary and there were no known nation-state opponents. Technology provided new, more lethal weapons, notably the tank and the airplane, which the Army sought to use effectively. The Army began to put intellectual effort into determining both the best ways to use existing technology and in how to best defend from current or future threats realizing that warfare, tactics, weapons and priorities would also change over time.

This situation, in some ways similar to the Transformation process our Army is undergoing today, took advantage of an expected respite from major conflicts. The Army conducted wargames, simulations and in-depth studies during the 1920s and 1930s. While industry continued to develop better radios, tanks, planes, and other tools of war, the Army continued to think through the problems of integrating the new technology, training soldiers, mobilization, and supporting mechanized forces. But the Army had a serious drawback in the inability to conduct large-scale exercises to confirm theory. Officers could visualize new techniques *might* work, but could not prove them nor incorporate valid lessons learned from actual application.

During this period the Army spent a great deal of its scarce resources on educating officers so they could be adaptive and versatile leaders. The Command and Staff College at Fort Leavenworth and the Infantry School at Fort Benning were two of the most important centers, not only in the educational processes, but also in the development of doctrine and concepts.

2-105. The "war to end all wars,"—World War I—was poorly named. A number of conflicts erupted in the 1920s and in 1931 the Japanese army seized Manchuria. Japan quit the League of Nations and a few years later renounced naval limitation treaties. In Europe, Adolf Hitler came to power in Germany in 1933, and by 1936 Nazi Germany had denounced the Treaty of Versailles, began rearming, and reoccupied the demilitarized Rhineland. Italy's Benito Mussolini began his career of aggression by attacking Ethiopia in 1935. A revolution in Spain in 1936 not only produced another fascist dictatorship but also a war that became a proving ground for World War II. The neutrality acts passed by the US Congress between 1935 and 1937 were a direct response to these European developments. The United States opened diplomatic relations with Soviet Russia in 1933 and in 1934 promised eventual independence to the Philippines.

2-106. The Army concentrated on equipping and training its combat units for mobile warfare rather than for the static warfare that had characterized operations on the western front in the First World War. To increase the maneuverability of its principal ground unit, the division, the Army decided after field tests to reorganize the infantry division by reducing the number of its infantry regiments from four to three, and to make it more mobile by using motor transportation only. The planned wartime strength of the new division was to be little more than half the size of its World War I counterpart.

## WORLD WAR II

2-107. The German annexation of Austria in March 1938 followed by the Czech crisis in September of the same year showed the United States and the other democratic nations that another world conflict was likely. War had already begun in the far east when Japan invaded China in 1937. After Germany seized all of Czechoslovakia in March 1939, war in Europe became inevitable. Hitler had no intention of stopping with that move and Great Britain and France decided that they must fight rather than yield anything more. On 23 August 1939 Nazi Germany and the Soviet Union agreed to a non-aggression pact, a partition of Poland and a Soviet free hand in Finland, Estonia, Latvia, and Lithuania. On 1 September 1939 Germany invaded Poland. France and Great Britain responded by declaring war on Germany, a course that could not lead to victory without aid from the United States. Still the majority of Americans wanted to stay out of the new war if possible, and this tempered the Nation's responses to the international situation.

2-108. Immediately after the European war started, President Franklin D. Roosevelt proclaimed a limited national emergency and authorized increases in regular Army and National Guard enlisted strengths to 227,000 and 235,000 respectively. At his urging Congress soon gave indirect support to the western democracies by ending the prohibition on sales of munitions to nations at war. British and French orders for munitions helped to prepare American industry for the large-scale war production that was to come.

### Expansion of the Army

2-109. Under the leadership of the Chief of Staff of the Army, General George C. Marshall, in the summer of 1940 **the Army began** a large expansion designed to protect the United States and the rest of the Western Hemisphere against any hostile forces from Europe. To fill the ranks of the newly expanded Army, Congress approved induction of the National Guard into federal service and the calling up of the Organized Reserves. Then it approved the first peacetime draft of untrained civilian manpower in the Nation's history in the Selective Service and Training Act of 14 September 1940. Units of the National Guard, draftees and the Reserve officers to train them, entered service as rapidly as the Army could build camps to house them. During the last six months of 1940 the active Army more than doubled in strength, and by mid-1941 it achieved its planned strength of one and a half million officers and men. The increase in ground units and in the Army Air Corps laid the foundation for even larger expansion when war came the following year.

2-110. On the eve of France's defeat in June 1940 President Roosevelt had directed the transfer or diversion of large stocks of Army World War I weapons, and of ammunition and aircraft, to both France and Great Britain. The foreign aid program culminated in the Lend-Lease Act of March 1941, which openly avowed the intention of the United States to become an "arsenal of democracy" against aggression. Prewar foreign aid was a measure of self defense; its basic purpose was to help contain the military might of the Axis powers until the United States could complete its own protective mobilization.

2-111. The Nazis invaded the Soviet Union on 22 June 1941. Three days later US Army troops landed in Greenland to protect it against German attack and to build bases for the air route across the North Atlantic. The President also decided that Americans should relieve British troops guarding Iceland. The initial contingent of American forces reached there in early July followed by a sizable Army expeditionary force in September. In August the President and British Prime Minister Winston Churchill met in Newfoundland and drafted the Atlantic Charter, which defined the general terms of a just peace for the world. The overt American moves in 1941 toward involvement in the war against Germany had solid backing in public opinion, but Americans were still not in favor of a declaration of war.

2-112. As the United States prepared for war in the Atlantic, American policy toward Japan toughened. Although the United States wanted to avoid a two-front war, it would not do so by surrendering vital areas or interests to the Japanese as the price for peace. When in late July 1941 the Japanese moved large forces into former French colonies in southern Indochina (now Vietnam), the United States responded by freezing Japanese assets and cutting off oil and steel shipments to Japan. The US demanded Japanese withdrawal from the occupied areas. Although the Japanese were unwilling to give up their newly acquired territory, they could not maintain operations for long without US oil and steel. They continued to negotiate with the United States but tentatively decided in September to embark on a war of conquest in Southeast Asia and the Indies as soon as possible. To enable this they would attack the great American naval base of Pearl Harbor in Hawaii. When intensive last-minute negotiations in November failed to produce any accommodation, the Japanese made their decision for war irrevocable.

### The United States Enters World War II

2-113. The Japanese attack of December 7, 1941 on Pearl Harbor and the Philippines at once ended any division of American opinion toward participation in the war. America went to war with popular support that was unprecedented in the military history of the United States. This was also the first time in its history that the United States had entered a war with a large Army in being and an industrial system partially retooled for war. The Army numbered 1,643,477 and was ready to defend the Western Hemisphere against invasion. But it was not ready to take part in large-scale operations across the oceans. Many months would pass before the United States could launch even limited offensives. Still, General Marshall had overseen a huge expansion of the Army and ensured its soldiers received the best training possible to prepare them for war.

*Once again, the destiny of our country is in the hands of the individual soldier. Upon your courage and efficiency depends the salvation of all that we hold dear. Prepare yourselves, then, to become good soldiers. For you will strike the mighty blows that will surely destroy the evil tyrants who menace our freedom, our homes, and our loved ones.*

**Message from President Franklin D. Roosevelt,** *The Army and You,* **1941**

2-114. During the first year after the Japanese attack on Pearl Harbor in December 1941, the Army's major task was to prevent disaster and preserve American morale while building strength for the eventual counteroffensive. Cut off from relief, American and Philippine soldiers under General Douglas MacArthur held out for over four months against superior Japanese air, naval, and ground power before they were forced to surrender. MacArthur obeyed President Roosevelt's orders to evacuate to Australia prior to the final capitulation. But he vowed to return to the Philippines, a promise which, combined with the heroism of the American and Philippine defenders, gave the Nation a needed symbol of defiance.

2-115. In India Lieutenant General Joseph W. "Vinegar Joe" Stilwell surveyed the remnants of his Chinese army after an arduous retreat from Burma and frankly admitted, "We got a hell of a beating... I think we ought to find out what caused it, go back, and retake it." The bombing raid on Tokyo in April 1942 led by Colonel James H. Doolittle gave American morale a boost. The US Navy's victory in the Battle of Midway helped to seize the initiative away from the Japanese forces. But it was not until November 1942 that American soldiers could take the offensive on a large scale, with the invasion of North Africa and the campaigns on Guadalcanal and New Guinea. When they did so, they learned hard lessons in the demands of modern combat. At Buna they bogged down in the jungle against strong Japanese positions. After having overrun Morocco and Algeria against little opposition, they took heavy losses at the hands of the German *Afrika Korps* near Kasserine Pass in Tunisia.

2-116. During 1943 and early 1944, the Army overcame its early mistakes and helped turn the tide against the Axis. In Tunisia, American troops recovered from the defeat at Kasserine Pass to participate in an offensive that forced the surrender of Axis forces in North Africa. Under the leadership of General Dwight D. Eisenhower and Lieutenant General George S. Patton, Jr., they joined with Allied forces to drive the Germans and Italians from the island of Sicily. American and Allied troops then landed on the Italian mainland and, against fierce German opposition, slowly advanced up the peninsula to Rome by early June 1944. As early as 1942, US Army Air Force bombers took the war to the German heartland and began preparing the way for the invasion of France.

*A veteran of the last war pretty well summed up the two wars when he said, "this is just like the last war, only the holes are bigger."*

**Ernie Pyle**

2-117. In the Pacific, MacArthur's forces captured Buna and leapfrogged their way along the northern New Guinea coastline. Soldiers, marines and sailors advanced through the Solomon and Marshall Islands of the South and Central Pacific. In northern Burma Stilwell's Chinese army, aided by a specially trained force of Americans known as Merrill's Marauders, drove back Japanese defenders and laid siege to the key crossroads city of Myitkyina. By restoring land communications with China, Stilwell hoped to supply the Chinese with the means to defeat the Japanese on the Asian mainland while American forces converged on Japan from the Pacific.

**"Tip of the Avalanche."**
**The 36th Infantry Division Lands at Salerno, Italy on 9 September 1943.**

2-118. The immense mobilization of resources and the long drive back from initial defeat led ultimately to the advance into the Axis homelands. In mid 1944, Allied forces everywhere were advancing. In the Pacific, US forces continued a methodical island-hopping campaign and prepared for the liberation of the Philippines. Allied forces in Italy struggled with the terrain, weather, and the German army, but made progress anyway, capturing Rome on 4 June 1944. In Great Britain, the Allies were ready to spring across the English Channel to the coast of Normandy.

2-119. On D-Day, 6 June 1944, General Dwight D. Eisenhower's Allied armies landed in France. The 82d and 101st Airborne Divisions parachuted into Normandy in the early morning darkness. Just after dawn, the 1st, 4th, and 29th Infantry Divisions assaulted the beaches codenamed Utah and Omaha. At the same time, British and Canadian soldiers were landing further east on the beaches known as Gold, Juno and Sword.

2-120. The US airborne drops scattered soldiers inland from Utah beach, causing extreme confusion among the enemy. The 4th Infantry Division got ashore at Utah with few losses. On Omaha beach the 1st and 29th Infantry Divisions had more difficulty. Veteran German soldiers occupied strong fortifications on bluffs overlooking the beaches. Their heavy fire at first put the success of the landings in jeopardy. But the personal courage and adaptability of individual soldiers allowed them to eventually get across the beach, up the bluffs, and inland. The cost of gaining the foothold in France was high. Over 6,000 Americans were killed, wounded, or missing.

---

### A Company, 116<sup>th</sup> Infantry on D-Day

Many soldiers of the 116<sup>th</sup> Infantry Regiment were National Guardsmen who had originally signed on with units in Virginia and Maryland. They were part of the 29<sup>th</sup> Infantry Division and their regiment was in the first wave of the landing on Omaha beach. 200 soldiers of A Company, 116<sup>th</sup> Infantry were in seven of the first landing craft to hit the beach that morning. Many of them came from Bedford, Virginia.

Strong currents had pushed many landing craft off target that morning, but A Company was right on target—the sector codenamed Dog Green. These soldiers landed almost alone as adjacent units landed further east. With no other Americans in sight, German defenders there concentrated all their fire on those seven landing craft.

One of the landing craft exploded after hitting a mine or being struck by a German artillery shell. Another dropped its ramp right in front of a German machine gun nest that killed every soldier before he could get off the boat. In ten minutes, every officer and every noncommissioned officer were dead or wounded. As A Company struggled ashore, German fire eventually hit all but a few dozen soldiers.

But their sacrifice brought weapons, explosives, and ammunition ashore, even if strewn across the beach, which was critical to the following waves of soldiers coming ashore. As the tide rose, these soldiers would abandon their equipment in the deep water but retrieved and used what A Company soldiers had died to bring to the beach.

Bedford, at the time a town of a little over 3,000, lost 19 of her sons on D-Day and 4 more before the war was won.

---

2-121. Also in June 1944 American soldiers and marines came ashore on the Mariana Islands, part of the inner ring of Japan's Pacific defenses. After two months of near stalemate in the hedgerows of Normandy, American troops under Lieutenant Generals Omar N. Bradley and Patton broke through the German lines and raced across France. In little over a month following the breakout, Allied armies had liberated nearly the whole country. A second invasion near Toulon on 15 August sealed the German army's fate in France.

2-122. The Allied advance slowed in September due to gasoline shortages brought on by the lack of a large, nearby port and the high tempo of operations. The respite gave the Germans time to reorganize their defenses along the French-German border. By stripping units and reinforcements from the Russian front, Hitler gambled on a surprise counteroffensive in the Ardennes in December that became known as the Battle of the Bulge.

2-123. The German attack in the Ardennes on 16 December 1944 was a surprise for the Allies because it fell on a sector that General Eisenhower thought was poorly suited for decisive offensive operations. In defensive positions early that morning were units that were brand new to the European Theater of Operations (ETO) or those that were recovering from extended duty on the line. The German attack also surprised these soldiers. But it wasn't long before they began to resist, slowing the German attack.

---

### Krinkelt-Rocherath during the Battle of the Bulge

Krinkelt-Rocherath was the name of two adjacent villages on the northern shoulder of the Ardennes attack. Defending these villages were a patchwork of units, including parts of the 2d Infantry Division.

On 19 December 1944 Technician Fourth Grade (Tech/4) Truman Kimbro, Company C, 2d Engineer Combat Battalion, led a squad to emplace mines on a crossroads near Rocherath. Nearing the objective, he and his squad were driven back under withering fire from an enemy tank and at least 20 infantrymen. All approaches to the crossroads were covered by intense enemy fire. Tech/4 Kimbro left his squad in a covered position and crawled alone, with mines, toward the crossroads. Close to his objective he was severely wounded, but continued to drag himself forward and placed his mines across the road. As he tried to return to his squad he was killed by enemy fire. The mines laid by Tech/4 Kimbro delayed the enemy armor and prevented attacks on withdrawing columns. He received the Medal of Honor posthumously.

Even though Americans would soon withdraw from Krinkelt-Rocherath, soldiers were fighting hard and delaying the enemy at nearly every crossroad and village. The northern shoulder would hold.

---

2-124. The Ardennes battle ended 31 January 1945 and cost over 80,000 American casualties, but the Allies ultimately prevailed due to the courage and skill of US Army soldiers. While very difficult fighting remained, German offensive power was seriously weakened. The fighting near Colmar, France, was as difficult as any thus far in the war. At nearby Holtzwihr 2LT Audie Murphy performed the actions for which he would receive the Medal of Honor.

2-125. In the east, the Soviet Army was within reach of Berlin while in Italy the Allies were steadily moving north to the Po River Valley. In Germany itself, US and British forces were poised to cross the Rhine River. On 7 March 1945 soldiers of the 9th Armored Division found an intact bridge at Remagen, Germany. Realizing the importance of the opportunity, they stormed across without hesitation, the first Allied soldiers to cross the Rhine. Other crossings followed on 22 and 23 March 1945.

2-126. Once across the Rhine, German resistance soon crumbled and the Army raced across Germany, into Czechoslovakia and Austria, linking up with Allied units coming up from Italy and with the Soviet Army at Torgau, Germany on 25 April 1945. The war in Europe ended 8 May 1945.

2-127. In Burma, the fall of Myitkyina in August 1944 and further Chinese and American advances to the south finally reopened the Burma Road in February 1945. In the Pacific, American soldiers and marines captured the Marianas in July 1944, bringing US Army Air Force B-29 bombers within range of the Japanese home islands. General MacArthur's forces landed at Leyte in October, fulfilling his promise to return to the Philippines. By February 1945 the US Sixth Army had recaptured Manila after bitter house-to-house fighting and was securing the main Philippine island of Luzon. The campaign would take a total of seven months and cost 40,000 American casualties.

**A squad leader of the 25th Infantry Division points out a suspected enemy position near Baugio, Luzon on 23 March 1945.**

2-128. Soldiers and marines invaded the island of Okinawa, part of Japan itself, on 1 April 1945. Defending the island were 120,000 Japanese soldiers and sailors, occupying strong fortifications inland. Capturing the island took nearly three months of bitter fighting. All but 7,000 enemy soldiers died, as did tens of thousands of Okinawan civilians caught in the terrible battle. Over 7,000 American soldiers and marines were killed at Okinawa. Army and Marine divisions suffered a 35% casualty rate. The US Navy was under near constant Kamikaze attack as the battle wore on and 5,000 American sailors also lost their lives.

## Private First Class Desmond T. Doss at Okinawa

Private First Class Doss was a company medic with the 307th Infantry Regiment in the 77th Infantry Division near Urasoe Mura, Okinawa. On 29 April 1945, the 1st Battalion assaulted a high escarpment. As our soldiers reached the top, enemy artillery, mortar, and machinegun fire inflicted about 75 casualties and drove the others back. PFC Doss refused to seek cover and remained in the fire-swept area with the wounded, carrying them one by one to the edge of the escarpment. There he lowered them on a rope-supported litter down the face of a cliff to friendly hands.

On 4 May PFC Doss treated four men who had been cut down while assaulting a strongly defended cave. He advanced through a shower of grenades to within 8 yards of the enemy in the cave's mouth, where he treated the wounded before making four separate trips under fire to evacuate them to safety.

On 5 May, when an American was severely wounded by fire from a cave, PFC Doss crawled to him where he had fallen 25 feet from the enemy position, rendered aid, and carried him 100 yards to safety while continually exposed to enemy fire.

During a night attack on 21 May, PFC Doss remained exposed while the rest of his company took cover, giving aid to the injured until he was himself seriously wounded in the legs by the explosion of a grenade. Rather than call another medic from cover, he cared for his own injuries and waited 5 hours before litter bearers reached him and started carrying him to cover. PFC Doss, seeing a more critically wounded man nearby, crawled off the litter and insisted the bearers give their first attention to the other man. Awaiting the litter bearers' return, he was again struck, this time suffering a compound fracture of an arm. He bound a rifle stock to his shattered arm as a splint and then crawled 300 yards over rough terrain to the aid station.

PFC Doss received the Medal of Honor from President Harry S. Truman on 12 October 1945.

2-129. When American soldiers and marines completed the campaign on Okinawa in June, they had closed the ring around Japan. This effectively isolated it from its conquered territories in Asia and continued bombing by Army Air Force B-29's crippled its industry. But since the Japanese government continued to ignore Allied demands for surrender, an invasion of Japan seemed necessary. The Battle of Okinawa showed what the cost might be if the United States had to invade the Japanese home islands. Estimates of total American casualties in an invasion of Japan ran from 100,000 to as high as one million. Japanese casualties, both combatant and noncombatant, would have been far heavier.

2-130. With this knowledge, President Truman authorized the use of two atomic bombs against Japan, destroying Hiroshima on 6 August 1945 and Nagasaki on 9 August 1945. Faced with the prospect of utter destruction of his country and people, Japan's Emperor Hirohito ordered his armed forces to cease resistance. In Tokyo Bay on 2 September 1945, Japan and the Allies signed the document that ended the most destructive war in history. Over 405,000 Americans had died, including 235,000 soldiers killed in action.

## COLD WAR

2-131. The Army was the principal occupation force in Europe and in Japan after the war ended. As after all of America's wars, the Nation demobilized rapidly, so that by 1950 the active Army had a total of 591,000 soldiers in 10 Divisions in Japan, Europe, and the US. The reserve component included 730,000 soldiers and 27 divisions.

The 7<sup>th</sup> Infantry Division Band on the capital grounds in Seoul in 1945.

2-132. The end of WWII left the United States and the Soviet Union as the greatest military powers in the world. Within two years after Hiroshima, Americans found themselves in a "Cold War," a long-term global struggle of power and ideology against the Soviet Union and international communism. Aware that technology and changes in world politics had ended the age of free security, the nation could no longer afford to leave to others the task of fending off aggressors while it belatedly mobilized. Americans gradually came to accept alliance commitments, such as the North Atlantic Treaty Organization (NATO), a sizable professional military establishment that stressed readiness and even a peacetime draft.

**Equipment of the US Army Constabulary.**
**Army units occupying Germany in the years after World War II were called constabulary units. Shown here are vehicles used by the Constabulary in 1946—from left to right: M8 armored car, M24 Chaffee light tank, 1/4-ton jeep. Overhead is an L-5 Sentinel observation aircraft.**

2-133. The National Security Act of 1947 was a sweeping reorganization of the US military. It established the Department of Defense and separate military departments of the Army, Navy, and a new, separate United States Air Force made up of the former Army Air Force. The US Air Force today cherishes as its own the traditions and stalwart service of the Air Service, Army Air Corps, and Army Air Force.

2-134. The United States had demobilized after WWII but nonetheless attempted to contain Soviet expansion. Eastern Europe was inextricably under communist control, but the western Allies did help Greece avoid falling under communist domination. In 1949 the Soviet Union successfully tested an atomic bomb, an event that possibly emboldened communist expansion. While the next 40 years were free of direct conflict between the US and USSR, a number of smaller wars erupted as the US and western Allies attempted to contain this expansion.

### KOREA

2-135. The first major test of the US resolve to contain communist expansion came on 25 June 1950 when seven infantry divisions and a tank brigade of the North Korean People's Army (NKPA) struck south across the 38th parallel. That was the line that in the last days of WWII the US and USSR agreed would be the demarcation line between the occupation forces of those two countries as they moved onto the Korean peninsula. The NKPA invasion was, at the time, thought to be part of a grand plan by the USSR to achieve world domination through force of arms.

2-136. The North Korean forces quickly overran the poorly equipped army of the Republic of Korea (ROK), and North Korean troops entered Seoul on 28 June. President Truman decided that the United States, with the United Nations (UN), had to assist with military forces if the ROK was to remain a free and independent nation. The United States alerted and deployed Army forces from occupation duty in Japan, and a task force first met the enemy north of Osan on 5 July 1950. Task Force Smith was overwhelmed by NKPA forces in that first engagement, but despite the loss, America continued to help South Korea resist the aggression.

---

### Task Force Smith

The first ground combat unit in Korea was a task force built from the 1st Battalion, 21st Infantry of the 24th Infantry Division, then on occupation duty in Japan. Commanded by LTC Charles Smith, the task force arrived in Pusan without two of its companies. The mission was to move to Taejon and block the enemy as far north as possible. On 4 July 1950 a battery of 105-mm artillery joined the task force. The infantry dug in north of Osan on high ground that had visibility all the way to the next town of Suwon, and the artillery emplaced a mile back. The road on which any NKPA force must advance led right through the task force.

Despite the excellent position, the task force had serious disadvantages. It was alone, with no support on the left or right. It was armed with few anti-tank weapons and most of these would not penetrate the frontal armor of an enemy T-34 tank, and no anti-tank mines were available.

At 0730 on 5 July 1950, a column of T-34 tanks approached from Suwon. The soldiers of the task force stayed at their posts while 33 tanks bore down on them. The artillery, recoilless rifles, and bazooka teams engaged these tanks but most of them passed through the task force's positions undamaged. They kept moving south, cutting comunications with the artillery.

About an hour after the tanks had passed through, LTC Smith saw trucks and over 1000 infantry approaching from Suwon. The task force repelled all attempts at frontal attacks, but soon the enemy was moving on the flanks. Without artillery support, low on ammunition, and with more and more enemy infantry moving around his force, LTC Smith decided at 1430 to disengage and head toward Ansong, east of Osan. Most of the task force's casualties occurred while withdrawing, but the whole force might have been lost had they stayed any longer. The task force lost its cohesion and small units and even individual soldiers made their way to friendly lines. By 7 July LTC Smith could account for only 250 of his 400 soldiers. It was a rough start in a long war.

---

2-137. Two years before the Korean War started, President Truman had directed the Armed Forces to integrate, that is, to end the practice of segregating African-Americans into separate units. But the Army had not fully implemented that executive order when fighting began in Korea. As casualties mounted and manpower needs increased, large numbers of replacements, including African-American soldiers, came into the Korean Theater of Operations. It became clear that to be effective and efficient, the Army in Korea had to accelerate integration. The Army began to assign soldiersto units regardless of race. By mid-1951 no segregated units remained in Korea.

**Artillery gun crew waits for the order to fire on the enemy, 25 July 1950.**

2-138. During the first few months of the war the US Army and UN forces fought a series of defensive actions to buy time to bring sufficient combat power into Korea to attack. By the end of August 1950, the UN was entrenched in the southeastern tip of the Korean peninsula called the Pusan Perimeter. Air and ground action had reduced NKPA forces to the point where the UN could counterattack. In conjunction with a US Army and Marine amphibious assault on 15 September 1950 at Inch'on, west of Seoul, the UN forces broke out of the Pusan perimeter. The NKPA was soon in full retreat and the UN began a pursuit. On 26 October 1950 the ROK Army 6th Division reached the Yalu River, along the Chinese border and the US 7th Infantry Division did so on 21 November 1950.

2-139. As the US led UN forces passed the 38th Parallel on 7 October 1950, The People's Republic of China (PRC) warned the UN through intermediaries that it would not allow an approach to the Chinese border. The UN Command ignored these warnings, as well as subsequent evidence of Chinese intervention in Korea. The UN advance was halted by Communist Chinese Forces (CCF) along the Ch'ong'Chon River and around the Changjin (Chosin) Reservoir. UN forces transitioned to the defense as

300,000 CCF soldiers poured into, around, and through UN lines. The UN retreated through the fierce winter of 1950-1951. But soldiers regained their confidence with a series of offensives beginning in January 1951 that led to the recapture of Seoul, stabilizing the situation.

---

### Chaplain Emil J. Kapaun in Korea

On 2 November 1950 the 8th Regiment of the 1st Cavalry Division, especially the 3d Battalion, suffered heavy losses in fighting with Chinese forces. Chaplain (CPT) Emil J. Kapaun, a veteran of the Burma-India Theater in World War II, was with them.

The battalion was nearly destroyed in the battle. Enemy soldiers captured Chaplain Kapaun while he was with a group of over 50 wounded he had helped gather in an old dugout. Ordered to leave many of those for whom he had risked his life, Kapaun and a few ambulatory wounded eventually reached a prison camp. For 6 months, under the most deprived conditions, he fought Communist indoctrination among the men, ministered to the sick and dying, and stole food from the enemy in trying to keep his fellow soldiers alive. Eventually, suffering from a blood clot, pneumonia, and dysentery, he died there on 23 May 1951. Chaplain Kapaun received the Legion of Merit posthumously.

At a memorial service for Chaplain Kapaun in 1954, Chief of Chaplains Patrick J. Ryan relayed the feelings of former prisoners, "Men said of him that for a few minutes he could invest a seething hut with the grandeur of a cathedral... he was able to inspire others so that they could go on living—when it would have been easier for them to die."

---

2-140. The United States and South Korea provided the vast majority of the manpower and America provided most of the materiel to fight the Korean War. Great Britain, Australia, New Zealand, Canada, Turkey, and other nations also provided cobat forces. In addition, the US Army could not have succeeded without the National Guard and US Army Reserve units that mobilized and went to Korea.

2-141. While both sides had indicated willingness to end the war roughly along the current front lines, they would continue to fight it out for 2 ½ more years as negotiators attempted to find a formula for peace. This period was marked by offensives on each side that tried to gain concessions in the negotiations with pressure on the battlefield. Some of the bloodiest actions of the war occurred in these battles that tested the will of the UN or the Chinese to continue the war. The problem at the truce negotiations rested primarily on the issue of the return of prisoners of war (POW). The communists wanted all POWs returned without qualification while the UN, recognizing that many enemy soldiers had been forced into service, wanted to allow those who wished to stay in South Korea to do so.

2-142. When Dwight D. Eisenhower became President of the United States and Stalin died in the Soviet Union, uncertainty enveloped the communist cause. In addition, Chinese leader Mao Zedong began to see that the war in Korea was detracting from his ability to address issues inside China. These factors contributed to a new commitment to end the war. As peace became closer and closer a reality, so too did both sides desire to gain as favorable terrain as possible. This led to a number of battles in the last days before the truce was signed. The Armistice became effective on 27 July 1953.

---

### Corporal Gilbert G. Collier, the Last Army Medal of Honor Recipient of the Korean War

Corporal Collier was assigned to F Company, 2d Battalion, 223d Infantry Regiment, 40th Infantry Division. On 20 July 1953, Corporal Collier was point man and assistant leader of a night combat patrol when he and his commanding officer slipped and fell from a sixty-foot cliff. The leader, incapacitated by a badly sprained ankle, ordered the patrol to return to the safety of friendly lines. Although suffering from a painful back injury, Corporal Collier voluntarily remained with his leader.

The two managed to crawl over the ridgeline to the next valley, where they waited until the next nightfall to continue toward their company's position. Shortly after leaving their hideout, they were ambushed and in the ensuring firefight, Corporal Collier killed two of the enemy but was wounded and separated from his companion. Ammunition expended, he closed with four of the enemy, killing, wounding, and routing them with his bayonet. Mortally wounded in this fight, he died while trying to reach and assist his leader. He was posthumously promoted to sergeant and then received the 130th Medal of Honor of the Korean War.

The Armistice that ended the Korean War went into effect 7 days later on 27 July 1953.

---

## VIETNAM

2-143. The containment policy, drawing a line against communism throughout the world, led the Army to the Republic of Vietnam. In 1950 the United States began aiding the French colonial rulers of Indochina, who were attempting to suppress a revolt by the Communist-dominated Viet Minh. When the French withdrew from Indochina in 1954, the former colony became the nations of Laos, Cambodia, and North and South Vietnam. US Army personnel played a key role in American assistance to the fledgling South Vietnamese state. This aid increased in the early 1960s as the Kennedy administration came to view Vietnam as a test case of American ability to resist Communist wars of national liberation. Army Special Forces teams formed paramilitary forces and established camps along the border to cut down the infiltration of men and materiel from North Vietnam, and other Army personnel trained South Vietnamese troops and accompanied them as advisers in field operations.

2-144. Despite American efforts, the South Vietnamese government seemed near to collapse through late 1963 and 1964, as repeated coups and ongoing Communist infiltration and subversion undermined the regime's stability. In early 1965 President Johnson began a process of escalation that put 184,000 American troops in South Vietnam by year's end.

## Landing Zone (LZ) X-Ray in the Ia Drang Valley

On 14 November 1965, the 1st Battalion, 7th Cavalry, an understrength infantry battalion of the 1st Cavalry Division, conducted an air assault to find and destroy enemy forces suspected to be on the Chu Pong Mountain near the Ia Drang Valley. What they found was a "reinforced North Vietnamese regiment of 2000 soldiers fresh off the Ho Chi Minh trail who were aggressively motivated to kill Americans."

The first helicopter touched down at 1048 hours. Shortly after that, while the rest of the battalion was still flying in, the enemy struck. Over the next three days the 450 soldiers of 1-7 Cav fought waves of North Vietnamese infantry who were determined to wipe out the Americans. Alternately attacking and plugging gaps to prevent the enemy from closing the LZ, soldiers fought with what they had available. SPC Willard Parish was a mortar gunner in C Company. But at LZ X-Ray, he took up an M60 machinegun. On the second morning the enemy had brought hundreds of soldiers right up to the battalion's lines. When they attacked, SPC Parish's training took over and, unaware of time, fought until he ran out of 7.62 mm ammunition. Then he stood up and kept firing at the enemy with a pistol in each hand. When all was quiet later, there were over 100 enemy bodies in front of his position. SPC Parish received the Silver Star for his actions.

The battalion had suffered over 100 killed and wounded and the enemy was close to overrunning the LZ which would isolate the battalion. The commander LTC Harold G. Moore committed his last reserve, the reconnaissance platoon, to counterattack and stabilize the C and D Company sectors. Then, after his soldiers marked their units' positions, he ordered strikes by over two dozen aircraft and called on the fires of four batteries of artillery. That ended the immediate threat long enough for reinforcements from the 2d Battalion, 5th Cavalry to arrive, having moved cross-country from another LZ.

Some of these fresh troops took part in an attack that rescued a platoon from B Company, 1-7 which had been cut off since shortly after the battle began. Those soldiers, after being pinned down and isolated from the rest of their company, had drawn up a tight perimeter and expertly used artillery fires to defeat numerous enemy attacks. SGT Ernie Savage had not lost another soldier since he took command of the platoon after its other leaders had been killed.

Early the next morning, the North Vietnamese attacked with 300 soldiers against B Company, 2-7 Cavalry, reinforcements who had arrived late the first day. Three times they attacked and three times the B Company troopers threw them back with heavy casualties. Just after daylight the North Vietnamese tried again. In less than 15 minutes, the field was piled with enemy dead, but B Company had only 6 wounded. The enemy had had enough in this fight. 1-7 Cav and the attached units had lost 79 soldiers killed and 121 wounded in the three days of combat but had inflicted over 1,300 casualties on the enemy.

2-145. From 1965 to 1969 American troop strength in Vietnam rose to 550,000. The Johnson administration sought to force the North Vietnamese and their Viet Cong allies in the South to either negotiate or abandon their attempts to reunify Vietnam by force. Barred by policy from invading North Vietnam, General William C. Westmoreland adopted a strategy of attrition, seeking to inflict enough casualties on the enemy in the South to make him more amenable to American objectives. In the mountains of the Central Highlands, the jungles of the coastal lowlands, and the plains near the South Vietnamese capital of Saigon, American forces attempted to locate the elusive enemy and bring him to battle on favorable terms. As the North Vietnamese admitted after the war, these operations inflicted significant losses but never forced the communists to abandon their efforts.

---

### Specialist Fifth Class Dwight H. Johnson

Specialist Fifth Class (SP5) Johnson, a tank driver with B Company, 1st Battalion, 69th Armor, was a member of a reaction force near Dak To, Vietnam on 15 January 1968. The force was moving to aid other elements of his platoon, which was in contact with a battalion size North Vietnamese force. SP5 Johnson's tank, upon reaching the battle, threw a track and became immobilized. He climbed out of the vehicle armed only with a .45 caliber pistol. Despite intense hostile fire, SP5 Johnson killed several enemy soldiers before he had expended his ammunition.

Returning to his tank through a heavy volume of antitank rocket, small arms and automatic weapons fire, he obtained a submachinegun with which to continue his fight against the advancing enemy. Armed with this weapon, SP5 Johnson again braved deadly enemy fire to return to the center of the ambush site where he eliminated more of the determined foe. When the last of his ammunition was expended, he killed an enemy soldier with the stock end of his submachinegun. Now weaponless, SP5 Johnson ignored the enemy fire around him, climbed into his platoon sergeant's tank, extricated a wounded crewmember, and carried him to an armored personnel carrier. He then returned to the same tank and assisted in firing the main gun until it jammed.

In a magnificent display of courage, SP5 Johnson exited the tank and again armed only with a .45 caliber pistol, engaged several North Vietnamese troops in close proximity to the vehicle. Fighting his way through devastating fire and remounting his own immobilized tank, he remained fully exposed to the enemy as he engaged them with the tank's externally-mounted .50 caliber machinegun until the situation was brought under control. SP5 Johnson received the Medal of Honor.

---

### The Tet Offensive

2-146. On 29 January 1968 the Allies began the Tet-lunar new year expecting the usual 36-hour peaceful holiday truce. Instead, determined enemy assaults began in the northern and central provinces before daylight on 30 January and in Saigon and the Mekong Delta regions that night. About 84,000 VC and North Vietnamese soldiers attacked or fired upon 36 of 44 provincial capitals, 5 of 6 autonomous cities, 64 of 242 district capitals and 50 hamlets. In addition, the enemy raided a number of military installations including almost every airfield.

2-147. The attack in Saigon began with an assault against the US Embassy. Other assaults were directed against the Presidential Palace, the compound of the Vietnamese Joint General Staff, and nearby Ton San Nhut air base. At Hue, eight enemy battalions infiltrated and fortified the city. It took three US Army, three US Marine Corps, and eleven South Vietnamese battalions to expel the enemy in fighting that lasted a month. American and South Vietnamese units lost over 500 killed in recapturing Hue, while enemy battle deaths may have been nearly 5,000. Among civilian casualties were over 3,000 civic leaders executed by the communists. Heavy fighting also occurred around the Special Forces camp at Dak To in the central highlands and around the US Marine Corps base at Khe Sanh. In both areas, the Allies defeated all attempts to dislodge them.

2-148. In tactical and operational terms, Tet proved a major defeat for the communists. Instead of gathering support from the South Vietnamese, it further alienated the people of the South and in fact pushed them toward greater cooperation with their government. The soldiers of the Army of the Republic of Vietnam performed professionally and inflicted heavy casualties on the enemy. All told, the Viet Cong and North Vietnamese suffered over 40,000 casualties in the month-long battle. But strategically, images of dead Americans in the US Embassy and the unexpected fury of the offensive discouraged the US public and eroded support for seeing the war through to victory.

2-149. Over the next five years, the Army slowly withdrew from Vietnam while carrying out a policy of "Vietnamization" that transferred responsibility for the battlefield to the South Vietnamese. Throughout the process, President Richard M. Nixon sought to balance the need to respond to domestic pressure for troop withdrawals with diplomatic and military efforts to preserve American honor and ensure the survival of South Vietnam. While some American units departed, other formations continued operations in South Vietnam and even expanded the war into neighboring Cambodia and Laos.

> *It's time that we recognized that ours was in truth a noble cause.*
>
> **President Ronald Reagan**

2-150. By the end of 1971, the American military presence in Vietnam had declined to a level of 157,000, and a year later it had decreased to 24,000. In the spring of 1972, Army advisers played a key role in defeating the Easter offensive, an all-out conventional attack by the North Vietnamese Army. But within two years of the Paris Peace Accords of 1973, Saigon fell in April 1975 to the North Vietnamese communists.

## WOMEN'S EXPANDED ROLE

2-151. Although women had long served proudly as nurses, clerks, and telephone operators and in other supporting roles, they only officially become part of the Army with the Army Nurse Corps' formation in 1901. They achieved full military status only with the creation of the Women's

Army Corps (WAC) in 1943. Even after World War II, WACs faced numerous restrictions. They could not constitute over 2 percent of the Army, serve in the combat arms, or obtain promotion to general officer rank. They also faced discharge if they married or became pregnant. With the reexamination of the role of women in American society during the 1960s and 1970s, and given the Army's need for qualified recruits for the post-Vietnam all-volunteer Army, these restrictions began to dissolve.

**A female soldier assigned to the 725ᵗʰ Ordnance Company (Explosive Ordnance Disposal) removes missiles and rocket-propelled-grenades from an Iraqi armored vehicle during Operation Iraqi Freedom.**

2-152. In 1967 President Lyndon B. Johnson eliminated the restrictions on percentages of women and promotions, opening the door to the first female generals in the Army in 1970. During the 1970s the Army expanded the number of military occupational specialties (MOSs) open to women and moved to ensure equal opportunity within those MOSs. The Army abolished involuntary separation for parenthood, allowed women to command men in noncombat units, and established innovative programs to assist military couples with assignments, schooling, and dependent care. In 1972 women first entered ROTC, and in 1976 they entered the US Military Academy.

## POST-VIETNAM AND THE VOLUNTEER ARMY

2-153. The end of the draft and the advent of the all-volunteer Army soon followed the end of the Vietnam War. While the Army struggled with the same problems as the rest of American society, it built an enlisted education system that helped overcome those problems. The NCO

Education System is not only the envy of the world; it has produced a professional, competent and dedicated corps of noncommissioned officers.

2-154. The Army maintained readiness to defend America's interests throughout the 1970s and 1980s, opposite Soviet-led Warsaw Pact forces in Europe. It demonstrated that readiness in annual REFORGER (REturn of FORces to GERmany) exercises and constant training at Hohenfels, Grafenwohr and other training areas. The vigilance of the Army and hundreds of thousands of soldiers over decades along the German border was rewarded in 1989 when the Berlin Wall was dismantled. Soon thereafter the Soviet Union itself unraveled and the Cold War ended.

2-155. US Army soldiers serving in the Republic of Korea have deterred aggression on that peninsula since the end of the Korean War. Despite periodic clashes and incidents along the DMZ soldiers have helped prevent another outbreak of war.

### URGENT FURY AND JUST CAUSE

2-156. Both Operations Urgent Fury (Grenada, 1983) and Just Cause (Panama, 1989) were US interventions to protect American citizens in those countries. The murder of Grenada's prime minister in October 1983 created a breakdown in civil order that threatened the lives of American medical students living on the island. At the request of allied Caribbean nations, the United States invaded the island to safeguard the Americans there. Operation Urgent Fury included Army Rangers and paratroopers from the 82d Airborne Division. This action succeeded in the eventual reestablishment of a representative form of government in Grenada at the cost of 18 soldiers, sailors, and marines killed in action (KIA).

2-157. Manuel Noriega took control of Panama in 1983. Corruption in the Panamanian government became widespread and eventually Noriega threatened the security of the United States by cooperating with Colombian drug producers. Harassment of American personnel increased and after a US marine was shot in December 1989, the US launched Operation Just Cause. This invasion, including over 25,000 soldiers, quickly secured its objectives although 23 Americans were KIA. Noriega surrendered on 3 January 1990 and was later convicted on drug trafficking charges.

### THE PERSIAN GULF WAR

2-158. Saddam Hussein's armies overran Kuwait in August 1990 and appeared poised for a further advance on Saudi Arabia. Rapid deployment by the US XVIII Airborne Corps and US Marine Corps, as well as air and sea power, deterred an Iraqi attack and bought time for the US VII Corps and allied forces to take position along the Saudi-Kuwaiti border. By January 1991 logisticians had built an enormous infrastructure in the desert to support a force of 500,000 troops.

**On the move during Operation Desert Storm.**

2-159. After negotiations failed to dislodge Iraqi forces from Kuwait and an overwhelming bombing offensive softened the enemy defenses, General H. Norman Schwarzkopf and his Saudi counterpart Lieutenant General Khalid ibn Sultan sent their multinational ground forces across the border in late February 1991. Within 100 hours, the coalition destroyed almost 4,000 Iraqi tanks, captured an estimated 60,000 Iraqis, and ruined 36 Iraqi divisions at the cost of 148 American KIA. Although Saddam Hussein remained in power in Iraq, Operation Desert Storm liberated Kuwait and destroyed much of the offensive capability of the Iraqi army.

## RELIEF IN AFRICA

2-160. In the early 1990s Somalia was in the worst drought in over a century and its people were starving. The international community responded with humanitarian aid but clan violence threatened international relief efforts. As a result the United Nations formed a US-led coalition, Operation Restore Hope, to protect relief workers so aid could continue to flow into the country and end the starvation of the Somali people. US soldiers also assisted in civic projects that built and repaired roads, schools, hospitals, and orphanages.

2-161. On 5 June 1993, Pakistani forces operating under UN command were ambushed during a mission to find and destroy arms caches, killing 24 soldiers. The UN resolved to capture all those responsible for their deaths, including Mohammed Aideed, leader of the powerful Somali National Alliance (SNA). In August, US Special Operations Forces (Task Force Ranger) deployed to Somalia to assist in the manhunt. As the search intensified, increasing violence caused the various national contingents on the UN force to curtail or even withdraw from operations entirely. But Task Force (TF) Ranger successfully captured several SNA leaders on a number of missions.

---

### Task Force Ranger

On 3 October 1993 TF Ranger descended on the Olympic Hotel in Mogadishu to capture key members of Aideed's group. As Rangers established security around the hotel, helicopters loitered to provide support. Other US Special Operations soldiers entered the building and took custody of Aideed's operatives. Soon small arms fire began, wounding several members of the security team. The SNA had reacted a few minutes faster than in previous raids. At that moment the US ground convoy pulled up, ready to extract the team and its prisoners.

Then SNA forces shot down one of the hovering helicopters. Rangers and Air Force personnel secured the crash site only 300 meters away from the hotel. But when a second helicopter was hit by a rocket-propelled grenade (RPG) it crashed 3 kilometers away. A ground rescue attempt of this crew failed but two US Special Operations soldiers in another helicopter saw growing numbers of SNA approaching the crash site and volunteered to attempt a rescue. They landed near the downed helicopter but the aircraft that inserted them was itself hit by RPG fire and had to withdraw. With no air cover and little hope of rescue, MSG Gary Gordon and SFC Randall Shughart defended the downed crew against overwhelming numbers of SNA gunmen. They were killed, but the pilot survived. MSG Gordon and SFC Shughart received the Medal of Honor posthumously.

As darkness fell, TF Ranger soldiers near the hotel and the first crash site were under constant attack by SNA forces. Ammunition, water and medical supplies were running dangerously low and there were many wounded. Pakistani and Malaysian armor joined American infantry and Rangers in forming two relief columns to break through to the surrounded Task Force Ranger soldiers. After fighting street by street for two hours, the relief forces found and evacuated the soldiers from the raid and first crash site, but found no one at the second crash site.

The mission succeeded in capturing a number of SNA leaders; 18 Americans died and 84 were wounded. But those who fought there refused to leave any of their fellow soldiers behind.

---

2-162. America withdrew completely from Somalia in 1994. That same year, ethnic hatred in Rwanda led to murder on a genocidal scale. Up to a million Rwandans were killed and two million Rwandans fled and settled in refugee camps in several central African locations. Appalling conditions, starvation, and disease took even more lives. The international community responded with one of the largest humanitarian relief efforts ever mounted. The US military quickly established an atmosphere of collaboration and coordination setting up the necessary infrastructure to complement and support the humanitarian response community. In Operation Support

Hope, US Army soldiers provided clean water, assisted in burying the dead, and integrated the transportation and distribution of relief supplies.

## HAITI

2-163. In December 1990 Jean-Bertrand Aristide was elected President of Haiti in an election that international observers deemed largely free and fair. However, once Aristide took office in February 1991 Haitian military officers deposed him and he fled the country. The human rights climate deteriorated as the military and the de facto government allowed atrocities in defiance of the international community's condemnation. Large numbers of Haitians attempted to flee by boat to the United States, many losing their lives in the process. The United States led a Multinational Force to return the previously elected Aristide regime to power, ensure security, assist with the rehabilitation of civil administration, train a police force, help prepare for elections, and turn over responsibility to the UN. Operation Uphold Democracy succeeded both in restoring the democratically elected government of Haiti and in stemming emigration. In March 1995 the United States transferred the peacekeeping responsibilities to the United Nations.

## THE BALKANS

2-164. During the mid-1990s Yugoslavia was in a state of unrest as various ethnic groups tried to create separate states for themselves. Serbia attempted through military force to prevent any group from gaining autonomy from the central government. After four years of conflict, the warring parties reached a negotiated settlement in 1995. NATO forces, including US Army units, bridged the Sava River and moved into Bosnia to keep the peace intact in Operation Joint Endeavor. Army soldiers continue to help maintain stability in the region and by so doing have saved many thousands of lives in Bosnia because of their service.

2-165. In 1999 it became evident to the world that Serbian forces brutally suppressed the separatist movement of ethnic Albanian Muslims in the province of Kosovo, leaving hundreds dead and over 200,000 homeless. The refusal of Serbia to negotiate peace and strong evidence of mass murder by Serbian forces resulted in the commencement of Operation Allied Force. Air strikes against Serbian military targets continued for 78 days in an effort to bring an end to the atrocities that continued to be waged by the Serbs. Serbian forces withdrew and NATO deployed a peacekeeping force, including US Army soldiers, to restore stability to the region and assist in the repair of the civilian infrastructure.

# THE WAR ON TERRORISM

## AFGHANISTAN

2-166. Terrorists of the al-Qaeda network attacked the United States on 11 September 2001, killing nearly 3000 people, damaging the Pentagon, and destroying the World Trade Center in New York City. The United States, with enormous support from the global community, responded 7 October

2001 with attacks on the al-Qaeda network and the Taliban-controlled government of Afghanistan that was supporting it. In Operation Enduring Freedom, US and allied forces quickly toppled the Taliban regime and severely damaged the al-Qaeda forces in Afghanistan. Special Operations Forces led the way in ground operations and conventional Army units began arriving in Afghanistan 4 December 2001. On 2 March 2002, Operation Anaconda began, in which US Army and allied units began assaults on Taliban and al-Qaeda forces still remaining in southeastern Afghanistan. Enemy forces that stood and fought were destroyed and the rest scattered.

Soldiers assigned to the 101st Airborne Division (Air Assault), fold the American Flag during a retreat ceremony at Kandahar International Airport, Afghanistan.

2-167. The Army, through its continuing operations in Afghanistan, provides support to its fledgling democracy and continues to seek out remnants of the al-Qaeda network remaining in that nation. The goal is to help Afghanis rebuild their country and give their people the benefits of a truly representative government while at the same time reducing the threat of terrorism to the US.

## IRAQ

2-168. After the Persian Gulf War, Saddam Hussein had retained power in Iraq. In defiance of numerous resolutions in the United Nations, despite the presence of inspection teams, and ignoring the world's demands that Iraq disarm, Saddam Hussein continued to build weapons of mass destruction (WMD). By late 2002 it had become evident to the United States that the Baathist regime of Saddam Hussein was providing weapons, training and other support to terrorists around the world. Intense diplomatic efforts by the United States were unable to remove of Hussein and his regime. The United States deployed its Armed Forces to the Gulf and prepared for Operation Iraqi Freedom.

2-169. With a coalition that included Great Britain, Australia, Poland and 44 other nations, the United States on 20 March 2003 began offensive military operations to remove Saddam Hussein from power and liberate Iraq. US Army, US Marine Corps and British forces entered Iraq and in only two weeks of simultaneous air and ground attacks had defeated most organized Iraqi forces and were on the outskirts of Baghdad.

**Soldiers from the 3d Infantry Division (Mechanized) in firing positions during Operation Iraqi Freedom.**

2-170. The 3d Infantry Division seized the main airport of Baghdad and began powerful armored incursions into the city itself. The 101st Airborne Division and US marines likewise closed in on Baghdad. In northern Iraq, the 173d Airborne Brigade and Special Operations Forces alongside free Iraqi forces from Kurdish areas defeated enemy units and liberated most of the northern area of the country. In the west, Special Operations Forces neutralized enemy units while searching for sites containing WMD. Throughout the country, Special Operations Forces provided intelligence and targeting data. In numerous, sharp engagements, Army units performed with bravery and great skill in defeating enemy regular and irregular forces while limiting US and civilian casualties. Operation Iraqi Freedom succeeded in liberating Iraq from a despot and bringing the hope for peace to the troubled Mideast. By the time major combat ended on 1 May 2003, 115 Americans had been killed in action, including 53 soldiers.

2-171. Despite continued attacks by remnants of Hussein's regime, the Army has helped create a secure environment for providing increased humanitarian assistance to impoverished areas. Stability and support operations continue to eliminate remaining pockets of Baathist resistance, restore utilities and services to the Iraqi people and create the conditions in which the people of Iraq can form a new and peaceful government.

2-172. US Army soldiers play a leading role in the war on terrorism and providing security to the Nation. Make no mistake about it: you are defending not only the Constitution and our way of life, but the very lives of our people and your own loved ones. Our enemies will try to strike us again. But the Army and all the Armed Forces, working with civilian branches of government and our allies, will make every effort to prevent such attacks.

2-173. The Army performs a long list of missions in support of American foreign policy and in response to domestic needs. The collapse of the Warsaw Pact in the early 1990s shifted the main focus of the Army's activities since World War II. Ancient hatreds and old rivalries have created conflict and chaos in many parts of the world. In Korea the Army still helps defend an armed border against a powerful enemy dedicated to the forced reunification of the country under Communist rule. The Army also has supported American foreign policy with peacekeeping or support operations in Macedonia, the Sinai and East Timor, and it has worked extensively with foreign and domestic agencies to curb terrorism. Since the 1980s the Army has worked closely with the Drug Enforcement Agency, the US Customs Service, and foreign agencies to halt the flow of illicit drugs into the United States. Initially, the Army merely loaned equipment; now it also trains and transports personnel and shares intelligence.

2-174. From California and Florida to Kurdistan and Somalia, the Army has aided victims of floods, earthquakes, hurricanes, war, famine, forest fires, and other natural and man-made disasters. It has helped with toxic waste removal as part of the Superfund cleanup program. It has provided helicopters and paramedics to communities lacking the resources to respond to medical emergencies. America's Army has given hope to oppressed peoples around the world. While performing all these contemporary missions, the Army has sought to anticipate and prepare for the future.

2-175. The more activist role of the federal government in American life since 1900 has resulted in the Army responding more often to such challenges as disaster relief, international terrorism, and organized crime. Still, a review of American history makes clear that the missions of the Army have always included a number of tasks beyond warfighting. The precise character of the Army's missions has varied depending on the needs of the nation at a particular time, whether fighting a war for survival, developing a transportation network and skilled engineers to support it, providing disaster relief, keeping the peace, or supporting American diplomacy. Throughout our long history, one can truly say of the Army, "When we were needed, we were there."

# HISTORY

2-176. To fully understand the events of history, how battles unfolded, and why things occurred the way they did, it is often helpful to walk the ground on which they happened. If you have the opportunity, go see the Gettysburg Battlefield. You may be surprised at how big the overall battlefield is or what a small area the 20th Maine fought in at the Little Round Top. If you see Pointe du Hoc near Omaha Beach in Normandy, France, you can better appreciate why Allied planners thought it had to be taken. Verdun, France was the scene of a bitter struggle between France and Germany in the First World War. There you can begin to understand some of the terrible and heroic sacrifices of both sides. Some battlefields, like Antietam near Sharpsburg, Maryland are well preserved and maintained by the National Park Service. Volunteers or state agencies maintain other battlefields, such as Mine Creek near Pleasonton, Kansas. Still others are on private property and you need permission to enter, like the fields near Varennes, France where the 3d Infantry Division and its 38th Infantry Regiment earned the nickname "Rock of the Marne."

2-177. But history isn't just about battlefields, of course. The Grand Canyon will take your breath away the first time you see it. Riding to the top of the "Gateway Arch" in St. Louis is worth the trip. You can't help but feel pride and awe visiting the Smithsonian in Washington, DC. The contrast between the roar of Niagara Falls and the quiet isolation of the Badlands is amazing. It is no less amazing than the diversity of our people. We Americans have our differences; in origin, in appearance, in priorities and in how to get things done. But still we are one nation, and when something is important enough, we unite to accomplish a task like no other nation on earth can. Go see for yourself. You are defending America, go see what she is all about.

## SECTION II - THE OPERATIONAL ENVIRONMENT

2-178. The operational environment is the "composite of the conditions, circumstances, and influences that affect the employment of military forces and bear on the decisions of the unit commander" (Joint Pub 1-02). The operational environment that exists today and in the near future (out to the year 2020) includes threats that extend from small, lower-technology opponents using more adaptive, guerrilla or terrorist type methods to large, modernized forces able to engage deployed US forces in more conventional ways. In some possible conflicts combinations of these types of threats could be present.

2-179. Although we may sense dangerous trends and potential threats, there is little certainty about how these threats may be used against America. Uncertainty marks the global war on terrorism, and soldiers will continue to operate in small scale contingencies and conflicts. These may require small, dispersed teams of junior officers, NCOs and junior enlisted soldiers and even civilians or contractors. Yet large scale conventional combat operations will also be possible. Victory in battle will require versatile units and agile soldiers, who can deploy rapidly, undertake a number of different missions, operate continuously over extended distances without large logistics bases, and quickly maneuver with precision to gain positional advantage. Soldiers must be capable of conducting prompt and sustained land operations at varying intensity resulting in decisive victory.

2-180. The operational environment now and in the near future has the following characteristics:

- Constant, high intensity, close combat.
- No rear areas, no sanctuary.
- Information operations effects down to the tactical level.
- Constantly changing rules of engagement (ROE) and tactics.
- Combatant and non-combatant roles blurred.
- Extreme stress, leader fatigue.

2-181. Soldiers in the operational environment must understand the following:

- All soldiers, regardless of battlefield location, must be fully prepared to engage in close combat.
- Rapid changes will require quick and accurate assessment of combat situations.
- Rapid individual judgment and decision-making function at lower levels.
- Dispersed distances will challenge discipline, motivation, and confidence in self and team.
- Presence of media will test soldiers' poise, bearing, and understanding of commander's intent.
- Increased physical and psychological stress over longer time frame.

2-182. Soldiers who succeed in the operational environment are imbued with the warrior ethos and are physically and mentally tough. They are also confident, decisive, and exercise sound judgment in their decisions. Successful soldiers are self-disciplined and capable of taking the intiative in a disciplined manner that helps the team accomplish the mission. Such soldiers are also self-motivated and take active roles in their teams.

2-183. Soldiers who succeed in the operational environment are expert in both warfighting and in the use of emerging technology. In the operational environment soldiers will have to be versatile, taking on new tasks and able to learn quickly to adapt to changes in the environment. Because of the probability of operating in dispersed, small teams, successful soldiers have leader potential and can step up to the challenge of leading other soldiers when required. Above all, soldiers in the operational environment know their own strengths, weaknesses, and take action to improve themselves.

# FULL SPECTRUM OPERATIONS

2-184. The Army operates in war or military operations other than war (MOOTW) by conducting offense, defense, and stability and support operations. These make up the full spectrum of military operations and may occur in a variety of missions extending from humanitarian assistance to disaster relief to peacekeeping and peacemaking to major theaters of war. These missions could occur simultaneously or transition from one to another. For example, a unit may be conducting an operation to destroy a cache of weapons while only a few kilometers away other soldiers are providing medical services to some of the local population. Full spectrum operations require skillful assessment, planning, preparation and execution. In order to successfully accomplish these missions, commanders focus their mission essential task list (METL), training time, and resources on combat tasks and conduct battle-focused training (for more on training see Chapter 5).

2-185. The challenge soldiers face in full spectrum operation means that you should conduct good training and always reach or surpass the standard. Effective training is the cornerstone of success on the battlefield or in other missions. Training to high standards is essential because the Army cannot predict every operation it deploys to. Battle-focused training on combat tasks prepares soldiers, units and leaders to deploy, fight and win. Upon alert, initial-entry Army forces deploy immediately, conduct operations and complete any needed mission-specific training in country. Follow-on forces conduct pre- or post-deployment mission rehearsal exercises, abbreviated if necessary, based on available time and resources.

# HOMELAND SECURITY

2-186. Homeland security is the sum total of operations intended to prepare for, prevent, deter, preempt, defend against, and respond to threats and aggressions directed towards US territory, sovereignty, domestic population and infrastructure. It also includes crisis management, consequence management, and other domestic civil support. It encompasses five distinct missions: domestic preparedness and civil support in case of attacks on civilians, continuity of government, continuity of military operations, border and coastal defense, and national missile defense. The objectives of Homeland Security are to prevent terrorist attacks within the United States, reduce America's vulnerability to terrorism, minimize the damage, and recover from attacks that do occur. The Army's role in Homeland Security falls within Homeland Defense or Civil Support.

> *Your value to the fight is not determined by your proximity to the target.*
>
> **GEN Peter J. Schoomaker**

2-187. Under homeland defense the Army has requirements in four areas: defense of US territory, air and missile defense, information assurance and weapons of mass destruction (WMD) defense and response. The Army supports civil authorities with disaster response, civil disturbance response, and support to special events. Examples of these areas are the National Guard support to airport security and the WMD Civil Support Teams (CST). These WMD-CSTs support civil authorities in incidents involving chemical, biological, radiological, nuclear or high-yield explosive devices. Both of these National Guard missions illustrate the importance of the reserve component in the Army's role in homeland defense.

## ARMY TRANSFORMATION

2-188. Change is a constant. People, organizations, cultures and even geography change with time. Change is necessary to remain competitive and relevant. The Army is no different. Periodic modernization has been required throughout the Army's history.

2-189. The Army is transforming itself into a force that is more strategically responsive and dominant at every point on the spectrum of military operations. Transformation is about changing the way we fight so we can continue to decisively win our Nation's wars. The 21st century operational environment and the potential of emerging technologies require Army Transformation. The global war on terrorism reinforces the need for a transformed Army that is more deployable, lethal, agile, versatile, survivable, and sustainable than current forces.

2-190. The Army is implementing change across its doctrine, training, leader development, organization, materiel, and soldier systems, as well as across all of its components. Transformation will result in a different Army, not just a modernized version of the current Army.

2-191. Transformation consists of three related parts—the Future Force, the Stryker Force, and the Current Force. We will develop concepts and technologies for the Future Force while fielding the Stryker Force to meet the near-term requirement to bridge the operational gap between our heavy and light forces. The third element of transformation is the modernization of existing systems in the Current Force to provide these systems with enhanced capabilities through the application of information technologies.

2-192. As the Army transforms, the Current Force will remain ready to provide the Nation with the warfighting capability needed to keep America strong and free. Through selective modernization the Current Force allows the Army to meet today's challenges and provides the time and flexibility to get transformation right. The Army is focusing resources on systems and units that are essential to both sustaining near-term readiness and fielding the Future Force while taking prudent risk with the remainder of the force. In this the Army will rebuild or selectively upgrade existing weapons systems and tactical vehicles, while also developing and procuring new systems with improved warfighting capabilities.

**A Stryker Infantry Carrier Vehicle squad follows their vehicle out of an Air Force C130 Hercules aircraft after landing at Bicycle Lake Army Airfield at the National Training Center, Fort Irwin, California.**

2-193. The Stryker Force is a transition force that bridges the near-term capability gap between our heavy and light forces. It combines the best characteristics of current heavy, light and special operations forces. Organized in Stryker Brigade Combat Teams (SBCT), it combines today's technology with selected capabilities of the Current Force to serve as a link to the Future Force. Most importantly, the Stryker Force allows exploration of new operational concepts relevant to the Future Force.

> *One thing some soldiers may not fully understand yet is that transformation involves a lot more than two brigades up at Fort Lewis - it's about the future and what kind of Army we'll have for decades to come. We will continue to man, modernize and train our current forces throughout the transformation.... We will continue to need sharp, quick-thinking leaders. The variety of missions and volume of information they'll be given will place a lot of responsibility on them.*
>
> *Transformation could cause as many changes in training and developing leaders in our schools as tactics and equipment. The result will be a future that lets us put a more powerful force on the ground faster and that will save a lot of lives...*
>
> SMA Jack L. Tilley

2-194. The end result of transformation is a new, more effective, and more efficient Army with a new fighting structure—the Future Force. It will provide our Nation with an increased range of options for crisis response, engagement, or sustained land force operations. The Future Force will have the capability to fight in a dispersed and non-linear manner if that provides a military advantage over its opponent. Future Force units will be highly responsive, deploy rapidly because of reduced platform weight and smaller logistical footprints, and arrive early to a crisis to deter conflict. These forces will be capable of moving by air and descending upon multiple points of entry. By applying their judgment to a detailed and accurate common operational picture, Future Force soldiers will identify and attack critical enemy capabilities and key vulnerabilities throughout the depth of the battle area.

2-195. Transformation is not something the Army is doing alone. The Army is coordinating transformation efforts with similar efforts by the other Services, business and industry, and science and technology partners.

## SECTION III - HOW THE US GOVERNMENT WORKS

2-196. The Declaration of Independence is an important document in US history. It says that all people have rights that no government may deny. This document signified the colonies' separation from England and the rule of George III. When the Second Continental Congress formed a committee to write the Declaration, the Committee thought it would be better for only one person to write it—Thomas Jefferson. It took Jefferson seventeen days to write the Declaration of Independence. On 2 July 1776 the Congress voted to declare independence from England. After two days of debate and some changes to the document, the Congress voted to accept the Declaration of Independence. This is why we celebrate the 4th of July as our Independence Day.

> *You have rights antecedent to all earthly governments, rights that cannot be repealed or restrained by human law.*
>
> **President John Adams**

## THE CONSTITUTION

2-197. The Declaration of Independence is an important document, but the foundation of our American government and its purpose, form, and structure are found in the Constitution of the United States. We didn't always have the Constitution. During the Revolutionary War, the states formed a "league of friendship" under the Articles of Confederation, which was ratified in 1781. The Articles provided for a national legislature but little else because the states feared a strong central government like the one they lived with under England's rule. Americans soon discovered that this weak form of government could not effectively respond to outside threats and so they called for a convention in 1787 to revise the Articles. Discussions and debate led the participants to draft an entirely new document and government.

2-198. The Constitution was adopted 17 September 1787 and ratified 21 June 1788. It is the supreme law of the land because no law may be passed that contradicts its principles and no person or government is exempt from following it. Members of the Armed Forces all promise to support and defend the Constitution in recognition of its importance. Without the Constitution, there would be no United States of America.

> *We the People of the United States, in Order to form a more perfect Union, establish Justice, insure domestic Tranquility, provide for the common defence, promote the general Welfare, and secure the Blessings of Liberty to ourselves and our Posterity, do ordain and establish this Constitution for the United States of America.*

**Preamble to the Constitution of the United States**

2-199. The Preamble of the Constitution describes the purpose of the Constitution and, by extension, our Federal, that is, national Government. In order to achieve this purpose the writers of the Constitution established three main principles on which our Government is based:

- Inherent rights: Rights of all persons living in the United States.

- Self-government: Government by the people; citizens selected by fellow citizens to govern.

- Separation of powers: Branches of government with different powers that provide checks and balances to the other branches.

2-200. The United States Constitution is a remarkable document. In about 4,500 words it lays out the framework of our system of government and in another 3,000 (the Amendments) enumerates individual rights and changes to the basic document. It provides us with a firm foundation and yet also, with effort, can change as our country changes. The Constitution establishes a republic, an indivisible union of 50 sovereign States. In our Nation, we the people, govern ourselves. We do this by choosing elected officials through free and secret ballot at regular intervals—elections. In this way, our Government derives its power from the people. The Constitution—

- Defines and limits the power of the national government.

- Defines the relationship between the national government and individual state governments.

- Describes some of the rights of the citizens of the United States.

2-201. The Constitution specifies the powers of the federal government, and all other power remains with the people or the states. This government system based on federalism shares power given by the people between the national and state (local) governments. Issues like defense are at the federal level where sufficient resources are available to accomplish the tasks required to defend our Nation. On the other hand, local issues like licensing, building codes or zoning laws have been left up to the individual states to decide based upon its people's needs and philosophies.

2-202. The Constitution can be changed through amendments to the document. It is a difficult process that requires a 2/3 majority of Congress agree to any proposed amendment and further that 3/4 of all the states also ratify (agree to) the amendment. The Constitution may also be amended in a Constitutional Convention if 2/3 of the states call for it but any changes and amendments must still be ratified by 3/4 of the states. Currently there are 27 amendments to the Constitution. The first ten amendments, accepted at the same time as the Constitution itself, are also called the Bill of Rights.

## BRANCHES OF GOVERNMENT

2-203. The delegates to the Constitutional Convention wanted to ensure a strong, cohesive central government, yet they also wanted to ensure that no individual or small group in the government would become too powerful. Under the Articles of Confederation, the national government lacked authority and the delegates didn't want to have that problem again. To solve these problems, the delegates to the Constitutional Convention created a government with separate branches, each with its own distinct powers. This system would establish a strong central government, while insuring a balance of power.

*The liberties and heritage of the United States... are priceless.*
*The Noncom's Guide*, 1957

2-204. Governmental power and functions in the United States rest in three branches of government: the legislative, judicial, and executive. Article I of the Constitution defines the legislative branch and gives power to make laws to the Congress of the United States. The executive powers of the President are defined in Article 2. Article 3 places judicial power in the hands of one Supreme Court and any lower courts Congress establishes.

2-205. In this system each branch operates independently of the others—a separation of powers. However, there are built in checks and balances to prevent concentration of power in any one branch and to protect the rights and liberties of citizens. For example, the President can veto (disapprove) bills approved by Congress, and the President nominates individuals to serve in the Federal courts. The Supreme Court rules on the constitutionality of a law enacted by Congress or an action by the President. Congress approves whether tax dollars may be spent on a particular action or program and can impeach and remove the President and Federal court justices and judges. See the organization of the government of the United States in Figure 2-1.

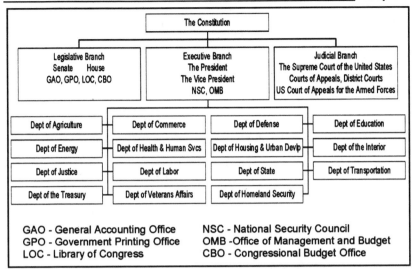

GAO - General Accounting Office     NSC - National Security Council
GPO - Government Printing Office     OMB -Office of Management and Budget
LOC - Library of Congress     CBO - Congressional Budget Office

**Figure 2-1. Organization of the US Government**

## LEGISLATIVE BRANCH

2-206. After much debate the delegates to the Constitutional Convention agreed on the creation of the House of Representatives and the Senate. A major issue involved how to determine representation in the legislative body. The delegates from larger and more populated states argued that only the size of a state's population should determine congressional representation. Fearing domination, delegates from smaller states were just as adamant for equal representation. A delegate from Connecticut, Roger Sherman, resolved the issue when he proposed a two-part (bicameral) legislature, with representation based on population in one (the House of Representatives) and with equal representation in the other (the Senate).

2-207. Congress refers many measures that may become law to various committees of legislators in each chamber. These committees consider each measure and select which will be actually brought to a vote and debated. The vast majority of issues are not brought for a vote and no other action occurs. An issue or "bill" that reaches the floor of the two chambers may not become law until both House and Senate pass it with a majority vote in each chamber. Then the bill is sent to the President for his signature, making it law. The President may also exercise his veto power, disapproving the bill and sending it back to the legislature with his reasons why it should not become law. Congress may override the veto if 2/3 of both House and Senate approve the bill. If the President takes no action, the bill becomes law after 10 days.

2-208. The Constitution specifies certain powers of Congress with respect to the military. Congress has the power to declare war and to set and collect taxes (which pay for soldiers' salaries, weapons, training, etc.). Congress determines the strength (number of people) of the Armed Forces and how much money the Armed Forces may spend. Congress also makes the basic rules for the Armed Forces and the Uniform Code of Military Justice. Congress established the US Court of Appeals for the Armed Forces based on its power to regulate the armed forces and to establish courts lower than the Supreme Court.

## EXECUTIVE BRANCH

2-209. When the delegates to the Constitutional Convention created the executive branch of government, they were afraid of putting too much power in the hands of one person and intensely debated the concept. In the end, with the checks and balances included in the Constitution, the delegates provided for a single President with a limited term of office to manage the executive branch of government. This limited term was different from any form of government in Europe at the time.

2-210. The executive branch of the government is responsible for enforcing the laws of the land. The Vice President, department heads (Cabinet members), and heads of independent agencies assist in this capacity. Unlike the powers of the President, their responsibilities are not defined in the Constitution but each has special powers and functions. The Cabinet includes the Vice President and, by law, the heads of 15 executive departments as shown in Figure 2-1. The National Security Council (NSC) supports the President, as commander-in-chief, with the integration of domestic, foreign, and military policies on National security.

2-211. The Constitution specifies that the President is the Commander-in-Chief of the US Armed Forces. Presidents have initiated military activities abroad over 200 times in our history, though Congress has declared war only five times. The President's signature on a bill is required before it can become law, unless 2/3 of Congress vote for its passage. The President nominates the Department of Defense and service secretaries (and other cabinet chiefs), the Chairman of the Joint Chiefs of Staff, and the service Chiefs of Staff. He also nominates the judges of the Supreme Court and those who sit on the US Court of Appeals for the Armed Forces. Each of these nominations requires confirmation by a majority of the Senate. The President commissions the officers of the Armed Forces. The President may also veto bills of Congress.

## JUDICIAL BRANCH

2-212. Article III of the Constitution established the judicial branch of government with the creation of the Supreme Court. It is the highest court in the country and vested with the judicial powers of the government. There are lower Federal courts that Congress deemed necessary and established using power granted in the Constitution, such as the US Court of Appeals for the Armed Forces.

2-213. Courts decide arguments about the meaning of laws and how they are applied. The Supreme Court also has the authority to declare acts of Congress, and by implication acts of the president, unconstitutional if they exceeded the powers granted by the Constitution. The latter power is known as judicial review and it is this process that the judiciary uses to provide checks and balances on the legislative and executive branches. Judicial review is not specified in the Constitution but it is an implied power, explained in a landmark Supreme Court decision, Marbury versus Madison (1803). Most courts don't rule on the constitutionality of laws but rather decide matters of guilt or innocence in criminal proceedings or adjudicate differences between civil parties.

## DEPARTMENT OF DEFENSE

2-214. Among the departments within the executive branch of the federal government is the Department of Defense. The National Security Act Amendments of 1949 designated the National Military Establishment as the Department of Defense with the Secretary of Defense as its head. The Department of Defense is composed of the following

- Office of the Secretary of Defense.
- The military departments and the military services within those departments.
- The Chairman of the Joint Chiefs of Staff and the Joint Staff.
- The unified combatant commands.
- The defense agencies and DOD field activities.
- Other organizations as may be established or designated by law, the President or the Secretary of Defense.

2-215. The Secretary of Defense is the principal defense policy adviser to the President and is responsible for the formulation of general defense policy and policy related to DOD, and for the execution of approved policy. Under the direction of the President, the Secretary exercises authority, direction, and control over the Department of Defense.

2-216. Each military department is separately organized under its own secretary and functions under the authority, direction, and control of the Secretary of Defense. The Secretary of each military department is responsible to the Secretary of Defense for the operation and efficiency of that department. Orders to the military departments are issued through the secretaries of these departments or their designees, by the Secretary of Defense, or under authority specifically delegated in writing by the Secretary of Defense, or provided by law. The organization of the Department of Defense is shown in Figure 2-2.

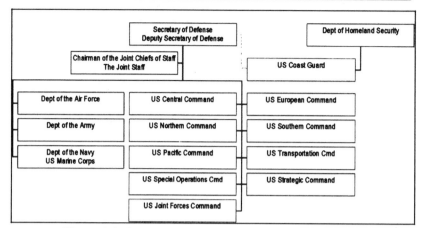

**Figure 2-2. Organization of the Department of Defense**

## JOINT CHIEFS OF STAFF

2-217. The Joint Chiefs of Staff consist of the Chairman; the Vice Chairman; the Chief of Staff of the Army; the Chief of Naval Operations; the Chief of Staff of the Air Force; and the Commandant of the Marine Corps. The Chairman of the Joint Chiefs of Staff is the principal military adviser to the President, the National Security Council, and the Secretary of Defense. The other members of the Joint Chiefs of Staff are military advisers who may provide additional information upon request from the President, the National Security Council, or the Secretary of Defense. They may also submit their advice when it does not agree with that of the Chairman. Subject to the authority of the President and the Secretary of Defense, the Chairman of the Joint Chiefs of Staff is responsible for—

- Assisting the President and the Secretary of Defense in providing for the strategic direction and planning of the Armed Forces and allocating resources to fulfill strategic plans.

- Making recommendations for the assignment of responsibilities within the Armed Forces in accordance with and in support of those logistic and mobility plans.

- Comparing the capabilities of American and allied Armed Forces with those of potential adversaries.

- Preparing and reviewing contingency plans that conform to policy guidance from the President and the Secretary of Defense.

- Preparing joint logistic and mobility plans to support contingency plans.

- Recommending assignment of logistic and mobility responsibilities to the Armed Forces to fulfill logistic and mobility plans.

## UNIFIED COMMANDS

2-218. The Unified Commands are geographically (like Central Command) or functionally (like Transportation Command) oriented. The commanders of the unified commands are responsible to the President and the Secretary of Defense for accomplishing the military missions assigned to them and exercising command authority over forces assigned to them. The operational chain of command runs from the President to the Secretary of Defense to these commanders. The Chairman of the Joint Chiefs of Staff functions within the chain of command by transmitting the orders of the President or the Secretary of Defense to the commanders of the unified commands.

2-219. Within each unified command is an Army component command. These Army component commands provide command and control to Army units that are or become part of the Unified Command. Army units may be assigned to the command; for example, the 35th Supply and Services Battalion, assigned to the 10th Area Support Group, part of US Army, Japan and 9th Theater Support Command. US Army, Japan and 9th TSC is further assigned to US Army, Pacific Command: the Army component of Pacific Command. Army units may also be temporarily part of a Unified Command for a specific mission. For example, Army Forces, Central Command (ARCENT) exerts operational control over Army units deployed to Iraq supporting Operation Iraqi Freedom.

# DEPARTMENT OF THE ARMY

2-220. In our Constitution we read, "We the people... provide for the common Defence," that the Congress raises the Army, and that the President is the Commander-in-Chief. The United States Army exists to serve the American people, protect enduring national interests, and fulfill national military responsibilities. The Army performs this by deterring and, when deterrence fails, by achieving quick, decisive victory anywhere in the world and under virtually any conditions as part of a joint team.

2-221. The institution of the Army is its essence, traditions, history, and lineage. It includes leader development, doctrine, training, professionalism, integrity, and the Army's tradition of responsibility to the nation. The Army's enduring values flow from the American ideals embodied in the Constitution and Declaration of Independence. And serve to guide the actions of soldiers as individuals and groups. Throughout American military history, these values have provided a firm foundation for military leaders and soldiers. They provide all soldiers with principles of conduct and standards of behavior that exemplify those ideals and values.

2-222. The Army maintains a relationship between the institutional Army, with its enduring values, and the organizational Army, the strategic force capable of decisive victory. Institutional changes occur slowly through deliberate evolution and are indistinguishable to the public at large. The organization changes more rapidly and visibly to meet requirements presented by national and international realities. In maintaining the balance between capabilities and requirements in the organization, the institution must not lose its enduring values. They are the foundation during periods of change and uncertainty. The challenge is to manage change, increase capability, maintain stability, and foster innovation.

2-223. The objective of Army forces is to dominate land operations by defeating enemy land forces, seizing and controlling terrain and destroying the enemy's will to resist. Supported by the Air Force and Navy, the Army can forcibly enter an area and conduct land operations anywhere in the world. The Army also can achieve quick and sustained land dominance across the spectrum of conflict. Its capabilities help achieve national political and military objectives.

2-224. The Army tailors forces with unique capabilities to achieve military objectives during major theater wars or smaller-scale operations. Army forces are assigned to a joint force commander under the direct command of an Army component commander or a joint force land component commander. In a joint force, a single commander exercises command authority or operational control over elements of two or more services. Within a joint force, service forces may work under subordinate joint commands or single service commands. Each military department (Army, Navy, and Air Force) retains responsibility for administration and logistic support of those forces it has allocated. You can see the organization of the Department of the Army in Figure 2-3.

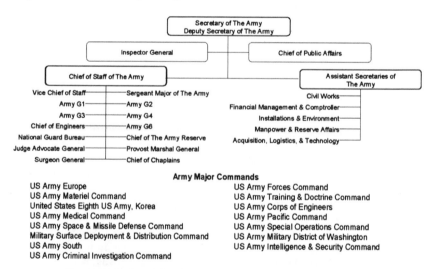

**Figure 2-3. Organization of the Department of the Army**

2-225. The Army is composed of two distinct and equally important components: the active component and the reserve components. The reserve components are the United States Army Reserve and the Army National Guard. The active component is a federal force of full-time soldiers and Department of the Army civilians. They make up the operational and institutional organizations engaged in the day-to-day missions of the Army.

Congress annually determines the number of soldiers that the Army may maintain in the active component.

2-226. Department of the Army civilians perform critical technical and administrative tasks that release soldiers for training and performance of other operational and institutional missions. In addition, many contractors work for the Army to support our forces at home and deployed around the world. While not members of the Army, these contractors provide vital services that sustain and enhance the Army's service to the Nation.

2-227. The US Army Reserve is the active component's primary federal reserve force. The US Army Reserve is made up of soldiers in the Selected Reserve, Individual Ready Reserve (IRR), and Retired Reserve, totaling over 1,000,000 soldiers. In the Selected Reserve you find soldiers in troop program units (TPU), active guard and reserve (AGR) soldiers, and Individual Mobilization Augmentees (IMA). The troop program units are made up of highly trained combat support and combat service support soldiers that can move on short notice. The US Army Reserve gives the Army the resources it needs to deploy overseas and sustain combat troops during wartime, contingencies, or other operations. It is the Army's main source of transportation, medical, logistic, and other combat support and combat service support units and it is the Army's only source of trained individual soldiers readily available to augment headquarters staffs and fill vacancies in units.

2-228. The Army National Guard has a unique, dual mission that consists of both federal and state roles. Although its primary mission is to serve as a federal reserve force, the Guard has an equally important role supporting the states. Until mobilized for a federal mission, their state executive (usually the governor) commands Army National Guard units. In the state role, the Army National Guard must maintain trained and disciplined forces for domestic emergencies or other missions that state law may require. In this capacity, they serve as the first military responders within states during emergencies; in their federal role, Army National Guard units must maintain trained and ready forces, available for prompt mobilization for war, national emergency, or other missions.

> *Our guardsmen, those who live and work within all of our nation's communities, are the Army's greatest link to the American people.*
>
> **Former Secretary of the Army Thomas E. White**

2-229. Regardless of component, the Army conducts both operational and institutional missions. The operational Army consists of numbered armies, corps, divisions, brigades, and battalions that conduct full spectrum operations around the world. They include the combat arms, combat support and combat service support units that deploy and operate to accomplish missions that support the overall objectives of the Nation. Both active and reserve component units take part in operational missions. Institutional missions include recruiting and training new soldiers, developing, acquiring and maintaining equipment, and managing the force, just to name a few. Regardless of where you are, you are part of a team that has important functions to support the Army's overall tasks. Your job is important. You are important to the Army whether you are active or reserve, combat arms, combat support or combat service support, infantry division or training brigade.

2-230. The active component of the Army has nearly 480,000 soldiers. The active component has 10 combat divisions, three cavalry regiments and two separate maneuver brigades. The Selected Reserve of the US Army Reserve consists of about 205,000 soldiers. It fields a large portion of the Army's support units, especially in civil affairs, engineering, transportation, and maintenance. The Army National Guard (ARNG) has approximately 350,000 soldiers. Upon mobilization, the Army National Guard can provide up to eight combat divisions, two Special Forces groups, and 15 enhanced Separate Brigades. Figure 2-4 below shows about what percentage of the Army's soldiers are in the active component, USAR Selected Reserve (SR), and ARNG.

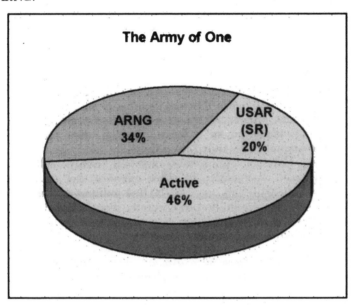

Figure 2-4. Make up of The Army of One

2-231. The Major Commands of the Army and the Army components of the Unified commands are in the active component. The Army provides units to the unified commands for specific purposes and duration. The Army component commanders of each unified command have command and control over these units. For example, Central Command normally has no Army combat units assigned to it. In the case of Operation Enduring Freedom, since 2001 a number of different divisions and smaller units have deployed to Southwest Asia (SWA) under US Army Central Command. The largest Army component is the US Army Forces Command (FORSCOM), which executes the land defense of the US. It also provides military support to civil authorities and trains, sustains, mobilizes and protects strategic land forces worldwide.

2-232. The teams and units of the Army are generally built upon the squad, the basic unit in the army structure. Squads are made up of 8 to 11 soldiers and are normally led by a staff sergeant. In some types of units, the crew is the basic element, as in armor units. Crews are made up of the soldiers who operate a particular weapon system. Tanks, for example, have a crew of four soldiers usually led by a SSG (though some crews may include higher ranking soldiers). Squads and crews combine to build nearly every MTOE unit in the Army, as follows—

- The platoon usually consists of two to four squads or crews. A lieutenant usually leads platoons, with a sergeant first class as second in command.

- Company, battery (in the artillery) or troop (in the cavalry) is made up of three to five platoons and is typically commanded by a captain. It usually has a first sergeant as the senior noncommissioned officer.

- The battalion or squadron (cavalry) is composed of four to six companies/batteries/troops and is commanded by a lieutenant colonel with a command sergeant major as the senior NCO. The battalion is tactically and administratively self-sufficient and can conduct independent operations of a limited scope. A cavalry unit of similar size to a battalion is called a squadron.

- The brigade, regiment or group is made up of two to five battalions under the command of a colonel with a command sergeant major as the senior NCO. Armored cavalry and ranger units of similar size and organization are called regiments, while Special Forces and some other units are known as groups.

- The division is typically made up of three maneuver brigades, as well combat support brigades. A division is commanded by a major general. The division performs major tactical operations for the corps and is capable of sustained operations. A command sergeant major is the senior NCO of the division.

- A corps is made of two or more divisions commanded by a lieutenant general with a command sergeant major as the senior NCO. Corps bring additional support assets and can comand and control large operations over great distances.

- Armies contain corps and other supporting assets. For example, the Third United States Army (TUSA) is also known as Army Forces, Central Command (ARCENT) and provides command and control for Army forces deployed in SWA.

2-233. We look to the past for lessons, we analyze the operational environment, and we adapt to win our Nation's wars. We remember that our purpose is to serve the Nation, defend the Constitution, and our way of life. But throughout all this, the Army—past, present, and future—is people.

2-234. Soldiers have made the US Army the world's most respected land force. That respect is a direct result of the values that soldiers embrace. As FM 1, *The Army* points out, "there is no moral comparison between American Soldiers and their adversaries in wars throughout our history. Thus, it is easy for Soldiers to believe in what they do."

**Chapter 3**

# Duties, Responsibilities, and Authority of the Soldier

Being an effective part of a team as a soldier means knowing your role and the rules for that team. This chapter explains the meaning of duty, responsibility, and authority and how these apply to every soldier in the Army. You'll find a quick reference to some of the rules soldiers live by in the sections on wear, appearance, and fit and standards of conduct. The discussion of the Uniform Code of Military Justice (UCMJ) explains some of the procedures in the use of military justice. This chapter provides brief overviews of these topics and for additional detailed information refer to the appropriate manuals.

For more information on duties, responsibilities and authority see AR 600-20, *Army Command Policy*, FM 6-0, *Command and Control*, FM 6-22 (22-100), *Army Leadership*, and FM 7-22.7, *The Army Noncommissioned Officer Guide*.

For more information on the wear and appearance of Army uniforms and insignia, see AR 670-1, *Wear and Appearance of Army Uniforms and Insignia*.

For more information on the Uniform Code of Military Justice, see FM 1-04.14 (27-14). *Legal Guide for Soldiers*, AR 27-10, *Military Justice*, AR 27-3, *The Army Legal Assistance Program*, and the *Manual for Courts-Martial*.

For more information on the law of land warfare, see FM 1-04.10 (27-10), *The Law of Land Warfare*.

For more information on Army standards of conduct, see AR 600-20 and DOD 5500.7-R, *Joint Ethics Regulation (JER)*.

For more information on the Code of Conduct, see AR 350- 30, *Code of Conduct/ Survival, Evasion, Resistance and Escape (SERE) Training* and DA Pam 360-512, *Code of the US Fighting Force*.

*Every soldier has a specific job to do and makes a unique contribution to the Army. But always remember you are a soldier first.*

## SECTION I - DUTIES, RESPONSIBILITIES, AND AUTHORITY

3-1.  Every soldier has certain duties, responsibilities, and most have some level of authority. You should know what these are and how they apply to you. One of your obligations as a soldier is to carry out your duties to standard and the best of your ability. Bear your responsibilities knowing that you are part of a great team that only works well when each of its members do their best. If you are in a leadership position, exert authority to build the team and develop your soldiers. Your fellow soldiers are depending on you each and every day to make tough decisions based on your rank and duty position.

*Serving my country is the best thing I can do with my life.*

**1SG Isaac Guest**

## DUTIES

3-2.  Duties are general requirements to be performed. Duty begins with everything required of you by law, regulation, and orders; but it includes much more than that. A duty is a legal or moral obligation. For example, soldiers have a legal duty to obey the lawful orders of their leaders. Likewise, all officers and NCOs have a duty to "Take care of their soldiers."

3-3.  Professionals do their work not just to the minimum standard, but to the very best of their ability. Soldiers and Department of the Army civilians (DAC) commit to excellence in all aspects of their professional responsibility so that when the job is done they can look back and honestly say, "I have given my all each and every day." Duty also means being able to accomplish tasks as part of a team. You must fulfill your obligations as a part of your unit. That means, for example, voluntarily assuming your share of the workload, willingly serving as a member of a team, or assuming a leadership role when appropriate.

3-4.  Commissioned officers are direct representatives of the President. The President uses commissions as legal instruments to appoint and exercise direct control over qualified people who act as his legal agents and help him carry out duties. The Army retains this direct-agent relationship with the President through its commissioned officers. The commission serves as the basis for a commissioned officer's legal authority. Commissioned officers command, establish policy, and manage Army resources.

3-5.  Warrant officers are highly specialized, single-track specialty officers who receive their authority from the Secretary of the Army upon their initial appointment. However, Title 10 USC authorizes the commissioning of warrant officers (WO1) upon promotion to chief warrant officer (CW2). These commissioned warrant officers are direct representatives of the President of the United States. They derive their authority from the same source as commissioned officers, but remain specialists in their field. Warrant officers can and do command detachments, units, activities, and vessels as well as lead, coach, train and counsel subordinates. As leaders and technical experts, they provide valuable skills, guidance, and expertise to commanders and organizations in their particular field.

3-6.    Noncommissioned officers, the backbone of the Army, train, lead, and take care of enlisted soldiers. They also provide advice to officers in every aspect of unit operations. NCOs often represent officers and DAC leaders in their absence. They ensure their soldiers, along with their personal equipment, are prepared to function as effective unit and team members. While commissioned officers command, establish policy, and manage resources, NCOs conduct the Army's daily business.

3-7.    Junior enlisted soldiers are where the rubber meets the road. Junior enlisted soldiers perform their duties to standard AND to the best of their ability. This means perfroming individual tasks identified by first line supervisors based on the unit's mission essential task list (METL). All soldiers must be able to do those individual tasks to standard because that is where every successful operation begins—at the individual task level. Junior enlisted soldiers can seek help from first-line supervisors for problems they are unable to solve. Like every soldier in the Army, junior enlisted soldiers have a duty to obey the lawful orders of superiors. Even junior enlisted soldiers can make on-the-spot corrections—they shouldn't walk by a deficiency without tactfully correcting the problem. That's professionalism.

3-8.    Department of the Army civilians are members of the executive branch of the federal government and are a vital part of the Army. DACs fill positions in staff and base sustaining operations that might otherwise have to be filled by officers and NCOs. Senior DACs establish policy and manage Army resources, but they do not have the authority to command. The complementary relationship and mutual respect between the military and civilian members of the Army is a long-standing tradition. Since the Army's beginning in 1775, military and civilian roles have stayed separate, yet necessarily related. Taken in combination, traditions, functions, and laws also help clarify duties of military and civilian members of the Army.

## SPECIFIED DUTIES

3-9.    Specified duties are those related to jobs and positions. Directives such as Army regulations, Department of the Army (DA) general orders, the Uniform Code of Military Justice (UCMJ), soldier's manuals, Army Training and Evaluation Program (ARTEP) or Mission Training Plan (MTP) publications, and Military Occupational Specialty (MOS) job descriptions specify the duties. They spell out what soldiers must do and the standards they must meet.

## DIRECTED DUTIES

3-10.   Directed duties are not specified as part of a job position or MOS or other directive. A superior gives them orally or in writing. Directed duties include being in charge of quarters (CQ) or serving as sergeant of the guard, staff duty officer, company training NCO, and nuclear, biological and chemical (NBC) NCO where these duties are not found in the unit's organizational charts.

## IMPLIED DUTIES

3-11.   Implied duties often support specified duties, but in some cases they may not be related to the military occupational specialty (MOS) job position. These duties may not be written but implied in the instructions. They're duties that improve the quality of the job and help keep the unit functioning at an optimum level. In most cases, these duties depend on individual initiative. They improve the work environment and motivate soldiers to perform because they want to, not because they have to.

# RESPONSIBILITIES

3-12.   Responsibility is the legally established and moral obligation a soldier assumes for his own actions, accomplishments and failures. Leaders also assume responsibility for the actions, accomplishments, and failures of their units and decisions. Above all, the leader is responsible for accomplishing his assigned missions. Then, he is responsible for his soldiers' health, welfare, morale, and discipline. The leader is responsible for maintaining and employing the resources of his force. In most cases, these responsibilities do not conflict. But sometimes they do. For example, SPC Hull has requested a three day pass, Friday through Sunday, because an old friend is visiting for the weekend. But Friday the company is going to the range to qualify on individual weapons. There is no other range time scheduled for the next three months. If such a conflict cannot be resolved, accomplishing the mission must come first. In the example, SPC Hull's commander disapproves the pass.

3-13.   Related to responsibility is accountability. This is the requirement to answer to superiors (and ultimately the American people) for mission accomplishment, for the lives and care of assigned soldiers, and for effectively and efficiently using Army resources. It also includes an obligation to answer for properly using delegated authority. Leaders are accountable for what they do or fail to do. For example, SSG Calhoun must explain to the platoon leader and platoon sergeant why three tires on one of her squad's vehicles are not inflated to the air pressure specified in the technical manual. Soldiers account for their actions to their fellow soldiers or organization, their leaders, the Army and the American people.

3-14.   Officers, NCOs, and DACs lead other officers, NCOs, junior enlisted soldiers, and DACs and help them carry out their responsibilities. Commanders set overall policies and standards, but all leaders guide, assist, and supervise subordinates, who assist and advise their leaders.

Mission accomplishment demands that officers, NCOs and DACs work together to advise, assist and learn from each other.

*Responsibility is a unique concept. It can only reside and inhere in a single individual. You may share it with others, but your portion is not diminished... Even if you do not recognize it or admit its presence, you cannot escape it. If responsibility is rightfully yours, no evasion, or ignorance, or passing the blame can shift the burden to someone else.*

Admiral Hyman G. Rickover

## INDIVIDUAL RESPONSIBILITY

3-15.   Every soldier is responsible for performing his duty to the very best of his ability—and for trying to improve his performance. You are also responsible for your personal conduct and appearance. You and every other soldier in the Army assumed this personal responsibility when you took your enlistment oath or oath as an officer. For example, every soldier is responsible for his own physical fitness. Commanders set aside time on the training schedule for physical training (PT), designate soldiers to lead PT and even ensure all soldiers complete unit runs. But only you can make yourself physically fit.

3-16.   Every soldier is responsible for treating other people with dignity and respect. You may not engage in nor tolerate sexual, racial or other types of discrimination or harassment. Such behavior is morally wrong in both modern society and our Army of values. In addition, it rapidly destroys unit cohesion and team integrity. That could result in lives unnecessarily lost in combat or failure to accomplish assigned missions. Neither of these possible results is acceptable. .

3-17.   Soldiers also have unique responsibilities based on rank, duty position and even geographical location. This manual won't go into all those unique jobs soldiers of different MOSs have. The next few paragraphs describe some of the more general responsibilities of all soldiers. Just remember this—regardless of rank or MOS or specialty—you are a soldier first.

3-18.   The general roles and responsibilities of the commissioned officer are as follows:

- Commands, establishes policy, and manages Army resources.
- Integrates collective, leader, and soldier training to accomplish mission.
- Deals primarily with units and unit operations.
- Concentrates on unit effectiveness and readiness.

3-19. The general roles and responsibilities of the warrant officer are as follows:

- Provides quality advice, counsels and solutions to support the command.
- Executes policy and manages the Army's system.
- Commands special-purpose units and task-organized operational elements.
- Focuses on collective, leader, and individual training.
- Operates, maintains, administers, and manages the Army's equipment, support activities, and technical systems.
- Concentrates on unit effectiveness and readiness.

3-20. The general roles and responsibilities of the noncommissioned officer are as follows:

- Trains soldiers and conducts the daily business of the Army within established policy.
- Focuses on individual soldier and small unit collective training.
- Deals primarily with individual soldier training and team leading.
- Ensures that subordinate teams, NCOs, and soldiers are prepared to function as effective unit and team members.

3-21. The general roles and responsibilities of the junior enlisted soldier are as follows:

- Obeys the lawful orders of NCOs and officers.
- Completes each task to the very best degree possible and not just to standard.
- Maintains a military appearance.
- Maintains individual physical fitness standards and readiness.
- Maintains individual equipment and clothing to standard.

3-22. As members of the executive branch of the federal government, Department of the Army civilians (DAC) are part of the Army team. The DAC provides unique skills that are essential to victory. The general roles and responsibilities of the DAC are as follows:

- Fills positions in staff and base sustaining operations that otherwise would have to be filled by soldiers.
- Provides specialized skills that are difficult to maintain in uniformed components.
- Provides continuity in organizations where soldiers are not available or regularly rotate.

- Applies technical, conceptual, and interpersonal skills to operate, maintain, and administer Army equipment and support, research, and technical activities—in a combat theater, if necessary.

- In addition, the DAC leader also—

  ▪ Establishes and executes policy, leads other DACs, and manages programs, projects, and Army systems.

  ▪ Concentrates on DAC individual and organizational effectiveness and readiness.

## AUTHORITY

3-23. Authority is the legitimate power of leaders to direct subordinates or to take action within the scope of their position. Military authority begins with the Constitution, which divides it between Congress and the President. Congress has the authority to make laws that govern the Army. The President, as Commander in Chief, commands the Armed Forces, including the Army. Two types of military authority exist: command and general military.

### COMMAND AUTHORITY

3-24. Command authority originates with the President and may be supplemented by law or regulation. It is the authority that a leader exercises over subordinates by virtue of rank and assignment to a position of leadership. Command authority is exercised when a member of the Army is assigned to or assumes a position requiring the direction and control of other members of the Army.

3-25. Command authority is not necessarily limited to commissioned (including warrant) officers. Any soldier assigned to a leadership position has the authority inherent in the position to issue orders necessary to accomplish his mission or for the welfare of his soldiers, unless contrary to law or regulation. A tank commander, squad leader, section or platoon sergeant uses this authority to direct and control his soldiers. In these cases, the authority the leader exercises is restricted to the soldiers and facilities that make up that leader's unit.

> *A colonel does not just command 3,000 men, a battalion commander 1,000, and a captain 250. A colonel commands three battalions, a battalion commander four companies, a captain four platoons, and a platoon leader four squads. Let us not forget that.*
>
> *Instruct your subordinates directly; do not command their people. Above all, do not do their jobs, or you will not do yours.*
>
> Colonel Louis de Maud'Huy

3-26. Don't confuse command authority with "Command." Except in emergency situations, only commissioned and warrant officers may command Army units and installations. Army regulations define

"Command" as a military organization or prescribed territory that is recognized as a command under official directives. DA civilians may exercise general supervision over an Army installation or activity, but they act under the authority of a military supervisor; they do not command.

## GENERAL MILITARY AUTHORITY

3-27.  General military authority originates in oaths of office and enlistment, law, rank structure, traditions, and regulations. This broad-based authority allows leaders to take appropriate corrective actions whenever a member of any armed service, anywhere, commits an act involving a breach of good order or discipline. Army Regulation 600-20, *Army Command Policy*, states this specifically, giving commissioned, warrant, and noncommissioned officers authority to "quell all quarrels, frays, and disorders among persons subject to military law." The purpose of this authority is to maintain good order and discipline.

3-28.  For NCOs, another source of general military authority stems from the combination of the chain of command and the NCO support channel. The chain of command passes orders and policies through the NCO support channel to provide authority for NCOs to do their job.

## DELEGATION OF AUTHORITY

3-29.  Just as Congress and the President cannot personally direct every aspect of Armed Forces operations, commanders at all levels cannot directly handle every action. To meet the organization's goals, these officers must delegate authority to subordinate commissioned and noncommissioned officers and, when appropriate, to DACs. These subordinate leaders, in turn, may further delegate that authority.

3-30.  Unless restricted by law, regulation, or a superior, leaders may delegate any or all of their authority to their subordinate leaders. However, such delegation must fall within the leader's scope of authority. Leaders cannot delegate authority they do not have and subordinate leaders may not assume authority that their superiors do not have, cannot delegate, or have retained. The task or duty to be performed limits the authority of the leader to whom it is assigned.

3-31.  When a leader assigns a subordinate a task, he delegates the requisite authority to accomplish the task as well. The subordinate accepts both the responsibility for accomplishing the task and the authority necessary to make it happen. The leader, however, always retains overall responsibility for the task's outcome, being ready to answer for all actions or omissions related to the outcome.

3-32.  For example, let's say the first sergeant told the 1st platoon sergeant to have a detail police an area outside the orderly room, and the platoon sergeant further assigns the task to SPC Green and two PFCs. The platoon sergeant delegates to SPC Green the authority to direct the two PFCs. In this way, SPC Green has the authority to complete the task and is accountable to the platoon sergeant for accomplishing it to standard.

# THE CHAIN OF COMMAND AND NCO SUPPORT CHANNEL

3-33.   Communication among soldiers, teams, units, and organizations is essential to efficient and effective mission accomplishment. Two-way communication is more effective than one-way communication. Mission accomplishment depends on information passing accurately to and from subordinates and leaders, up and down the chain of command and NCO support channel, and laterally among adjacent organizations or activities. In garrison operations, organizations working on the same mission or project should be considered "adjacent."

## CHAIN OF COMMAND

3-34.   The Army has only one chain of command. Through this chain of command, leaders issue orders and instructions and convey policies. An effective chain of command is a two-way communication channel. Its members do more than transmit orders; they carry information from within the unit or organization back up to its leader. They furnish information about how things are developing, notify the leader of problems, and provide request for clarification and help. Leaders at all levels use the chain of command—their subordinate leaders—to keep their people informed and render assistance. They continually facilitate the process of gaining the necessary clarification and solving problems.

3-35.   Beyond conducting their normal duties, NCOs train soldiers and advises commanders on individual soldier readiness and the training needed to ensure unit readiness. Officers and DAC leaders should consult their command sergeant major, first sergeant, or NCOIC, before implementing policy. Leaders must continually communicate to avoid duplicating instructions or issuing conflicting orders. Continuous and open lines of communication enable leaders to freely plan, make decisions, and program future training and operations.

## NONCOMMISSIONED OFFICER SUPPORT CHANNEL

3-36.   The NCO support channel parallels and reinforces the chain of command. NCO leaders work with and support the commissioned and warrant officers of their chain of command. For the chain of command to work efficiently, the NCO support channel must operate effectively. At battalion level and higher, the NCO support channel begins with the command sergeant major, extends through first sergeants, platoon sergeants and ends with section chiefs, squad leaders or team leaders.

> *The NCO support channel...is used for exchanging information; providing reports; issuing instructions, which are directive in nature; accomplishing routine but important activities in accordance with command policies and directives. Most often, it is used to execute established policies, procedures, and standards involving the performance, training, appearance, and conduct of enlisted personnel. Its power rests with the chain of command.*
>
> FM 22-600-20, *The Duties, Responsibilities, and Authority of NCOs*, 1977

3-37. The connection between the chain of command and the NCO support channel is the senior NCO. Commanders issue orders through the chain of command, but senior NCOs must know and understand the orders to issue effective implementing instructions through the NCO support channel. Although the first sergeant and command sergeant major are not part of the formal chain of command, leaders should consult them on all enlisted soldier matters and individual training.

3-38. Successful leaders have good relationships with their senior NCOs. Successful commanders have a good leader-NCO relationship with their first sergeants and command sergeant major. The need for such a relationship applies to platoon leaders and platoon sergeants as well as to staff officers and NCOs. Senior NCOs have extensive experience in successfully completing missions and dealing with enlisted soldier issues. Also, senior NCOs can monitor organizational activities at all levels, take corrective action to keep the organization within the boundaries of the commander's intent, or report situations that require the attention of the officer leadership. A positive relationship between officers and NCOs creates conditions for success.

3-39. The NCO support channel assists the chain of command in accomplishing the following:

- Transmitting, instilling and ensuring the efficacy of the Army ethic.
- Planning and conducting the day-to-day unit operations within prescribed policies and directives.
- Training enlisted soldiers in their MOS as well as in the basic skills and attributes of a soldier.
- Supervising unit physical fitness training and ensuring that soldiers comply with the height/weight and appearance standards in AR 600-9, *The Army Weight Control Program*, and AR 670-1, *Wear and Appearance of Army Uniforms and Insignia*.
- Teaching soldiers the history of the Army, to include military customs, courtesies, and traditions.
- Caring for individual soldiers and their families both on and off duty.
- Teaching soldiers the mission of the unit and developing individual training programs to support the mission.
- Accounting for and maintaining individual arms and equipment of enlisted soldiers and unit equipment under their control.
- Administrating and monitoring the NCO professional development program and other unit training programs.
- Achieving and maintaining Army values.
- Advising the commander on rewards and punishment for enlisted soldiers.

3-40.   Soldiers should use the chain of command or the NCO support channel (as appropriate) to help solve problems, whether small or large. The chain of command and the NCO support channel are also effective and efficient means of communication from where the rubber meets the road to the very highest echelons of the Army. Whether you have a problem, suggestion, complaint or commendation the chain and the channel are the means to communicate to the leaders who need to know.

## INSPECTIONS AND CORRECTIONS

3-41.   Why do we have inspections? From long experience, the Army has found that some soldiers, if allowed to, will become careless and lax in the performance of minor barracks, office, and work area maintenance. They become accustomed to conditions in their immediate surroundings and overlook minor deficiencies. Should a soldier fall below the Army standard of performance someone will notice those deficiencies immediately. All soldiers have the responsibility to uphold the Army standard.

3-42.   Your supervisors will order inspections to see that soldiers have all the equipment and clothing issued to them and that it is serviceable. Inspections serve this practical purpose; they are not harassment. You will probably agree that inspections often correct small problems before they become big problems. Sharp appearance, efficient performance, and excellent maintenance are important considerations that affect you directly. They are the visible signs of a good organization in which any soldier would be a proud member. First-line leaders should inspect their soldiers daily and should regularly check soldiers' rooms, common areas, offices and work areas of their soldiers. First-line leaders should also make arrangements with soldiers who live in quarters (on or off post) to ensure the soldier maintains a healthy and safe environment for himself and his family.

### TYPES OF INSPECTIONS

3-43.   There are two categories of inspections for determining the status of individual soldiers and their equipment: in-ranks and in-quarters. An in-ranks inspection is of personnel and equipment in a unit formation. The leader examines each soldier individually, noticing their general appearance and the condition of their clothing and equipment. When inspecting crew-served weapons and vehicles, the soldiers are normally positioned to the rear of the formation with the operators standing by their vehicle or weapon. Leaders may conduct an in-quarters (barracks) inspection to include personal appearance, individual weapons, field equipment, displays, maintenance, and sanitary conditions. Organizations will have inspection programs that will help determine the status and mission readiness of the unit and its components. These include command inspections, staff inspections, and Inspector General inspections.

### On-the-Spot Corrections

3-44.   One of the most effective administrative corrective measures is the on-the-spot correction. Use this tool for making the quickest and often most effective corrections to deficiencies in training or standards. Generally, a soldier requires an on-the-spot correction for one of two reasons. Either the soldier you are correcting does not know what the standard is or does not care what the standard is. If the soldier was aware of the standard but chose not to adhere to it, this may indicate a larger problem that his chain of command should address. In such a situation you might follow up an on-the-spot correction with a call to the soldier's first sergeant or commander. Figure 3-1 shows the steps in properly making an on-the-spot correction.

---

- Correct the soldier.

- Attack the performance, never the person.

- Give one correction at a time. Do not dump.

- Don't keep bringing it up. When the correction is over, it is over.

---

**Figure 3-1. On-the-Spot Correction Steps**

3-45.   Keeping a soldier on track is the key element in solving performance problems. Motivated soldiers keep the group functioning and training productive. Ultimately soldiers accomplish the training objectives, and most importantly, the mission. Some leaders believe that soldiers work as expected simply because that is their job. That may be true, but soldiers and leaders also need a simple pat-on-the-back once in a while, for a job well done. Good leaders praise their soldiers and care about the job they are doing. Soldiers not performing to standard need correction.

---

**Making an On-the-Spot Correction**

PFC Bucher returned to the battery area after PT and got out of his car to go to formation. He noticed CPL Mays had arrived and waited for him to walk up to the unit together. CPL Mays locked his car and said hello to PFC Bucher but still hadn't put his beret on. PFC Bucher was unsure what to do but knew that he wasn't supposed to walk by a deficiency.

PFC Bucher said, "Good morning, CPL Mays." He looked around to ensure no one could hear him and went on, "You really should put your headgear on, Corporal. An impressionable young troop like me might get the wrong idea and think it's okay to walk around without cover."

CPL Mays wasn't amused but took the hint. "Thanks, Bucher, I forgot," he said, pulling his beret out of his cargo pocket. "And thanks for not making a big deal out of it. Let's go to formation before we're late."

---

3-46.   Often the on-the-spot correction is the best tool to get soldiers back on track. But even after making an on-the-spot correction, additional training may be necessary. Figure 3-2 shows the guidelines in using corrective training.

> - The training, instruction or correction given to a soldier to correct deficiencies must be directly related to the deficiency.
>
> - Orient the corrective action to improving the soldier's performance in their problem area.
>
> - You may take corrective measures after normal duty hours. Such measures assume the nature of the training or instruction, not punishment.
>
> - Corrective training should continue only until the training deficiency is overcome.
>
> - All levels of command should take care to ensure that training and instruction are not used in an oppressive manner to evade the procedural safeguards in imposing nonjudical punishment.
>
> - Do not make notes in soldiers' official records of deficiencies satisfactorily corrected by means of training and instruction.

**Figure 3-2. Corrective Training Guidelines**

3-47.    More often than not, soldiers do good things that deserve some recognition. In the same way as on-the-spot corrections (but obviously for different reasons), leaders praise soldiers' good work by telling them the specific action or result observed and why it was good. This will tend to encourage soldiers to continue doing those good things and motivate other soldiers to reach that standard, too.

3-48.    Making an informal, unscheduled check of equipment, soldiers, or quarters is called an on-the-spot inspection. Stopping to check the tag on a fire extinguisher as you walk through a maintenance bay is an example of an on-the-spot inspection. Another example is checking the condition of the trash dumpster area in back of the orderly room. For any inspection, the steps are the same: preparation, conduct, and follow-up.

### PCCs / PCIs

3-49.    Pre-combat checks (PCCs), Pre-combat inspections (PCIs) and Pre-execution checks are key to ensuring leaders, trainers, and soldiers are adequately prepared to execute operations and training to Army standard. PCC/PCIs are the bridge between pre-execution checks and execution of training. They are also detailed final checks that all units conduct before and during execution of training and combat operations. Conduct PCC/PCIs at the beginning of each event or exercise as part of troop leading procedures to check soldiers, equipment, vehicles, and mission knowledge.

3-50.    The chain of command is responsible for developing, validating, and verifying all PCC/PCIs. Pre-execution checks ensure that all planning and prerequisite training (soldier, leader, and collective) are complete prior to the execution of training. They systematically prepare soldiers, trainers,

the bulk or length of hair may not interfere with the
dgear, protective masks, or equipment. Males are not
braids, cornrows, or dreadlocks (unkempt, twisted,
parts of hair) while in uniform or in civilian clothes on
ipped closely or shaved to the scalp is authorized.

keep sideburns neatly trimmed. Sideburns may not be
the sideburn will be a clean-shaven, horizontal line.
extend below the lowest part of the exterior ear opening.

keep their face clean-shaven when in uniform or in
duty. Mustaches are permitted. If mustaches are worn,
trimmed, tapered, and tidy. Mustaches will not present
ushy appearance, and no portion of the mustache will
line or extend sideways beyond a vertical line drawn
orners of the mouth. Handlebar mustaches, goatees, and
uthorized. If appropriate medical authority prescribes
length required for treatment must be specified. For
gth of the beard will not exceed ¼ inch." Soldiers will
trimmed to the level specified by appropriate medical
are not authorized to shape the growth into goatees, or
andlebar mustaches.

prohibited from wearing wigs or hairpieces while in
lian clothes on duty, except to cover natural baldness or
tion caused by accident or medical procedure. When worn,
will conform to the standard haircut criteria.

**dards**

ldiers will ensure their hair is neatly groomed, that the
of the hair are not excessive, and that the hair does not
unkempt, or extreme appearance. Likewise, trendy styles
aved portions of the scalp (other than the neckline) or
the hair are prohibited. Females may wear braids and
g as the braided style is conservative, the braids and
gly on the head, and any holding devices comply with the
llocks (unkempt, twisted, matted individual parts of hair)
uniform or in civilian clothes on duty. Hair will not fall
s or extend below the bottom edge of the collar at any time
ctivity or when standing in formation. Long hair that falls
the bottom edge of the collar, to include braids, will be
spicuously fastened or pinned, so no free-hanging hair is
cludes styles worn with the improved physical fitness

at are lopsided or distinctly unbalanced are prohibited.
ls, or braids that are not secured to the head (allowing hair
widely spaced individual hanging locks, and other extreme
rude from the head are prohibited. Extensions, weaves,
ieces are authorized only if these additions have the same

and resources to ensure training execution starts properly. Pre-execution checks provide the attention to detail needed to use resources efficiently.

*In no other profession are the penalties for employing untrained personnel so appalling or so irrevocable as in the military.*

General of the Army Douglas MacArthur

## SECTION II - WEAR AND APPEARANCE

3-51.    This section provides an overview of Army Regulation 670-1, *Wear and Appearance of Army Uniforms and Insignia*. It is a quick reference to personal appearance policies and uniform appearance and fit. For details refer to the regulation.

## PERSONAL APPEARANCE POLICIES

3-52.    In the Army discipline is judged, in part, by the manner in which a soldier wears the uniform, as well as by the soldier's personal appearance. Therefore, a neat and well-groomed appearance by all soldiers is fundamental to the Army and contributes to building the pride and esprit essential to an effective military force. A part of the Army's strength and military effectiveness is the pride and self-discipline that American soldiers display in their appearance.

3-53.    Commanders ensure that military personnel under their command present a neat and soldierly appearance. In the absence of specific procedures or guidelines, commanders must determine a soldier's appearance complies with standards in AR 670-1. Soldiers must take pride in their appearance at all times, in or out of uniform, on and off duty. Pride in appearance includes soldiers' physical fitness and adherence to acceptable weight standards in accordance with AR 600-9, *The Army Weight Control Program*.

### RELIGIOUS ITEMS

3-54.    Soldiers may wear religious apparel, articles, or jewelry subject to some limitations based on mission or other requirements.    The term "religious apparel" applies to articles of clothing worn as part of the observance of the religious faith practiced by the soldier. These religious articles include, but are not limited to, medallions, small booklets, pictures, or copies of religious symbols or writing carried by the individual in wallets or pockets. See AR 600-20, *Army Command Policy*, paragraph 5-6g for more information on accommodating religious practices.

3-55.    Soldiers may wear religious apparel, articles, or jewelry with the uniform,  to include the physical fitness uniform, if they are neat, conservative, and discreet. "Neat, conservative, and discreet" means it meets the uniform criteria of AR 670-1. In other words, when religious jewelry is worn, the uniform must meet the same standards of wear as if the religious jewelry were not worn. For example, a religious item worn on a chain may not be visible when worn with the utility, service, dress or mess uniforms. When worn with the physical fitness uniform, the item should be no more visible than identification (ID) tags would be in the same uniform. The width of chains worn with religious items should be approximately the same size as the width of the ID tag chain.

3-56.    Soldiers may not wear these items when doing so would interfere with the performance of their duties or cause a safety problem. Soldiers may not be prohibited, however, from wearing religious apparel, articles or jewelry meeting the criteria of AR 670-1 simply because they are religious in nature if wear is permitted of similar items of a nonreligious nature. A specific example would be wearing a ring with a religious symbol. If the ring meets the uniform standards for jewelry and is not worn in a work area where rings are prohibited because of safety concerns, then wear is allowed and may not be prohibited simply because the ring bears a religious symbol.

3-57.    During a worship service, rite, or ritual, soldiers may wear visible or apparent religious articles, symbols, jewelry, and apparel that do not meet normal uniform standards. Commanders, however, may place reasonable limits on the wear of non-subdued items of religious apparel during worship services, rites, or rituals conducted in the field for operational or safety reasons. When soldiers in uniform wear visible religious articles on such occasions, they must ensure that these articles are not permanently affixed or appended to any prescribed article of the uniform.

3-58.    Chaplains may wear religious attire as described in AR 670-1, CTA 50-909, *Field and Garrison Furnishings and Equipment*, and AR 165-1, *Chaplain Activities in the United States Army*, in the performance of religious services and other official duties, as required. Commanders may not prohibit chaplains from wearing religious symbols that are part of the chaplain's duty uniform.

3-59.    Soldiers may wear religious headgear while in uniform if the headgear meets the following criteria:

- It must be subdued in color (black, brown, green, dark or navy blue, or a combination of these colors).
- It must be of a style and size that can be completely covered by standard military headgear and it cannot interfere with the proper wear or functioning of protective clothing or equipment.
- The headgear cannot bear any writing, symbols or pictures.
- Soldiers will not wear religious headgear in place of military headgear when military headgear is required (outdoors or indoors when required for duties or ceremonies).

## HAIR STANDARDS

3-60.    Army Regulation 670-1 governs hair and grooming practices or accommodations based on religious practices. Exceptions based on religious

practices that were give[n]
prior to 1 January 1986
otherwise qualified for re[t]

3-61.    The requirement
maintain uniformity wit[h]
acceptable, as long as the
address every acceptabl[e]
conservative grooming. It
exercise good judgment in
comply with the hair, f[i]
military uniform or while i[n]

3-62.    Leaders judge the
appearance of headgear
described in the applicable
and comfortably, without di[s]
hairstyles that do not allow
the proper wear of the prote[ctive]

3-63.    Extreme, eccentric,
authorized. If soldiers use d[yes]
that result in natural hair
military appearance are pro[hibited]
result in an extreme appea[rance]
include, but are not limited t[o]
engine) red, and fluorescent c[olors]
to use good judgment in dete[rmining]
upon the overall effect on the

3-64.    Soldiers who have a te[ndency]
cut a part into the hair. The
curved, and will fall in the ar[ea]
hair. Soldiers will not cut desi[gns]

3-65.    Soldiers may not wear
safety, or duty performance (s[uch]
is authorized in lieu of the hair
to the soldier at no cost.

### Male Hair Standards

3-66.    Male haircuts will conf[orm]
the head must be neatly groom[ed]
be excessive or present a ragg[ed]
hair must present a tapered
where the outline of the soldie[r]
curving inward to the natural
The hair will not fall over the e[ars]
for the closely cut hair at the ba[ck]
back is permitted to a moderat[e]
maintained.

3-67.    In all cases,
normal wear of hea[d]
authorized to wear
matted, individual
duty. Hair that is c[lose]

3-68.    Males will
flared; the base of
Sideburns will not

3-69.    Males will
civilian clothes on
they will be neatly
a chopped off or b
cover the upper li[p]
upward from the c
beards are not a
beard growth, the
example, "The le[ngth]
keep the growth
authority, but the[y]
"Fu Manchu" or h[a]

3-70.    Males are
uniform or in civi[l]
physical disfigura
wigs or hairpieces

### Female Hair Stan[dards]

3-71.    Female s[oldiers]
length and bulk
present a ragged[,]
that result in s[hort]
designs cut into
cornrows as lon[g]
cornrows lie snu[g]
standards. Drea[d]
are prohibited i[n]
over the eyebrow[s]
during normal a
naturally below
neatly and inco[nspicuously]
visible. This in
uniform (IPFU)

3-72.    Styles t[hat]
Ponytails, pigta[ils]
to hang freely),
styles that pro
wigs, and hairp[ieces]

general appearance as the individual's natural hair. Additionally, any wigs, extensions, hairpieces, or weaves must comply with grooming policies.

3-73.    Females will ensure that hairstyles do not interfere with proper wear of military headgear, protective masks, or equipment at any time. When headgear is worn, the hair will not extend below the bottom edge of the front of the headgear or below the bottom edge of the collar.

3-74.    Hair-holding devices may be used only for securing the hair. Soldiers will not place hair-holding devices in the hair for decorative purposes. All hair-holding devices must be plain and of a color as close to the soldier's hair as is possible or clear. Authorized devices include, but are not limited to, small, plain scrunchies (elastic hair bands covered with material), barrettes, combs, pins, clips, rubber bands, and hair bands. Devices that are conspicuous, excessive or decorative are prohibited. Some examples of prohibited devices include, but are not limited to, large, lacy scrunchies; beads, bows, or claw clips; clips, pins, or barrettes with butterflies, flowers, sparkles, gems, or scalloped edges; and bows made from hairpieces.

## COSMETICS

3-75.    As with hairstyles, the requirement for standards regarding cosmetics is necessary to maintain uniformity and to avoid an extreme or unmilitary appearance. Males are prohibited from wearing cosmetics, to include nail polish. Females are authorized to wear cosmetics with all uniforms, provided they are applied conservatively and in good taste and complement the uniform. Leaders at all levels must exercise good judgment in the enforcement of this policy.

3-76.    Females may wear cosmetics if they are conservative and complement the uniform and their complexion. Eccentric, exaggerated, or trendy cosmetic styles and colors, to include makeup covering tattoos, are inappropriate with the uniform and are prohibited. Permanent makeup, such as eyebrow or eyeliner, is authorized if it conforms to standards.

3-77.    Females will not wear shades of lipstick and nail polish that contrast with their complexion, detract from the uniform, or that are extreme. Some examples of extreme colors include, but are not limited to, purple, gold, blue, black, white, bright (fire-engine) red, khaki, camouflage colors and fluorescent colors. Soldiers will not apply designs to nails or apply two-tone colors to nails. Females will comply with the cosmetics policy while in any military uniform or while in civilian clothes on duty.

## FINGERNAILS

3-78.    All soldiers will keep fingernails clean and neatly trimmed. Males will keep nails trimmed so as not to extend beyond the fingertip. Females will not exceed a nail length of ¼ inch, as measured from the tip of the finger. Females will trim nails shorter if the commander determines that the longer length detracts from the military image, presents a safety concern, or interferes with the performance of duties.

## HYGIENE AND BODY GROOMING

3-79. Soldiers will maintain good personal hygiene and grooming on a daily basis. Not only is this an indicator of a disciplined soldier, but also demonstrates respect for others and for the uniform.

## TATTOOS

3-80. Tattoos or brands that are visible in a class A uniform (worn with slacks/trousers) are prohibited (see exception in paragraph 3-84 below). Tattoos or brands that are extremist, indecent, sexist or racist are prohibited, regardless of location on the body, as they are prejudicial to good order and discipline within units. Extremist tattoos or brands are those affiliated with, depicting, or symbolizing extremist philosophies, organizations or activities.

3-81. Indecent tattoos or brands are those that are grossly offensive to modesty, decency, or propriety; shock the moral sense because of their vulgar, filthy, or disgusting nature or tendency to incite lustful thought; or tend reasonably to corrupt morals or incite libidinous thoughts. Sexist tattoos or brands are those that advocate a philosophy that degrades or demeans a person based on race, ethnicity, or national origin. Racist tattoos or brands are those that advocate a philosophy that degrades or demeans a person based on race, ethnicity, or national origin.

3-82. Commanders must ensure soldiers understand the tattoo policy. For soldiers who are not in compliance, commanders may not order the removal of a tattoo or brand. However, the commander must counsel soldiers, and afford them the opportunity to seek medical advice about removal or alteration of the tattoo or brand.

3-83. If soldiers are not in compliance with the policy, and refuse to remove or alter the tattoos or brands, commanders—

- Ensure the soldier understands the policy.
- Ensure the soldier has been afforded the opportunity to seek medical advice about the removal or alteration.
- Counsel the soldier in writing. The counseling form will state that the soldier's refusal to remove extremist, indecent, sexist, or racist tattoos or brands anywhere on the body, or refusal to remove any type of tattoo or brand visible in the class A uniform (worn with slacks/trousers) will result in discharge.
- Existing tattoos or brands on the hands that are not extremist, indecent, sexist, or racist, but are visible in the class A uniform are authorized for soldiers who entered the Army before 1 July 2002. Soldiers who entered the Army 1 July 2002 and later may not have tattoos that are visible in the Class A uniform.
- Soldiers may not cover tattoos or brands in order to comply with the tattoo policy.

3-84. Unit commanders or executive officers make determinations on the appropriateness of tattoos for soldiers currently on active duty. This authority cannot be further delegated. Any such determination must be fully documented in writing and include a description of existing tattoos or brands and their location on the body. The soldier will receive a copy of the determination.

## UNIFORM APPEARANCE AND FIT

3-85. All soldiers must maintain a high standard of dress and appearance. Uniforms will fit properly; trousers, pants, or skirts should not fit tightly; and soldiers must keep uniforms clean and serviceable and press them as necessary.

### APPEARANCE

3-86. Soldiers must project a military image that leaves no doubt that they live by a common military standard and are responsible to military order and discipline. Soldiers will ensure that articles carried in pockets do not protrude from the pocket or present a bulky appearance.

> *That uniform stood for something to me—and it still does, something pretty grand and fine.*
>
> SGT Henry Giles

3-87. When required and prescribed by the commander, soldiers may attach keys or key chains to the uniform when performing duties such as charge of quarters, armorer, duty officer/NCO, or other duties as prescribed by the commander. Keys or key chains will be attached to the uniform on the belt, belt loops, or waistband.

3-88. At the discretion of the commander and when required in the performance of duties soldiers may wear an electronic device on the belt, belt loops, or waistband of the uniform. Only one electronic device may be worn. It may be either a pager or a cell phone. The body of the device may not exceed 4x2x1 inches, and the device and carrying case must be black; no other colors are authorized. If security cords or chains are attached to the device, soldiers will conceal the cord or chain from view. Other types of electronic devices are not authorized for wear on the uniform. If the commander issues and requires the use of other electronic devices in the performance of duties, the soldier will carry them in the hand, pocket, briefcase, purse, bag, or in some other carrying container.

3-89. Soldiers will not wear keys, key chains, or electronic devices on the uniform when the commander determines such wear is inappropriate, such as in formation, or during parades or ceremonies. Soldiers will not wear items or devices on the uniform when not performing required duties.

3-90. While in uniform, soldiers will not place their hands in their pockets, except momentarily to place or retrieve objects. Soldiers will keep uniforms buttoned, zipped, and snapped. They will ensure metallic devices such as metal insignia, belt buckles, and belt tips are free of scratches and corrosion and are in proper luster or remain properly subdued, as applicable; and that all medals and ribbons are clean and not frayed. Soldiers will keep shoes and boots cleaned and shined. Soldiers will replace the rank insignia, name and US Army distinguishing tapes (nametapes), nameplates, unit patches, and combat and skill badges when unserviceable or no longer conform to standards.

3-91.    Lapels and sleeves of service, dress, and mess coats and jackets will be roll-pressed, without creasing. Skirts will not be creased. Trousers, slacks, and the sleeves of shirts and blouses will be creased. Soldiers may add military creases to the AG shade 415 shirt and the battle dress uniform (BDU) coat (not the field jacket). Soldiers will center the front creases on each side of the shirt, centered on the pockets, for those garments that have front pockets. Soldiers may press a horizontal crease across the upper back of the shirt or coat (not necessary on the male shirt due to the yoke seam), and they may press three equally spaced vertical creases down the back, beginning at the yoke seam or horizontal crease. Additionally, soldiers may crease the sleeves of the BDU coat. Soldiers are not authorized to sew military creases into the uniform.

3-92.    Although some uniform items are made of wash-and-wear materials or are treated with a permanent-press finish, soldiers may need to press these items to maintain a neat, military appearance. However, before pressing uniform items, soldiers should read and comply with care instruction labels attached to the items. Soldiers may starch BDUs and the maternity work uniform, at their option. Commanders will not require soldiers to starch these uniforms, and soldiers will not receive an increase in their clothing replacement allowance to compensate for potential premature wear that may be caused by starching uniforms.

## THE BERET

3-93.    The beret is the basic headgear for utility uniforms in garrison environments. The beret is not worn in the field, in training environments, or in environments where the wear of the beret is impractical, as determined by the commander. Additionally, the beret is not worn on deployments unless authorized by the commander. Soldiers being transferred from one organization to another may continue to wear the beret and flash of the former unit until they report for duty at the new organization.

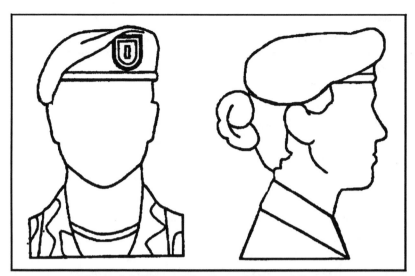

**Figure 3-3. Wear of the Beret, Male and Female**

3-94.   The beret is worn so that the headband (edge binding) is straight across the forehead, one (1) inch above the eyebrows. The flash is positioned over the left eye, and the excess material is draped over to the right ear, extending to at least the top of the ear, and no lower than the middle of the ear. Soldiers will cut off the ends of the adjusting ribbon and secure the ribbon knot inside the edge binding at the back of the beret. When worn properly, the beret is formed to the shape of the head; therefore, soldiers may not wear hairstyles that cause distortion of the beret. See Figure 3-3, Wear of the Beret, Male and Female.

3-95.   Soldiers who are not assigned to units or positions authorized wear of the tan, green, or maroon berets will wear the black beret. This includes senior and junior Reserve Officer Training Corps (ROTC) instructors, unless otherwise indicated. Soldiers are issued the black beret upon assignment to their first permanent duty assignment after the completion of initial entry training or officer/warrant officer basic courses. Cadets and officer/warrant officer candidates will not wear the black beret. Split-option soldiers or soldiers in the simultaneous membership program will wear the black beret only when performing duties with their units, and they will wear the patrol cap with the BDU, when in a cadet or trainee status.

3-96.   Soldiers who have not been issued or who do not wear the black beret will wear the patrol cap with the BDU. In those cases where beret sustainment levels are not sufficient for turn-in and reissue of unserviceable berets, the commander can authorize the temporary wear of the patrol cap until the beret can be replaced. The Army flash is the only flash authorized for wear on the black beret, unless authorization for another flash was granted before the implementation of the black beret as the standard Army headgear (for example, Opposing Forces elements).

### Ranger Tan Beret

3-97. Soldiers assigned to the following units are authorized wear of the Ranger tan beret. Soldiers will wear the approved flash of the unit to which they are assigned:

- 75th Ranger Regiment.
- Ranger Training Brigade.
- Ranger-qualified soldiers in the following units or positions, if they previously served in the 75th Ranger Regiment.
  - US Special Operations Command.
  - US Army Special Operations Command.
  - US Special Operations Command Joint Task Force.
  - Theater Special Operations Command.

### Green Beret

3-98. If approved by local commanders, all Special Forces-qualified soldiers (those carrying the Special Forces MOSs of 18A or 180A, CMF 18, and CSMs reclassified from 18Z to 00Z) are authorized to wear the Green Beret. This includes ROTC instructors and those attending training at an Army service school in a student status. Special Forces (SF) soldiers will wear the approved flash of the unit to which they are assigned. Special Forces soldiers who are assigned to an organization without an approved flash will wear the generic SF flash (the flash approved for soldiers assigned to SF positions, but not assigned to SF units).

### Maroon Beret

3-99. All soldiers assigned to airborne units whose primary missions are airborne operations wear the maroon beret. The airborne designation for a unit is found in the unit modification table of organization and equipment (MTOE). Other soldiers authorized to wear the maroon beret are as follows:

- Active Army advisors to reserve airborne units on jump status.
- Soldiers assigned to the airborne departments of the US Army Infantry School and the US Army Quartermaster School.
- Soldiers assigned to long-range surveillance detachments designated as airborne.
- Soldiers assigned to the airborne/airlift action office.
- Recruiters of the Special Operations Recruiting Company (SORC), US Army Recruiting Command, will wear the USASOC flash.
- Soldiers assigned to the airborne procurement team.
- Soldiers assigned to 55th Signal Company Airborne Combat Camera Documentation Team.
- Soldiers assigned to 982d Combat Signal Company airborne platoons.
- Soldiers assigned to rigger detachments.

## FIT

3-100. Fitting instructions and alterations of uniforms will be made in accordance with AR 700-84, *Issue and Sale of Personal Clothing*, and TM 10-227, *Fitting of Army Uniforms and Footwear*. The following is a summary of general fitting guidelines:

- Black all-weather coat. The length of the sleeves of the all-weather coat will be ½ inch longer than the service coat.

  - Males. The bottom of the black all-weather coat will reach to a point 1 ½ inches below the center of the knee.

  - Females. The bottom of the coat will reach a point at least 1 inch below the skirt hem, but not less than 1-½ inches below the center of the knee.

- Uniform coats and jackets (male and female). The sleeve length will be 1 inch below the bottom of the wrist bone.

- Trousers will be fitted and worn with the lower edge of the waistband at the top of the hipbone, plus or minus ½ inch. The front crease of the trousers will reach the top of the instep, touching the top of the shoe at the shoelaces.

- Trousers will be cut on a diagonal line to reach a point approximately midway between the top of the heel and the top of the standard shoe in the back. The trousers may have a slight break in the front.

- Knee-length skirts. Skirts lengths will be no more than 1 inch above or 2 inches below the center of the knee.

- Long-sleeved shirts. The sleeve length will extend to the center of the wrist bone.

- Soldiers will wear appropriate undergarments with all uniforms.

## WHEN THE WEAR OF THE ARMY UNIFORM IS REQUIRED OR PROHIBITED

3-101. All soldiers will wear the Army uniform when on duty, unless granted an exception to wear civilian clothes. The following personnel may grant exceptions:

- Commanders of major Army commands (MACOMs).

- Assistant Secretaries, the Secretary of Defense or his designee, or Secretary of the Army.

- Heads of Department of Defense agencies.

- Heads of Department of the Army Staff agencies.

3-102. Soldiers traveling on Air Mobility Command (AMC) and non-AMC flights on permanent change of station (PCS) orders, temporary duty (TDY), emergency leave, or space-available flights, are authorized to wear civilian clothes. Soldiers must ensure clothing worn is appropriate for the occasion and reflects positively on the Army. Travel to certain countries requires wear of civilian clothing. For up-to-date information concerning mandatory wear of civilian clothing in foreign countries, see DOD 4500.54G, *The Department of Defense Foreign Clearance Guide* (available online at http://www.fcg.pentagon.mil/fcg/fcg.htm). The individual's travel orders will reflect information authorizing the wear of civilian clothing.

3-103. Soldiers may wear the BDU when deploying as part of a unit move and the mode of transportation is for the exclusive use of the military. Embarkation and debarkation points will be in military-controlled areas.

3-104. Army National Guard technicians who are also members of the Army National Guard will wear the appropriate Army duty uniform while engaged in their civil service status.

3-105. Wearing Army uniforms is prohibited in the following situations:

- In connection with the furtherance of any political or commercial interest, or when engaged in off duty civilian employment.

- When participating in public speeches, interviews, picket lines, marches, rallies, or public demonstrations, except as authorized by competent authority.

- When attending any meeting or event that is a function of, or is sponsored by, an extremist organization.

- When wearing the uniform would bring discredit upon the Army.

- When specifically prohibited by Army regulations.

3-106. Soldiers will wear headgear with the Army uniform, except under the following circumstances:

- Headgear is not required if it would interfere with the safe operation of military vehicles.

- The wear of military headgear is not required while in or on a privately owned vehicle (POV), a commercial vehicle, or on public conveyance (such as a subway, train, plane or bus).

- Soldiers will not wear headgear indoors unless under arms in an official capacity or when directed by the commander, such as for indoor ceremonial activities.

- Soldiers will carry their headgear, when it is not worn, in their hand while wearing service, dress, and mess uniforms.

- Soldiers are not required to wear headgear to evening social events (after Retreat) when wearing the Army blue and white uniforms, the enlisted green dress uniform, the Army green maternity dress uniform, or the mess and evening mess uniforms.

- Soldiers are authorized storage of the headgear, when it is not worn, in the BDU cargo pockets. Soldiers must fold the headgear neatly as not to present a bulky appearance.

- Soldiers will not attach the headgear to the uniform, or hang it from the belt.

3-107. Soldiers may continue to wear uniform items changed in design or material as long as the item remains in serviceable condition, unless specifically prohibited. See Appendix D, "Mandatory Possession and Wear-out Dates," of AR 670-1.

## WEAR OF MILITARY AND CIVILIAN ITEMS

3-108. Generally speaking, the wear of a combination of civilian and military clothing is prohibited. However, when local commanders have authorized it, some uniform items, like the IPFU and the Army black all-weather coat may be worn with civilian clothing (provided rank insignia is removed). Wear of other items such as black oxford shoes (low quarters), combat boots, belts or gloves with civilian clothing are also allowed.

### Civilian Bags

3-109. Soldiers may carry civilian gym bags, civilian rucksacks, or other similar civilian bags while in uniform. Soldiers may carry these bags by hand, on one shoulder using a shoulder strap, or over both shoulders using both shoulder straps. If the soldier opts to carry a bag over one shoulder, the bag must be carried on the same side of the body as the shoulder strap. Soldiers may not carry the bag slung across the body with the strap over the opposite shoulder.

3-110. If soldiers choose to carry a shoulder bag while in uniform, the bag must be black with no other colors and may not have any logos. The contents of the bag may not be visible; therefore, see-through plastic or mesh bags are not authorized. There is no restriction on the color of civilian bags carried in the hand. Commanders govern the wear of organizational issue rucksacks in garrison and field environments.

### Handbags

3-111. Female soldiers may carry black handbags in the hand or over one shoulder. Soldiers may not wear the shoulder bag in such a manner that the strap is draped diagonally across the body with the purse resting on the hip opposite the shoulder holding the strap.

3-112. Civilian clothing is considered appropriate attire for individuals who are participating in civilian outdoor activities such as hikes or volksmarches, orienteering, or similar activities. Soldiers who are spectators at these activities may wear utility or field uniforms. However, commanders of participating units that provide support personnel, such as medical and traffic control personnel, may prescribe appropriate uniforms, to include utility or organizational uniforms, if warranted by the occasion, weather conditions, or activity.

3-113. Soldiers may wear experimental uniform items while actively engaged in an experimental uniform test program approved by HQ, US Army training and Doctrine Command (TRADOC), HQ, US Army Materiel Command (AMC), or the Army Uniform Board, HQDA. Soldiers will not wear experimental items after completion of the test unless such wear is approved by HQDA.

## UNIFORMITY OF MATERIAL

3-114. When soldiers exercise their option to choose among various fabrics authorized for uniforms, they must ensure that all garments (coats, trousers, skirts and slacks) are made of the same material. When gold lace (sleeve or trouser ornamentation) or gold bullion is prescribed for wear with uniforms, soldiers may substitute gold-colored nylon, rayon, or synthetic metallic gold. If trouser and sleeve ornamentation is gold bullion, the cap ornamentation and shoulder strap insignia must also be gold bullion. Anodized aluminum white-gold colored buttons are not authorized for wear.

## WEAR OF JEWELRY AND ACCESSORIES

3-115. Soldiers may wear a wristwatch, a wrist identification bracelet, and a total of two rings (a wedding set is considered one ring) with Army uniforms, unless prohibited by the commander for safety or health reasons. Any jewelry soldiers wear must be conservative and in good taste. Identification bracelets are limited to medical alert bracelets and missing in action/prisoner of war (MIA/POW) bracelets. Soldiers may wear only one item on each wrist.

3-116. No other jewelry will appear exposed while wearing the uniform; this includes watch chains or similar items, pens, and pencils. The only authorized exceptions are religious items described at the beginning of this section. Other exceptions are a conservative tie tack or tie clasp that male soldiers may wear with the black four-in-hand necktie and a pen or pencil that may appear exposed on the hospital duty, food service, combat vehicle crewman (CVC), or flight uniforms.

### Body Piercing

3-117. When on any Army installation or other places under Army control, soldiers may not attach, affix, or display objects, articles, jewelry, or ornamentation to or through the skin while they are in uniform, in civilian clothes on duty, or in civilian clothes off duty (this includes earrings for male soldiers). The only exception is for female soldiers as follows (the term "skin" is not confined to external skin, but includes the tongue, lips, inside the mouth, and other surfaces of the body not readily visible):

- Females are authorized to wear prescribed earrings with the service, dress, and mess uniforms, or while on duty in civilian attire.

- Earrings may be screw-on, clip-on, or post-type earrings, in gold, silver, white pearl, or diamond. The earrings will not exceed six-mm or ¼ inch in diameter, and they must be unadorned and spherical.

- When worn, the earrings will fit snugly against the ear. Females may wear earrings only as a matched pair, with only one earring per ear.

- Females are not authorized to wear earrings with any Class C (utility) uniform (BDU, hospital duty, food service, physical fitness, and field or organizational).

- When females are off duty, there are no restrictions on the wear of earrings.

3-118. Ankle bracelets, necklaces, faddish (trendy) devices, medallions, amulets, and personal talismans or icons are not authorized for wear in any military uniform, or in civilian clothes on duty. Soldiers may not wear these items when doing so would interfere with the performance of their duties or present a safety concern. Soldiers may not be prohibited, however, from wearing religious apparel, articles, or jewelry meeting the criteria of AR 670-1 simply because they are religious in nature, if wear is permitted of similar items of a nonreligious nature. A specific example would be wearing a ring with a religious symbol. If the ring meets the uniform standards for jewelry and is not worn in a work area where rings are prohibited because of safety concerns, then wear is allowed and may not be prohibited simply because the ring bears a religious symbol.

### Eyeglasses and Sunglasses

3-119. Soldiers may wear conservative civilian prescription eyeglasses with all uniforms. Conservative prescription and nonprescription sunglasses are authorized for wear when in a garrison environment, except when in formation and while indoors. Individuals who are required by medical authority to wear sunglasses for medical reasons other than refractive error may wear them, except when health or safety considerations apply. Soldiers may not wear sunglasses in the field unless required by the commander for safety reasons in high-glare field environments.

3-120. Eyeglasses or sunglasses that are trendy, or have lenses or frames with initials, designs, or other adornments are not authorized for wear. Soldiers may not wear lenses with extreme or trendy colors, which include but are not limited to red, yellow, blue, purple, bright green, or orange. Lens colors must be traditional gray, brown, or dark green shades. Soldiers will not wear lenses or frames that are so large or so small that they detract from the appearance of the uniform. Soldiers will not attach chains, bands, or ribbons to eyeglasses. Eyeglass restraints are authorized only when required for safety purposes. Soldiers will not hang eyeglasses or eyeglass cases on the uniform, and may not let glasses hang from eyeglass restraints down the front of the uniform.

### Contact Lenses

3-121. Tinted or colored contact lenses are not authorized for wear with the uniform. The only exception is for opaque lenses medically prescribed for eye injuries. Additionally, clear lenses that have designs on them that change the contour of the iris are not authorized for wear with the uniform.

### IDENTIFICATION TAGS AND SECURITY BADGES

3-122. Soldiers will wear ID tags at all times when in a field environment, while traveling in aircraft, and when outside the continental United States (OCONUS). Soldiers will wear ID tags around the neck, except when safety considerations apply. See AR 600-8-14, *Identification Cards for Members of the Uniformed Services, Their Family Members, and Other Eligible Personnel*, for more information on the wear of ID tags.

3-123. In restricted areas, commanders may prescribe the wear of security identification badges, in accordance with AR 600-8-14 and other applicable regulations. Soldiers will not wear security identification badges outside the area for which they are required. Soldiers will not hang other items from the security badge(s). The manner of wear will be determined by the organization that requires wear of the badges.

## WEAR OF PERSONAL PROTECTIVE OR REFLECTIVE CLOTHING

3-124. Soldiers are authorized to wear commercially designed, protective headgear with the uniform when operating motorcycles, bicycles or other like vehicles, and are required to do so when installation regulations mandate such wear. Soldiers will remove protective headgear and don authorized Army headgear upon dismounting from the vehicle.

3-125. Soldiers may wear protective/reflective outer garments with uniforms when safety considerations make it appropriate and when authorized by the commander. When safety considerations apply, commanders may require the wear of organizational protective or reflective items, or other occupational health or safety equipment with the uniform (such as during physical fitness training). If required, commanders will furnish protective or reflective clothing to soldiers at no cost.

## WEAR OF CIVILIAN CLOTHING

3-126. Civilian clothing is authorized for wear when off duty, unless the wear is prohibited by the installation commander in the continental United States (CONUS) or by the Major Army Command (MACOM) commander OCONUS. Commanders down to unit level may restrict the wear of civilian clothes by those soldiers who have had their pass privileges revoked under the provisions of AR 600-8-10, *Leaves and Passes*. When on duty in civilian clothes, soldiers will conform to the appearance standards in AR 670-1 unless exempted by the commander for specific mission requirements.

## SECTION III - UNIFORM CODE OF MILITARY JUSTICE

3-127. This section provides an overview of selected chapters and articles from the Uniform Code of Military Justice (UCMJ). Military law or military justice is the branch of the law that regulates military activity. It is generally penal or disciplinary in nature and in the US, includes and is comparable to civilian criminal law. Its sources are many and varied, with some considerably pre-dating the US and its Constitution. However, since it is through the Constitution that our Public Law began to exist, the Constitution can properly be considered the primary source of the law governing our military.

> *American military justice is the best in the world and includes open trials, right to counsel, and judicial review.*
>
> Senator Patrick Leahy

3-128. The source of military law comes from two provisions of the US Constitution, those vesting certain powers in the legislative branch and those granting certain authority to the executive branch. In addition, the Fifth Amendment recognizes that offenses in the Armed Forces are dealt with in accordance with military law.

3-129. Along with the Constitution, there are other sources, both written and unwritten, that govern the military. International law and numerous treaties affecting the military have contributed to define the law of war. Congress contributed the UCMJ and other statutes; Executive orders, including the Manual for Courts-Martial (MCM); service regulations; and usages and customs of the Armed Forces form the foundation of military law. The civilian and military court systems have contributed decisions to clarify the gray areas. The UCMJ is federal law, enacted by Congress. The law authorizes the Commander-in-Chief (President of the United States) to implement the provisions of the UCMJ. The President does this via an executive order known as the Manual for Courts-Martial.

3-130. Military discipline is founded upon self-discipline, respect for authority, and the embracing of the professional Army ethic with its supporting individual values. Military discipline is developed through individual and group training to create a mental attitude that will result in proper conduct and prompt obedience to lawful military authority. Soldiers demonstrate their discipline in many ways, including the prompt and correct execution of orders and compliance with regulations.

> *When soldiers get into trouble, they need firm but constructive support and guidance for correcting the problem at hand; they are not seeking sympathy or self-pity. Soldiers expect to see a role model, someone with knowledge of what needs to be done, the physical conditioning to lead by example, the self-discipline to set standards, and the maturity to recognize, acknowledge, and reward success.*
>
> GEN Colin L. Powell and CSM Robert F. Beach

3-131. It is your duty to abide by law and regulation, 24 hours a day, seven days a week, for as long as you're in the Army. Soldiers obey and promptly execute the legal orders of their lawful superiors. Laws and regulations are part of everyday life. The UCMJ gives us judicial authority, which is essential to the Army's ability to accomplish its mission. The UCMJ is the statute that defines criminal offenses for soldiers.

## ARTICLES OF THE MANUAL FOR COURTS-MARTIAL

3-132. The Manual for Courts-Martial (MCM) is a pretty big book. It contains the Uniform Code of Military Justice and instructs military lawyers and judges on how to conduct courts-martial. It is also where nonjudicial punishment (Article 15) is found. There are a total of 140 articles in the MCM. The MCM explains what conduct is in violation of the

UCMJ, sets forth rules of evidence, contains a list of maximum punishments for each offense and explains types of court-martials. Articles 1 through 146 are in the following categories:

- General Provisions—Articles 1 through 6.

- Apprehension and Restraint—Articles 7 through 14.

- Nonjudicial Punishment—Article 15

- Court-Martial Jurisdiction—Articles 16 through 21.

- Composition of Courts-Martial—Articles 22 through 29.

- Courts-Martial Procedures and Sentences—Articles 30 through 58.

- Post-Trial Procedures and Review of Courts-Martial—Articles 59 through 76.

- Punitive Articles—Articles 77 through 133. Also known as the "punitive offenses," these describe specific offenses that can result in punishment by court-martial or nonjudicial punishment.

- Article 134 is a "catch-all" that covers any offenses not specifically named in Articles 77-133.

- Miscellaneous Provisions—Articles 135 through 146.

3-133. Soldiers have rights under the UCMJ. In some ways, the USMJ provides even greater protections of soldiers' rights than under strictly civilian jurisdiction. A soldier has the following rights:

- The right to remain silent.

- The right to counsel.

- The right to demand trial.

- Under Article 15, the right to present his case, in the presence of the imposing commander.

- The right to call witnesses (if they are reasonably available).

- The right to present evidence.

- Under Article 15, the right to request a spokesperson (but not an attorney at the hearing).

- The right to request an open hearing.

- The right to examine all evidence.

3-134. Most courts-martial are preceded by an Article 32 investigation. This is an investigation by an officer, probably from the same installation, that tries to determine if there is enough evidence to go to a court-martial. It can be thought of as a little like a grand jury in the civilian legal system. The Article 32 investigation will also consider if the charges are correct and how to proceed with the case, whether by court-martial, nonjudicial punishment, administrative action, or even no action at all.

3-135. Refer to AR 27-10, *Military Justice*, the *Manual for Courts-Martial (MCM), United States*, or visit your installation legal office for additional information. Also see Chapter 7 for information on the effects of the character of discharge on benefits after separation. Making the right decision is critical for the soldier receiving the punishment as well as the individual administering punishment under the UCMJ.

## ARTICLE 15

3-136. Within the UCMJ is a provision for punishing misconduct through judicial proceedings like a court-martial. The UCMJ also gives commanders the authority to impose nonjudicial punishment, described in the UCMJ under Article 15. Article 15 provides commanders an essential tool in maintaining discipline. The Article allows commanders to impose punishment for relatively minor infractions. Only commanders may impose punishment under Article 15. A commander is any warrant officer or commissioned officer that is in command of a unit and has been given authority under AR 600-20, either orally or in writing, to administer nonjudical punishment.

3-137. When reviewing the circumstances surrounding an incident of misconduct, the commander will ensure that prior to processing an Article 15, an actual offense under the UCMJ was committed. He ensures the alleged offense violated the UCMJ, Army Regulations, Army Policy, a lawful order, local laws or some other rule the soldier had a duty to obey.

3-138. The soldier is informed that the commander has started nonjudicial punishment (Article 15) procedures against him. Once the commander has conducted the hearing and if he decides that the accused is (a) guilty and (b) needs to be punished, he will prescribe punishment that fits the offense(s). Soldiers may present evidence at Article 15 hearings. Evidence would be something that shows a soldier is not guilty of the alleged offense(s). A soldier may also present matters in extenuation and mitigation, which are reasons why he should be punished less or not at all.

3-139. The level of proof is the same at both an Article 15 hearing and a court-martial; the imposing commander must be convinced of the accused soldier's guilt by the evidence presented before the soldier can be found guilty. Whatever the outcome of the hearing, an Article 15 is not considered a conviction and will not appear in your civilian record. On the other hand, if you demand a trial by court-martial and are convicted, this would be a federal conviction that would stay with you even after you leave the Army. No lawyers are involved in the Article 15 hearing however, the soldier has the right to speak with an attorney prior to accepting proceedings under Article 15. There is also no prosecutor at an Article 15 hearing. At a court-martial, a military lawyer may represent the accused at no cost to the soldier, and there would also be a prosecutor present.

3-140. If a soldier thinks he has been punished excessively, or evidence was not properly considered, he may appeal to the next level of command within five days. The soldier is not entitled to a personal appearance in front of the appeal authority (although he may request one) so he should include written statements as to why the appeal should be granted. If the soldier doesn't submit these statements, the appeal authority may never get his side of what happened. The appeal authority can take any action to lessen the punishment but may NOT INCREASE the punishment given by the original commander.

3-141. Article 15s come in different levels: Summarized, Company Grade and Field Grade. They differ in two main respects: the severity of the punishment and in how the record of it can affect a soldier's future in the Army. Maximum punishments are shown in Table 3-1 below.

**Table 3-1. Maximum Punishments in Article 15**

|  | Summarized | Company Grade | Field Grade |
|---|---|---|---|
| **Restriction** | 14 days | 14 days | 60 days |
| **Extra Duty** | 14 days | 14 days | 45 days |
| **Pay Forfeiture** | None | 7 days | ½ month for 2 months |
| **Rank Reduction (E4 & below)** | None | 1 grade | 1 or more grades |
| **Rank Reduction (E5 & E6)** | None | None | 1 grade |
| **Rank Reduction (E7 & up)** | None | None | None |

Note: If both restriction and extra duty are imposed they must be served at the same time. Pay forfeiture, restriction and extra duty may be all or partially suspended.

3-142. Article 15s can affect a soldier's future. Summarized Article 15s are filed in the local files (at the installation Staff Judge Advocate office) for a period of two years or until the transfer of the soldier, whichever occurs first. Company and Field Grade Article 15s can be filed in the soldier's official military personnel file (OMPF). The commander in each case decides where to file the Article 15. An Article 15 in a soldier's official records will affect promotions, clearances, and special assignments.

## ADMINISTRATIVE TOOLS

3-143. The Army has administrative means of discharging enlisted soldiers earlier than their original service obligation. These are not part of the UCMJ but are other tools commanders can use to maintain unit readiness. The reasons a commander may take such action vary from the extreme of soldier misconduct to the soldier's request because of some hardship that necessitates his discharge. These "chapters" are actually chapters of AR 635-200, *Personnel Separations—Enlisted Personnel*. Other regulations also authorize discharge for certain reasons: AR 600-43, *Conscientious Objection;* AR 635-40, *Physical Evaluation for Retention, Retirement, or Separation;* and AR 604-10, *Military Personnel Security Program.* The chapters in AR 635-200 are listed below in Table 3-2.

### Table 3-2. Types of Chapter Discharges

| | |
|---|---|
| Chapter 3 | Character of Service. |
| Chapter 4 | Separation for Expiration of Service Obligation. |
| Chapter 5 | Separation for Convenience of the Government. |
| Chapter 6 | Separation Because of Dependency or Hardship. |
| Chapter 7 | Defective Enlistment/Reenlistment and Extensions. |
| Chapter 8 | Separation of Enlisted Women—Pregnancy. |
| Chapter 9 | Alcohol or Other Drug Abuse Rehabilitation Failure. |
| Chapter 10 | Discharge in Lieu of Trail by Court-Martial. |
| Chapter 11 | Entry Level Performance and Conduct. |
| Chapter 12 | Retirement for Length of Service. |
| Chapter 13 | Separation for Unsatisfactory Performance. |
| Chapter 14 | Separation for Misconduct. |
| Chapter 15 | Discharge for Homosexual Conduct. |
| Chapter 16 | Selected Changes in Service Obligations. |
| Chapter 18 | Failure to Meet Body Fat Standards. |
| Chapter 19 | Qualitative Management Program. |

### DISCHARGE

3-144. If separated, the soldier could receive one of three types of discharges (depending on the type of chapter): honorable, general (under honorable conditions) also called a general discharge, or a discharge under other-than-honorable-conditions, also called an "OTH." An honorable discharge is the best discharge a soldier can receive from the service. A general discharge affects some of the benefits a veteran is eligible for. An OTH discharge will deprive you of most of the benefits you would receive with an honorable discharge and may cause you substantial prejudice in civilian life. Generally, an OTH discharge is only possible under Chapters 14 and 15. Before you can be given an OTH, you have the right to have your case heard by an administrative separation board.

3-145. The benefits available to you under the different types of discharges are listed in Chapter 7. Note that with a general discharge, you keep most of the pay entitlements or Veterans Administration (VA) benefits that you might have accrued thus far. For example, you can still cash in your accrued leave. However, you do lose any Montgomery GI Bill (MGIB) contributions and any civil service retirement credit (that is, credit toward federal civil service retirement for your active duty military time) to which you would otherwise be entitled. The biggest problem with a general discharge is that it is the second best type of discharge. As such, a future employer may inquire as to why you didn't get the best type.

3-146. The separation authority (your battalion or brigade commander, or the commanding general, depending on your type of chapter) decides whether or not you should be separated, and, if so, what type of discharge you should get. There are three ways to have input into those decisions.

3-147. If you have less than six years of military service you may submit statements in your own behalf. If you have six years or more of military service, or you are being considered for an OTH discharge, you have two additional options. You may request a hearing before an administrative separation board. The board's job is to recommend to the separation authority whether you should be separated and, if so, with what kind of discharge. The separation authority makes the final decision but cannot do anything less favorable to you than the board recommended. At the board you have the right to legal representation

3-148. You also may submit a conditional waiver. A conditional waiver is a document you send to the separation authority telling him that you will agree to give up your right to a board hearing if he promises to give you a better type of discharge (usually a general discharge). If the separation authority agrees, you get that better type of discharge. If he turns down your proposal, you still have the right to a board. In any case, you have the right to consult with a military lawyer to decide which option is best.

# LAW OF LAND WARFARE

3-149. American traditions and morals require us to educate and enforce the laws of war among members of the Armed Forces. Throughout the history of armed conflict, lives have been lost and property destroyed because combatants failed to abide by the laws of war. Some of these violations are caused by a blatant disregard for the international laws of war, and some are a result of pure ignorance. The laws are not new. Some versions of the present laws of war have been around a long time. Over 100 years ago most civilized nations recognized a need to prevent unnecessary destruction of lives and property on the battlefield. Most nations endorse these laws but do not always abide by them. The law of war today, embodied by the Hague and Geneva Conventions, can be generally divided into four categories:

- Conduct of hostilities, forbidden targets, illegal tactics, and unlawful warfare techniques.
- Treatment of wounded and sick on land and sea.
- Treatment of prisoners of war.
- Treatment of civilians.

3-150. The conduct of armed hostilities on land is regulated by the law of land warfare which is both written and unwritten. It is inspired by the desire to diminish the evils of war. The purposes of the law of war are as follows:

- Protect combatants and noncombatants from unnecessary suffering.
- Safeguard certain fundamental human rights of persons who fall into the hands of the enemy, particularly prisoners of war, the wounded and sick, and civilians.
- Facilitate the restoration of peace.

## BASIC PRINCIPLES

3-151. The law of war places limits on employing any kind or degree of violence that is not actually necessary for military purposes. The law of war also requires belligerents to conduct hostilities with regard for the principles of humanity. The law of war is binding not only upon states but also upon individuals and the members of their armed forces. American soldiers must know and abide by the law of land warfare—even if the enemy does not.

3-152. Any person, whether a member of the armed forces or a civilian who commits an act which constitutes a crime under international law is responsible and liable for punishment. The term "war crime" is a technical expression for violation of the law of war by any person or persons, military or civilian. Every violation of the law of war is a war crime.

3-153. In some cases, military commanders may be responsible for war crimes committed by subordinate members of the armed forces or other persons subject to their control. For example, if soldiers commit atrocities against prisoners of war, the responsibility may rest not only with the actual perpetrators but also with the commander, especially if the acts occurred by an order of the commander concerned. The commander is also responsible if he has or should have knowledge that soldiers or other persons subject to his control are about to commit or have committed a war crime and he fails to take steps to prevent such crime or to punish violators.

3-154. The United States normally punishes war crimes as such only if they are committed by enemy nationals or by persons serving the interests of the enemy state. Violations of the law of war committed by persons subject to military law of the United States usually constitute violations of the Uniform Code of Military Justice and are prosecuted under the UCMJ. Commanders must insure that war crimes committed by members of their forces against enemy personnel are promptly and adequately punished.

## DEFENSE OF SUPERIOR ORDERS

3-155. The fact that the law of war has been violated even if on the order of a superior authority, whether military or civil, does not change the act in question of its character as a war crime. It does not constitute a defense in the trial of an accused individual unless he did not know and could not reasonably have been expected to know that the act was unlawful. In all cases where the order is held not to constitute a defense to an allegation of war crime, the fact that the individual was acting pursuant to orders may be considered in mitigation of punishment.

3-156. In considering the question of whether a superior order constitutes a valid defense, a court-martial takes into consideration the fact that obedience to lawful military orders is the duty of every member of the armed forces. At the same time, remember that members of the armed forces are bound to obey only lawful orders.

*I've long since forgotten the name of the speaker, but I'll never forget what he said. 'Imagine this. In the spring of 1945, around the world, the sight of a twelve-man squad of teenage boys, armed and in uniform, brought terror to people's hearts. Whether it was a Red Army squad in Berlin, Leipzig, or Warsaw, or a German squad in Holland, or a Japanese squad in Manila, Seoul, or Beijing, that squad meant rape, pillage, looting, wanton destruction, senseless killing. But there was one exception: a squad of GIs, a sight that brought the biggest smiles you ever saw to people's lips, and joy to their hearts.'*

**Stephen H. Ambrose**

## THE GENEVA CONVENTIONS ON THE LAWS OF WAR

3-157. Noncombatants are persons not taking part in hostilities, including members of armed forces who have laid down their arms and those incapacitated by sickness, wounds, detention, or any other cause. Noncombatants shall in all circumstances be treated humanely without exception. The following acts are and shall remain prohibited at any time and in any place whatsoever with respect to noncombatants:

- Violence to life and person, in particular murder of all kinds, mutilation, cruel treatment, and torture.

- Taking of hostages.

- Outrages upon personal dignity, in particular humiliating and degrading treatment.

- Passing sentences and carrying out executions without previous judgment of a regularly constituted court that affords all the judicial guarantees recognized as indispensable by civilized peoples.

3-158. For more information about the law of land warfare, see FM 1-04.10 (27-10), *The Law of Land Warfare*.

## SECTION IV - STANDARDS OF CONDUCT

3-159. Department of the Army personnel must place loyalty to country, ethical principles, and law above private gain and other personal interests. Army Regulation 600-20, *Army Command Policy* and DOD 5500.7-R, *Joint Ethics Regulation* are the regulatory documents that affect Army standards of conduct.

# RELATIONSHIPS BETWEEN SOLDIERS OF DIFFERENT RANK

3-160. Relationships between soldiers of different rank are prohibited if they—

- Compromise, or appear to compromise, the integrity of supervisory authority or the chain of command.

- Cause actual or perceived partiality or unfairness.
- Involve, or appear to involve, the improper use of rank or position for personal gain.
- Are, or are perceived to be, exploitative or coercive in nature.
- Create an actual or clearly predictable adverse impact on discipline, authority, morale, or the ability of the command to accomplish its mission.

---

### Platoon Sergeant and Enlisted Soldier Relationship

SSG Young, a single male platoon sergeant of the 3rd Platoon, C Company, is dating PV2 Owens, a single female soldier in A Company, both in the same battalion. Their relationship is known to the command and throughout both units since they have lunch together and hold hands while walking in uniform. Both individuals say their relationship is serious but marriage has not been discussed. Both commanders do not believe that the relationship is presently affecting either unit. Should their respective unit commanders counsel SSG Young and Private Owens regarding this relationship?

Yes. They must be informed that holding hands while in uniform or while in public places is inappropriate. In addition, they must avoid behavior that could be perceived by other soldiers as suggesting that Private Owens is receiving special treatment because of her relationship with SSG Young.

---

3-161. Certain types of personal relationships between officers and enlisted soldiers are prohibited. Prohibited relationships include on-going business relationships between officers and enlisted soldiers. This prohibition does not apply to landlord/tenant relationships or to one-time transactions such as the sale of an automobile or house but does apply to borrowing or lending money, commercial solicitation, and any other type of on-going financial or business relationship. In case of Army National Guard (ARNG) or United States Army Reserve (USAR) personnel, this prohibition does not apply to relationships that exist due to their civilian occupation or employment.

3-162. Other prohibited relationships are dating, shared living accommodations other than those directed by operational requirements, and intimate or sexual relationships between officers and enlisted soldiers. This prohibition does not apply to marriages prior to 1 March 2000. Other exceptions are the following:

- Relationships that comply with this policy but then become non-compliant due to a change in status of one of the members (for example, two enlisted members are married and one is subsequently selected as a warrant officer).
- Personal relationships outside of marriage between members of the ARNG or USAR, when the relationship primarily exists due to civilian acquaintances.

- Personal relationships outside of marriage between members of the regular Army and members of the ARNG or USAR when the relationships primarily exist due to civilian association.

3-163. All soldiers must ensure that these relationships do not interfere with good order and discipline. Commanders will ensure that personal relationships, which exist between soldiers of different ranks emanating from their civilian careers, will not influence training.

---

### Officer - Enlisted Gambling

A long-standing tradition in the battalion has been to have weekly poker games involving members of the staff. While both officers and enlisted soldiers participate regularly, no one plays against other soldiers in the same chain of command. They also enjoy office pools like football and other sports events. Is this a problem?

Army regulation prohibits gambling between officers and enlisted soldiers. Some states may also prohibit gambling, regardless of who is playing the game. The Joint Ethics Regulation (JER) prohibits certain gambling by DOD employees while on duty or on federally owned or leased property. Soldiers must be aware of both Army policy and applicable state law restrictions. Assuming this scenario does not violate the JER or state or federal law, officers may participate in poker games or pools only with other officers and enlisted only with enlisted soldiers. In any case leaders should beware of potential problems of how such activity is perceived.

---

3-164. All military personnel share the responsibility for maintaining professional relationships. However, in any relationship between soldiers of different grade or rank the senior member is generally in the best position to terminate or limit the extent of the relationship. Nevertheless, all members may be held accountable for relationships that violate this policy.

3-165. Commanders should seek to prevent inappropriate or unprofessional relationships through proper training and leadership by example. Should inappropriate relationships occur, commanders have available a wide range of responses. These responses may include counseling, reprimand, order to cease, reassignment, or adverse action. Potential adverse action may include official reprimand, adverse evaluation report(s), non-judicial punishment, separation, bar to reenlistment, promotion denial, demotion, and courts-martial.

3-166. These prohibitions are not intended to preclude normal team building associations, which occur in the context of activities such as community organizations, religious activities, family gatherings, unit-based social functions, or athletic teams or events.

### OTHER PROHIBITED RELATIONSHIPS

3-167. Trainee and soldier relationships between permanent party personnel and Initial Entry Training (IET) trainees not required by the training mission are prohibited. This prohibition applies to permanent party personnel without regard to the installation of assignment of the permanent party member or the trainee.

3-168. Recruiter and recruit relationships between permanent party personnel assigned or attached to the United States Army Recruiting Command and potential prospects, applicants, members of the Delayed Entry Program (DEP), or members of the Delayed Training Program (DTP) not required by the recruiting mission is prohibited. This prohibition applies to United States Army Recruiting Command personnel without regard to the unit of assignment of the permanent party member and the potential prospects, applicants, DEP or DTP members.

## EXTREMIST ORGANIZATIONS AND ACTIVITIES

3-169. Participation in extremist organizations and activities by Army personnel is inconsistent with the responsibilities of military service. The Army provides equal opportunity and treatment for all soldiers without regard to race, color, religion, gender, or national origin. Commanders enforce this Army policy because it is vitally important to unit cohesion and morale, and is essential to the Army's ability to accomplish its mission.

3-170. All soldiers must reject participation in extremist organizations and activities. Extremist organizations and activities are those that advocate racial, gender or ethnic hatred or intolerance. They are also those that advocate, create, or engage in illegal discrimination based on race, color, gender, religion, or national origin. Extremist organizations are also those that advocate the use of or use force or violence or unlawful means to deprive individuals of their rights under the United States Constitution or the laws of the United States or any state, by unlawful means.

3-171. Soldiers are prohibited from the following actions in support of extremist organizations or activities. Penalties for violations of these prohibitions include the full range of statutory and regulatory sanctions, both criminal (UCMJ), and administrative:

- Participating in public demonstrations or rallies.
- Attending a meeting or activity with the knowledge that the meeting or activity involves an extremist cause.
- Fund-raising activities.
- Recruiting or training members.
- Creating, organizing or leading such an organization or activity.
- Distributing literature that supports extremist causes.

3-172. Commanders have the authority to prohibit soldiers from engaging in or participating in any other activities that the commander determines will adversely affect good order and discipline or morale within the command. Commanders may order the removal of symbols, flags, posters, or other displays from barracks. Commanders may also place areas or activities off-limits, or to order soldiers not to participate in those activities that are contrary to good order and discipline or morale of the unit or pose a threat to health, safety, and security of military personnel or a military installation. Commanders have options for dealing with soldiers that are in violation of the prohibitions. For example, the commander may use Article 15, bar to reenlistment or other administrative or disciplinary actions.

3-173. Commanders must investigate any soldier involved with an extremist organization or activity. Indicators of such involvement are membership, receipt of literature, or presence at an event that could threaten the good order and discipline of the unit. Soldiers should be aware of the potential adverse effects that violation of Army policy may have upon good order and discipline in the unit and upon their military service.

## HOMOSEXUAL CONDUCT

3-174. A person's sexual orientation is considered a personal and private matter and is not a bar to entry or continued service unless manifested by homosexual conduct. Homosexual conduct is grounds for separation from the Army. "Homosexual conduct" is a homosexual act, a statement by a soldier that demonstrates a propensity or intent to engage in homosexual acts, the solicitation of another to engage in homosexual act or acts, or a homosexual marriage or attempted marriage.

3-175. Only a soldier's commander is authorized to initiate fact-finding inquiries involving homosexual conduct. A commander may initiate a fact-finding inquiry only when he has received credible information that there is a basis for discharge. Commanders are accountable for ensuring that inquiries are conducted properly and that no abuse of authority occurs. It is the commander's responsibility alone to investigate and take action in cases of alleged homosexual conduct. Other soldiers must not engage in behavior that may injure unit cohesion and team integrity, such as repeating rumors or harassing a soldier they believe has a different sexual orientation.

## HAZING

3-176. The Army is a values-based organization where everyone is encouraged to do what is right by treating others as they should be treated—with dignity and respect. Hazing is in opposition to our values and is prohibited. Hazing is any conduct whereby one military member or employee, regardless of service or rank, unnecessarily causes another military member or employee, regardless of service or rank, to suffer or be exposed to an activity which is cruel, abusive, oppressive or harmful.

3-177. Hazing includes, but is not limited to any form of initiation, "rite of passage" or congratulatory act that involves inflicting pain or encouraging others to engage in illegal, harmful, demeaning or dangerous acts. Physically striking another in order to inflict pain; piercing another's skin in any manner; forcing or requiring the consumption of excessive amounts of food, alcohol, drugs, or other substances can be considered hazing. Simply telling another soldier to participate in any such activity is also considered hazing. Hazing need not involve physical contact among or between military members or employees; it can be verbal or psychological in nature.

3-178. Hazing is not limited to superior-subordinate relationships. It may occur between peers or even, under certain circumstances, may involve actions directed towards senior military personnel by those juniors in rank or grade to them. Hazing has at times occurred during graduation ceremonies or similar military "rites of passage." However, it may also happen in day-to-day military settings. It is prohibited in all cases, to include off duty or "unofficial" celebrations or unit functions. Express or implied consent to hazing is not a defense to violation of AR 600-20.

## CODE OF CONDUCT

3-179. The Code of Conduct applies to all members of the US Armed Forces. It is the duty of individual soldiers who become isolated from their unit in the course of combat operations to continue to fight, evade capture, and regain contact with friendly forces. But if captured, individual soldiers must live, act and speak in a manner that leaves no doubt that they adhere to the traditions of the US Army and resist enemy attempts of interrogation, indoctrination and other exploitation. Individual soldiers are accountable for their actions even while isolated from friendly forces or held by the enemy. See The Code of Conduct in Figure 3-4.

---

### The Code of Conduct

I am an American fighting in the forces that guard my country and our way of life; I am prepared to give my life in their defense.

I will never surrender of my own free will. If in command, I will never surrender the members of my command while they still have the means to resist.

If I am captured I will continue to resist by all means available. I will make every effort to escape and aid others to escape. I will accept neither parole nor special favors from the enemy.

If I become a prisoner of war, I will keep faith with my fellow prisoners. I will give no information or take part in any action, which might be harmful to my comrades. If I am senior, I will take command. If not, I will obey the lawful orders of those appointed over me and will back them up in every way.

Should I become a prisoner of war, I am required to give name, rank, service number, and date of birth. I will evade answering further questions to the utmost of my ability. I will make no oral or written statements disloyal to my country and its allies.

I will never forget that I am an American fighting for freedom, responsible for my actions, and dedicated to the principles which made my country free. I will trust in my God and in the United States of America.

---

**Figure 3-4. The Code of Conduct**

3-180. Soldiers must take every reasonable step to prevent enemy exploitation of themselves and the US Government. If unable to completely prevent such exploitation, soldiers must limit exploitation as much as possible. In a sense, detained soldiers often are catalysts for their own release, based upon their ability to become unattractive sources of exploitation. That is, one who resists successfully may expect captors to lose interest in further exploitation attempts. Detainees or captives very often must use their judgment as to which actions will increase their chances of returning home with honor and dignity. Without exception, the soldier who can say honestly that he has done his utmost to resist exploitation upholds national policy, the founding principles of the United States, and the highest traditions of military service.

3-181. Regardless of the type of detention or captivity or harshness of treatment, soldiers will maintain their military bearing. They should make every effort to remain calm and courteous and project personal dignity. This is particularly important during the process of capture and the early stages of internment when the captor may be uncertain of his control over the captives. Rude behavior seldom serves the long-term interest of a detainee, captive or hostage. Additionally, it often results in unnecessary punishment, which in some situations can jeopardize survival and severely complicate efforts to gain release of the detained or captured soldiers.

3-182. There are no circumstances in which a detainee or captive should voluntarily give classified information or materials to unauthorized persons. To the utmost of their ability, soldiers held as detainees, captives, or hostages will protect all classified information. An unauthorized disclosure of classified information, for whatever reason, does not justify further disclosures. Detainees, captives, and hostages must resist, to the utmost of their ability, each and every attempt by their captor to obtain such information.

3-183. In situations where detained or captured soldiers are held in a group, soldiers will organize, to the fullest extent possible, in a military manner under the senior military member present (regardless of service). Historically, establishment of a military chain of command has been a tremendous source of strength for all captives. In such circumstances, make every effort to establish and sustain communications with other detainees, captives, or hostages. Military detainees, captives, or hostages will encourage civilians being held with them to participate in the military organization and accept the authority of the senior military member. The senior military member is obligated to establish a military organization and to ensure that the guidelines in support of the Department of Defense (DOD) policy to survive with honor are not compromised. Army Regulation 350-30, *Code of Conduct, Survival, Evasion, Resistance, and Escape (SERE) Training* covers the Code of Conduct.

# GIFTS AND DONATIONS

3-184. Army standards of conduct affect whether soldiers and Department of the Army civilians (DAC) may give gifts to each other. A "gift" includes nearly anything of monetary value, including services. A gift to the spouse of a soldier or DAC with the knowledge and permission of the soldier/DAC is considered a gift to that person. Items not considered gifts are—

- Coffee, doughnuts and similar modest items of food and refreshments when offered other than as part of a meal.

- Greeting cards, most plaques, certificates and trophies, which are intended solely for presentation.

- Any prize, commercial discount, or other benefit which is available to the general public, all federal employees, or all military members (e.g., military discounts).

## GIFTS BETWEEN SOLDIERS

3-185. As a general rule, soldiers may not directly or indirectly, give a gift to or make a donation toward a gift for an official superior. Soldiers likewise may not accept a gift from a subordinate. An exception to the general rule is that on an occasional basis, including any occasion on which gifts are traditionally given or exchanged, the following may be given to an official superior or accepted from a subordinate:

- Items, other than cash, with an aggregate market value of $10 or less per occasion.

- Items such as food and refreshments to be shared in the office among several soldiers/DACs.

- Personal, customary hospitality provided at a residence, for example, inviting your supervisor over for dinner.

- Items given in connection with the receipt of personal hospitality if of a type and value customarily given on such occasions, for example, bringing your dinner party hostess a bouquet of flowers.

3-186. The other exception to the general rule is in giving gifts in recognition of infrequently occurring occasions of personal significance. Examples of these are as marriage, illness, the birth or adoption of a child, or upon occasions that terminate a subordinate-superior relationship, such as retirement, resignation, or transfer. The following limitations exist for this infrequent occasion exception:

- The fair market value of a gift or gifts from a single donating group should not exceed $300.

- The maximum amount that may be solicited for a gift or gifts for a special, infrequent occasion is $10.

- The cost of food, refreshments, and entertainment provided to mark the occasion for which the gift is given do not have to be included in the $300/10 limitations.

## GIFTS FROM OUTSIDE SOURCES

3-187. Soldiers and DACs may not ask for gifts. Additionally, they may not accept gifts from a "prohibited source" (generally defined as any person or entity who does, or seeks to do, business with DOD). Even if an item would otherwise be considered a prohibited gift from an outside source, there are a few exceptions which permit acceptance. These include the following:

- Gifts with a retail value of $20 or less per occasion, provided that the aggregate value of gifts received from any one person or entity does not exceed $50 in a calendar year.

- Gifts which are clearly motivated by a family relationship or personal friendship.

- Gifts resulting from the outside business activities of soldiers or their spouses.

- Free attendance provided by the sponsor of an event for the day on which a soldier is speaking or presenting information at the event.

- Free attendance provided by the sponsor of a widely attended gathering of mutual interest that clearly has government interest.

- Gifts accepted by the soldier under a specific statute or regulation (for example, foreign gifts valued at $260 or less accepted in accordance with AR 1-100, *Gifts and Donations*).

## GIFTS FROM FOREIGN GOVERNMENTS

3-188. Congress has consented to the receipt of certain foreign gifts of minimal value, i.e., with a retail value of $260 or less. It is the recipient's burden to establish value. A personal memorandum for record should be made and kept for all foreign gifts received under $260 for the recipient's personal protection.

3-189. Gifts over the $260 limit should be refused; however, if doing so will result in embarrassment, or would offend or otherwise adversely affect the foreign government giving the gift, then the gift may be accepted. In this case the recipient must make a full record of the event, including the circumstances surrounding the gift, the date and place of presentation.

3-190. Ordinarily, the gift, and supporting information above must be forwarded to Commander, US Army Total Personnel Command (PERSCOM), within 60 days of gift receipt. Gifts are then normally forwarded to the General Services Agency for proper disposition. Organizations may request to retain gifts locally for use in an official capacity, (e.g., to display in the unit). Those requests also go to PERSCOM but the gifts may be retained at the unit pending PERSCOM approval. In some circumstances, the recipient may also purchase gifts for their full retail value.

3-191. For additional information on giving or receiving gifts refer to AR 1-100, *Gifts and Donations.*

## FUND-RAISING

3-192. Fund-raising events and activities for organizations may not conflict or interfere with the annual Combined Federal Campaign (CFC) and Army Emergency Relief (AER) fund drives. Generally, CFC and AER are the only fund-raising authorized throughout the Army. Such fund-raising must be conducted in accordance with (IAW) AR 600-29, *Fund-Raising Within the Department of the Army*, or AR 930-4, *Army Emergency Relief.*

3-193. Provided no on-the-job fund-raising is involved, installation commanders may authorize the following fund-raising activities—

- Fund-raising in support of installation Morale, Welfare and Recreation (MWR) activities IAW AR 215-1, *Morale, Welfare, and Recreation Activities And Nonappropriated Fund Instrumentalities*, and AR 600-29.

- Occasional fund-raising in support of on-post-private organizations IAW AR 600-29.

- Other limited fund-raising activities to assist the unfortunate. These activities may include the use of "poppies" or other similar tokens by veterans' organizations, or the placement of collection boxes in public use areas of Army buildings or installations for the voluntary donation of foods or goods for charitable cause. Such activities must be consistent with AR 600-29.

3-194. Fund-raising by religious organizations or their affiliates is authorized only in connection with religious services and must be conducted in accordance with AR 165-1, *Chaplain Activities in the United States Army*.

## LAUTENBERG AMENDMENT

3-195. The Lautenberg Amendment to the Gun Control Act of 1968, effective 30 September 1996, makes it a felony for those convicted of misdemeanor crimes of domestic violence to ship, transport, possess, or receive firearms or ammunition. The Amendment also makes it a felony to transfer a firearm or ammunition to an individual known, or reasonably believed, to have such a conviction. Soldiers are not exempt from the Lautenberg Amendment.

3-196. Summary court-martial convictions, nonjudicial punishment under Article 15, UCMJ, and deferred prosecutions (or similar alternative dispositions) in civilian court do not constitute qualifying convictions within the meaning of the Lautenberg Amendment. The prohibitions do not preclude a soldier from operating major weapons systems or crew served weapons such as tanks, missiles, and aircraft. The Lautenberg Amendment applies to soldiers with privately owned firearms and ammunition stored on or off post.

3-197. Army policy is that all soldiers known to have, or soldiers whom commanders have reasonable cause to believe have, a conviction of a misdemeanor crime of domestic are non-deployable for missions that require possession of firearms or ammunition. Soldiers affected by the Lautenberg Amendment are not eligible for overseas assignment. However, soldiers who are based outside the continental United States (OCONUS) will continue to comply with their assignment instructions.

3-198. Soldiers with qualifying convictions may not be assigned or attached to tables of organization and equipment (TOE) or modified TOE (MTOE) units. Commanders will not appoint such soldiers to leadership positions that would give them access to firearms and ammunition. Soldiers with qualifying convictions may not attend any service school where instruction with individual weapons or ammunition is part of the curriculum.

3-199. Soldiers whom commanders know, or have reasonable cause to believe have, a qualifying conviction may extend if otherwise qualified, but are limited to a one year extension. Affected soldiers may not reenlist and are not eligible for the indefinite reenlistment program. Soldiers barred from reenlistment based on a Lautenberg qualifying conviction occurring after 30 September 1996 may not extend their enlistment. However, such soldiers must be given a reasonable time to seek removal of the conviction or a pardon.

3-200. Officers are subject to the provisions of the Lautenberg Amendment like any other soldier. The effects of are somewhat different if an officer has a qualifying conviction. Officers may request release from active duty or submit an unqualified resignation under AR 600-8-24, *Officer Transfers and Discharges.*

**Chapter 4**

# Customs, Courtesies, and Traditions

The Army is an organization that instills pride in its members because of its history, mission, capabilities, and the respect it has earned in the service of the Nation. A reflection of that pride is visible in the customs, courtesies, and traditions the Army holds. Adherence to them connects us with soldiers throughout America's history.

For more information on Customs, Courtesies and Traditions see Army Regulation 600-20, *Army Command Policy*, paragraph 4-3; AR 600-25, *Salutes, Honors and Visits of Courtesy*; DA Pam 600-60, *A Guide to Protocol and Etiquette*; and FM 3-21.5, *Drill and Ceremonies*.

For more information on Department of the Army policy for unit and individual flags, guidons, and streamers see AR 840-10, *Heraldic Activities—Flags, Guidons, Streamers, Tabards, and Automobile and Aircraft Plates*.

## CUSTOMS

4-1. The Army has its own customs, both official and social. Some have been handed down from the distant past while others are of comparatively recent origin. Those customs that endure stand on their own merits. As a long established social organization, the Army observes a number of customs that add to the interest, pleasure, and graciousness of Army life.

> *Often it is these customs and traditions, strange to the civilian eye but solemn to the soldier, that keep the man in the uniform going in the unexciting times of peace. In war they keep him fighting at the front. The fiery regimental spirit fondly polished over decades and centuries possesses him in the face of the enemy. [The soldier] fights for the regiment, his battalion, his company, his platoon, his section, his comrade.*

4-2. A **custom** is an established practice. Customs include positive actions—things you do, and taboos—things you avoid. All established arts, trades, and professions, all races of people, all nations, and even different sections of the same nation have their own practices and customs by which they govern a part of their lives.

4-3. Many Army customs compliment procedures required by military courtesy, while others add to the graciousness of garrison life. The breach of some Army customs merely brands the offender as ignorant, careless, or ill bred. Violations of other Army customs, however, will bring official censure or disciplinary action. The customs of the Army are its common law. These are a few:

- Never criticize the Army or a leader in public.
- Never go "over the heads" of superiors—don't jump the chain of command.
- Never offer excuses.
- Never "wear" a superior's rank by saying something like, "the first sergeant wants this done now," when in fact the first sergeant said no such thing. Speak with your own voice.
- Never turn and walk away to avoid giving the hand salute.
- Never run indoors or pretend you don't hear (while driving, for example) to avoid standing reveille or retreat.
- Never appear in uniform while under the influence of alcohol.
- If you don't know the answer to a superior's question, you will never go wrong with the response, "I don't know sir, but I'll find out."

## COURTESIES

4-4. **Courtesy** among members of the Armed Forces is vital to maintain discipline. Military courtesy means good manners and politeness in dealing with other people. Courteous behavior provides a basis for developing good human relations. The distinction between civilian and military courtesy is that military courtesy was developed in a military atmosphere and has become an integral part of serving in uniform.

4-5. Most forms of military courtesy have some counterpart in civilian life. For example, we train soldiers to say sir or ma'am when talking to a higher ranking officer. Young men and women are sometimes taught to say sir to their fathers or ma'am to their mothers and likewise to other elders. It is often considered good manners for a younger person to say sir or ma'am when speaking to an older person. The use of the word sir is also common in the business world, such as in the salutation of a letter or in any well-ordered institution.

4-6. Military courtesy is not a one-way street. Enlisted personnel are expected to be courteous to officers and likewise officers are expected to return the courtesy. Mutual respect is a vital part of military courtesy. In the final analysis, military courtesy is the respect shown to each other by members of the same profession. Some of the Army's more common courtesies include rendering the hand salute, standing at attention or parade rest, or even addressing others by their rank.

## THE HAND SALUTE

4-7. The salute is not simply an honor exchanged. It is a privileged gesture of respect and trust among soldiers. Remember the salute is not only prescribed by regulation but is also recognition of each other's commitment, abilities, and professionalism.

4-8. Some historians believe the hand salute began in late Roman times when assassinations were common. A citizen who wanted to see a public official had to approach with his right hand raised to show that he did not hold a weapon. Knights in armor raised visors with the right hand when meeting a comrade. This practice gradually became a way of showing respect and, in early American history, sometimes involved removing the hat. By 1820, the motion was modified to touching the hat, and since then it has become the hand salute used today. You salute to show respect toward an officer, flag, or our country.

4-9. The salute is widely misunderstood outside the military. Some consider it to be a gesture of servility since the junior extends a salute to the senior, but we know that it is quite the opposite. The salute is an expression that recognizes each other as a member of the profession of arms; that they have made a personal commitment of self-sacrifice to preserve our way of life. The fact that the junior extends the greeting first is merely a point of etiquette—a salute extended or returned makes the same statement.

---

### The Salute

1LT Thompson and his platoon's newest NCO, SGT Jemison, were walking toward the orderly room one morning. As they turned the corner and approached the building, PFC Robertson walked out carrying a large box. PFC Robertson said, "Good morning, sir," and kept walking past the two. As his hands were occupied, he didn't salute.

But 1LT Thompson saluted and replied with the unit motto, "First Tank!"

After the soldier had passed, SGT Jemison asked the lieutenant why he saluted since the soldier did not.

"He did by rendering the greeting of the day. If I had been carrying something and he wasn't, he would have saluted. It's a privilege, not a chore," said 1LT Thompson. "It's just as important for me to return a salute as for a soldier to render it."

---

4-10. The way you salute says a lot about you as a soldier. A proud, smart salute shows pride in yourself and your unit and that you are confident in your abilities as a soldier. A sloppy salute might mean that you're ashamed of your unit, lack confidence, or at the very least, that you haven't learned how to salute correctly.

4-11. In saluting, turn your head and eyes toward the person or flag you are saluting. Bring your hand up to the correct position in one, smart motion without any preparatory movement. When dropping the salute, bring your hand directly down to its natural position at your side, without slapping your leg or moving your hand out to the side. Any flourish in the salute is improper.

4-12. The proper way to salute when wearing the beret or without headgear is to raise your right hand until the tip of your forefinger touches the outer edge of your right eyebrow (just above and to the right of your right eye). When wearing headgear, the forefinger touches the headgear slightly above and to the right of your right eye. Your fingers are together, straight, and your thumb snug along the hand in line with the fingers. Your hand, wrist, and forearm are straight, forming a straight line from your elbow to your fingertips. Your upper arm (elbow to shoulder) is horizontal to the ground.

4-13. All soldiers in uniform are required to salute when they meet and recognize persons entitled (by grade) to a salute except when it is inappropriate or impractical (in public conveyances such as planes and buses, in public places such as inside theaters, or when driving a vehicle). A salute is also rendered:

- When the United States National Anthem, "To the Color," "Hail to the Chief," or foreign national anthems are played.
- To uncased National Color outdoors.
- On ceremonial occasions such as changes of command or funerals.
- At reveille and retreat ceremonies, during the raising or lowering of the flag.
- During the sounding of honors.
- When pledging allegiance to the US flag outdoors.
- When turning over control of formations.
- When rendering reports.
- To officers of friendly foreign countries.

4-14. Salutes are not required when:
- Indoors, unless reporting to an officer or when on duty as a guard.
- A prisoner.
- Saluting is obviously inappropriate. In any case not covered by specific instructions, render the salute.
- Either the senior or the subordinate is wearing civilian clothes.

4-15. In general, you don't salute when you are working (for example, under your vehicle doing maintenance), indoors (except when reporting), or when saluting is not practical (carrying articles with both hands, for example). A good rule of thumb is this: if you are outdoors and it is practical to salute, do so. Outdoors includes theater marquees, shelters over gas station pumps, covered walkways, and other similar shelters that are open on the sides.

## OTHER COURTESIES

4-16. Military courtesy shows respect and reflects self-discipline. Consistent and proper military courtesy is an indicator of unit discipline, as well. Soldiers demonstrate courtesy in the way we address officers or NCOs of superior rank. Some other simple but visible signs of respect and self-discipline are as follows:

- When talking to an officer of superior rank, stand at attention until ordered otherwise.

- When you are dismissed, or when the officer departs, come to attention and salute.

- When speaking to or being addressed a noncommissioned officer of superior rank, stand at parade rest until ordered otherwise.

- When an officer of superior rank enters a room, the first soldier to recognize the officer calls personnel in the room to attention but does not salute. A salute indoors is rendered only when reporting.

- When an NCO of superior rank enters the room, the first soldier to recognize the NCO calls the room to "At ease."

- Walk on the left of an officer or NCO of superior rank.

- When entering or exiting a vehicle, the junior ranking soldier is the first to enter, and the senior in rank is the first to exit.

- When outdoors and approached by an NCO, you greet the NCO by saying, "Good morning, Sergeant," for example.

- The first person who sees an officer enter a dining facility gives the order "At ease," unless a more senior officer is already present. Many units extend this courtesy to senior NCOs, also.

- When you hear the command "At ease" in a dining facility, remain seated, silent and continue eating unless directed otherwise.

4-17. When you report to an officer of superior rank, approach the officer to whom you are reporting and stop about two steps from him, assuming the position of attention. Give the proper salute and say, for example, "Sir, Private Smith reports." If you are indoors, use the same procedures as above, except remove your headgear before reporting. If you are armed, however, do not remove your headgear.

## Parade Rest

PV2 Robbs was new to the company and was on his way to see SGT Putnam, his section leader, for reception and integration counseling. SFC Stone, the platoon sergeant was present to monitor the counseling.

PV2 Robbs entered the room and immediately assumed the position of parade rest but before he could report, SGT Putnam said, "You don't have to do that."

But SFC Stone interjected, "Go ahead and stay at parade rest, Private, you're doing the right thing." He continued, "You both need to know we don't want to lower any standards, here. Standing at parade rest is what junior enlisted soldiers do when speaking with or being addressed by an NCO. And by the way, Sergeant, we NCOs stand at parade rest when speaking with NCOs of superior rank. Besides, you know the proper command would be 'at ease,' 'stand at ease,' or 'carry on.' OK?"

"Hooah, Sergeant Stone," said SGT Putnam and turned back to PV2 Robbs. "Welcome, Private Robbs. This is a great unit to soldier in..."

4-18. A soldier addressing a higher ranking officer uses the word sir or ma'am in the same manner as a polite civilian speaking with a person to whom he wishes to show respect. In the military service, the matter of who says sir or ma'am to whom is clearly defined; in civilian life it is largely a matter of discretion. In the case of NCOs and soldiers, we address them by their rank because they've earned that rank.

4-19. Simple courtesy is an important indicator of a person's bearing, discipline, and manners. It is a fact that most people respond positively to genuine politeness and courtesy. Walk down a street in most towns and cities and see the response you get from people when you just say "good morning." It is no different for soldiers. Some units substitute the greeting with their unit motto, such as "Deeds, not Words," or "Keep up the Fire." These reiterate pride in the unit and demonstrate the discipline and professionalism of a unit's soldiers.

> When I walk up to a soldier he should go to parade rest. Not because I'm better than he is, but because he respects who he is and who I am based on what we both do. It's professionalism.
>
> SMA Jack L. Tilley

## RENDERING HONOR TO THE FLAG

4-20. The flag of the United States is the symbol of our nation. The union, white stars on a field of blue, is the honor point of the flag. The union of the flag and the flag itself, when in company with other flags, are always given the honor position, which is on the right. The rules for displaying the flag are contained in AR 840-10, *Heraldic Activities—Flags, Guidons,*

*Streamers, Tabards, and Automobile and Aircraft Plates*. Some of the rules for displaying the flag are as follows:

- All Army installations will display the flag of the United States outdoors.

- Continental United States (CONUS) Army installations will fly only one flag of the United States at a time except as authorized by the commanding generals of major Army commands.

- Installations will display the flag daily from reveille to retreat.

- When a number of flags are displayed from staffs set in a line, the flag of the United States will be at the right; to the left of an observer facing the display. If no foreign national flags are present, the flag of the United States may be placed at the center of the line providing it is displayed at a higher level.

- When the flag of the United States is displayed with state flags, all of the state flags will be of comparable size.

4-21. When the flag is being raised in the morning, you should stand at attention on the first note of "Reveille" and salute. In the evening "Retreat" is played prior to "To the Colors." ("Colors" refer to the flag of the United States and can also include the unit flag). When you hear the first note of "Retreat" come to the position of attention and face the flag (or the direction the music is coming from if the flag is not visible). Render the hand salute at the first note of "To the Colors." You normally face the flag when saluting, unless duty requires you to face in some other direction. At the conclusion of the music, resume your regular duties. If you are involved in some duty that would be hampered by saluting, you do not need to salute.

4-22. When in a formation or a group, the senior soldier present will call the group to "Attention" and then "Parade, Rest" at the first note of "Retreat." That soldier will then call the group to "Attention" and "Present, Arms" at the first note of "To the Colors" and then "Order, Arms" at the conclusion. When in civilian clothing, the only change is to place your right hand over your heart instead of saluting. Vehicles in motion should stop. If you are in a car or on a motorcycle, dismount and salute. If you are with a group in a military vehicle or bus, remain in the vehicle. The individual in charge will dismount and salute. These honors also apply to the national anthems of foreign countries during ceremonies or parades.

4-23. When you are passing or being passed by colors that are being presented, paraded, or displayed, salute when the colors are six paces from you. Hold the salute until the colors are six paces beyond you.

4-24. The Pledge of Allegiance is not recited in military formations or in military ceremonies. At other functions where the Pledge of Allegiance is recited, a soldier in uniform silently stands at attention facing the flag and renders the hand salute. If indoors a soldier in uniform silently stands at attention facing the flag. Where other participants are primarily civilians or in civilian attire, soldiers in uniform indoors may recite the pledge if they desire. A soldier in civilian clothing recites the pledge while standing at attention, facing the flag with the right hand over the heart. Male soldiers in civilian clothing should remove headgear with their right hand and hold it over the left shoulder so that the right hand is over the heart.

## TRADITIONS

4-25. **Tradition** is a customary pattern of thought, action, or behavior help by an identifiable group of people. It is information, beliefs, and customs handed down by word of mouth or by example from one generation to another without written instruction. Our military traditions are really the "Army Way" of doing and thinking. An interesting thing about traditions is that many of our Army traditions started out as something quite different from what they are now.

4-26. Military tradition is an interesting and often amusing subject. It gives a soldier a feeling of pride to understand just why we do things the way we do. Traditions are expressed in the things we do, the uniform we wear, and the things we say. Many of the words we use in the Army are unique and have been added to our vocabulary from different parts of the world and at different times in history.

4-27. Army traditions are the things that everyone in the Army does, everywhere. Unit traditions are the unique things that you do in your unit that other units may or may not do. Some unit traditions are—

- Ceremonial duties. Soldiers of the Old Guard, the 3d Infantry, have been Sentinels of the Tomb of the Unknown Soldier since 1948.
- The green berets of the Army's Special Forces.
- Airborne units' maroon beret.
- Cavalry units' spurs and hats.
- Special designations (authorized unit nicknames) such as Cottonbalers, the 7th Infantry Regiment.
- Distinctive items of clothing worn in your unit such as headgear, belt buckles, and tankers' boots.
- The promotion party.
- Unit mottoes such as "Victory!" or "Send me!"
- "Hooah!" This informal but always understood sound is less a word than an audible affirmation of the warrior ethos. The soldier that utters that sound understands his task and will not quit until it is completed. That sound means soldiers are ready and willing to accomplish the mission at hand.

## THE BUGLE CALL

4-28. The music you hear at various hours of the day (for example, "Reveille," "Retreat," and "Taps") or during ceremonies (funerals, change of command, etc.) has come to us from the days when bugles were used to communicate orders to large groups of soldiers on noisy battlefields.

Military buglers have been communicating with soldiers for centuries. Bugle calls told troops when to go to bed, when to wake up, when to eat, when to attack, and when to retreat. There were stable calls, water calls, drill calls, sick calls, and church calls on Sunday.

4-29. The Twilight Tattoo is a time honored military tradition that dates back to the British Army 300 years ago when bugle calls were designed to notify the troops to return to the barracks from the local towns. The familiar tune of "Tattoo" signaled tavern owners to "doe den tap toe" or "turn off the taps." The troops knew the call meant "taps off," and minutes later they were back in their tents.

4-30. Bugles were first used for signaling in America by the British army during the Revolutionary War. The sound of the bugle made it possible to convey commands over a great distance and could usually be heard above the roar of battle. Right up to the beginning of the First World War, bugles were important tools in the control of units.

**Bugler from the Army Band**

4-31. As weapons became more lethal, with longer ranges, and required greater dispersal of units, bugles lost effectiveness in controlling units. But the Army still retains bugles and the music with which they communicate to soldiers is another reminder of our heritage. With every note of Reveille or Retreat we call to mind our common bond with soldiers of the Continental Army and the sacrifices soldiers have made ever since. You can hear the bugle calls still used today on the Army Homepage at www.army.mil/armyband/listen/spirit.htm.

## COLORS, FLAGS, AND GUIDONS

4-32. The National and organizational flags carried by Color-bearing units are called the National Color and the organizational color respectively (the word color is capitalized when referring to the National flag only). When used singularly, the term "Color" implies the National Color. The term "Colors" means the national and organizational colors.

4-33. The Colors originated as a means of battlefield identification and performed this function for many years. The old rank of Ensign—originally an Army title, now used only in the Navy—was assigned to the regiment's junior officer who carried the flag (ensign) into battle. Because the color party marched into battle at the front and center of the regiment, casualties were high. Victories in the old days were sometimes expressed in terms of the number of enemy colors captured. The practice of carrying colors into battle persisted through the American Civil War; the last Medals of Honor awarded during this conflict were for capturing Confederate colors. Modern armies now carry colors only in ceremonies.

> ... *a small group of Union soldiers, held prisoners by the Confederates, made a Stars and Stripes from their own clothing, flew it for a few minutes from the rafters of the old warehouse in which they were imprisoned, and then tore it into 22 pieces, one for each man who helped make it. Every one then hid the piece of flag in his clothing and took it with him when released from prison. In the years following the war, the pieces were finally recovered and sewed together again to form the flag, which is still in existence.*
>
> FM 21-13, *The Soldier's Guide*, 1952

4-34. Regiments and separate battalions are the only units that carry colors. Divisions, brigades and other organizations have a distinguishing standard that shows the shoulder-sleeve insignia. Company-size units carry guidons (small flags) in the colors of their branches.

4-35. United States Army flags traditionally have been used for purposes of identification and the fostering of esprit de corps. The present policies stem from ideas and practices dating back to the Revolutionary War. In turn, those were influenced by the military traditions of Western Europe to a great extent. The English, French, Dutch, Spanish, and others brought to North America their flags, military uniforms, and other official symbolism. Also, leaders of the colonists were familiar with military traditions and particularly those of England and France.

4-36. With the Declaration of Independence and the formation of troops, came the need for items to identify the soldiers and military units. On February 20, 1776, General Washington's headquarters issued an order on flags. It said that regiments should each have distinctive colors similar to the uniforms of the regiment and that "the Number of the Regiment is to be mark'd on the Colours, and such a Motto, as the Colonel may choose..."

4-37. General Washington's order emphasized the significance of organizational colors to the Army by directing quick design and procurement. As late as 1779, the designs of regimental and national colors to be carried by Army organizations were the subject of correspondence between Washington and the Board of War. The Americans intended to follow the British practice of using two different designs for the National flag: one for the naval or marine flag and the other for the battle or Army flag. By 1780, the stars and stripes design adopted by the United States in 1777 was generally known as the marine (maritime) flag used extensively at sea, but no Army National flag had been adopted prior to 1780.

4-38. The first Army National Color was blue incorporating the design of an eagle displayed (somewhat similar to that in the coat of arms adopted for the United States) and the name of the regiment. That National Color of the Army was carried until 1841 when it became the regimental color. From that blue flag evolved the eagle on regimental and battalion flags and, finally, on Major Army Command flags. Continuous recognition of the significance of flags to the soldiers' morale resulted in a well-defined system of flags for organizations at all echelons. In general, flags incorporate design elements that are identical to or relate to the insignia worn by the members of the organization.

## THE ARMY FLAG AND ITS STREAMERS

4-39. Until 1956 no flag represented the Army as a whole. The first official US Army flag was unfurled on 14 June 1956 at Independence Hall in Philadelphia, Pennsylvania, by then Secretary of the Army Wilbur M. Brucker. This flag was designed to meet the need for one banner to represent the entire Army.

4-40. The Army flag is in the national colors of red, white, and blue with a yellow fringe. It has a white field with the War Office seal in blue in its center. Beneath the seal is a scarlet scroll with the inscription "United States Army" in white letters. Below the scroll the numerals "1775" appears in blue to commemorate the year in which the Army was created with the appointment of General George Washington as Commander in Chief.

4-41. The historic War Office seal, somewhat modified from its original, is the design feature that gives to the Army flag its greatest distinction. The center of the seal depicts a roman breastplate over a jupon, or a leather jacket. Above the breastplate rises a sword upon which rests a Phrygian cap. Rising from the breastplate to the left (facing the viewer) is a pike, or esponton, flanked by an unidentified organizational color. On the right side rises a musket with fixed bayonet flanked by the National Color. Above the sword is a rattlesnake holding in its mouth a scroll inscribed "This We'll Defend." To the lower left of the breastplate is a cannon in front of a drum with two drumsticks. Below the cannon are three cannon balls and to the right is a mortar on a trunnion with two powder flasks below. See the Army flag in figure 4-1 below.

**Figure 4-1. The Army Flag and Streamers**

4-42. From its colors to its heraldic devices, the Army flag is rich in symbolism that speaks of our nation's and the Army's origin and heritage. The colors used in the flag were selected for their traditional significance. Red, white, and blue are the colors, of course, of the national flag. Furthermore, those colors symbolize in the language of heraldry the virtues of hardiness and valor (red), purity and innocence (white), and vigilance, perseverance, and justice (blue). Blue is especially significant since it has been the unofficial color of the Army for more than two hundred years.

4-43. The meaning of the symbols that make up the heraldic design of the seal can be fully understood only in terms of its eighteenth century origin. For example, the placement of the two flags shown on the seal, the organizational and the national flags are reversed in violation of heraldic custom. The placing of the United States flag on the left (from the flag's point of view) rather than on the right reflected the tendency of the leaders of the Revolutionary War period to discard traditional European concepts. The display of both an organizational color and the national flag was a common practice of the Continental Army during the Revolutionary War. See the Army seal in figure 4-2 below.

**Figure 4-2. The Army Seal**

4-44. The implements of warfare, cannon, cannon balls, mortar, powder flasks, pike, and rifle, are all of the type used in the Revolutionary War. Their inclusion in the seal reflects the powers and duties of the revolutionary era Board of War for the procurement and handling of artillery, arms, ammunition, and other war-like stores belonging to the United States. The pike is of the type carried by subordinate officers of infantry. The drum and drumsticks are symbols of public notification, reflecting the tradition of a citizen militia. Drums also served various military purposes in the eighteenth century, such as the regulation of firing in battle by the drummer's beat. The Phrygian cap atop the sword's point is the type of cap given to ancient Roman slaves when they were granted freedom. However, during the French Revolution, the cap was adopted and worn as a "Cap of Liberty," and is now a traditional symbol of liberty. The coiled rattlesnake and scroll was a symbol that appeared frequently on colonial flags, particularly those representing groups opposed to some aspect of British rule.

4-45. The Army flag reflects our history and touches the lives of generations of Americans. In 1956, Chief of Staff of the Army General Maxwell D. Taylor called it the "American soldier's Flag... for those who have gone before us, for those who man our ramparts today, and for those who will stand guard over our freedoms in all of our tomorrows." The Army flag remains today a symbol of the Army's achievements in the past and of its readiness to meet the challenges of the future.

> *The Army is hundreds of years older than you are and proud of its experience. It draws strength from the past and offers some of that strength to you through symbols.*

FM 21-13, *The Soldier's Guide*, 1952

4-46. The streamers attached to the Army flag staff denote campaigns fought by the Army throughout our Nation's history. Each streamer (2 ¾ inches wide and 4 feet long) is embroidered with the designation of a campaign and the year(s) in which it occurred. The colors derive from the campaign ribbon authorized for service in that particular war.

4-47. The concept of campaign streamers came to prominence in the Civil War when Army organizations embroidered the names of battles on their organizational colors. This was discontinued in 1890 when units were authorized to place silver bands, engraved with the names of battles, around the staffs of their organizational colors. When American Expeditionary Force (AEF) units in World War I were unable to obtain silver bands, General Pershing authorized the use of small ribbons bearing the names of the World War I operations. In 1921 all color-bearing Army organizations were authorized to use the large campaign streamers currently displayed. To properly display the campaign streamers, a soldier ensures the first (Lexington) and last (Kosovo Defense Campaign) campaign streamers are visible.

## The Campaigns of the United States Army

4-48. These are the campaigns the Army has been a part of:

### Revolutionary War

- Lexington 19 Apr 1775
- Ticonderoga 10 May 1775
- Boston 17 Jun 1775-17 Mar 1776
- Quebec 28 Augt 1775-3 Jul 1776
- Charleston 28-29 Jun 1776; 29 Mar-12 May 1780
- Long Island 26-29 Aug 1776
- Trenton 26 Dec 1776
- Princeton 3 Jan 1777
- Saratoga 2 Jul-17 Oct 1777
- Brandywine 11 Sep 1777
- Germantown 4 Oct 1777
- Monmouth 28 Jun 1778
- Savannah 29 Dec 1778; 16 Sep-10 Oct 1779
- Cowpens 17 Jan 1781
- Guilford Court House 15 Mar 1781
- Yorktown 28 Sep-19 Oct 1781

### War of 1812

- Canada 18 Jun 1812-17 Feb 1815
- Chippewa 5 Jul 1814
- Lundy's Lane 25 Jul 1814
- Bladensburg 17-29 Aug 1814

- McHenry 13 Sep 1814
- New Orleans 23 Sep 1814-8 Jan 1815

**Mexican War**

- Palo Alto 8 May 1846
- Resaca de la Palma 9 May 1846
- Monterey 21 Sep 1846
- Buena Vista 22-23 Feb 1847
- Vera Cruz 9-29 Mar 1847
- Cerro Gordo 17 Apr 1847
- Contreras 18-20 Aug 1847
- Churubusco 20 Aug 1847
- Molino del Rey 8 Sep 1847
- Chapultepec 13 Sep 1847

**Civil War**

- Sumter 12-13 Apr 1861
- Bull Run 16-22 Jul 1861
- Henry & Donelson 6-16 Feb 1862
- Mississippi River 6 Feb 1862-9 Jul 1863
- Peninsula 17 Mar-3 Aug 1862
- Shiloh 6-7 Apr 1862
- Valley 15 May-17 Jun 1862
- Manassas 7 Aug-2 Sep 1862
- Antietam 3-17 Sept 1862
- Fredericksburg 9 Nov-15 Dec 1862
- Murfreesborough 26 Dec 1862-4 Jan 1863
- Chancellorsville 27 Apr-6 May 1863
- Gettysburg 29 Jun-3 Jul 1863

- Vicksburg 29 Mar-4 Jul 1863
- Chickamauga 16 Aug-22 Sep 1863
- Chattanooga 23-27 Nov 1863
- Wilderness 4-7 May 1864
- Atlanta 7 May-2 Sep 1864
- Spotsylvania 8-21 May 1864
- Cold Harbor 22 May-3 Jun 1864
- Petersburg 4 Jun 1864-2 Apr 1865
- Shenandoah 7 Aug-28 Nov 1864
- Franklin 17-30 Nov 1864
- Nashville 1-16 Dec 1864
- Appomattox 3-9 Apr 1865

**Indian Wars**

- Miami Jan 1790-Aug 1795
- Tippecanoe 21 Sep-18 Nov 1811
- Creeks 27 Jul 1813-Aug 1814; Feb 1836-Jul 1837
- Seminoles 20 Nov 1817-31 Oct 1818; 28 Dec 1835-14 Aug 1842; 15 Dec 1855-May 1858
- Black Hawk 26 Apr-20 Sep 1832
- Comanches 1867-1875
- Modocs 1872-1873
- Apaches 1873; 1885-1886
- Little Big Horn 1876-1877
- Nez Perces 1877
- Bannocks 1878
- Cheyennes 1878-1879
- Utes Sep 1879-Nov 1880
- Pine Ridge Nov 1890-Jan 1891

**War with Spain**

- Santiago 22 Jun-11 Jul 1898

- Puerto Rico 25 Jul-13 Aug 1898

- Manila 31 Jul-13 Aug 1898

### China Relief Expedition

- Tientsin 13 Jul 1900

- Yang-tsun 6 Aug 1900

- Peking 14-15 Aug 1900

### Philippine Insurrection

- Manila 4 Feb-17 Mar 1899

- Iloilo 8-12 Feb 1899

- Malolos 24 Mar-16 Aug 1899

- Laguna de Bay 8-17 Apr 1899

- San Isidro 12 Apr-30 May 1899; 15 Oct-19 Nov 1899

- Zapote River 13 Jun 1899

- Cavite 7-13 Oct 1899; 4 Jan-9 Feb 1900

- Tarlac 5-20 Nov 1899

- San Fabian 6-19 Nov 1899

- Mindanao 4 Jul 1902-31 Dec 1904; 22 Oct 1905

- Jolo 1-24 May 1905; 6-8 Mar 1906; 6 Aug 1906; 11-15 Jun 1913

### Mexican Expedition

- Mexico 1916-1917 14 Mar 1916-7 Feb 1917

### World War I

- Cambrai 20 Nov-4 Dec 1917

- Somme Defensive 21 Mar-6 Apr 1918

- Lys 9-27 Apr 1918

- Aisne 27 May-5 Jun 1918

- Montdidier-Noyon 9-13 Jun 1918

- Champagne-Marne 18 Jul-6 Aug 1918

- Aisne-Marne 15-18 Jul 1918

- Somme Offensive 8 Aug-11 Nov 1918

- Oise-Aisne 18 Aug-11 Nov 1918

- Ypres-Lys 19 Aug-11 Nov 1918

- St. Mihiel 12-16 Sep 1918

- Meuse-Argonne 26 Sept-11 Nov 1918

- Vittoria Veneto 24 Oct-4 Nov 1918

### World War II

### American Theater

- Antisubmarine 7 Dec 1941-2 Sep 1945

### Asiatic-Pacific Theater

- Philippine Islands 7 Dec 1941-10 May 1942

- Burma 7 Dec 1941-26 May 1942

- Central Pacific 7 Dec 1941-6 Dec 1943

- East Indies 1 Jan-22 Jul 1942

- India-Burma 2 Apr 1942-28 Jan 1945

- Air Offensive, Japan 17 Apr 1942-2 Sep 1945

- Aleutian Islands 3 Jun 1942-24 Aug 1943

- China Defensive 4 Jul 1942-4 May 1945

- Papua 23 Jul 1942-23 Jan 1943

- Guadalcanal 7 Aug 1942-21 Feb 1943

- New Guinea 24 Jan 1943-31 Dec 1944

- Northern Solomons 22 Feb 1943-21 Nov 1944

- Eastern Mandates 31 Jan-14 Jun 1944

- Bismarck Archipelago 15 Dec 1943-27 Nov 1944

- Western Pacific 15 Jun 1944-2 Sep 1945

- Leyte 17 Oct 1944-1 Jul 1945

- Luzon 15 Dec 1944-4 Jul 1945

- Central Burma 29 Jan-15 Jul 1945

- Southern Philippines 27 Feb-4 Jul 1945

- Ryukyus 26 Mar-2 Jul 1945

- China Offensive 5 May-2 Sep 1945

**European-African-Middle Eastern Theater**

- Egypt-Libya 11 Jun 1942-12 Feb 1943

- Air Offensive, Europe 4 Jul 1942-5 Jun 1944

- Algeria-French Morocco 8-11 Nov 1942

- Tunisia 17 Nov 1942-13 May 1943

- Sicily 9 Jul-17 Aug 1943

- Naples-Foggia Air: 18 Aug 1943-21 Jan 1944; Ground: 9 Sep 1943- 21 Jan 1944

- Anzio 22 Jan-24 May 1944

- Rome-Arno 22 Jan-9 Sep 1944

- Normandy 6 Jun-24 Jul 1944

- Northern France 25 Jul-14 Sep 1944

- Southern France 15 Aug- 14 Sep 1944

- Northern Apennines 10 Sep 1944-4 Apr 1945

- Rhineland 15 Sep 1944-21 Mar 1945

- Ardennes-Alsace 16 Dec 1944-25 Jan 1945

- Central Europe 22 Mar-11 May 1945

- Po Valley 5 Apr-8 May 1945

**Korean War**

- UN Defensive 27 Jun-15 Sep 1950

- UN Offensive 16 Sep-2 Nov 1950

- CCF Intervention 3 Nov 1950-24 Jan 1951

- First UN Counteroffensive 25 Jan-21 Apr 1951

- CCF Spring Offensive 22 Apr-8 Jul 1951

- UN Summer-Fall Offensive 9 Jul-27 Nov 1951

- Second Korean Winter 28 Nov 1951-30 Apr 1952

- Korea, Summer-Fall 1952 1 May-30 Nov 1952

- Third Korean Winter 1 Dec 1952-30 Apr 1953

- Korea, Summer 1953 1 May-27 Jul 1953

**Vietnam**

- Advisory 15 Mar 1962-7 Mar 1965

- Defense 8 Mar-24 Dec 1965

- Counteroffensive 25 Dec 1965-30 Jun 1966

- Counteroffensive, Phase II
  1 Jul 1966-31 May 1967

- Counteroffensive, Phase III
  1 Jun 1967-29 Jan 1968

- Tet Counteroffensive
  30 Jan-1 Apr 1968

- Counteroffensive, Phase IV
  2 Apr-30 Jun 1968

- Counteroffensive, Phase V
  1 Jul-1 Nov 1968

- Counteroffensive, Phase VI
  2 Nov 1968-22 Feb 1969

- Tet 69 Counteroffensive
  23 Feb-8 Jun 1969

- Summer-Fall 1969 9 Jun-
  31 Oct 1969

- Winter-Spring 1970
  1 Nov 1969-30 Apr 1970

- Sanctuary
  Counteroffensive 1 May -
  30 Jun 1970

- Counteroffensive, Phase
  VII 1 Jul 1970-31 Jun
  1971

- Consolidation I 1 Jul-
  30 Nov 1971

- Consolidation II    1
  Dec 1971-29 Mar 1972

- Cease-Fire 30 Mar 1972-
  28 Jan 1973

**Armed Forces Expeditions**

- Dominican Republic 28 Apr
  1965-21 Sep 1966

- Grenada 23 Oct-21 Nov 1983

- Panama 20 Dec 1989- 31 Jan
  1990

**Southwest Asia**

- Defense of Saudi Arabia
  2 Aug 1990-16 Jan 1991

- Liberation and Defense of
  Kuwait 17 Jan-11 Apr 1991

- Cease-Fire 12 Apr 1991-
  30 Nov 1995

**Kosovo**

- Kosovo Air Campaign
  24 Mar - 10 Jun 1999

- Kosovo Defense Campaign
  11 Jun 1999 - (Closing date to
  be determined)

## OFFICER AND NCO PRIVILEGES OF RANK

4-49. As you continue in your Army career, you will find there are privileges that come with rank and responsibility. Some of these privileges are higher pay, different housing or more barracks space, NCO or Officers' clubs, and dedicated vehicles or office space. Remember first that with higher rank comes greater responsibility.

> *Each step up the ladder of leadership brings you a larger share of pay, prestige, and privileges. These are earned rewards for your willingness to accept greater responsibilities. They are not outright gifts. You are expected to pay back every dollar... in work and conscientious concern for your men and your unit, in many jobs well done.*
>
> *The Noncom's Guide,* 1962

4-50. The acceptance of greater responsibility merits greater compensation to be sure. The other privileges are given to help the leader do the job. The battalion command sergeant major, for example, performs duties that are made more efficient and effective by having an office in garrison.

4-51. The most important thing to remember in any discussion about the "privileges of rank" is that with them come profound responsibilities. That responsibility is for the performance of the team and the very lives of the soldiers in it. Leaders willingly accept this responsibility as a privilege in itself.

> *It is said that 'rank has its privileges.' This is as it should be, particularly when we remember that one of the primary privileges of rank is to be entrusted with responsibility.*
>
> MSG Frank K. Nicolas

## LINEAGE AND HONORS

4-52. In combat, individual exploits and personal valor are important, but team effort wins the fight. The Army pays close attention to team performance, to the organizations in which soldiers serve and fight, and to the flags and colors that symbolize those organizations.

4-53. The older an organization, the more soldiers, both active and retired, have had the opportunity of serving in and identifying with it and the more opportunities the organization has had to win battle honors. As the Army got smaller, posts closed and units inactivated, flags and colors moved around to ensure certain units continued. Such actions have occurred throughout the Army's history, but increased after World War II as the Army placed more emphasis on retaining units with the most history and honors.

4-54. For those who say, "What does it matter" there is no response since for those outside the military unit numbers mean little and their history is unimportant—one organization is much the same as any other. But for those soldiers who have served in the "Big Red One," the "Wolfhounds," the "Rainbow Division," or the "Buffalos" (a misspelling that just stuck), unit pride is very much a part of their lives.

4-55. US Army units, like soldiers, have an individual service record. Units display their unit history and battle honors on their colors. These honors are a source of unit pride and whenever soldiers gather to compare the unit decorations on their uniforms there is an inherent competition between them.

4-56. The Army did not originally have a system for tracing unit history and honors. Units simply embroidered on their colors the names of the battles in which they fought, but units often disagreed about what differentiated a "skirmish" from a "battle" or a "campaign." By the 1920s, however, the Army found that it needed to standardize its battle honors and began to perform impartial research on unit histories (often tracing them through a variety of redesignations) and to determine campaign participation credit.

4-57. The Army, despite vigorous reorganization in the 1950s and 1960s, carried on the lineage and honors in units that exist still today. Unit esprit de corps and unit cohesion are essential characteristics of an effective fighting organization. Military history has demonstrated that units with high esprit, a sense of tradition and pride in past achievements, perform well in combat. Soldiers still proudly learn and remember the history, customs, and traditions behind the regiments.

4-58. The customs, courtesies, and traditions of our Army provide a connection with soldiers throughout the history of the Nation. As you continue in your service, remember that these also help in unit and self-discipline, building the team and demonstrating your professionalism.

**Chapter 5**

# Training

Soldiers prepare to fight the Nation's wars through tough, realistic and relevant training. That training pushes soldiers to their limit and beyond while maintaining high standards. This chapter will familiarize you with the system the Army uses to plan for, execute and assess the effectiveness of training and your responsibilities in making it happen. You must understand the importance of being proficient in your individual tasks so that the team can accomplish its collective tasks and mission. Force protection is a part of every operation and you can enhance force protection by knowing the rules of engagement.

For more information on training, see FM 7-0 (25-100), *Training the Force*, FM 7-1 (25-101), *Battle Focused Training*, and AR 350-1, *Army Training and Education.*
For more information on common tasks and skills, see STP 21-1-SMCT, *Soldier's Manual of Common Tasks*, and FM 3-21.75 (21-75), *Combat Skills of the Soldier.*

For more information on physical training, see FM 3-22.20 (21-20), *Physical Fitness Training.*

For more information on safety, see FM 5-19 (100-14), *Risk Management*, AR 385-10, *Army Safety Program*, and DA PAM 385-1, *Small Unit Safety Officer/NCO Guide.*

For more information on force protection and antiterrorism, see FM 3-07.2 (100-35), *Force Protection*, and AR 525-13, *Antiterrorism.*

For more information on guard duty, see FM 3-21.6 (22-6), *Guard Duty.*

# SECTION I: ARMY TRAINING MANAGEMENT

5-1.    Every soldier, NCO, warrant officer, and officer has one primary mission—to be trained and ready to fight and win our Nations wars. Success in battle does not happen by accident; it is a direct result of tough, realistic, and challenging training. We exist as an Army to deter war, or if deterrence fails, to reestablish peace through victory in combat. To accomplish this, our Armed Forces must be able to perform their assigned strategic, operational, and tactical missions. Now for deterrence to be effective, potential enemies must know with certainty that the Army has the credible, demonstrable capability to mobilize, deploy, fight, sustain, and win any conflict.

> *Let every nation know, whether it wishes us well or ill, that we shall pay any price, bear any burden, meet any hardship, support any friend, oppose any foe, to assure the survival and success of liberty.*
>
> John F. Kennedy

5-2.    Training is that process that melds human and materiel resources into these required capabilities. The Army has an obligation to the American people to ensure its soldiers go into battle with the assurance of success and survival. This is an obligation that only rigorous and realistic training, conducted to standard, can fulfill.

5-3.    We train the way we fight because our history shows the direct relation between realistic training and success on the battlefield. Today's leaders must apply the lessons of history in planning training for tomorrow's battles. We can trace the connection between training and success in battle to our Army's earliest experiences during the American Revolution. General George Washington had long sensed the need for uniform training and organization, so he secured the appointment of Baron Von Steuben as Inspector General in charge of training. Von Steuben clearly understood the difference between the American citizen soldier and the European professional. He noted that American soldiers had to be told why they did things before they would do them well, and he applied this same philosophy in his training which helped the continental soldiers understand and endure the rigorous and demanding training he put them through. After Valley Forge, Continentals would fight on equal terms with British regulars. Von Steuben began the tradition of effective unit training that today still develops leaders and forges battle-ready units for the Army.

> *With 2,000 years of examples behind us we have no excuses when fighting, for not fighting well.*
>
> T.E. Lawrence

5-4.    Field Manual 7-0, *Training the Force*, points out that today our Army must meet the challenge of a wider range of threats and a more complex set of operating environments while incorporating new and diverse technologies. The Army meets these challenges through its core competencies: shape the security environment, prompt response, mobilization, forcible entry operations, sustained land dominance, and support civil authorities. Field Manual 7-0 is the Army's capstone training doctrine and is applicable to all units, at all levels, and in all components. While its focus is principally at division and below, FM 7-0 provides the essential fundamentals for all individual, leader and unit training.

5-5.    Training for warfighting is our number one priority in peace and war. Warfighting readiness comes from tactical and technical competence and confidence. Competence relates to the ability to fight our doctrine through tactical and technical execution. Confidence is the individual and collective belief that we can do all things better than the adversary and that our units possess the trust and will to accomplish the mission.

*To lead an untrained people to war is to throw them away.*
Confucius

5-6.    Field Manual 7-0 provides the training and leader development methods that are the basis for developing competent and confident soldiers and the units that will win decisively in any environment. Training is the means to achieve tactical and technical competence for specific tasks, conditions, and standards. Leader Development is the deliberate, continuous, sequential and progressive process, based on values, that develops soldiers and civilians into competent and confident leaders capable of decisive action.

5-7.    Closing the gap between training, leader development, and battlefield performance has always been the critical challenge for any Army. Overcoming this challenge requires achieving the correct balance between training management and training execution. Training management focuses leaders on the science of training in terms of resource efficiencies (People, time, ammo, etc.) measured against tasks and standards. Training execution focuses leaders on the art of leadership to develop trust, will, and teamwork under varying conditions. Leaders integrate this science and art to identify the right tasks, conditions, and standards in training, foster unit will and spirit, and then adapt to the battlefield to win decisively.

## HOW THE SYSTEM OPERATES

5-8.    Soldier and leader training and development continue in all units in the active and reserve components. Using the institutional foundation as the basis, training in organizations and units focuses and hones individual and team skills and knowledge. This requires all soldiers, at some level, to take responsibility for the training and readiness of the unit.

*For they had learned that true safety was to be found in long previous training, and not in eloquent exhortations uttered when they were going into action.*

Thucydides, *History of the Peloponesian Wars*

5-9. Unit training consists of three components: collective training, leader development and individual training. Collective training comes from the unit's mission essential task list (METL) and mission training plans (MTP). Leader development is embedded in collective training tasks and in some separate individual leader focused training. Individual training establishes, improves, and sustains individual soldier proficiency in tasks directly related to the unit's METL. Commanders plan and conduct unit collective training to prepare soldiers and leaders for unit missions.

## COMMANDER'S RESPONSIBILITY

5-10. The commander is responsible for the wartime readiness of the entire unit. The commander is therefore the primary trainer of the organization and is responsible for ensuring that all training is conducted to standard. This is a top priority of the commander, and the command climate must reflect this priority. He analyzes the unit's wartime mission and develops the unit's METL. Then, using appropriate doctrine and the MTP, the commander plans training and briefs the training plan to the next higher commander. The next higher commander provides resources, protects the training from interference, and assesses the training.

5-11. The commander's involvement and presence in planning, preparing, executing and assessing unit training to standards is key to effective unit training. They must ensure MTP standards are met during all training. If a squad, platoon, or company fails to meet the established standard for identified METL tasks, the unit must retrain until the tasks are performed to standard. Sustaining METL proficiency is the critical factor commanders adhere to when training small units.

## NCO RESPONSIBILITY

5-12. A great strength of the US Army is its professional NCO Corps. NCOs take pride in being responsible for the individual training of soldiers, crews, and small teams. They continue the development of new soldiers when they arrive in the unit. NCOs train soldiers to the non-negotiable standards published in MTPs and soldier's training publications (STPs), including the common task manual. NCOs provide commanders with assessments of individual and crew/team proficiency to support the training management process.

5-13. Individual and crew/team training is an integral part of unit training. Taking advantage of every training opportunity is a valuable talent of NCOs. NCOs routinely help integrate individual training with unit training to ensure soldiers can perform their tasks to prescribed standard as a team member. In this way they assist the commander in forging a team capable of performing the unit's METL to the prescribed standard and accomplishing all assigned missions.

## YOUR RESPONSIBILITY

5-14.   You, as an individual soldier, are responsible for performing your individual tasks to the prescribed standard. Training is the cornerstone of success. It is a full time job in peacetime and continues in wartime. In battle, you and your unit will fight as well or as poorly as you and your fellow soldiers trained. Your proficiency will make a difference.

---

### The Best Machinegunner in the 101st

Private "Tex" McMorries was a machine gunner in Company G, 501st Parachute Infantry Regiment, during World War II. During Operation Market Garden, the 501st landed in drop zones near the city of Veghel, Holland. On 24 September 1944 the Germans attacked to recapture the town. Private McMorries and his squad were holding a critical roadblock on the Germans' likeliest avenue of approach to the village.

When German reconnaissance had determined that the roadblock was a weak area in the American line, they attacked. In the initial firefight the Germans poured a tremendous amount of firepower on the American position and six soldiers were wounded. The enemy advanced to within 100 yards of the position when Private McMorries opened fire with his machine gun, halting the German advance. The Germans attacked again several times but the Americans threw them back each time.

Private McMorries never received an award for his action that day. When asked about his feelings on not being recognized with an award, Tex McMorries replied, "I wanted no credit for my little part in 101st history. I am only proud that if you asked a man of Company G, 501st, who was the best machine gunner in the 101st, he will name me. That is my decoration. It can't be worn, only felt. It is the only one I care for now." He fulfilled his obligations to his unit and to his country. His actions as an infantryman characterized the requirements that must be possessed by all soldiers to ensure their effectiveness and ability to fight and win on the battlefield.

---

5-15.   You received a lot of critical skills training in Basic Combat Training (BCT) and Advanced Individual Training (AIT) or in officer basic course. But in your unit you learn more skills and how to function as a member of the team under conditions that approximate battlefield conditions. To maintain proficiency and gain new skills requires continual self-development, which may take the form of training or education.

5-16.   Soldier Training Publications (STPs) contain individual critical tasks, professional development information, and other training information that are important to your success as a soldier. Your MOS-specific STP helps you maintain your task performance proficiency and it aids unit leaders, unit trainers, and commanders to train subordinates to perform their individual critical tasks to the prescribed standard. STPs help standardize individual training for the whole Army.

*Gunners that can't shoot will die.*
**The Battalion Commander's Handbook**

5-17.   Individual tasks are the building blocks to collective tasks. Your first-line supervisor will identify those individual tasks that support your units mission essential task list (METL). If you have questions about which tasks you must perform, ask your first-line supervisor for clarification, assistance and guidance. Your first-line supervisor knows how to perform each task or can direct you to the appropriate soldier training publications, field manuals, technical manuals, and Army regulations. A good habit is to periodically ask your supervisor or fellow soldier to check your task performance to ensure that you can perform each task you are responsible for to the prescribed standard.

*Training then—both good and bad—is habit forming. The difference is that one develops the battlefield habits that win; the other gets you killed.*
**SMA Glen E. Morrell**

## LEADER TRAINING AND DEVELOPMENT

5-18.   Competent and confident leaders are a prerequisite to training ready units. Leader training and leader development are integral parts of unit readiness. Leaders are soldiers first and must be technically and tactically proficient in basic soldier skills. They are also adaptive, capable of sensing their environment, adjusting the plan when appropriate and properly applying the proficiency acquired through training.

5-19.   Leader training is an expansion of these skills that qualifies them to lead other soldiers. As such, the doctrine and principles of training leader tasks is the same as that for any other task. Leader training occurs in the institutional Army, the unit, the combat training centers, and through self-development. Leader training is a part of leader development.

5-20.   Leader development is the deliberate, continuous, sequential and progressive process, grounded in Army values, that grows soldiers into competent and confident leaders capable of decisive action. Leader development comes from the knowledge, skills, and experiences gained through institutional training and education, organizational training, operational experience, and self-development. In always doing your best during training you are developing leader skills and attributes. But this won't be enough to provide the insight, intuition and judgment necessary in combat. Self-study and training is also essential. It begins with a candid assessment of your strengths and weaknesses and then, with your supervisor, develop a program to build on those strengths and minimize those weaknesses. Often this involves reading about leadership, military history, or MOS-related subjects, for example. But it also may include other activities, such as college or correspondence courses.

*The most enduring legacy that we can leave for our future generations of noncommissioned officers will be leader development.*

**SMA Julius W. Gates**

5-21.   Another great resource available to help you in self-development and leaders for training subordinates is US Army Training and Doctrine Command's digital library at http://www.adtdl.army.mil/atdls.htm. The digital library database contains publications and additional information not included in your STP. You can access this information through the internet and through your Army Knowledge Online (AKO) account.

## BATTLE FOCUS TRAINING MANAGEMENT

5-22.   The foundation of the training process is the Army training management cycle. The training management cycle and the necessary guidelines on how to plan, execute, and assess training and leader development is also found in FM 7-0. Understanding how the Army trains the Army to fight is key to successful joint, multinational, interagency, and combined arms operations. Effective training leads to units that execute the Army's core competencies and capabilities.

5-23.   Training management starts with the unit mission. From mission, unit leaders develop the mission essential task list (METL). The METL is an unconstrained statement of the tasks required to accomplish wartime missions. The availability of resources does not affect METL development, but resources for training are constrained and compete with other missions and requirements. Therefore, leaders develop the long-range, short-range, and near-term training plans to effectively utilize available resources to train for proficiency on METL tasks.

5-24.   Planning is an extension of the battle focus concept that links organizational METL with the subsequent preparation, execution, and evaluation of training. The planning process ensures continuous coordination from long range planning, through short-range planning to near-term planning, which ultimately leads to training execution.   The commander's assessment provides direction and focus to the planning process. Through the training planning process, the commander's guidance (training vision, goals, and priorities) is melded together with the METL and the training assessment into manageable training plans.

5-25.   Long-range training plans:
- Are about one year out for AC battalion level organizations.
- Are about three years out for RC battalion level organizations.
- Disseminate METL and battle tasks.
- Establish training objectives for each METL.

- Schedule projected major training events.
- Identify long lead-time resources and allocate major resources such as major training area rotations.
- Identify major training support systems products and services and identify new requirements.

5-26.  Short-range training plans:

- Are about three months for AC battalion level organizations.
- Are about one year out for RC battalion level organizations.
- Refine and expand upon appropriate portions of long-range plan.
- Cross-reference each training event with specific training objectives.
- Identify and allocate short-range lead time resources such as local training facilities.

5-27.  Near-term training plans:

- Refine and expand upon short-range plan through conduct of training meetings.
- Determine best sequence for training.
- Provide specific guidance for trainers.
- Allocate training support systems, products and services, simulators and simulations, and similar resources to specific trainers.
- Publish detailed training schedules.
- Provide basis for executing and evaluating training.

5-28.  Properly developed training plans will—

- Maintain a consistent battle focus.
- Be coordinated with habitually task organized supporting organizations.
- Focus on the correct time horizon.
- Be concerned with future proficiency.
- Incorporate risk management into all training plans.
- Establish organizational stability.
- Make the most efficient use of resources.

5-29.  After training plans are developed, units execute training by preparing, conducting, and recovering from training. The process continues with training evaluations that provide bottom-up input to the organizational assessment. These assessments provide necessary feedback to the senior commander that assist in preparing the training assessment.

## TRAINING AND TIME MANAGEMENT

5-30.  The purpose of time management is to achieve and sustain technical and tactical competence and maintain training proficiency at an acceptable level. Time management systems identify, focus and protect prime time training periods and the resources to support the training. There are three periods in this time management cycle: green, amber and red.

### Green

5-31.   The training focus of units in green periods is multiechelon; collective training that leads to METL proficiency. This period coincides with the availability of major training resources and key training facilities and devices. Organizations in Green periods conduct planned training without distraction and external taskings.

### Amber

5-32.   The focus of units in amber periods is on training proficiency at the platoon, squad and crew level. Individual self-development is maximized through the use of education centers and distributed learning. Organizations in Amber periods are assigned support taskings beyond the capability of those units in the Red period. Commanders must strive for minimal disruption to Amber units' training programs.

### Red

5-33.   The training focus of units in the Red periods is on maximizing self-development opportunities to improve leader and individual task proficiency. Units in the Red periods execute details and other administrative requirements and allow the maximum number of soldiers to take leave. Block leave is a technique that permits an entire unit to take leave for a designated period of time. Commanders maintain unit integrity when executing administrative and support requirements i.e. Squad, Team, Platoon integrity. This exercises the chain of command and provides individual training opportunities for first line leaders.

### TOP-DOWN/BOTTOM-UP APPROACH TO TRAINING

5-34.   The Top-Down/Bottom-Up approach to training is a team effort in which senior leader provide training focus, direction and resources, and junior leaders provide feedback on unit training proficiency, identify specific unit training needs, and execute training to standard in accordance with the approved plan. It is a team effort that maintains training focus, establishes training priorities, and enables effective communication between command echelons.

5-35.   Guidance based on wartime mission and priorities flows from the top-down and results in subordinate units having to identify specific collective and individual tasks that support the higher unit's mission. Input from the bottom up is essential because it identifies training needs to achieve task proficiency on identified collective and individual tasks. Leaders at all levels communicate with each other about requirements and planning, preparing, executing, and evaluating training.

5-36.   Some leaders centralize planning to provide a consistent training focus throughout the organization. However, they decentralize execution to ensure that the conduct of mission-related training sustains strengths and overcomes the weakness unique to each unit. Decentralize execution promotes subordinates leaders' initiative to train their units, but does not mean senior leaders give up their responsibilities to supervise training, develop leaders, and provide feedback.

## BATTLE FOCUS

5-37. Battle focus is a concept used to derive peacetime training requirements from assigned and anticipated missions. The priority of training in units is to train to standard on wartime missions. Battle focus guides the planning, preparation, executing, and assessment of each organization's training programs to ensure its members train as they will fight. Battle focus training is critical throughout the entire training process and is used by commanders to allocate resources for training based on wartime and operational mission requirements.

5-38. Battle focus enables commanders and staffs at all echelons to structure a training program that copes with non-mission related requirements while focusing on mission essential training activities. In garrison, peacetime operations most units cannot attain proficiency to standard on every task whether due to time or other resource constraints. Battle focus helps the commander to design a successful training program by consciously focusing on a reduced number of critical tasks that are essential to mission accomplishment.

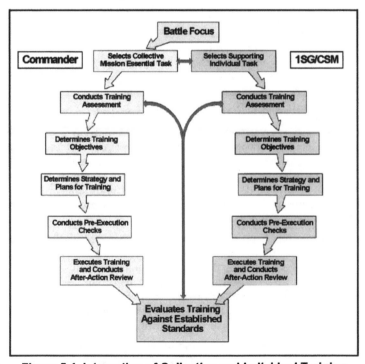

**Figure 5-1. Integration of Collective and Individual Training**

5-39. A critical aspect of the battle-focus concept is to understand the responsibility for and the linkage between the collective mission essential tasks and the individual tasks that support them. The commander and the command sergeant major or the first sergeant (CSM/1SG) must jointly coordinate the collective mission-essential tasks and individual training tasks on which the unit will concentrate its efforts during a given period. The CSM/1SG must select the specific individual tasks that support each collective task to be trained. Although NCOs have a primary role in training and sustaining individual soldier skills, officers at every echelon remain responsible for training to established standards during both individual and collective training. Battle focus is applied to all missions across the full spectrum of operations. Figure 5-1 shows this process.

## TRAINING SCHEDULES

5-40. Near-term planning results in a detailed training schedule. Backward planning is used to ensure that all tasks can be executed in the time available and that tasks depending on other tasks are executed in the correct sequence. Training is considered "Locked In" when the battalion commander signs the training schedule. At a minimum, it should—

- Specify when training starts and where it takes place.
- Allocate adequate time for scheduled training and additional training as required to correct anticipated deficiencies.
- Specify individual, leader, and collective tasks to be trained.
- Provide concurrent training topics that will efficiently use available training time.
- Specify who conducts the training and who evaluates the training.
- Provide administrative information concerning uniform, weapon, equipment, references, and safety precautions.

5-41. Senior commanders establish policies to minimize changes to the training schedule. Training is locked in when training schedules are published. Command responsibility is established to as follows—

- The company commander drafts the training schedule.
- The battalion commander approves and signs the schedule and provides necessary administrative support.
- The brigade commander reviews each training schedule published in his command.
- The division commander reviews selected training schedules in detail and the complete list of organization wide training highlights developed by the division staff.

## CONDUCT OF TRAINING

5-42. Ideally, training is executed using the crawl-walk-run approach. This allows and promotes an objective standard-based approach to training. Training starts at this level. Crawl events are relatively simple to conduct and require minimum support from the unit. But after the crawl stage, training becomes incrementally more difficult, requiring more resources from the unit and home station and increasing the level of realism. At the run stage, the level of difficulty for the training event intensifies. Run stage training requires optimum resources and ideally approaches the level of realism expected in combat. Progression from the walk to the run stage for a particular task may occur during a one-day training exercise or may require a succession of training periods over time. Achievement of the Army standard determines progression between stages.

5-43.　In crawl-walk-run training, the tasks and the standard remain the same; however, the conditions under which they are trained change. For example, commanders may change the conditions by increasing the difficulty of the conditions under which the task is being performed, increasing the tempo of the task training, increasing the number of tasks being trained, or by increasing the number of personnel involved in the training. Whichever approach is used, it is important that all leaders and soldiers involved understand which stage they are currently training and understand the Army standard.

5-44.　An example of the crawl-walk-run approach occurs in the execution of the infantry platoon task "conduct an attack." In the crawl stage, the platoon leader describes the task step-by-step, including what each soldier does. In the walk stage, the platoon conducts a rehearsal of the attack at a step-by-step pace. In the run stage, the platoon executes the task at combat speed under tactical conditions against an opposing force (OPFOR). Ideally this includes multiple iterations under increasingly difficult conditions—at night, for example. Each time they practice the attack, the platoon strives to achieve the tactical objective to the standard described in the training and evaluation outline (T&EO) for "conduct an attack."

## THE AFTER-ACTION REVIEW

5-45.　The After-action Review (AAR) is a structured review process that allows all training participants to discover for themselves what happened, why it happened, and how it can be done better. The unit leader or an observer of the training can lead the discussion, but the key to having an effective AAR is active involvment by all the soldiers who took part in the training. All soldiers have a unique perspective of any given event and should contribute to the AAR.

5-46.　An effective AAR will focus on the training objectives and whether the unit met the appropriate standards (not on who won or lost). The result of an AAR is that soldiers learn lessons from the training. That requires maximum participation of soldiers and leaders (including OPFOR) so those lessons learned can be shared.

*Most coaches study the films when they lose, I study them when we win—to see if I can figure out what I did right.*

**Coach Paul "Bear" Bryant**

5-47. There are four distinct parts of an AAR. First, soldiers who participated in the training review what was supposed to happen. Secondly, you have to establish what, in fact, did happen, including the OPFOR's point of view. Then you determine what was right or wrong with what happened, with respect to applicable standards. Finally—and this is vitally important—you have to determine how the task should be done differently next time.

**Hotwash—An AAR at the Combat Maneuver Training Center Hohenfels, Germany.**

5-48. An AAR should occur immediately after a training event and may result in some additional training. You should expect to retrain on any task that was not conducted to standard. That retraining will probably happen at the earliest opportunity, if not immediately. Training is incomplete until the task is trained to standard. Soldiers will remember the standard enforced, not the one discussed. This same approach is useful in virtual and constructive simulation as a means to train battle staffs and subordinate organizations.

> *AARs are one of the best tools we have... AARs must be a two-way communication between the NCO and the soldiers. They are not lectures.*
>
> **Center for Army Lessons Learned**

## SERGEANT'S TIME TRAINING

5-49. Some training time during the week should be devoted to the small-unit leader (such as a squad leader or a vehicle commander) to train his soldiers. This enhances readiness and cohesion and it also allows the junior NCO to learn and exercise the Army's training-management system at the lowest level. *The key is to train the trainer so that he can train his soldiers.* This requires the NCO to identify essential soldier and small-unit and team tasks (drills) that support unit METL.

5-50. NCOs are the primary trainers of junior enlisted soldiers. Sergeant's Time Training (STT) affords a prime opportunity for developing first line leaders while they gain their soldier's confidence. Active component commanders should institute STT as a regular part of the units training program. This will allow NCOs to train their soldiers on certain tasks in a small group environment.

5-51. Sergeant's Time Training is a hands-on, practical training for soldiers given by their NCOs. It provides the NCO with resources and the authority to bring training publications or technical manuals to life and develops the trust between leader and led to ensure success in combat. In the active component, the chain of command and the NCO support channel implement this training by scheduling five continuous uninterrupted hours each week to STT. STT may be difficult for reserve component (RC) units to accomplish during a typical training assembly or even during annual training, but RC units should plan and conduct STT after mobilization.

5-52. NCOs or first line leaders are the primary trainers during STT and should strive for 100% of their soldiers present for training. Platoon sergeants assist in the preparation and execution of training and officers provide the METL resources (time, personnel and equipment) to conduct training and provide feedback to commanders. Senior NCOs should protect this program against distractions and provide leadership and guidance as necessary to the first-line leaders. NCOs conduct a training assessment and recommend what individual tasks or crew and squad collective training they need to conduct during STT. Topics are based on the small unit leader's assessment of training areas that need special attention. Sergeant's Time Training may be used to train soldiers in a low-density MOS by consolidating soldiers across battalion/brigade and other organizations.

5-53. Many units have their own way of conducting STT but some aspects are universal. For example, STT is standard oriented and not time oriented. In other words, expect to train on a task until soldiers are proficient in that task. In addition, all first-line supervisors maintain a file with the task, conditions, and standards for each task and each soldier's proficiency in those tasks.

5-54. At the end of Sergeant's Time Training, the supervisor will assesses the training conducted and makes recommendations for future training. If the task could not be trained to standard, then the supervisor should reschedule the same task for a future Sergeant's Time.

## TASK, CONDITIONS, AND STANDARDS

5-55.  Task, conditions, and standards are the Army's formula for training tasks to standard. You should learn the specific conditions and standards before training a task so you understand what is expected of you.

- **Task:** A clearly defined and measurable activity accomplished by individuals and organizations. Tasks are specific activities that contribute to the accomplishment of encompassing missions or other requirements.

- **Conditions:** The circumstances and environment in which the task is to be performed.

- **Standard:** The minimum acceptable proficiency required in the performance of the training task under a specific set of conditions.

## SECTION II: INDIVIDUAL SOLDIER TRAINING

5-56.  The competence of the individual soldier is the heart of any unit's ability to conduct its mission. Individual training is the instruction of soldiers to perform their critical individual tasks to the prescribed standard. A soldier must be capable of performing these tasks in order to serve as a viable member of a team and to contribute to the accomplishment of a unit's missions. Maintain proficiency in your individual tasks to build self-confidence and trust among your fellow soldiers.

5-57.  Individual training is initially conducted in the training base in a formal school setting but subsequently may also be provided via distributed learning that a soldier must complete in his unit or at a distance learning site. Initial individual training is often conducted with commercial firms, by specialized Army activities at civilian institutions, and units in the field.

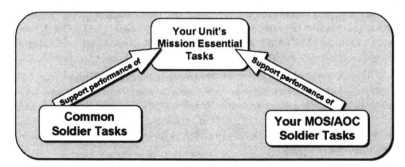

**Figure 5-2. Individual Task to METL Relationship**

5-58.  Individual training is also conducted in the unit on tasks not trained in formal training or to sustain task performance proficiency. Army training is task based. This is how the Army ensures units and soldiers are trained to accomplish unit missions. Army units identify their mission essential tasks, the collective tasks that the unit must be able to perform to accomplish its mission. For your unit to accomplish its mission, every soldier in your unit must first be able to perform his individual tasks that support those mission essential tasks. Figure 5-2 shows this relationship between individual tasks and the METL.

# PHYSICAL FITNESS

5-59. Your physical fitness has a direct impact on combat readiness. A soldier who is physically unfit for duty is as much a casualty as if an enemy bullet had hit him. When that unfitness is a result of the soldier's own carelessness or, worse yet, of his own misconduct, he is guilty of a breach of trust with his comrades, the Army and his fellow Americans. The Army expects you to keep in top physical condition and for that purpose provides you with good food, clothing, sanitary facilities, physical training, and medical care.

5-60. Your unit's physical fitness program is but one component of total fitness. Some of the others are weight control, diet and nutrition, stress management, dental health, and spiritual and ethical fitness, as well as the avoidance of hypertension, substance abuse, and tobacco use.

5-61. Even though soldiers are physically fit some still may become ill. Daily "sick call" is aimed at revealing and halting illness at its beginning. If you feel below par in the morning, Army doctors want to see you immediately. They will diagnose and treat your ailment before it gets worse. This is true regardless of where you are stationed. Army medical experts have made and continue to make surveys of much of the world so that they can diagnose, treat, and control the diseases found there.

## PHYSICAL TRAINING

5-62. An important part of overall fitness is physical training. The objective of physical training in the Army is to improve soldiers' abilities to meet the physical demands of war. Any physical training that results in numerous injuries or accidents works against this goal. Good, sound physical training challenges soldiers but does not place them at undue risk nor lead to situations where accidents or injuries are likely to occur.

5-63. The Army's physical fitness training program includes the USAR and ARNG, encompasses all ages and ranks, and both male and female soldiers. Its purpose is to physically condition all soldiers throughout their careers beginning with basic combat training (BCT). It also includes soldiers with limiting physical profiles who must also participate in physical fitness training.

### Unit Programs

5-64. There are many types of units in the Army, and their missions often require different levels of fitness. TOE and TDA units must emphasize attaining and maintaining the fitness level required for the mission. The unit's standards may exceed the Army's minimums. Army Regulation 350-1 authorizes commanders to set higher standards that are justified by mission requirements.

5-65. The considerations for the active component also apply to the reserve component. However, since members of RC units cannot participate together in collective physical training on a regular basis, RC unit programs must focus on the individual's fitness responsibilities and efforts. But commanders must still ensure that the unit's fitness level and individual PT programs are maintained. Master Fitness Trainers (MFT) can assist RC commanders and soldiers.

5-66. Soldiers everywhere must accept responsibility for their own physical fitness. This is especially true for those assigned to duty positions and organizations that offer little opportunity to participate in collective unit PT programs. Some examples are Headquarters, Department of the Army (HQDA) and Major Army Command (MACOM) staffs, hospitals, service school staff and faculty, and recruiting.

### Special Programs

5-67. The day-to-day unit PT program conducted for most soldiers may not be appropriate for all unit members. Some of them may not be able to exercise at the intensity or duration best suited to their needs. At least three groups of soldiers may need special PT programs. They are as follows:

- Those who fail the APFT and do not have medical profiles.
- Those who are overweight/overfat according to AR 600-9.
- Those who have either permanent or temporary medical profiles.

5-68. Leaders should also give special consideration to soldiers who are age 40 or older and to recent arrivals who cannot meet the standards of their new unit. Special programs must be tailored to each soldier's needs, and trained, knowledgeable leaders should develop and conduct them. This training should be conducted with the unit. If this is impossible, it should at least occur at the same time. There must be a positive approach to all special fitness training.

## FIELDCRAFT

5-69. Much can be done to discipline soldiers in garrison; however, in the field, whether in training, combat or on an operational mission, whether under blue skies, in storms, cold and heat, or marching, all soldiers must endure regardless of the hardships. Fieldcraft are skills, knowledge and adaptability that helps soldiers operate in the field so as to spend less effort fighting the elements and more effort fighting the enemy. Being an expert in fieldcraft reduces the likelihood of you being a casualty due to cold or heat injuries, for example.

5-70. Another challenge for leaders is to develop and implement sleep plans that will recharge soldiers and accomplish the mission. All soldiers, but particularly leaders, are susceptible to sleep deprivation. Many poor decisions have been made by leaders who went without sleep for unnecessarily long periods of time, putting their soldiers and units at additional risk. Leaders must balance sleep and mission requirements to maintain mental alertness and physical readiness.

## INDIVIDUAL COMBAT SKILLS

5-71.    Regardless of where you expect to be on or near the battlefield, every soldier must be proficient in the performance of certain tasks to give him the best possible chance for survival. Listed below are selected combat tasks that are important for every soldier whether in combat arms (CA), combat support (CS), and combat service support (CSS) branches or MOSs. The inclusion or exclusion on this list of any particular individual task does not imply that other common tasks are less important or that any MOS-specific tasks are less important.

**Building an individual fighting position during Operation Iraqi Freedom.**

5-72.    You can find the complete tasks with the performance measures in Appendix A or in STP 21-1-SMCT, *Soldier's Manual of Common Tasks*. Tasks, conditions and standards sometimes change, so periodically check for them in STP 21-1-SMCT and ensure that you can perform the listed tasks to the prescribed standard.

### SHOOT

5-73.    Action: Engage Targets with an M16A1 or M16A2 Rifle. For more information see FM 3-22.9, *M16A1 and M16A2 Rifle Marksmanship*.

- Conditions: Given an M16A1 or M16A2 rifle, magazines, ammunition, individual combat equipment, and stationary or moving targets (personnel or equipment) at engageable ranges.

- Standards: Detected and determined range to targets. Fired the M16A1 or M16A2 rifle, engaged targets in assigned sector of fire. Applied correct marksmanship fundamentals and target engagement techniques so that each target was hit or suppressed. Hit 60 percent or more of the targets in assigned sector of fire.

## MOVE

5-74.   Task : Navigate from One Point on the Ground to Another Point while dismounted (071-329-1006).

- Conditions: Given a standard topographic map of the area, scale 1:50,000, a coordinate scale and protractor, a compass, and writing material.

- Standards: Move on foot to a designated point at a rate of 3,000 meters in an hour.

5-75.   Task: Move Over, Through, or Around Obstacles (Except Minefields) (071-326-0503).

- Conditions: Given individual weapon, load-carrying equipment (LCE), one smoke grenade, wood or grass mats or chicken wire, a grappling hook, wrapping material, wire cutters (optional) and a buddy. During daylight or darkness, you are at a field location, moving over a route with natural and man-made crossings and obstacles (walls and barbed wire entanglements).

- Standards: Approached within 100 meters of a suspected enemy position over a specified route, negotiated each obstacle encountered within the time designated while retaining all of your equipment without becoming a casualty to a bobby trap or early warning device.

## COMMUNICATE

5-76.   Task: Perform Voice Communication (113-571-1022).

- Conditions: Given: 1) One operational radio set for each member, warmed up and set to the net frequency. 2) A call sign information card consisting of: Net member duty position, net call sign, suffix list, and a message to be transmitted. 3) Situation: the net is considered to be secure and authenication is not required.

- Standards: Enter a radio net, send a message, and leave a radio net using the proper call signs, call sign sequence, prowords, and phonetic alphabet and numerals with 100 percent accuracy.

## SURVIVE

5-77.   Task: React to Chemical or Biological Attack/Hazard (031-503-1019).

- Conditions: Given mission-oriented protective posture (MOPP) gear, a protective mask, individual decontaminating kits, and a tactical environment in which chemical and biological (CB) weapons have been or may be used by the enemy. You are in MOPP Level 1, and one or more of the following automatic masking criteria happens:

    a. A chemical alarm sounds.

    b. A positive reading is obtained on detector paper.

    c. Individuals exhibit symptoms of CB agent poisoning.

    d. You observe a contamination marker.

    e. Your supervisor tells you to mask.

    f. You see personnel wearing protective mask.

    g. You observe other signs of a possible CB attack.

- Standards: Do not become a casualty. Identify chemical contamination markers with 100 percent accuracy, and notify your supervisor. Start the steps to decontaminate yourself within 1 minute of finding chemical contamination. Decontaminate your individual equipment after you have completely decontaminated yourself.

5-78.    Task: Decontaminate Yourself and Individual Equipment Using Chemical Decontaminating Kits (031-503-1013).

- Conditions: You are at mission-oriented protection posture (MOPP) 2 with remaining MOPP gear available. You have a full canteen of water, a poncho, load bearing equipment (LBE), assigned decontaminating kit(s), and applicable technical manuals (TMs). Your skin is contaminated or has been exposed to chemical agents, or you have passed through a chemically contaminated area.

- Standards: Start the steps to decontaminate your skin and/or eyes within 1 minute after you find they are contaminated. Decontaminate all exposed skin and your eyes as necessary before chemical agent symptoms occur. Decontaminate all personal equipment for liquid contamination after decontaminating your skin, face and eyes.

5-79.    Task: Evaluate a Casualty (081-831-1000).

- Conditions: You have a casualty who has signs and/or symptoms of an injury.

- Standards: Evaluated the casualty following the correct sequence. All injuries and /or conditions were identified. The casualty was immobilized if a neck or back injury is suspected.

5-80.    Task: Perform First Aid for Nerve Agent Injury (081-831-1044).

- Conditions: You and your unit have come under a chemical attack. You are wearing protective overgarments and/or mask, or they are immediately available. There are casualties with nerve agent injuries. Necessary materials and equipment: chemical protective gloves, overgarments, overboots, protective mask and hood, mask carrier, and nerve agent antidote autoinjectors. The casualty has the following:

- Three antidote treatment, nerve agent, autoinjectors (ATNAA) and one convulsant antidote for nerve agents (CANA) autoinjector.

- OR three sets of MARK I nerve agent antidote autoinjectors.

- Standards: Administered correctly the antidote to self or administered three sets of MARK I nerve agent antidote autoinjectors or three ATNAAs followed by the CANA to a buddy following the correct sequence. Take appropriate action to react to the chemical hazard and treat yourself for nerve agent poisoning following the correct sequence.

5-81.  Task: React to Indirect Fire While Dismounted (071-326-0510).

- Conditions: You are a member (without leadership responsibilities) of a section, squad or team. You are either in a defensive position or moving on foot. You hear incoming rounds, shells exploding or passing overhead, or someone shouting "incoming!"

- Standards: React to each situation by shouting "incoming," following the leaders direction if available and taking or maintaining cover.

5-82.  Task: React to Direct Fire While Mounted (071-410-0002).

- Conditions: In a combat environment, given a tracked/wheeled vehicle and a requirement to react to direct fire.

- Standards: The vehicle has returned fire and taken appropriate action after analysis of the situation based on an order received from the chain of command.

5-83.  Task: Select Temporary Fighting Positions (071-326-0513).

- Conditions: You must select a temporary fighting position, when at an overwatch position, after initial movement into a tentative defensive position, at a halt during movement, or upon receiving direct fire.

- Standards: Select a firing position that protected you from the enemy observation and fire, and allowed you to place effective fire on enemy positions without exposing most of your head and body.

## OPPORTUNITY TRAINING

5-84.  Opportunity training is the conduct of pre-selected, prepared instruction on critical tasks that require little explanation. Sometimes called "hip-pocket" training, it is conducted when proficiency has been reached on the scheduled primary training task and time is available. Unscheduled breaks in exercises or assembly area operations, or while waiting for transportation, provide time for opportunity training.

5-85. Creative, aggressive leaders and soldiers use this time to sustain skills. For example, a Bradley Stinger Fighting Vehicle commander might conduct opportunity training on aircraft identification while waiting to have his crew's multiple integrated laser engagement system (MILES) re-keyed during an (FTX). Good leader books are necessary to select tasks for quality opportunity training.

5-86. Leaders, especially NCOs who are first line supervisors, must be prepared to present these impromptu classes at any opportunity. Any time the squad leader has five minutes, he should also be prepared to instruct squad members on subjects such as safety, personal hygiene, or maintenance of equipment. In addition, most junior enlisted soldiers are very capable of preparing and giving short blocks of instruction on Skill Level 1 individual tasks.

## DRILLS

5-87. Drills provide small units standard procedures for building strong, aggressive units. A unit's ability to accomplish its mission depends on soldiers, leaders, and units executing key actions quickly. All soldiers and their leaders must understand their immediate reaction to enemy contact. They must also understand squad or platoon follow-up actions to maintain momentum and offensive spirit on the battlefield. Drills are actions in situations requiring instantaneous response. Soldiers must execute drills instinctively. This results from continual practice and rehearsals.

5-88. Drills provide standardized actions that link soldier and collective tasks at platoon level and below. At company and above, integration of systems and synchronization demand an analysis of mission, enemy, terrain and weather, troops, time available, civil consideration (METT-TC). Standard tactics, techniques and procedures (TTP) help to speed the decision and action cycle of units above platoon level, but they are not drills. There are two types of drills—battle drills and crew drills.

5-89. A battle drill is a collective action rapidly executed without applying a deliberate decision-making process. The following are characteristics of battle drills:

- They require minimal leader orders to accomplish and are standard throughout the Army.
- They continue sequential actions that are vital to success in combat or critical to preserving life.
- They apply to platoon or smaller units.
- They are trained responses to enemy actions or leader's orders.
- They represent mental steps followed for offensive and defensive actions in training and combat.

5-90. Crew drill is a collective action that the crew of a weapon or system must perform to employ the weapon or equipment. This action is a trained response to a given stimulus, such as a leader order or the status of the weapon or equipment. Like a battle drill, a crew drill requires minimal leader orders to accomplish and is standard throughout the Army.

### ENVIRONMENTAL PROTECTION

5-91. Every soldier must protect the environment from damage when conducting or participating in training. This means you personally must know and take actions necessary to prevent that damage. Task performance information, such as that in the STPs, identify environmental considerations that you must take into account when performing the task. Technical manuals and other how-to books also contain information. You can also ask your leader for information and advice.

5-92. The Army has made great progress in protecting the environment while conducting productive training. It is not just the protection of wildlife or vegetation that is of concern to the Army. Many installations have sites of archaeological significance and others restrict vehicular traffic to prevent excessive soil erosion. The reason for these restrictions is to preserve the environment for future Americans.

## SAFETY

5-93. Every soldier is responsible to ensure realistic training is safe; safety awareness protects combat power. Historically, more casualties occur in combat due to accidents than from enemy action. Ensuring that realistic training is safe instills the awareness that will save lives in combat. Conducting realistic training is challenging business. The goal of the chain of command is *not* training first *nor* safety first, but *training safely.*

> *Units that participate in tough, well-disciplined training, with technically and tactically competent leaders present, have significantly fewer accidents.*
>
> **BG James E. Simmons, Director of Army Safety**

5-94. The commander is the unit safety officer. He is ultimately responsible for unit safety; however; every soldier is responsible for safe training. This includes leaders throughout the chain of command and the NCO support channel, not just range safety officers and NCOs, observer controllers (OCs), and soldiers conducting training. Well-trained junior enlisted soldiers are often the first to observe unsafe actions or conditions.

5-95. Safety does not mean we won't perform tasks or missions that carry some amount of risk. In fact, safe training requires recognition of the risk involved, determining the degree of risk and then applying effort to reduce the risk while accomplishing the mission. This process is risk management, and is a key part of planning all training and operations. The result of this process is that soldiers are aware of potential safety problems in a task or mission but also know that leaders have taken steps to reduce or eliminate the effects of those problems.

## COMBAT STRESS

5-96. The purpose of training is to prepare you and your unit to accomplish missions in combat or other operations. Combat is an environment that will push you to your physical and emotional limits—and beyond. Fear, fatigue, pressure to accomplish the mission and other factors combine to raise stress to seemingly unbearable levels. That stress could cause soldiers to exhibit unusual behavior in combat. Combat stress behavior is the generic term that covers the full range of behaviors in combat, from behaviors that are highly positive to those that are totally negative. Keep in mind that such stress can occur in the combat-like conditions of operations other than war, also. There is nothing wrong in experiencing combat stress or exhibiting the resulting reactions, as long it does not include misconduct.

5-97. Positive combat stress behaviors include heightened alertness, strength, endurance, and tolerance to discomfort. Examples of positive combat stress behaviors include the strong personal bonding between combat soldiers and the pride and self-identification that they develop with the unit's history and mission. These provide unit cohesion, the binding force that keeps soldiers together and performing the mission in spite of danger and death. The ultimate positive combat stress behaviors are acts of extreme courage and action involving almost unbelievable strength. They may even involve deliberate self-sacrifice.

5-98. The citations for recipients of the Medal of Honor or other awards for valor in battle describe almost unbelievable feats of courage, strength, and endurance. The recipient overcame the paralysis of fear, and in some cases, also called forth muscle strength far beyond what he had ever used before. He may have persevered in spite of wounds that would normally be so painful as to be disabling. Some of these heroes willingly sacrificed their lives for the sake of their buddies.

5-99. Positive combat stress behaviors and misconduct stress behaviors are to some extent a double-edged sword. The same physiological and psychological processes that result in heroic bravery in one situation can produce criminal acts such as atrocities against enemy prisoners or civilians in another. Stress may drag the sword down in the direction of the misconduct edge, while sound, moral leadership and military training and discipline must direct it upward toward the positive behaviors.

5-100. Examples of misconduct stress behaviors range from minor breaches of unit orders or regulations to serious violations of the Uniform Code of Military Justice (UCMJ). Misconduct stress behaviors are most likely to occur in poorly trained and undisciplined soldiers. But these behaviors can possibly occur in good, even heroic soldiers under extreme combat stress. Misconduct stress behavior can be prevented by stress control measures, but once serious misconduct has occurred, it must be punished to prevent further erosion of discipline. Combat stress, even with heroic combat performance, cannot justify criminal misconduct.

## COMBAT STRESS REACTION

5-101. Combat stress reaction is common, predictable, negative, emotional and physical reaction of normal soldiers to the abnormal stressors of combat. By definition, any such reactions interfere with mission performance or well being but can be treated. These reactions do not include misconduct stress behaviors. They range from fear, anxiety and depression in minor cases to memory loss, physical impairment and even hallucinations in the more severe cases. On the lower end of the scale the behaviors are normal and common signs. As behaviors become progressively more severe in their effects they are warning signs of serious problems. Warning signs deserve immediate attention by the leader, medic, or buddy to prevent potential harm to the soldier, others, or the mission.

5-102. Warning signs do not necessarily mean the soldier must be relieved of duty or evacuated if they respond quickly to helping actions. However, soldiers may need evaluation at medical treatment facilities to rule out other physical or mental illness. If combat stress reaction persists and makes the soldier unable to perform duties reliably, then further treatment such as by specialized combat stress control teams, may be necessary. But prompt treatment close to the soldier's unit provides the best potential for returning the soldier to duty.

*Just because you're trained for something doesn't mean you're prepared for it.*

**Anonymous**

5-103. No training will completely prepare you for combat, but with proper training, discipline and unit cohesion you will be able to do your job and function as a member of the team. Stress in combat is unavoidable, but you can minimize combat stress reaction by continuing to do your job and talking to your fellow soldiers and leaders. Remember that your buddies are under the same stress. They experience many of the same feelings as you do so just talking about it can help them, too. Previous combat experience does not immunize a soldier from the effects of combat stress, either. For more information about the causes, effects, and treatment of combat stress, see FM 6-22.5, *Combat Stress.*

## SECTION III: FORCE PROTECTION

5-104. The operational environment demands that all soldiers are proficient in certain combat tasks. This environment does not have rear areas that are free of enemy interference. We must expect and plan for a potential adversary to oppose Army operations from deployment to the conclusion of the fight, and beyond. For this reason it is vitally important soldiers take positive steps in force protection to minimize vulnerability to terrorist acts.

5-105. Force protection is action taken to prevent or mitigate hostile actions against Department of Defense (DOD) personnel (to include family members), resources, facilities, and critical information. These actions conserve the force's fighting potential so it can be applied at the decisive time and place, and incorporates the coordinated and synchronized offensive and defensive measures to enable the effective employment of the joint force while degrading opportunities for the enemy.

**A Military Police soldier inspects a vehicle entering an Army installation.**

5-106. Force protection is a security program to protect soldiers, civilian employees, family members, information, equipment, and facilities in all location and situations. This is accomplished through a combination of antiterrorism, physical security, and information operations; high-risk personnel security; and law enforcement operations, all supported by foreign intelligence, counter intelligence, and other security programs.

5-107. Force Protection does not include actions to defeat the enemy or protect against accidents, weather, or disease. The goal is to protect soldiers, DA civilians, their family members, facilities, information, and other material resources from terrorism. The objectives of force protection are to deter incidents, employ countermeasures, mitigate effects, and to recover from an incident.

5-108. The scope of force protection includes pre-incident, incident, and post-incident task and activities. The achievement of a comprehensive program requires that the full cycle of planning, preparation, execution, and continuous assessment be accomplished before, during, and after the threat event. A complete force protection operation crosses the entire spectrum from pre-incident to post-incident. Force protection is everyone's business. Be vigilant!

5-109. Standard descriptions of force protection requirements and states of readiness are called force protection conditions. There are five force protection condition levels: Normal and ALPHA through DELTA. Each has specified force protection tasks or security measures listed in AR 525-13, *Antiterrorism*. Army installations supplement these with specific actions for that installation. Force protection conditions are usually set by Army major commands but may be altered by installation or local commanders, based on local conditions, with higher approval.

5-110. How units conduct force protection may be different in a combat environment only in the specific tasks performed. Regardless of location or activity, the operational environment requires force protection awareness throughout the Army. It doesn't matter whether you are moving, resting or actually fighting. Be alert for indications of terrorist activity or surveillance and anything that seems out of place.

## TERRORISM

5-111. Terrorism is the calculated use of unlawful violence or threat of unlawful violence to instill fear; intended to coerce or to intimidate governments or societies in the pursuit of goals that are generally political, religious, or ideological. Terrorism has four key elements:

- It is premeditated—planned in advance rather than an impulsive act.
- It is political—designed to change the existing political order.
- It is usually aimed at civilians—not at combat-ready troops.
- It is carried out by subnational groups—not by the army of a country.

5-112. Every soldier has some role in fighting terrorism. Usually these are actions in an installation or unit antiterrorism (AT) plan. As a minimum, you should know what the likely terrorist threat is for your area. You should know who to call if you see or hear something that "isn't quite right." What would that be? Something that appears out of place: for example, a van parked across the street from an entry control point that reappears at the same time for several days. Reporting such unusual activity may seem an overreaction but is prudent. If it is an innocent citizen who just happened to be there by coincidence, no harm done. But if it was something more, then you may have saved lives. Remember when reporting, just like in giving a spot report by the SALUTE or SALT format, be accurate and as detailed as possible without adding any speculation.

## Khobar

6th Battalion, 52d ADA deployed in early 1996 to Southwest Asia (SWA) on a scheduled theater missile defense rotation. The unit was trained and evaluated in all facets of its mission and well prepared for it, but no more so than any other unit. Weeks passed, force protection condition (FPCON) levels fluctuated, and soldiers were tested time and time again. Staying focused was the watchword. Everything was clicking, and the unit was like a boxer getting instructions from the referee. The referee tells you to break from the tie-up but protect yourself at all times. Boxers have gotten knocked out on the break.

By the early summer of 1996, the battalion's rotation was coming to a close. Months of ups and downs in FPCON levels didn't break this disciplined, confident unit's morale. But at 2230 on the night of 25 June 1996, an explosion sent everyone in the Khobar Towers complex scrambling. Some scrambled for their lives and others to tend the numerous wounded. A large bomb had detonated just outside of the cantonment area, destroying and damaging buildings and sending window glass throughout the compound. Nineteen US Air Force airmen died and hundreds were injured.

But the combat lifesavers and medics of Headquarters and Headquarters Battery, 6-52 ADA quickly transitioned to their wartime mission. That mission was to help save lives by "evaluating casualties" and treating and caring for the wounded. But "treat mass casualties," a task performed so well by the unit on its external evaluation, was no longer a training task. It was real. Competence and confidence showed on the stern faces of the soldiers as they and others carefully looked through the debris for survivors to evaluate, treat, and evacuate from the horrible scene. A long day consequently turned into a very long night. Soldiers and airmen worked together as if they had been training for years and everyone did more than his or her part. Guard shifts doubled and sometimes tripled to ensure security was complete.

Later, SGT David Skinner, a combat medic for the battalion, was asked if he was afraid of the possibility of another bomb going off. "You didn't have time to think about another bomb. We get paid to save lives and that's what we tried to do." He praised the courage and dedication of the combat lifesavers that stood side by side with the medics. For the actions of the soldiers that night and through the next early morning hours, 6-52 ADA received the Army Superior Unit Award.

5-113. Level I antiterrorism training is required for all soldiers and DA civilians. Army Regulation 525-13 and Department of Defense Instruction 2000.16, *DOD Antiterrorism Standards* require this annual training. You can accomplish this training online using the DOD Antiterrorism Training System at http://at-awareness.org. Soldiers and DACs traveling outside the 50 United States, its territories and possessions for any reason must have an AOR update within two months of travel. Military and DAC family members must receive antiterrorism awareness training within 12 months of travel, on official orders, outside the US, its territories and possessions.

5-114. The purpose of the annual antiterrorism training is to increase your awareness of terrorism and to improve your ability to apply personal protective measures. The training includes the following subjects:

- Terrorist operations.
- Individual protective measures.
- Terrorist surveillance techniques.
- Improvised explosive device (IED) attacks.
- Kidnapping and hostage survival.
- Explanation of terrorism threat levels and Force Protection Condition (FPCON) system.

5-115. You may also receive antiterrorism training from a certified Level II antiterrorism instructor. The Army's goal is that all personnel are aware of the terrorist threat and adequately trained in the application of protective measures. Antiterrorism training should also be integrated into unit collective training at every opportunity.

5-116. You, your family, or your neighborhood may be terrorist targets; therefore, be prepared to alter your routine to disrupt surveillance. You should know where to go if communications are disrupted. Your installation and unit should have a force protection and antiterrorism plan. In these plans are instructions for implementing higher levels of security and what individual soldiers should be aware of. These plans also inform soldiers and DACs of where to go in the event of an attack or emergency and provide guidance on protecting family members and visitors on the installation. Critical tasks of installation plans include the following:

- Collect, analyze, and disseminate threat information.
- Increase antiterrorism in every soldier, civilian, and family member.
- Maintain installation defenses in accordance with force protection conditions (FPCON).
- Conduct exercises and evaluate/assess antiterrorism plans.

### RULES OF ENGAGEMENT AND RULES FOR THE USE OF FORCE

5-117. Rules of engagements (ROE), rules for the use of force (RUF) and the general orders help soldiers know how to react in difficult situations before they arise. The ROE are directives that describe the circumstances and limitations for military forces to start or continue combat engagement with other forces.

5-118. The ROE are normally part of every operations plan (OPLAN) and operations order (OPORD). The ROE help you in obeying the law of war and help prevent escalating a conflict. Know the ROE and actively determine if any changes to the ROE have occurred. The ROE will be different with each operation, in different areas, and will change as the situation changes. In no case, however, will the ROE limit your inherent right to self defense.

5-119. A thorough understanding of the specific ROE gives soldiers confidence that they can and will react properly in the event of an attack or encounter with local personnel. Confident soldiers do not hesitate to properly defend themselves and their fellow soldiers. Likewise, confident, disciplined soldiers will not take action that violates the ROE. In both cases, confident soldiers protect lives and demonstrate professionalism, both of which have positive effects on the local population and for the overall Army mission.

---

### Rules of Engagement

Company D, 1st Battalion, 41st Infantry, was assigned to Task Force Eagle as part of Operation Joint Endeavor. Power struggles taking place in Republika Srpsk sparked violent clashes in northeastern Bosnia-Herzegovina. One such clash involved D Company.

On 5 September 1997, about 110 angry Serbs boxed in 60 soldiers from D Company, guarding a checkpoint in Celopek, north of Zvornick. Twenty-five of the US soldiers faced 70 Serbs to the south of the checkpoint, while another 25 faced 40 Serbs to the north. The angry Serbs, throwing rocks, bottles, and light fixtures, punched at least three of D Company's soldiers and attempted to drive vehicles through the roadblock. At one point, as an automobile attempted to break through, the crowd surged forward. The soldiers, well disciplined through rigorous training and armed with a thorough understanding of the ROE, held their ground and focused on the mission. The crowd finally backed off after an hour and a half when the commander ordered his troops to load their weapons and the Serb police arrived to assist.

The soldiers of D Company accomplished their mission while displaying enormous restraint—the result of the discipline that had been strengthened in their training. But for that discipline and confidence, the incident might well have resulted in disaster, not only for the soldiers, but also for the diplomatic mission they were assigned to enforce. They were confident in the training they had conducted prior to and during deployment and in their leadership. Their discipline in adhering to the ROE allowed them to diffuse the situation using appropriate force and resulted in the protection of the unit, the soldiers, and the civilians.

---

5-120. A useful acronym for remembering some of the basics of the ROE is RAMP.

- R—Return Fire with Aimed Fire. Return force with force. You always have the right to repel hostile acts with necessary force.

- A—Anticipate Attack. Use force if, but only if, you see clear indicators of hostile intent.

- M—Measure the amount of Force that you use, if time and circumstances permit. Use only the amount of force necessary to protect lives and accomplish the mission.

- P—Protect with deadly force only human life, and property designated by your commander. Stop short of deadly force when protecting other property.

5-121. Rules on the use of force are escalating rules for US military personnel performing security duties within the United States. Like the ROE, RUF may vary depending on the operation and location, so be sure to understand the RUF. These rules primarily limit the use of deadly force to specifically defined situations. You have the inherent right of self-defense and the defense of others against deadly force. But use only the minimum force necessary to remove the threat. Deadly force is only used as the last resort, typically as follows:

- For immediate threat of death or serious bodily injury to self or others.

- For defense of persons under protection.

- To prevent theft, damage, or destruction of firearms, ammunition, explosives, or property designated vital to national security.

5-122. When the situation permits, security personnel utilize escalating degrees of force. The degrees are defined as follows:

- SHOUT—verbal warning to halt.

- SHOVE—nonlethal physical force.

- SHOW—intent to use weapon.

- SHOOT—deliberately aimed shots until threat no longer exists.

- Warning shots are not permitted.

5-123. Your training should include ROE or RUF. This should include classroom type instruction that states what the rules are but also should be a part of field training. For example, a field exercise could include situations training soldiers on what to do if a large group of local civilians appear outside the unit perimeter. In this way, soldiers can gain experience in handling potentially hostile crowds while complying with the ROE.

### Guard Duty

5-124. We can't leave the subject of ROE and RUF without a word on guard duty. Guard duty is important. It is a mission common to tactical and garrison operations and key to physical and operational security. It is also important in antiterrorism. A sentinel at a guard post is protecting his fellow soldiers and may be the first line of defense against enemy soldiers, thieves, spies, or even terrorists. It is for these reasons you should take guard duty seriously and approach it with the same professionalism that you do all your other duties. The General Orders are:

- General Order Number 1: I will guard everything within the limits of my post and quit my post only when properly relieved.

- General Order Number 2: I will obey my special orders and perform all my duties in a military manner.

- General Order Number 3: I will report all violations of my special orders, emergencies, and anything not covered in my instructions to the commander of relief.

## THE MEDIA

5-125. While not directly a part of force protection, interaction with the media has an impact because potential adversaries can get useful information about you, your unit, your mission, or even your family through news reports. Commanders will implement operational and information security programs to defeat terrorists' efforts to gain information, but in nearly every case, such programs involve knowledgeable and positive action on the part of individual soldiers.

5-126. The media, that is, the civilian news gathering organizations of the world, have a job to do—report what they see to the world. There are times when the media will be interested in your unit or your family members. Deployments and reunions are always newsworthy events that will attract press attention, and so will gate closures or reports of casualties. But every operation and every installation has specific guidance for speaking with the media. That guidance will tell you what are appropriate or inappropriate subjects to comment on and is intended to help you maintain operational security. In any case, you should have your commander's authorization to speak with a member of the media before doing so, particularly when the topic relates to the Army or the Department of Defense.

5-127. The military as an institution and the media have had their ups and downs, but the rapport between individual soldiers and members of the media has almost always been excellent and you should do your best to keep that up. America benefits from a well-informed public. While you do not have to speak if you do not feel comfortable, if you do communicate with someone from the media, keep the following general rules in mind:

- Do know the local public affairs guidance regarding media relations.
- Do give honest and forthright answers in matters of which you have direct knowledge.
- Do remember there is no such thing as "off the record"! Everything is on the record.
- Do use a media opportunity to tell your story as an unofficial ambassador for our nation and our Army.
- Don't guess or make something up to answer a question. If you don't know the answer, say so.
- Don't volunteer information that was not asked for.
- Don't answer a question that is inappropriate. Refer the reporter to the local Army public affairs officer.
- Don't discuss politics or foreign policy and avoid labeling events or actions. For example, only the Federal Bureau of Investigation and the Department of Justice may call a crime a "terrorist" incident. Until then, it is just an incident.

**Chapter 6**

# Developmental Counseling and Professional Development

You may or may not intend to make the Army a career, but it is important to the future of the Army that you develop and prepare to assume positions of greater responsibility. The demands of combat may put even junior enlisted soldiers into leadership positions in stressful situations. This is why the Army puts so much effort into developing soldiers and training them to lead. This chapter will provide you with a basic understanding of the importance of developmental counseling and its relation to professional development. The Army has well-developed professional development and education systems that will help you learn—but you will have to do the work and provide the motivation.

For more information on developmental counseling see FM 6-22 (22-100), *Army Leadership*, Appendix B and C and the Army counseling website at www.counseling.army.mil.

For more information on professional development see AR 350-17, Noncommissioned Officer Development Program, DA PAM 350-58, Leader Development for America's Army, and DA PAM 600-3, Commissioned Officer Development and Career Management, DA PAM 600-11, Warrant Officer Professional Development or DA PAM 600-25, US Army Noncommissioned Officer Professional Development Guide.

For more information on retention and reenlistment see AR 140-111, *US Army Reserve Reenlistment Program*, and AR 601-280, *Army Retention Program*.

## SECTION I - DEVELOPMENTAL COUNSELING

6-1. Development counseling is a type of communication that leaders use to empower and enable soldiers. It is much more than providing feedback or direction. It is communication to help develop a soldier's ability to achieve individual and unit goals. Leaders counsel soldiers to help them be successful. Effective developmental counseling is one of the ways you will learn and grow. Leaders owe their soldiers the best possible road map to success. Leaders help their soldiers solve complex problems by guiding them to workable solutions through effective counseling.

6-2. Developmental counseling is subordinate-centered communication that outlines actions necessary for soldiers to achieve individual and organizational goals and objectives. It is vital to the Army's future that all leaders conduct professional growth counseling with their soldiers to develop the leaders of tomorrow.

6-3. Subordinate-centered, two way communication is simply a style of communication where you as a subordinate are not a passive listener, but a vital contributor in the communication process. The purpose of subordinate-centered communication is to allow the subordinate to maintain control and responsibility for the issue. This type of communication where you as a subordinate take an active role takes longer. Subordinate participation is absolutely necessary when leaders are attempting to develop and not simply impart direction or advice.

## COUNSELING IS AN OBLIGATION

6-4. NCOs counsel their subordinate NCOs and junior enlisted soldiers, and officers will counsel subordinate leaders. For example, the company commander counsels the first sergeant. There may be situations where officers counsel junior enlisted soldiers. The point is this: every leader has an obligation to develop their subordinates through developmental counseling. The Army values play a very important role. Simply put the values of *loyalty, duty* and *selfless service* require leaders to counsel their soldiers. The values of *honor, integrity* and *personal courage* require both leaders and soldiers to give straightforward feedback and, if possible, goal-oriented tasks or solutions. The Army value of *respect* requires us all to find the best way to communicate that feedback and goals.

6-5. Some skills leaders use in effective counseling are the following:

- Active listening: Giving full attention to subordinates; listening to their words and the way they are spoken. Transmit and understanding of message through responding.

- Responding: Use appropriate eye contact and gestures. Check understandings, summarize, interpret and question.

- Questioning: Serves as a way to obtain valuable information and get subordinates to think. Most questions should be open-ended.

6-6.    Some soldiers may perceive counseling as an adverse action, perhaps because that is their experience. Developmental counseling most definitely is not supposed to be an adverse action. Regular developmental counseling is the Army's most important tool for developing future leaders at every level. Regular effective developmental counseling helps all soldiers become better members of the team, maintain or improve performance, and prepare them for the future. Regular counseling helps leaders and soldiers communicate more clearly and efficiently. Therefore soldiers should want to be counseled. Effective counseling must include some of the following elements:

- Purpose: Clearly define the purpose of the counseling.
- Flexibility: Fit the counseling style to the character of each soldier and to the relationship desired.
- Respect: View soldiers as unique, complex individuals, each with their own sets of values, beliefs, and attitudes.
- Communication: Establish open, two-way communication with the soldier using spoken language, non-verbal actions, and gestures and body language. Effective counselors listen more than they speak.
- Support: Encourage soldiers through actions while guiding them through their problems.

6-7.    Leaders conduct counseling to assist soldiers in achieving and developing personal, professional development and organizational goals, and to prepare them for increased responsibility. Leaders are responsible for developing soldiers through teaching, coaching, and counseling. This is done effectively by identifying weaknesses, setting goals, developing and implementing a plan of action, and providing oversight and motivation throughout the process. Leaders are responsible for everything their units do or fail to do; your leader is responsible for all your military actions. Inherent in that responsibility is the duty to help you develop, and, one day, make you ready to lead.

## EFFECTIVE COUNSELING PROGRAM

6-8.    It is in the unit's best interest to establish an effective counseling program. Four essential elements of an effective counseling program are education and training; experience; continued support; and enforcement.

6-9.    Education and training occurs in the institution (for example, Primary Leadership Development Course or Captain's Career Course) and unit (NCO Development Program and correspondence courses), and through mentorship and self-development. The Army provides a base line of education to its soldiers in order to "show what right looks like." The Noncommissioned Officer Education System (NCOES) is an example and educates the NCO Corps on counseling. However, NCOES cannot accomplish this alone. Unit NCO development programs conduct training to provide that base of education of what right looks like to all leaders.

6-10. Soldiers learn by doing and receive guidance from more senior leaders. After initial education and training, all leaders must put their skills to use. NCOs must practice counseling while at the same time receiving guidance and mentoring on how to improve counseling techniques.

6-11. Continued support from both the Army and leaders is available from the Army's counseling website (www.counseling.army.mil), FM 6-22 (22-100), Appendix B and C, and unit leaders (through spot checks and random monitoring of counseling sessions). These provide necessary support and critiques that will improve a young leader's counseling skills.

6-12. Enforcement is a key component of an effective developmental counseling program. Once leaders have the tools (both education and support) necessary for quality counseling, senior leaders must hold them accountable to ensure acceptable counseling standards for both frequency and content. This is often accomplished through some type of compliance inspections.

## THE DEVELOPMENTAL COUNSELING PROCESS

6-13. The Developmental Counseling process consists of four stages:
- Identify the need for counseling
- Prepare for counseling
  - Schedule the time.
  - Notify the counselee well in advance.
  - Organize information.
  - Outline the components of the counseling session.
  - Plan counseling strategy.
  - Establish the right atmosphere.
- Conduct the counseling session:
  - Open the session.
  - Discuss the issue.
  - Develop a plan of action (to include the leader's responsibilities).
  - Record and Close the Session.
- Follow-up.
  - Support Plan of Action Implementation.
  - Assess Plan of Action.

## TYPES OF DEVELOPMENTAL COUNSELING

6-14. Counseling serves many purposes. Each type of counseling has a unique goal or desired outcome and sometimes uses a different method. In some cases a specific event may trigger a need for developmental counseling. In all cases, the goal is to improve the team's performance by helping the counseled soldier become a more effective member of the team. As a counselee you should expect to be actively involved in the developmental counseling process. The leader is assisting you in identifying your strengths and weaknesses.

## EVENT-ORIENTED COUNSELING

6-15. Event-oriented counseling involves a specific event or situation. It may precede events, such as going to a promotion board or attending a school, or it may follow events, such as a noteworthy duty performance, a problem with performance of mission accomplishment, or a personal problem.

### Counseling for Specific Instances

6-16. Sometimes counseling is tied to specific instances of superior or substandard duty performance. For example, if you performed exceptionally well during an inspection, your squad leader might review your preparation for and conduct during the inspection. The key to successful counseling for specific performance is to conduct the counseling session as close to the time of the event as possible. It doesn't necessarily occur next to a desk with a counseling form in hand. It can occur in an informal setting. But it is important to have a record of some kind for reference later in a regular performance counseling.

---

### Informal "Footlocker" Counseling

Bravo Company had gotten back from the field on Wednesday, and by Thursday PFC Newman already had his HMMWV standing tall. SSG Ulbrich, his squad leader, was impressed that he had squared his vehicle away so quickly. She called him over to his vehicle and in a few minutes they reviewed together the work he had accomplished to conduct PMCS and get it ready to go again.

While she knew PFC Newman had worked through lunch, she also learned he had helped another soldier clean his personal gear in the barracks after duty hours.

"Keep this up, Newman," she said, "You are a great example to the other soldiers and are developing into a fine leader, too."

At the end of the day, the platoon leader called PFC Newman out in front of the formation and gave him a "pat on the back" in front of his fellow soldiers.

---

### Reception and Integration Counseling

6-17. Leaders must counsel new team members when they report in. Reception and integration counseling serves two purposes: first, it identifies and helps fix any problems or concerns that new members have, especially any issues resulting from the new duty assignment; second, it lets you know the unit standards and how you fit into the team. Reception and integration counseling starts the team building process. It clarifies your responsibilities and sends the message that the chain of command cares. Reception and integration counseling should begin immediately upon arrival so you can quickly become integrated into the organization.

### Promotion Counseling

6-18. Commanders or their designated representatives must conduct promotion counseling for all specialists, corporals, and sergeants who are eligible for advancement without waiver, but are not recommended for promotion to the next higher grade. Army Regulation 600-8-19, *Enlisted Promotions and Reductions*, requires that AC soldiers within this category receive initial (event-oriented) counseling when they attain full eligibility and then periodic (performance and personal growth) counseling at least quarterly.

---

### Promotion Counseling

SSG Dills counseled SPC Snyder on his eligibility for promotion and sadi he would recommend him for the next promotion board. After completion of the promotion point worksheet (DA Form 3355), SPC Snyder found out that he had only 200 points—just enough to appear before the board. The minimum requirement to be placed on the SGT promotion list is 350 points. SPC Snyder would need to get a maximum score on the board to obtain the additional 150 points required for promotion to SGT. SPC Snyder was confident that he would pass the board and assured SSG Dills, "This will be easy, I won't have a problem, Sergeant."

SPC Snyder got his chance and appeared before the sergeant promotion board. He received 149 points from the board members. Although SSG Dills recommended SPC Snyder for promotion he would have to counsel him again because he did not have enough points to be added to the list.

During the next promotion counseling session, SSG Dills had appropriate tools and paperwork available (AR 600-8-19, DA Form 3355-Promotion Point Worksheet, and DA Form 4856-E—Counseling Form) and a proposed plan of action that they talked over. SPC Snyder helped develop the plan of action for ensuring he had enough points for promotion next time.

---

### Crisis Counseling

6-19. You may receive counseling to help you get through the initial shock after receiving negative news, such as notification of the death of a loved one. Your leader will help you by listening and providing assistance as appropriate. That assistance may include help from a support activity or coordinating external agency support. Crisis counseling focuses on your immediate, short-term needs.

### Referral Counseling

6-20. Referral counseling helps soldiers work through a personal situation and may follow crisis counseling. Referral counseling also acts as preventative counseling before a situation becomes a problem. Usually, the leader assists the soldier in identifying the problem.

6-21. Outside agencies can help your leaders help you resolve problems. Although it is generally in your best interest to seek help first from your immediate supervisor, leaders will always respect your right to contact these agencies on your own. But leaders, through experience, have developed a feel for what agency can help in a given situation and can refer you to the appropriate resource, such as Army community services, a chaplain, or a substance abuse counselor. You can find more information on support activities in Appendix B, Army Programs or in FM 6-22 (22-100), Appendix C.

### Adverse Separation Counseling

6-22. Adverse separation counseling may involve informing a soldier of the administrative actions available to the commander in the event substandard performance continues and of the consequences associated with those administrative actions. Developmental counseling may not apply when a soldier has engaged in more serious acts of misconduct. In those situations, the leader should refer the matter to the commander or the servicing staff judge advocate's office.

## PERFORMANCE AND PROFESSIONAL GROWTH COUNSELING

### Performance Counseling

6-23. During performance counseling, you review your duty performance with your supervisor. You and your leader jointly establish performance objectives and standards for the next period. Rather than dwelling on the past, you both should focus the session on the strengths, areas needing improvement, and potential. Performance counseling communicates standards and is an opportunity for leaders to establish and clarify the expected values, attributes, skills, and actions. Performance counseling is required for noncommissioned officers; mandatory, face-to-face performance counseling between the rater and the rated NCO is required under the NCOER system. It is a generally accepted standard that all soldiers receive performance counseling at least monthly.

### Professional Growth Counseling

6-24. Professional growth counseling includes planning for the accomplishment of the individual and professional goals. You conduct this counseling to assist subordinates in achieving organizational and individual goals. Professional growth counseling begins with an initial counseling within the first 30 days of arrival. Additional counseling occurs quarterly thereafter with a periodic assessment (perhaps at a minimum of once a month). Counseling then is a continuous process.

6-25. During the counseling you and your leader will identify and discuss together your strengths/weaknesses and then create a plan of action to build upon your strengths and overcome weaknesses. The leader will help you help yourself and focus more towards the future. This future-oriented approach establishes short and long-term goals and objectives. FM 6-22 (22-100), Appendix B, provides the necessary tools to do a self-assessment to help you identify your weaknesses and strengths and provide a means of improving your abilities and skills.

## SECTION II – PROFESSIONAL DEVELOPMENT

6-26. Leader development in the Army occurs in three pillars: institutional training, operational assignments, and self development. The Army's education systems—institutional development—are key to leader development. These systems provides leader and skill training in an integrated system of resident training at multiple levels. In both the officer and NCO systems, this is a continuous cycle of education, training, experience, assessment, feedback, and reinforcement.

*Everybody's got to know how to be a leader.*

**GEN Peter J. Schoomaker**

6-27. The needs of the unit and the demonstrated potential of the leader are always kept in focus and balance at all times. The emphasis is on developing competent and confident leaders who understand and are able to exploit the full potential of current and future Army doctrine. Self-development ties together a soldiers' experience and training to make them better leaders, which ultimately benefit their units' combat readiness.

## INSTITUTIONAL TRAINING

6-28. Institutional training includes all the formal training you receive in the "schoolhouse." Institutional training provides the basic knowledge, technical, tactical, and leadership skills needed at appropriate levels in a soldier's career. Institutional training is primarily composed of the Officer, Warrant Officer , Noncommissioned Officer Education Systems.

### THE OFFICER EDUCATION SYSTEM (OES)

6-29. The OES prepares officers for increased responsibilities and successful performance at the next higher level. It provides precommissioning, branch, and leader development training to develop officers to lead platoon, company, battalion, and higher level organizations. The Officer Education System is a combination of branch-immaterial and branch-specific courses providing progressive and sequential training throughout an officer's career.

### Precommission Training

6-30. The United States Military Academy, ROTC, and Federal/State OCS educate and train cadets/officer candidates and assess their readiness and potential for commissioning as second lieutenants. Precommission sources share a common goal that each graduate possesses the character, leadership, and other attributes essential to progressive and continuing development throughout a career of exemplary service to the Nation.

### Officer Basic Course (OBC)

6-31. The OBC is a branch-specific qualification course that provides new second lieutenants an opportunity to acquire the basic leader, tactical, and technical skills needed to succeed at their first duty assignment. Some branch OBC graduates (military intelligence or chemical for example) are trained for success as a battalion staff officer.

### Captains Career Course (CCC)

6-32. The CCC is a multiple-phased course providing captains an opportunity to acquire the advanced leader, tactical, and technical skills needed to lead company-size units and serve at battalion and/or brigade staff levels. The first phase is branch-specific training. The second phase is branch-immaterial staff process training to provide skills necessary for success in single service, joint, and combined environments. Captains learn to function as staff officers by improving their abilities to analyze and solve military problems, communicate, and interact as members of a staff.

### Command and General Staff Officer Course (CGSOC)

6-33. The CGSOC educates promotable captains and majors in the values and practice of the profession of arms. It emphasizes tactical and operational skills required for warfighting at the corps and division levels. Graduates of CGSOC receive credit for Joint Professional Military Education Phase I. Alternate attendance may be at the Air Command and Staff College, the Naval War College, the U.S. Marine Corps Command and Staff College, the Western Hemisphere Institute for Security Cooperation Command and Staff College, and foreign military colleges approved/validated by CGSOC.

### Army War College (AWC)

6-34. Various senior service colleges (SSC) offer capstone professional military education. The Army SSC is AWC at Carlisle Barracks, PA. The AWC prepares selected military, civilian, and international leaders to assume strategic leadership responsibilities in military or national security organizations. It educates leaders and the Nation on the employment of land power as part of a unified, joint, or multinational force in support of the national military strategy; researches operational and strategic issues; and conducts outreach programs that benefit the AWC, the Army, and the Nation.

### WARRANT OFFICER EDUCATION SYSTEM (WOES)

6-35. The WOES prepares warrant officers to successfully perform in increasing levels of responsibility throughout an entire career. The WOES provides the preappointment, branch MOS-specific, and leader development training needed to produce technically and tactically competent warrant officer leaders for assignment to platoon, detachment, company, battalion, and higher level organizations. The WOES is a combination of branch-immaterial and branch-specific courses providing progressive and sequential training throughout a warrant officer's career.

### Warrant Officer Candidate Course (WOCC)

6-36. The WOCC is a MOS/branch immaterial course that assesses the potential of candidates to become successful Army warrant officers, and to provide training in basic officer and leader competencies. Evaluation and training occur in a mentally and physically demanding environment. Contingent upon certification by a branch proponent that they are technically and tactically qualified for award of an authorized warrant officer MOS, WOCC graduates are appointed to warrant officer, grade WO1.

### Warrant Officer Basic Course (WOBC)

6-37. The WOBC (including the Initial Entry Rotary Wing Qualification Course) is the MOS-specific training and technical certification process conducted by branch proponents to ensure all warrant officers have attained the degree of leadership, technical and tactical competence needed to perform in their MOS at the platoon through battalion levels. Training is performance-oriented and focuses on technical skills, leadership, effective communication, unit training, maintenance operations, security, property accountability, tactics, ethics, and development of and caring for subordinates and their families.

### Warrant Officer Advanced Course (WOAC)

6-38. The WOAC is MOS-specific designed to build on the tasks and VASA developed through previous training and experience. The course provides Chief Warrant Officers in grade CW3 the leader, tactical, and technical training to serve in company and higher-level positions. Primary focus is directed toward leadership skill reinforcement, staff skills, and advanced MOS-specific training. Warrant Officer Advanced Course training consists of a nonresident phase and a resident course.

### Warrant Officer Staff Course (WOSC)

6-39. The WOSC is a branch-immaterial resident course. The course focuses on the staff officer tasks, leadership skills, and knowledge needed to serve in grade CW4 positions at battalion and higher levels. Instruction includes decisionmaking, staff roles and functions, organizational theory, structure of the Army, budget formation and execution, communication, training management, personnel management, and special leadership issues.

### Warrant Officer Senior Staff Course (WOSSC)

6-40. The WOSSC is the capstone for warrant officer professional military education. This branch-immaterial resident course provides warrant officers with a broader Army perspective required for assignment to grade

CW5-level positions as technical, functional, and branch systems integrators and trainers at the highest organizational levels. Instruction focuses on "how the Army runs" (force integration) and provides up-to-date information on Army-level policy, programs, and special items of interest.

## THE NCO EDUCATION SYSTEM (NCOES)

6-41. Institutional training for enlisted soldiers probably began in Initial Entry Training (IET). But the continuing education of junior enlisted soldiers is why our Army's NCO corps is the best in the world. Soldiers who have the potential for greater responsibility and the willingness to accept it will receive training to prepare them for that responsibility.

### Primary Leadership Development Course (PLDC)

6-42. The first leadership course a promotable specialist or NCO will attend is the non-MOS specific Primary Leadership Development Course (PLDC) conducted at NCO Academies (NCOA) worldwide. Soldiers on a promotion list who have met a cutoff score and are otherwise qualified may receive conditional promotion to Sergeant before completion of PLDC.

### Basic Noncommissioned Officer Course (BNCOC)

6-43. Combat arms (CA), combat support (CS), and combat service support (CSS) basic course occurs at proponent service schools. Successful completion of BNCOC is a prerequisite for consideration for promotion to sergeant first class. Active component sergeants promotable to staff sergeant who have met an announced cutoff score can attend BNCOC but must complete the course within one year. Reserve component sergeants must first complete Phase I. Training varies in length from two to nineteen weeks with an average of nine weeks. A 12-day common core designed by the US Army Sergeants Major Academy supplements leadership training received at PLDC. The Department of the Army funds all BNCOC courses. Priority for attendance is SSGs and SGTs (P).

### Advanced Noncommissioned Officer Course (ANCOC)

6-44. Department of the Army selects ANCOC attendees by a centralized SFC/ANCOC selection board. The zone of consideration is announced by personnel services command (PERSCOM) before each board convenes. Promotable SSGs can be conditionally promoted prior to attending ANCOC but must complete the course within a year. Promotable SSGs who meet the announced promotion sequence number can be conditionally promoted prior to and during the course. All soldiers selected for promotion to SFC who have not previously attended ANCOC are automatic selectees. Priority of ANCOC attendance is for SFC and SSG (P).

### Sergeants Major Course (SMC)

6-45. The Sergeants Major Course is the senior level NCOES course and the capstone of NCO education. Soldiers selected for SMC attend a resident course or a non-resident course. A Department of the Army centralized selection board determines who attends resident or non-resident training. The nine month resident course is conducted at the US Army Sergeants Major Academy (USASMA) in Fort Bliss, Texas. Selected individuals may complete SMC through non-resident training, which includes a two week resident phase at USASMA. Soldiers selected for promotion to SGM who are not graduates will attend the next resident SMC. Soldiers may not decline once selected. Successful completion of SMC is a requirement for promotion to SGM. MSGs (P) can be conditionally promoted to SGM prior to and during the course. NCOs who complete SMC incur a two-year service obligation upon graduation.

## OPERATIONAL ASSIGNMENTS

6-46. Operational experience provides soldiers the opportunity to use and build upon what was learned through the process of formal education. Experience gained through a variety of challenging duty assignments prepares soldiers for combat or other operations. A soldier's MOS is usually the basis for operational assignment.

> *The successful leader knows that for him to excel, his soldiers must excel.*
>
> MAJ Don T. Riley

6-47. Developing leaders is a priority mission in command and organizations. Commanders, leaders and supervisors develop soldiers and ensure necessary educational requirements are met. Commanders establish formal unit LDPs that focus on developing individual leaders. These programs normally consist of three phases: reception and integration, basic skill development, and advanced development and sustainment.

- Reception and Integration. The squad leader and platoon sergeant interview new soldiers and discuss his duty position, previous experience and training, personal goals, and possible future assignments. Some units may administer a diagnostic test to identify strengths and weaknesses.

- Basic Skill Development. The new soldier attains a minimum acceptable level of proficiency in critical tasks necessary to perform his mission. The responsibility for this phase lies with the new soldier's immediate supervisor, assisted by other key NCOs and officers.

- Advanced Development and Sustainment. This phase sustains proficiency in tasks already mastered and develops new skills. This is often done through additional duty assignments, technical or developmental courses, and self-development.

6-48. Commanders and leaders use the unit Leader Development Program (LDP) and NCO Development Program (NCODP) to enhance NCO development during operational assignments. The unit NCODP is the CSM's leader development program for NCOs (CPL through CSM). The unit NCODP encompasses most training at the unit level and is tailored to the unique requirements of the unit and its NCOs. The unit NCODP should include primarily METL-driven tasks but may also include general military subjects such as customs, courtesies and traditions of the US Army.

## SELF-DEVELOPMENT

6-49. Self-development is a life-long, standards-based, and competency driven process that is progressive and sequential and complements institutional and operational experiences to provide personal and professional development. It is accomplished through structured and non-structured, technical and academic learning experiences conducted in multiple environments using traditional, technology-enhanced and self-directed methods. Self-development consists of individual study, education, research, professional reading, practice, and self-assessment. You can find a a list of Internet resources in Appendix D and a professional reading list in Appendix E.

> *A [soldier] cannot lead without... studying, reading, observing, learning. He must apply himself to gain the goal—to develop the talent for military leadership.*
>
> **MSG Frank K. Nicolas**

6-50. Self-development includes both structured and self-motivated development tasks. At junior levels, self-development is very structured and narrowly focused. It is tailored towards building the basic leader skills and closely tied with unit NCO development programs. The components may be distance learning, directed reading programs, or other activities that directly relate to building direct leader skills. As NCOs become more senior in rank, self-motivated development becomes more important—activities like professional reading or college courses that help the senior NCO develop organizational leadership skills.

6-51. Professional development models (PDM) are available for each career management field. You can find these at each career branch website and in DA PAM 600-25, *"The US Army Noncommissioned Officer Professional Development Guide."* PDMs provide both career and educational road maps for NCOs to assist in self-development.

### EDUCATIONAL ACTIVITIES IN SUPPORT OF SELF-DEVELOPMENT

6-52. Self-development activities recommended in PDMs draw on the programs and services offered through the Army Continuing Education System (ACES) which operate education centers throughout the Army. In addition, Army Knowledge Online (AKO) has links to computer-based training courses (e-learning) available to all soldiers and DA civilians. Some other educational services that may assist in self-development are the following:

- Education Center Counseling Service.
- Functional Academic Skills Training.

- College Courses.
- Testing.
- Language Training.
- Correspondence Courses.
- Army Learning Centers.

## PROMOTIONS

6-53. Promotions are one of the most visible means of recognizing the performance and potential of soldiers. With promotion to higher rank usually comes greater responsibility and more complex duties. In the next few pages are brief descriptions of the promotion systems of the active component, Army National Guard and US Army Reserve. Since promotion eligibility periodically changes, you should refer to the governing regulation to find out the most current criteria.

6-54. In general terms, promotions are accomplished in a decentralized, semi-centralized or centralized manner. Decentralized promotions are controlled and executed at the unit level. For example, active component commanders may promote an eligible PV2 to PFC in a decentralized system. In semi-centralized promotions, part of the process is at unit level (boards). For promotions to SSG, for example, units convene boards to recommend SGTs for promotion to SSG. Those SGTs the board recommends then receive promotion when they attain the number of promotion points required by centralized cut-off score lists. The Army convenes centralized promotion boards to consider soldiers for promotion to LTC, for example.

### ENLISTED PROMOTION OVERVIEW (ACTIVE COMPONENT)

6-55. The regulation that governs active component enlisted promotions and reductions is Army Regulation 600-8-19, *Enlisted Promotions and Reductions*. It provides the objectives of the Army's enlisted promotion system, which include filling authorized enlisted spaces with the best-qualified soldiers. The promotion system provides for career progression and rank that is in line with potential, recognizing the best qualified soldier to attract and retain the highest caliber soldier for a career in the Army. Additionally, it precludes promoting the soldier who is not productive or not best qualified, providing an equitable system for all soldiers.

6-56. Promotions for enlisted soldiers to PV2, PFC and SPC are decentralized. Soldiers receive automatic promotion to PV2 after 6 months time in service (TIS). Soldiers are automatically promoted to PFC after 12 months TIS and 4 months time in grade (TIG). Soldiers are automatically promoted to SPC after 26 months TIS and 6 months TIG. In all cases, promotions occur unless the commander takes action to prevent the promotion. Based on strength computations at the battalion level, there may be allocations available to promote soldiers earlier than the automatic TIG/TIS requirements. Table 6-1 shows TIG/TIS requirements for promotions PV2-SSG.

### Table 6-1. Promotion Criteria-Active Duty

| Rank | TIS | TIG | Waivable TIS | Waivable TIG | Authority |
|------|-----|-----|--------------|--------------|-----------|
| PV2 | 6 | | 4 | | Co Cdr |
| PFC | 12 | 4 | 6 | 2 | Co Cdr |
| SPC | 24 | 6 | 18 | 3 | Co Cdr |
| SGT | 36 | 8 | 33 | 4 | LTC |
| SSG | 84 | 10 | 48 | 5 | LTC |
| SFC-SGM | Announced by CDR, PERSCOM | | | | Selection Board |

Note: TIS/TIG in months

6-57. Precedence of relative rank. Among enlisted soldiers of the same grade or rank in active military service (to include retired enlisted soldiers on active duty) precedence of relative rank is determined as follows:

- Date of rank (DOR).

- Length of active Federal service in the Army when DORs are the same.

- By length of total active federal service when a and b above are the same.

- Date of birth when a, b, and c are the same. Older is more senior.

6-58. Date of rank and effective date:

- The DOR for promotion to a higher grade is the date specified in the promotion instrument or when no date is specified is the date of the instrument of promotion.

- The DOR in all other cases will be established as governed by appropriate regulation.

- The DOR in a grade to which reduced for inefficiency or failure to complete a school course is the same as that previously held in that grade. If reduction is a grade higher than that previously held, it is the date the soldier was eligible for promotion under the promotion criteria set forth for that grade under this regulation.

- The DOR on reduction for all other reasons is the effective date of reduction.

- The DOR and the effective date will be the same unless otherwise directed by the regulation.

6-59. Soldiers receive conditional promotion to SSG, SFC, and SGM. The Army is reemphasizing the requirement for soldiers to attend and graduate scheduled NCOES courses to retain conditional promotions. For SSGs, SFCs or SGMs to retain conditional promotions, they must complete BNCOC, ANCOC or the US Army Sergeants Major Course (respectively).

6-60. The conditional promotion is for a 12 month period. If conditionally promoted soldiers are enrolled in the appropriate NCOES course at the end of the 12 month period, they may complete the training and retain their promoted rank upon graduation. Soldiers who do not complete the training for justifiable reasons (as described in AR 600-8-19) will lose their conditional promotion and be reduced to the previous rank. Conditionally promoted soldiers who fail to complete the course for any of the following reasons will be reduced to the previous rank and removed from the promotion selection list:

- Soldiers who fail to attend their scheduled class (unjustified reason).
- Soldiers who are denied enrollment for failure to meet weight standard in AR 600-9, *The Army Weight Control Program.*
- Soldiers released from the course for failure to meet course standards.

6-61. Soldiers may receive conditional promotion to SGT. If a soldier meets the appropriate cutoff score and is otherwise qualified, but has not yet completed PLDC, the soldier receives conditional promotion under the following conditions:

- Soldier is on the unit order of merit list (OML) for attendance to PLDC.
- Soldier is operationally deployed (not including National Training Center or Joint Readiness Training Center).
- Soldier is on temproary profile that prohibits attendance at PLDC.

## ENLISTED PROMOTIONS OVERVIEW (ARMY NATIONAL GUARD)

6-62. Like its active counterpart the Army National Guard promotion system is designed to help fill authorized enlisted vacancies with the best qualified enlisted soldiers who have demonstrated the potential to serve at the next higher grade in line with each soldier's potential. For the NCO grades, it prescribes the NCOES requirement for promotion: the soldier on the list will attend the course required for promotion to that grade.

6-63. Table 6-2 shows the TIS/TIG requirements for enlisted promotions in the Army National Guard.

**Table 6-2. Promotion Criteria-Army National Guard**

| Rank | TIS | TIG | Waivable TIS | Waivable TIG | Authority |
|------|-----|-----|------------|------------|-----------|
| PV2 | 6 | | 4 | | Commander |
| PFC | 12 | 4 | 6 | 2 | Commander |
| SPC | 26 | 4 | 14 | 3 | Commander |
| SGT | N/A | 6 | N/A* | | LTC |
| SSG | N/A | 8 | N/A* | | LTC |
| SFC | 9 Years | 11 | 6 Years* | | Selection Board |
| MSG | 13 Years | 12 | 8 Years* | | Selection Board |
| SGM | 16 Years | 14 | 10 Years* | | Selection Board |

Note: TIS/TIG in months unless otherwise noted. * Cumulative Enlisted Service

6-64. The Chief, National Guard Bureau, is the convening and promotion authority for active guard and reserve (AGR) Title 10 enlisted soldier attached to NGB and active duty installations. State Adjutants General (AG) are convening and promotion authority for all promotion boards to SGT through and SGM. They may delegate their authority to their Assistant AG (Army) or Deputy State Area Reserve Command (STARC) commander. They also may delegate promotion authority to subordinate commanders as follows:

- Commanders in MG positions may promote soldiers to SGM.

- Commanders in COL or higher positions may promote soldiers to SFC and MSG.

- Commanders in LTC or higher positions may promote soldiers to SGT and SSG.

- All other commanders may promote soldiers to PV2 and SPC.

## ENLISTED PROMOTIONS OVERVIEW RESERVE (TROOP PROGRAM UNITS)

6-65. The promotion criteria for soldiers (PV2-SSG) in reserve troop program units (TPU) are shown in Table 6-3.

### Table 6-3. Promotion Criteria-Reserve TPU, PV2-SSG

| Rank | TIS | TIG | Waivable TIS | Waivable TIG | Authority |
|------|-----|-----|--------------|--------------|-----------|
| PV2 | 6 | | | | Commander |
| PFC | 12 | 4 | 6 | 2 | Commander |
| SPC/CPL | 24 | 6 | 12 | 3 | Commander |
| SGT | 36 | 12 | 18 | 6 | LTC |
| SSG | 84 | 15 | 48 | 8 | LTC |

Note: TIS/TIG in months.

6-66. For promotion to SFC and higher rank, soldiers in reserve TPU undergo a centralized selection process. The promotion criteria for these soldiers are shown in Table 6-4.

### Table 6-4. Promotion Criteria-Reserve TPU, SFC-SGM

| Rank | TIS (PZ) | TIG (PZ) | TIS (SZ) |
|------|----------|----------|----------|
| SFC | 11 Years | 21 Months | 9 Years |
| MSG* | 15 Years | 24 Months | 11 Years |
| SGM** | 18 Years | 28 Months | 13 Years |

Note: Promotion selection centralized at ARCOM/GOCOM/RSC headquarters and general officer commands OCONUS. * Must have 8 years CES. ** Must have 10 years CES

6-67. Active Guard and Reserve (AGR) soldiers promotion criteria are shown in Table 6-5.

### Table 6-5. Promotion Criteria-Active Guard and Reserve

| Rank | TIS | TIG | Waivable TIS | Waivable TIG | Authority |
|------|-----|-----|--------------|--------------|-----------|
| PV2 | 6 | | 4 | | Commander |
| PFC | 12 | 4 | 6 | 2 | Commander |
| SPC/CPL* | 15 | 9 | No Waivers | 4.5 | Commander |
| SGT** | 24 | 8 | 12 | 4 | LTC |
| SSG-SGM | Centralized Process Against Existing Vacancies | | | | Selection Board |

Note: TIS/TIG in months. * Must have completed a minimum of three continuous months on AGR status. ** Must have completed a minimum of 6 months on AGR status.

6-68. The promotion criteria for individual ready reserve (IRR), individual mobilization augmentee (IMA), and standby reserve (active list) soldiers are shown in table 6-6.

**Table 6-6. Promotion Criteria-IRR, IMA, and Standby Reserve (Active List)**

| Rank | TIG (in months) |
|---|---|
| PFC | 12 |
| CPL/SPC | 12 |
| SGT | 24 |
| SSG | 36 |
| SFC | 36 |
| MSG | 24 |
| SGM | 28 |

Commander, PERSCOM is the promotion authority for all IRR, IMA and Standby Reserve (Active List) soldiers.
All soldiers must be in the IRR or Standby Reserve (Active List) for a 1-year period to be considered for promotion.
The advancement and promotion of soldiers assigned to the IRR are limited to PV2 through SFC.
The advancement and promotion of soldiers assigned to IMA positions or Standby Reserve (Active List) are limited to PFC through SGM.
Soldier must have earned 27 retirement points in either of the two years preceding selection for promotion.

## OFFICERS PROMOTION OVERVIEW

6-69. All AC officer promotions are done through the centralized promotion system and are governed by procedures based on Title 10, United States code, Army Regulation (AR 600-8-29, *Officer Promotions*), and policy established by the Secretary of the Army and the Deputy Chief of Staff for personnel.

6-70. The basic concept of the promotion selection system is to select for promotion those officers who have demonstrated that they possess the professional and moral qualifications, integrity, physical fitness, and ability required to successfully perform the duties expected of an officer at the next higher grade. Promotion is not intended to be a reward for long and honorable service in the present grade but is based on overall demonstrated performance and potential abilities.

6-71. Promotion selection is conducted fairly and equitably by boards composed of mature, experienced senior officers. Each board consists of different members, and women and minority members are routinely appointed. Selection boards recommend those officers who, in the collective judgment of the board, are the best qualified for promotion.

6-72. The Army has established procedures to counsel, upon request, officers not selected for promotion. An officer may request reconsideration for promotion when an action, by a regularly scheduled selection board which considered him or her for promotion, was contrary to law or involved material error.

## SECTION III – RETENTION AND REENLISTMENT

---

### The Oath of Enlistment

I, (name of enlistee) do solemnly swear (or affirm) that I will support and defend the Constitution of the United States against all enemies, foreign and domestic; that I will bear true faith and allegiance to the same; that I will obey the orders of the President of the United States and the orders of the officers appointed over me, according to regulations and the Uniform code of Military Justice. So help me God!

---

6-73. All commanders are retention officers. Commanders and NCOs at all levels have the responsibilities to sustain Army personnel readiness by developing and implementing and maintaining aggressive local Army retention programs designed to accomplish specific goals and missions consistent with governing laws, policies, and directives.

*This country has done a lot for my family. This is a way to give back.*

SPC Luis Feliciano

6-74. The goals of the Army Retention Program are to—

- Reenlist on a long-term basis, sufficient numbers of highly qualified active Army soldiers.
- Enlist or transfer and assign sufficient numbers of highly qualified soldiers who are separating from the active Army into RC units, consistent with geographic constraints.
- Achieve and maintain Army force alignment through the retention, transfer, or enlistment of highly qualified soldiers in critical skills and locations.
- Adequately support special programs such as the US Military Academy Preparatory School (USMAPS) and ROTC "Green to Gold" programs.

6-75. Commanders are issued retention missions based upon their "fair share" ratio of enlistment eligible soldiers. Commanders receive missions in the following categories:

- Regular Army Initial Term mission.
- Regular Army Mid-Career mission. Soldiers serving on their second or subsequent term of service, having 10 or less years of Active Federal Service at ETS.

- RC enlistment/transfer mission. This mission is based upon the number of eligible in the ranks of CPL/SPC and SGT scheduled for ETS and may be assigned as required by HQDA.

- Missions as otherwise required by DA. Missions are to include the USMAPS and ROTC Green to Gold programs.

**Reenlisting in Kandahar, Afghanistan.**

6-76. DA policy states that only those soldiers who have maintained a record of acceptable performance will be offered the privilege of reenlisting within the active Army or transferring or enlisting into the RC. Other soldiers will be separated under appropriate administrative procedures or barred from reenlistment under Chapter 8, AR 635-200.

> *The end for which a soldier is recruited, clothed, armed, and trained, the whole object of his sleeping, eating, drinking, and marching is simply that he should fight at the right place and the right time.*
>
> Carl von Clausewitz

## BONUS EXTENSION AND RETRAINING (BEAR) PROGRAM

6-77. BEAR is a program designed to assist in force alignment. It allows eligible soldiers an opportunity to extend their enlistment for formal retraining into a shortage MOS that is presently in the Selective Reenlistment Bonus (SRB) program. Upon completion of retraining, the soldier is awarded the new primary military occupational specialty (PMOS), reenlists, and receives an SRB in the newly awarded MOS.

# TYPES OF DISCHARGES

6-78. The type of discharge that you will receive from the Army is based on your military record; for example, if you are separated for administrative reasons other than completion of term in service, you may receive the following types of discharge. For more information on the effects of discharges see Chapter 7.

- Honorable. This type of discharge depends on your behavior and performance of duty. Isolated incidents of minor misconduct may be disregarded if your overall record of service is good.

- General Discharge under Honorable Conditions. This discharge is appropriate for those whose military records are satisfactory but are not good enough to warrant an honorable discharge.

- Discharge under Other Than Honorable Conditions. This is the most severe of the administrative discharges. It may result in the loss of veteran's benefits. Such a discharge usually is given to those who have shown one or more incidents of serious misconduct.

- Entry-Level Separation. This discharge applies if you are within 180 days of continuous active duty and your records do not warrant a discharge under other than honorable conditions.

# BARS TO REENLISTMENT

6-79. The bar is a procedure to deny reenlistment to soldiers whose immediate separation under administrative procedures is not warranted, but whose reentry into or service beyond end of time in service (ETS) with the active Army is not in the best interest of the Army. Soldiers may not reenlist without the recommendation of the commander. However, if a commander wishes to disapprove a request for reenlistment of extension when submitted by a soldier who is fully qualified for reenlistment without waiver, he or she must concurrently submit a Bar to Reenlistment.

6-80. The Bar to reenlistment is not a punitive action but is designed for use as a rehabilitative tool. Imposition of a bar does not preclude administrative separation at a later date. The Bar to Reenlistment puts a soldier on notice that he is not a candidate for reenlistment. A soldier who is barred from reenlistment realizes he may be subject to separation if the circumstances that led to the Bar to Reenlistment are not overcome. The commander who imposes the bar will advise the soldier exactly what is expected in order to overcome the Bar to Reenlistment. Commanders must review the circumstances for imposing the bar every three months and either remove or continue the bar to reenlistment.

6-81. Commanders must initiate separation proceedings under AR 600-200 upon completion of the second 3-month review if the commander decides not to remove the bar. Initiation of separation action is not required for soldiers who, at the time of the second 3-month review, have more than 18 years of active federal service but less than 20 years. These soldiers will be required to retire on the last day of the month when eligibility is attained.

**Chapter 7**

# Benefits of Service

We serve the Nation in the Army for a number of reasons. Duty, honor, discipline, and the love of country are just a few of them. Many soldiers initially join the Army so they can afford college or to gain job skills for later in life. Considering the pay, allowances, and other benefits, American soldiers are among the best paid in the world. This chapter highlights some of the excellent benefits of serving in the US Army.

For more information on pay and allowances, see the Defense Finance and Accounting Service (DFAS) website at www.dfas.mil, and AR 37-104-4, *Military Pay and Allowances Policies and Procedures - Active Component*, 31 Oct 94.

For more information on financial readiness see TC 21-7, *Personal Financial Readiness and Deployability Handbook*, 17 November 1997.

For more information on Army housing, see the Army Housing website at www.housing.army.mil and AR 210-50, *Housing Management*, 26 Feb 99.

For more information on military retirement see AR 680-300, *Army Reserve Retirement Point Credit System*, 8 Jun 73, and AR 600-8-7, *Retirement Services Program*, 1 Jun 00.

# ARMY WELL-BEING

7-1.    The benefits of serving in the Army go beyond the paycheck you receive. Not only do you grow as a person, but you develop friendships that will last a lifetime. You also gain the satisfaction of having served your country and the pride that goes with it. Army well-being is the total package of programs and benefits with the ultimate purpose of maintaining combat readiness by caring for the needs of soldiers and their families.

7-2.    Well-being is "the personal—physical, material, mental, and spiritual—state of soldiers, civilians, and their families that contributes to their preparedness to perform the Army's mission." Soldiers have a responsibility to ensure that personal issues do not impair their ability to deploy and conduct the mission. Army well-being helps them fulfill this responsibility.

> *Army readiness is inextricably linked to the well being of our people. Our success depends on the whole team—soldiers, civilians, families—All of whom serve the Nation. Strategic responsiveness requires that our support structures provide soldiers and families the resources to be self-reliant both when the force is deployed and when it is at home. When we deploy, soldiers will know that their families are safe, housed, and have access to medical care, community services, and educational opportunities. We have a covenant with our soldiers and families, and we will keep faith with them.*
>
> General Eric K. Shinseki

7-3.    The goal of Army well-being is to improve and sustain the institutional strength of the Army. Institutional strength is the force behind the Army that distinguishes it from occupations and other professions. It is the force that binds us together as the Army Team.

7-4.    Well-being is the human dimension of Army Transformation. As the Army changes, well-being represents our resolute commitment to prepare now to meet future needs, as well as today's needs. Army well-being is closely linked to four key outcomes—performance, readiness, retention, and recruiting.

- Army well-being enhances performance by strengthening command climate and the bond between the leader and the led.

- Army well-being enhances readiness by producing self-reliant soldiers who are able to focus on their mission, confident in the preparedness and self-reliance of their families.

- Army well-being enhances retention and recruiting by creating the environment for positive decisions by the right men and women to join and stay in the Army.

## SECTION I – PAY AND ALLOWANCES

7-5.    You are among the best-paid soldiers in the world. With the other benefits of military service, the compensation provided members of the US Armed Forces compares very favorably with similar jobs in civilian life. Our country's leaders and our fellow citizens have decided that to maintain a professional, capable, and ready Army requires good compensation in pay, allowances, and benefits. You can find detailed information on pay and allowances at the Defense Finance and Accounting (DFAS) website at www.dfas.mil and in TC 21-7, *Personal Financial Readiness and Deployability Handbook.*

## PAY

7-6.    Soldiers receive a salary, that is, pay for duties performed under a contract of service. Soldiers do not receive a wage, which is a price for a set amount of labor, usually measured in hours. The distinction is made clear in the phrase "I'm a soldier everyday, all day—24/7." This distinction is important because the soldier has a duty to obey orders and to go where needed, regardless of when or where.

7-7.    There are various types of pay. Basic pay is received by all soldiers and is the main component of an individual's salary. Other types of payments, often referred to as special pay, are for specific qualifications or events. For example, there are special pays for aviators and parachutists. There is also special pay for dangerous or hardship duties.

### BASIC PAY

7-8.    Soldiers receive pay on a monthly basis (though active duty soldiers can elect to split their pay and receive a portion in the middle of the month). It is likely the largest part of your paycheck and is the amount you see on military pay charts. Nearly every year congress authorizes an increase to military pay and allowances. The DFAS website has the current basic pay charts for active duty and reserve soldiers. Basic pay generally increases every two years for soldiers in a given grade.

### SPECIAL PAY

7-9.    Soldiers may receive special pay for having certain skills (such as helicopter pilots) or for being in specified areas (such as in a combat zone). Table 7-1 shows some of these types of pay and why a soldier receives them. The DFAS website shows the most up-to-date amounts for these and other special pay categories. The source for this information is the Department of Defense Financial Management Regulation (DODFMR), Volume 7A: *Military Pay Policy and Procedures - Active Duty and Reserve Pay* (Military Pay Manual for short).

**Table 7-1. Other Pay**

| Pay Type | Who gets it | How much |
|---|---|---|
| Diving Duty | Qualified divers in designated diving slots | Up to $340/month |
| Sea Duty | Soldiers assigned to a vessel at sea or in port 50 miles from home port. Varies with rank and time in service. | Up to $400/month |
| Hardship Duty | For assignment to specific area (e.g., Kuwait outside Kuwait City) or to specific units (e.g., Joint Task Force—Full Accounting). | $8-150/month |
| Special Duty | Recruiters, drill sergeants, nominative CSMs | Up to $375/month |
| Enlistment Bonuses | Enlisted soldiers for specified MOSs | Varies |
| Reenlistment Bonuses | Enlisted soldiers for specified MOSs | Varies |
| Hostile Fire/ Imminent Danger | Soldiers in combat or designated imminent danger area * | $150-225/month |
| Overseas Extension Incentive | Soldiers in certain locations and MOSs, who extending their overseas tour. | Varies |
| Foreign Language | Qualified linguists in critical language MOS. May not receive pay for more than three language specialties | $100/month for each language |
| Flight | Soldiers on flight status. Pay is prorated depending on flying hours. | $150 – 250/month |
| Parachute (Jump) ** | Soldiers on jump status. HALO status is $225/month. | $150/month |
| Demolition ** | Explosive ordnance disposal (EOD) specialists assigned to EOD units | $150/month |
| Experimental Stress ** | Test subjects during testing | $150/month |
| Special Pay | Health professionals (physicians, dentists, nurses). | Up to $1000/month |

\* In a combat zone/hazardous duty area enlisted pay is nontaxable. A portion of officer pay is nontaxable.
\*\* Only two hazardous duty payments per month are authorized.

## ALLOWANCES

7-10.  Allowances are other payments to the soldier, usually nontaxable, that are in lieu of services the government does not provide. For example, if government quarters are not available, the Army pays a basic allowance for housing (BAH) to the soldier to allow him to find adequate housing off post in the civilian community. Soldiers who reside in government quarters receive reduced or no BAH. Soldiers have many different allowances available to them. Table 7-2 shows some of these. As with the different types of pay, you can find up-to-date eligibility requirements and amounts on the DFAS website and in the Military Pay Manual.

**Table 7-2. Allowances**

| Allowance | Who gets it |
|---|---|
| Basic Allowance for Housing (BAH) | Active duty soldiers who have not been furnished adequate government quarters for themselves or their dependents or who have been furnished inadequate quarters. BAH is intended to pay only a portion of the soldier's housing costs. |
| Basic Allowance for Subsistence (BAS) | All Active duty officers and active duty enlisted soldiers who are authorized to mess separately (separate rations) or soldiers who do not have a dining facility available. |
| Family Separation Allowance (FSA) | Active duty soldiers on permanent or temporary duty for 30 consecutive days at a location where dependents may not go to at government expense and where government quarters are unavailable for the dependents. Up to $250 per month. |
| Clothing Maintenance Allowance | Active duty enlisted soldiers on the anniversary of enlistment. Intended to pay for replacement of military unique items required for wear. Increases after the first three years. |
| Dislocation Allowance | Active duty soldiers who make a permanent change of station. Intended to defray costs associated with moving that are not reimbursed through other means. Equal to two months of BAH. |
| Cost of Living Allowance | Active duty soldiers assigned and residing in specified high-cost areas. Intended to compensate for a portion of non-housing costs that exceed the US average by 8% or more. |
| Additional Active Duty Uniform Allowance | Reserve component officers ordered to active duty or active duty for training (ADT) for 90 days or more. Payable after serving 90 consecutive days of active duty. |
| Per Diem Allowance | Soldiers on temporary duty (TDY) when government quarters and mess are unavailable. Per diem is a tax-free daily allowance for the added expenses of buying meals and/or living in hotels while on official business. |

# LEAVE

7-11.   Every active duty soldier may accrue (earn and build up) 30 days of leave each year. That comes out to 2.5 days per month. Reserve component soldiers on active duty earn leave, also, although not while on active duty for training unless the period exceeds 30 days. This benefit surpasses nearly any vacation plan available in the civilian labor world. When authorized to take leave, soldiers continue receiving full pay and allowances as while on duty—and accruing more leave. Soldiers who have more than 60 days of accrued leave on 1 October lose the portion in excess of 60 days. This is often referred to as "use or lose." Soldiers can request exceptions in cases of extended deployments or other extraordinary reasons.

7-12.   Soldiers may also cash in leave, that is, trade it for an equivalent amount of basic pay. Enlisted soldiers may do so when they reenlist while any soldier may do so upon departing the service. Soldiers may cash in no more than 60 days of leave in a career.

7-13.   At the end of your time in the Army, you may also choose to use your accrued leave as Terminal Leave. This is when you go on leave prior to the end of your service after outprocessing the Army, but continue to receive full pay and allowances up to your actual end of service date. Many soldiers find this option very helpful when leaving the Army to go to college or when starting a new career. You may also cash in a portion of your accrued leave while taking terminal leave. It all depends on your circumstances.

## SECTION II – HOUSING

7-14.    Active duty soldiers and their families are entitled to healthy, safe housing to live in. An entitlement in the Army is something that must be provided and may not be taken away without due process. In the case of housing, soldiers live in government furnished quarters in exchange for their BAH, or they keep their BAH to pay rent for civilian (off-post) housing. Government housing and BAH directly result from the Constitution. The third amendment of the Constitution forbids the government from quartering soldiers in housing without the owner's consent, so the government provides quarters or a housing allowance (BAH) to all active duty soldiers.

## GOVERNMENT HOUSING

7-15.    Government quarters are safe, maintained, and adequate for soldiers' needs. In some cases, because of great need, some government housing remains in use past its expected useful life. Installations continue to maintain these quarters and they are still safe to live in. In those unusual cases where soldiers reside in inadequate government furnished quarters, they receive a portion of BAH to compensate for the inconvenience. The standard of what is considered adequate quarters is in Chapter 4 of AR 210-50, *Housing Management*. Many commands or installations have supplements to AR 210-50 that further define adequate and inadequate quarters. The standards of adequacy generally are qualitative in nature and assess the size, configuration, and safety of the housing as well as its condition, services, and amenities.

7-16.    The Army owes decent housing to every active duty soldier and family. But living in government quarters come with responsibilities, such as following rules on appearance and use. For example, you may have to keep your grass cut to a certain length, or there may be limitations on when and how many lights you can put up for Christmas. These rules aren't intended to be a nuisance or a restriction of freedom. They are intended to help maintain a safe and pleasant environment for all soldiers and their families. Such rules are similar to those in civilian homeowners' associations, for example.

7-17.    Army installations have a system in place to assign soldiers and their families housing, maintain that housing, and to help soldiers leave those quarters upon reassignment. In cases where quarters are not available or the soldier (SFC and above) elects to live off-post, Army installations provide assistance in finding good housing in the civilian community. Living in government housing is an excellent value. In most locations, the BAH a soldier receives to pay for civilian housing does not cover the full cost of that housing—rent or mortgage, electricity, water and sewer, maintenance, etc. On the other hand, living in government housing prevents you from receiving BAH, but you won't have any of those bills (although telephone, internet access, and cable TV services are your responsibility to pay). You can often obtain supplies and hardware for the maintenance of your quarters at no cost to you from self-help stores on the installation.

7-18.    Few installations have enough housing units to accommodate every soldier and family assigned there. That is why you will often have to wait to get into government-furnished quarters. Installations have waiting lists that show every soldier and family who have requested government quarters. Your name is put on the list as of the day you sign in at your new unit. However, an interesting exception is when you return from a dependent-restricted (unaccompanied) overseas tour. At that time, you may be put on the list as of the day you departed your previous duty station for the unaccompanied tour, for a maximum 14-month credit. Watch out though: any voluntary extensions negate this credit.

## BASIC ALLOWANCE FOR HOUSING (BAH)

7-19.    Some soldiers receive Basic Allowance for Housing (BAH). This tax-free monthly allowance goes to stateside servicemembers who cannot get into government quarters or who choose to live off base. For most soldiers, BAH is the second-largest part of their compensation. Allowances are based on rank, dependent status, and location.

7-20.    The rates are calculated by surveying the civilian housing market in 370 locations across the United States. For example, BAH with dependents rates for senior enlisted members and officers are set by canvassing the rental costs of three and four-bedroom single-family homes in neighborhoods where the typical civilian income is $60,000 to $100,000 per year. For the BAH without dependents rate for junior enlisted personnel the survey focuses on one-bedroom apartments in neighborhoods where the typical civilian earns $20,000 to $30,000 per year.

7-21.    Different types of BAH are available. There is an allowance for soldiers on active duty (BAH-I) including RC soldiers on active duty, a BAH for RC soldiers on active duty for less than 140 days (BAH-II), and a partial rate BAH. As with all pay and allowances, you can find current rates on the DFAS website. With BAH-I, you may receive a "with-dependents" rate or "without-dependents" rate.

- The "with-dependents" rate goes to soldiers with at least one family member who meets the official definition of a dependent. The allowance does not increase with additional family members.

- If a husband and wife both are on active duty and have a child, the higher-ranking spouse receives BAH at the "with-dependents" rate. The other spouse receives BAH at the "without-dependents" rate.

- The "without-dependents" rate is for single people with no family members living with them. Dual military couples without children both receive BAH at the without-dependents rate.

- BAH-Differential (BAH-DIFF) is for soldiers paying child support and not receiving BAH at the "with dependent rate." To receive BAH-DIFF, the soldier's child support payment must equal or exceed the amount of the BAH-DIFF.

- Reserve component soldiers on active duty for fewer than 140 days are entitled to the monthly BAH-II. For BAH-II there is a married rate and a single rate.

- A soldier without dependents is authorized partial BAH (Rebate) when assigned to single-type government quarters (barracks, BOQ, BEQ) or when residing off post without a statement of nonavailability.

7-22. The actual amount a soldier pays "out-of-pocket" depends on the housing choices he makes. Thrifty soldiers can keep all the BAH due them even if their housing costs are less than their allowance. Those who choose a bigger or more expensive residence than the typical soldier in their pay grade will find that their out-of-pocket costs are higher.

7-23. Most soldiers stationed overseas who live off base receive an overseas housing allowance (OHA). While OCONUS soldiers receive OHA for the same pupose that CONUS soldiers receive BAH, OHA varies each month with currency exchange rates. Personnel assigned to unaccompanied tours overseas can collect BAH if their families live off base in the United States. In unusual cases, service secretaries can declare a tour within the United States as unaccompanied. For example, if a child is seriously ill and needs to remain near a medical center, the family can continue to receive a housing allowance in that location after the soldier has moved to another assignment.

## SECTION III – HEALTH

7-24. The Department of Defense (DOD) has developed a world class health care system for servicemembers and their families. It encourages total health fitness, delivers top quality health care, and focuses on medical readiness.

## TRICARE

7-25. In response to the challenge of maintaining medical combat readiness while providing the best health care for all eligible personnel, the Department of Defense introduced TRICARE (TRI—Army, Navy and Air Force and CARE—health care). TRICARE is a regionally managed health care program. TRICARE brings together the health care resources of the Army, Navy, and Air Force and supplements them with networks of civilian health care professionals to provide better access and high quality service while maintaining the capability to support military operations. TRICARE offers soldiers and their families affordable health care when they need it the most. Registration is important—be sure to enroll your family members in the Defense Enrollment Eligibility Reporting System (DEERS).

7-26. TRICARE affects soldiers and retirees in the US, Europe, Latin America, and the Pacific. Those eligible for TRICARE are—

- Active duty soldiers (including reserve component soldiers on active duty under Title 10) and their families.
- Retirees and their families (see Section VIII).
- Survivors of all uniformed services who are not eligible for Medicare.

7-27. TRICARE offers eligible beneficiaries three choices for their health care:

- TRICARE Prime—where military treatment facilities (MTFs) are the principal source of health care.
- TRICARE Extra—a preferred provider option that saves money.
- TRICARE Standard—a fee-for-service option (the old CHAMPUS program).

7-28. The main challenge for most eligible beneficiaries is deciding which TRICARE option; Prime, Extra or Standard is best for them. Active duty soldiers are enrolled in TRICARE Prime and pay no fees. Active duty family members pay no enrollment fees, but they must choose a TRICARE option and apply for enrollment in TRICARE Prime. There are no enrollment fees for active duty families in TRICARE Prime.

## TRICARE PRIME

7-29. With TRICARE Prime, most of your health care will come from an MTF, augmented by the TRICARE contractor's Preferred Provider Network (PPN). All active duty personnel are enrolled in TRICARE Prime. Soldiers receive most of their care from military medical personnel. Family members and survivors of active duty personnel may enroll. For active duty families, there is no enrollment fee for TRICARE Prime, but they must complete an enrollment form. Reserve component soldiers (and their family members) called to active duty for 30 days or more may enroll in TRICARE Prime or may be eligible for TRICARE Prime Remote.

7-30. Your primary care manager or team of providers will see you first for your health care needs. The primary care manager—

- Provides and/or coordinates your care.
- Maintains your health records.
- Refers you to specialists, if necessary. To be covered, specialty care must be arranged and approved by your primary care manager.

7-31.   Advantages of TRICARE Prime:

- No enrollment fee for active duty and families.
- Small fee per visit to civilian providers and no fee for active duty members.
- Guaranteed appointments.
- Primary care manager supervises and coordinates care.
- Away-from-home emergency coverage.

7-32.   Disadvantages of TRICARE Prime:

- Enrollment fee for retirees and their families.
- Provider choice limited.
- Specialty care by referral only.
- Not universally available.

**TRICARE STANDARD**

7-33.   TRICARE Standard is the new name for CHAMPUS. Under this plan, you can see the authorized provider of your choice. Those who are happy with coverage from a current civilian provider often opt for this plan. However, this flexibility generally means that care costs more. Treatment may also be available at an MTF if space allows and after TRICARE Prime patients have been served. Furthermore, TRICARE Standard may be the only coverage available in some areas.

7-34.   Active duty family members, family members of reserve component soldiers ordered to active duty for more than 30 days, and retirees drawing retired pay are eligible for TRICARE Standard. Active duty soldiers are enrolled in TRICARE Prime and not eligible for TRICARE Standard. The RC soldier ordered to active duty for more than 30 days is entitled to the TRICARE Prime benefit as soon as he is activated.

7-35.   Advantages of TRICARE Standard:

- Broadest choice of providers.
- Widely available.
- No enrollment fee.
- TRICARE Extra is an available option.

7-36.   Disadvantages of TRICARE Standard:

- No Primary Care Manager.
- Patient pays a deductible, co-payment and the balance of the medical bill if the provider does not participate in TRICARE Standard.
- Nonavailability statement may be required for civilian inpatient care for areas surrounding MTFs.
- Beneficiaries may have to do their own paperwork and file their own claims.

## TRICARE EXTRA

7-37. With TRICARE Extra, you will choose a doctor, hospital, or other medical provider listed in the TRICARE Provider Directory. If you need assistance, call the health care finder at your nearest TRICARE service center (TSC). Anyone who is eligible for TRICARE Standard may use TRICARE Extra.

7-38. Advantages of TRICARE Extra:

- Co-payment 5% less than TRICARE Standard.
- No balance billing.
- No enrollment fee.
- No deductible when using retail pharmacy network.
- No forms to file.
- You may use also TRICARE Standard.

7-39. Disadvantages of TRICARE Extra:

- No primary care manager.
- Provider choice is limited.
- Patient pays a deductible and co-payment.
- Nonavailability statement may be required for civilian inpatient care for areas surrounding MTFs.
- Not universally available.

## TRICARE OVERSEAS

7-40. The TRICARE Overseas programs are designed to provide health care to eligible beneficiaries who reside overseas, not in the 50 United States. TRICARE has three overseas regions: Europe, Pacific and Latin America & Canada.

7-41. The main difference for overseas prime enrollees is that the co-payment for civilian care is waived and no pre-authorization is required for TRICARE covered benefits received outside of Puerto Rico, even when traveling in CONUS. TRICARE Prime enrollees in Puerto Rico who are enrolled to an MTF must have authorization from their primary care manager to see a civilian provider for other than emergency care.

7-42. Other TRICARE options:

- TRICARE Prime Remote—designed for active duty family members in remote locations. This is similar to TRICARE Prime.
- TRICARE for Life—for Medicare-eligible beneficiaries age 65 and over.
- TRICARE Plus. Enrolled beneficiaries have priority access to care at military treatment facilities; however, beneficiaries who choose to use TRICARE Extra, TRICARE Standard or TRICARE for Life may also continue to receive care in an MTF as capacity exists.

7-43. The best source of information on current health care benefits is your health benefits advisor available at your local TSC or MTF. Look for additional information on the TRICARE website, www.tricare.osd.mil.

# DENTAL

7-44. The Tricare Dental Program (TDP) is a voluntary, comprehensive dental program offered worldwide for family members of all active duty soldiers. It may also be available to selected reserve and individual ready reserve (IRR) soldiers and/or their family members. Active duty soldiers get dental care through their servicing dental activity.

### ENROLLMENT BASICS

7-45. The TDP offers two plans: a single plan and a family plan. New enrollees must continue in the TDP for at least 12 months. Anyone failing to pay premiums or who disenrolls for other than a valid disenrollment reason may not re-enroll in the program for 12 months.

7-46. Under the single plan, one eligible member is covered. This can be one active duty family member, a selected reserve or IRR member, or one selected reserve or IRR family member. A family enrollment consists of two or more covered family members, either active duty, selected reserve or IRR. Under the TDP, however, all eligible family members of a sponsor must be enrolled if any are enrolled, except for the following:

- Sponsors may voluntarily enroll children under four years old. Upon their 4th birthday, they are automatically enrolled.

- If a sponsor has family members living in geographically separated locations, he may enroll only those family members residing in one location (e.g., children living with a divorced spouse).

- Selected reserve and IRR sponsors can enroll independently of their family members and family members can enroll independently of the sponsor.

- Two soldiers cannot enroll the same family members. If both husband and wife are soldiers, they cannot enroll each other in the plan.

### ELIGIBILITY

7-47. Active duty family members, selected reserve, and IRR members and/or their family members are eligible for the TDP if the sponsor has at least 12 months remaining on his or her service commitment at the time of enrollment. Family members of active duty, selected reserve and IRR soldiers, including spouses and unmarried children (natural, step, adopted and wards) under the age of 21, are eligible.

7-48. Child eligibility may be available after age 21 if—

- The dependent is a full time student at an accredited college or university and is more than 50% dependent on the sponsor for financial support.

- The dependent has a disabling illness or injury that occurred before his or her 21st birthday, or between the ages of 21 and 23 while enrolled as a full time student, and was more than 50% dependent on the sponsor for financial support.

7-49.    Upon mobilization, RC soldiers become eligible for the same health care benefits as active duty soldiers, including dental benefits. As a result, RC soldiers enrolled in the TDP who are activated for more than 30 days automatically are removed from the program and become eligible for dental care from military dental providers. Family members of mobilized reservists become eligible for the same lower premiums that active duty family members enjoy.

## REMOTELY STATIONED ACTIVE DUTY SOLDIERS

7-50.    The Tri-Service Remote Dental Program (RDP) is for military personnel serving on active duty in remote CONUS locations (50 miles or more from a military base). Soldiers enrolled in TRICARE Prime Remote (medical) are automatically eligible for the RDP. RDP eligible active duty soldiers can receive emergency dental care any time they are in an active duty status. RDP is not for family members.

7-51.    Soldiers that leave the Army with transitional assistance health care benefits may receive dental coverage for emergency care only. Soldiers that have served 180 days of continuous active duty or more may be eligible for dental care as a veteran's benefit following separation from active duty. The laws governing veteran's benefits change frequently. See current information on the Department of Veterans Affairs website at www.va.gov or visit your local VA office.

## SURVIVOR BENEFITS

7-52.    When an enrolled soldier dies while on active duty for a period of more than 30 days, the enrolled family members will continue to receive benefits for 3 years from the month following the month of the soldier's death. This applies only to family members enrolled at the time of death.

7-53.    This benefit also applies to enrolled family members of selected reserve and IRR—special mobilization category (IRR—SMC) sponsors who die while in selected reserve and IRR—SMC status regardless if the sponsor was enrolled at the time of death. Family members must be enrolled at time of death to receive these benefits. In these cases the government pays the entire TDP premium. The family members will be notified of coverage termination prior to disenrollment.

7-54.    For additional information regarding the Tricare Dental Program, visit your local TRICARE office or the website through the Army homepage.

## SUPPLEMENTAL INSURANCE

7-55.    If you receive medical care outside the military system, and you don't have any other health insurance (or a supplemental policy) to help pay your cost-shares or co-payments, you'll face out-of-pocket expenses.

Even though TRICARE pays a generous share of the cost of civilian medical bills, your share of the cost might be substantial.

7-56. Many associations, organizations, and insurance companies provide supplemental insurance. Supplemental insurance may cover co-payments and costs TRICARE does not pay. The TRICARE website has a list of some of the associations and organizations that offer supplemental insurance. Neither TRICARE nor the Department of Defense endorses any specific company, organization, or plan. Likewise, neither DOD nor the TRICARE Management Activity promotes any specific policy for purchase, nor recommends retention or cancellation of any coverage you may have. The decision to purchase supplemental insurance is **yours and yours alone.**

---

### Medical Bills

SFC Willer is married and has one daughter, Linda. While on leave recently, the family was involved in an auto accident and unfortunately Linda was seriously injured. There wasn't a military hospital located nearby and she required urgent medical attention.

Linda received proper and immediate medical care at a civilian hospital and recovered completely from the accident. But SFC Willer is now faced with substantial medical bills that he can't afford and TRICARE will not pay completely.

SFC Willer is enrolled in TRICARE Prime and his family is in TRICARE Standard. TRICARE paid about half of the bill for Linda's care. For care providers that are part of the TRICARE system that would be the end of the story because those providers agree to accept what TRICARE pays (along with any co-payment required). But the civilian hospital where Linda was treated is not part of the TRICARE system. It expects SFC Willer to pay what the hospital billed, above and beyond the amount TRICARE paid.

---

7-57. Most TRICARE supplemental insurance policies are designed to reimburse patients for the civilian medical care bills they must pay after TRICARE pays the government's share of the cost. Before you buy any supplement, carefully consider which plan is best suited to your individual needs. Each TRICARE supplemental policy has its own rules concerning acceptance for pre-existing conditions, eligibility requirements for the family, deductibles, mental health limitations, long-term illness, well-baby care, care provided to persons with disabilities, claims under the diagnosis-related group payment system for inpatient hospital charges, and rules concerning allowable charges. In some soldiers' situations, supplemental insurance may be appropriate while others may not need or want it. Look at your own circumstances and decide if the additional cost of supplemental insurance is something you think necessary. Either way, it is your decision.

## SECTION IV – FINANCIAL READINESS AND PLANNING

7-58.   First term soldiers get financial readiness training at their first duty station. Most installations also offer financial readiness training to other soldiers upon request, usually through the Army Community Service (ACS) or Community Service Center (CSC). Many units also have appointed a command financial NCO (CFNCO) who conducts training and financial counseling for assigned soldiers. The training you receive helps you manage your finances while in the service and can help you plan for the future as well. Training Circular 21-7, *Personal Financial Readiness and Deployability Handbook*, is a good reference for more details.

## READINESS

7-59.   Financial readiness for AC and RC soldiers means ensuring you and your family are provided for within the limits of your income. The reason it is a readiness issue is that soldiers with money problems may be unable to focus on their mission, especially if deployed. Training in financial matters can help you gain control over your finances and manage your money more effectively. The goal of the training is to provide you with the tools to handle your money wisely and to make informed purchasing decisions so you are better able to concentrate on your duties.

7-60.   The Consumer Affairs and Financial Assistance Program (CAFAP), offered through ACS, can train soldiers and spouses in money management, proper use of credit, basic financial planning, deployment, transition and relocation, insurance options, and check writing principles. If you don't already know how, CAFAP counselors and the CFNCO can teach you about budgeting. Budgeting can prevent financial difficulties before they arise.

7-61.   Service in the Army helps to save money. For example, shopping at the Commissary is usually less expensive than off-post. The MWR facilities on base are nearly always a better value than similar businesses in the civilian community. You also have access to free legal assistance that in the civilian world could cost hundreds or even thousands of dollars. Your health care costs very little in comparison to that of civilian workers. But you should take positive steps to ensure expenses don't exceed your income. One of the best tools is to create a budget. A budget is a list that shows your expected income and expenses on a periodic basis, usually monthly. The goal is to track your expenses and learn the discipline to spend money when you planned to.

7-62.   The key is discipline. Eating out less saves money immediately. If you are considering the purchase of a vehicle, make sure beforehand that the payments fit in your budget—and don't forget the insurance and operating costs. Save ahead of time for big purchases like TVs or appliances so you don't have to pay interest on credit cards or loans. These few little tips can help keep you on budget. Set financial goals that are reasonable and then make a plan for reaching them. Stay on budget by avoiding unnecessary expenses and smart purchases. It isn't easy, but soldiers have performed much more difficult tasks.

## PLANNING

7-63. Soldiers, through training and discipline, are planners by nature. So it shouldn't be any surprise that it's important to plan for the future financially. The trouble is soldiers often don't think of it until late in their careers. Our commitment to the Army, our fellow soldiers, and to our families occasionally leave little time for thinking about financial goals. However, someday you will leave the service and start a new career and someday you will also leave the civilian work force. The sooner you plan for that day, the more likely you will attain the goals you set.

7-64. In basic terms, there are three areas to consider: retirement planning, emergency savings, and insurance. Retirement planning is a long-term savings process to prepare for the day you are no longer in the work force or earning a regular paycheck. You should also try to save enough now to cover emergencies or unforeseen opportunities. That means having enough money in the bank, for example, to pay the deductible on your car insurance in case of an accident or to get home on emergency leave. Finally, life insurance is money that, in the event of your death, helps your family or beneficiaries get back on their feet.

### SERVICEMEMBERS' GROUP LIFE INSURANCE (SGLI)

7-65. Soldiers are involved in a dangerous profession in a dangerous world. As in civilian life, soldiers often purchase life insurance to protect their families in the case of the soldier's death. Since World War I the government has provided insurance of some type to all members of the Armed Forces. The origins of SGLI date back to the Vietnam War. As the Armed Forces began to suffer significant casualties, the private life insurance companies were unwilling to underwrite the coverage for members of the service. This created the need for a government sponsored life insurance program to cover soldiers placed in harms way. Servicemens' Group Life Insurance (SGLI) was instituted in 1965 to meet this need. The name changed in 1997 in recognition of the increasing numbers of women who serve in the Armed Forces.

7-66. SGLI initially covered only active duty personnel, but it has expanded over the years to cover certain reserve component soldiers. The maximum amount of protection has increased significantly since the program started. Originally, the coverage was limited to $10,000, but it has gradually increased over the years through legislation to its current maximum coverage level of $250,000. All eligible soldiers are automatically covered by SGLI for the maximum amount unless they decline or reduce the coverage in writing. The very low cost of SGLI makes it a wise choice while on active duty or in the reserve component.

7-67. The coverage expires 120 days after separation from the Army. Soldiers may continue the coverage for two reasons. First, if, upon separation, a soldier is not able to work due to disability, a disability extension of up to one year of free coverage is available. Second, any soldier can convert their SGLI coverage to either Veterans' Group Life Insurance (VGLI) or to a commercial life insurance policy. Both the disability extension and the VGLI conversion options require an application to the Office of Servicemembers' Group Life Insurance (OSGLI). Find more information on the VA Insurance website at www.insurance.va.gov.

7-68. Family coverage, which took effect on 1 November 2001, provides automatic coverage of $100,000 (or the SGLI coverage level of the soldier, whichever is less) on SGLI-insured soldiers' spouses. As with the basic SGLI, soldiers may in writing decline or reduce spousal coverage. Dependent children are also automatically insured, at no cost to the soldier, for $10,000 per child.

7-69. If you wish to increase your total life insurance coverage to more than that provided by SGLI, commercial life insurance in various forms is available. Some insurance products cover you for a specified period or term and are usually the least expensive initially. Permanent insurance (for example, Whole Life) is designed to last a lifetime and may provide a cash value after a few years but is generally the more expensive option at the time of purchase. There are a number of variations of each as well. But look before you leap—make sure you really need it, can afford it, and understand what you're paying for! For example, any insurance you purchase should have no restrictions as to occupation, aviation status, or military status (active or reserve) in peacetime or war. Read the fine print and ask questions.

7-70. As you progress in your career or even after you leave the Army, you should reevaluate both the amount and type of insurance you carry. Events such as the birth of children or buying a house may change the amount of insurance with which you want to protect your beneficiaries. It depends on what your beneficiary will need. For example, let's say a soldier wants her spouse to be able to pay off the house and still have money available to pay for four years of college for their three children. They would add the balance of the home loan to the expected cost of the tuition, then subtract any amount the government pays in the event of the soldier's death (so they don't pay for more insurance than they need). A single soldier paying child support or a soldier who designates his parents as the beneficiaries each would similarly calculate how much money would be needed in the event of the soldiers' death and insure for the amount they desire.

## RETIREMENT BENEFITS

7-71. Soldiers who complete at least 20 years of military service can receive outstanding retirement benefits, including retired pay. Military retired pay has a long history that is often misunderstood. It is not a pension. Pensions are primarily the result of financial need. Military retired pay is not based on financial need, but is regarded as delayed compensation for completing 20 or more years of active military service. The authority for nondisability retired pay, commonly known as "length-of-service" retired pay, is contained in Title 10 of the US Code.

7-72.    The military retirement system has four basic purposes:

- To provide the people of this nation a choice of career service in the armed forces that is competitive with reasonably available alternatives.

- To provide promotion opportunities for young and able-bodied members.

- To provide some measure of economic security to retired members.

- To provide a backup pool of experienced personnel in case of national emergency.

7-73.    If you decide to make the Army a career, you will retire at a relatively young age so you will probably begin another career. In fact, the leadership abilities and experience gained in the Army often make former soldiers highly valued employees. Even former soldiers who start their own businesses have a unique edge—they are confident, smart, and have outstanding initiative.

### Active Component Retirement

7-74.    For soldiers who retire from active duty, your retirement system is determined by your DIEMS, or date-initially-entered-military-service. Soldiers with DIEMS before 8 September 1980, receive a percentage of their final basic pay, calculated by multiplying 2.5% by the number of years of service. Those with DIEMS on or after 8 September 1980, receive a percentage of the average of their highest 36 months of basic pay, referred to as the high-three formula. Soldiers with DIEMS after 31 July 1986 may choose between the high-three formula and the Military Retirement Reform Act of 1986 (commonly called REDUX) formula.

7-75.    Under the high-three formula, monthly retirement pay is the average of the highest 36 months of basic pay, multiplied by 2.5 percent per year of service, up to a maximum of 75%. For example, a soldier who serves 24 years would receive monthly retirement pay of 60% of the average of his highest 36 months of basic pay.

7-76.    Soldiers who choose the REDUX option receive a $30,000 career-status bonus (CSB) during their 15th year of service and agree to serve five more years. Retired pay then equals the number of years of creditable service multiplied by 2.5 percent, minus 1 percent for each year of service under 30, multiplied by the average of the soldier's highest 36 months of basic pay. If you stay in for 30 years, the retirement pay will be the same as the high-three formula. The $30,000 CSB is taxable. At age 62, retired pay is recomputed under the high-three formula but will not be retroactive. Under REDUX, the longer one stays on active duty, the closer the percentage multiplier is to what it would have been under the high-three formula, up to the 30-year point at which the percentage multipliers are equal. Look for more details on active component retirement on the Army G1 website at www.armyg1.army.mil.

7-77.    In addition to retirement pay, soldiers may also participate in the TriCare for Retirees health care plan and the Delta Dental for Retirees plan. For low premium rates, Army retirees can continue to receive the same level of care they and their families enjoyed while on active duty. See Section VIII for more on these programs.

### Reserve Component Retirement

7-78.   Reserve component soldiers may also retire after 20 years of service. Reserve soldiers earn "retirement points" that are used to calculate the amount of retired pay in the following ways:

- Inactive duty for training (IDT) points earned as a troop program unit (TPU) member or as an IRR/IMA soldier attached to a TPU.
- Active duty (AD).
- Active duty for training (ADT).
- Annual training (AT).
- Active duty for special work (ADSW).
- Correspondence course points.
- Funeral honors duty.
- Points-only (non-paid) status (reinforcement training unit soldiers).

7-79.   As an RC soldier, you must earn at least 50 retirement points in a year for that year to count toward retirement. You may request retirement after you have 20 of these "good" years toward retirement. You will be eligible for a number of benefits but a monthly retirement check won't be one of them until you turn age 60. At that time you will receive retirement pay based on the highest rank you held, the number of qualifying years of service, the pay scale in effect at age 60, and the number of retirement points you earned. More detailed information is available on the Army Reserve Personnel Command website at www.2xcitizen.usar.army.mil.

7-80.   Section 3991, Title 10 United States Code provides that enlisted retirees may receive an additional 10% in retired pay (not to exceed 75% of active duty basic pay) if they are recipients of the Medal of Honor, Distinguished Service Cross, or the Navy Cross. In the case of retired Medal of Honor (MOH) recipients, this is in addition to the special pension of $1000 per month paid to all MOH recipients.

### RETIREMENT PLANNING

7-81.   Whether you stay in the Army or not, you should think now about that inevitable day in the future when you are out of the workforce. If you stay in the Army long enough to retire, that is part of the answer. Social Security payments won't start until you are about age 67. But even then, these together may not be enough to live on. Either way you should consider a strategy that will provide an income.

7-82.   Your installation's Consumer Affairs and Financial Assistance Program (CAFAP) counselor or your unit's CFNCO can describe some of the tools available to accomplish this. Some of those tools are traditional individual retirement accounts (IRA), Roth IRAs, 401(k), savings incentive match plan for employees (SIMPLE) IRAs, annuities, US savings bonds, Thrift Savings Plan (TSP), stocks, bonds, and mutual funds. The CAFAP counselor and your unit's CFNCO are not professional investment advisors, but they are able to give generic information on investing. They are not able to advise you on a particular investment or course of action. Those decisions are yours to make. Learn as much as you can and if you want professional investment advice, seek it from licensed professionals.

7-83. An investment program is not necessarily a luxury or even expensive. The key to investing is to start early and then stick with it. For example, let's assume you can afford to invest $25 per month and you invest in a long term tool like an IRA. Let's further assume that IRA averages a 10% rate of return per year. If you were to start this at the age of 20, by the time you were 65 you would have $227,000. Different investments have historically provided different returns so do a little homework before choosing one.

7-84. There is risk involved. Just because a particular mutual fund, for example, had a high rate of return for the last ten years does not mean it will for the next ten. Less risky investments may not keep up with inflation. Professional investment advisors can help if you need more details. But it's your future, your money, and your decision.

### Thrift Savings Plan (TSP)

7-85. The Thrift Savings Plan (TSP) is a retirement savings and investment plan created by Congress in 1986. Participation in the TSP is optional and is offered as a supplement to the traditional military pension benefit plan. TSP offers the same savings and tax advantages that 401(k) plans provide employees of private sector companies.

7-86. Some of the benefits of contributing to the TSP are the following:

- Immediate tax savings that reduce your taxable income by the amount contributed to the plan.

- Easy to start retirement savings plan for all members of the Army regardless of number of years of service.

- Ability to transfer or rollover IRAs, 401(k), or other eligible employer plans into TSP.

7-87. All soldiers, both active and reserve component while in a paid status may contribute to the TSP. An initial opportunity occurs within the first 60 days of becoming a member of the Army. After the initial opportunity ends, you may elect to start or change contribution amounts during designated TSP "open seasons." Also, members of the ready reserve can change or start their contributions when changes in military status occur such as transferring from the IRR to active duty, into a troop program unit (TPU), or becoming an individual mobilization augmentee (IMA).

7-88. The TSP is a defined contribution plan governed by Internal Revenue Service (IRS) codes that prohibit withdrawals of TSP money while still in the Army. The only exception to this rule is when certain types of financial hardships occur in a soldier's life or after a soldier reaches the age of 59½. A soldier may borrow money from his TSP account after obtaining a balance of a $1,000. Loans must be paid back with interest by allotment. Both the principal and interest are returned to the soldier's account.

7-89. After leaving the Army you have several options for withdrawing money from your TSP account. You can leave your balance in the TSP where it will continue to grow. You might decide to receive a single payment or transfer all or part of the account to other eligible employer plans or traditional IRAs. You might also decide to receive monthly payments in the amount you request or by the IRS life expectancy tables. In any case, the IRS requires that withdrawals from the account must start no later than age 70½.

7-90. Your personnel office and Army Community Service (ACS) representative can provide basic information regarding this program. However, soldiers should read the *Summary of the Thrift Savings Plan for the Uniformed Services* before deciding whether or not to enroll. The TSP also provides booklets on specific program features including the investment funds and loan and withdrawal programs. These booklets, along with informational fact sheets, can be viewed and downloaded on the TSP website at www.tsp.gov. The TSP website also has forms, calculators, current information on changes to the program, updates on rates of return, and access to options in your TSP account.

## Survivor Benefit Plan (SBP)

7-91. Congress established the Survivor Benefit Plan (SBP) to provide a monthly income to survivors of retired soldiers when retirement pay stops. The plan also protects survivors of soldiers on ac tive duty who die in the line of duty. Soldiers on active duty pay nothing for this benefit. The benefit is paid to the beneficiary of a soldier who dies in line-of-duty (LOD) and is not yet retirement eligible (has not accrued 20 years of service) on the date of death. The beneficiariy receives 55 percent of the retirement pay the soldier would receive if retired with a total disability rating on the date of death. This means that if you died while on active duty and in the line of duty, your spouse will receive a monthly check of 41.25% (55% X 75%) of your pay at the time of your death. But Dependency and Indemnity Compensation (DIC) payable by the Department of Veterans Affairs (VA), reduces a spouse's SBP annuity dollar-per-dollar.

7-92. Retirees pay for their survivor benefits in SBP. The cost varies with the amount the retiree elects to provide the spouse. The retiree may elect to provide up to 55% of his retired pay to his spouse. For those about to retire, this is an important decision because without SBP, the surviving spouse of a retiree no longer receives the monthly retirement check. Find out more at the website of the Army G1, Retirement Services Directorate.

## SECTION V – EDUCATION

7-93.   The Army Continuing Education System (ACES) through its many programs promotes lifelong learning opportunities and sharpens the competitive edge of the Army. ACES is committed to excellence in service, innovation, and deployability. For more information about Army education see Appendix B or the ACES website, www.armyeducation.army.mil.

## TUITION ASSISTANCE PROGRAM

7-94.   The Tuition Assistance (TA) Program provides financial assistance for voluntary off-duty education programs in support of a soldier's professional and personal self-development goals. All soldiers (officers, warrant officers, enlisted) on active duty (including RC soldiers on active duty pursuant to Title 10 or Title 32, USC) may participate in the TA program. Before obtaining TA, soldiers must visit an education counselor to declare an educational goal and create an educational plan. The counselor will help explain TA procedures, requirement for TA reimbursements, and, if necessary, officer active duty service obligation (ADSO). Find out more at your installation education center or in AR 621-5, *Army Continuing Education System.*

### MONTGOMERY GI BILL

7-95.   In some cases TA won't cover all the approved charges for a course. Soldiers eligible for MGIB can use MGIB as Top-Up to Tuition Assistance to cover the remaining charges. Top-Up pays the remaining TA costs up to the maximum of the MGIB rate payable to eligible individuals who have been discharged from active duty. Top-Up covers only the tuition and fees approved for TA.

7-96.   Soldiers eligible for the Montgomery GI Bill-Active Duty (MGIB-AD), can use these benefits while in service after two continuous years of active duty. However, using "regular" MGIB in service may not be to every individual's advantage. In most cases the amount eligible individuals can receive after discharge from active duty will be higher, even though the charge to their MGIB entitlement will be at the same rate. Using MGIB as Top-Up to Tuition Assistance may be more advantageous than using regular MGIB while in service. Soldiers should consult with an education counselor or with VA to make the best use of their MGIB benefits.

7-97.   Regular MGIB pays tuition and approved fees for approved courses. This payment can't exceed the amount that would be payable to individuals discharged from service, so it may not cover full tuition and fees for very expensive courses.

## EARMYU

7-98.   In July 2000, the Army announced a new education recruiting initiative entitled Army University Access Online (AUAO), now referred to as eArmyU. This program is entirely online, offering soldiers a streamlined portal approach to a wide variety of postsecondary degrees and technical certificates. All courses allow soldiers to study on their own schedule. Highly motivated soldiers can complete degree and certification requirements regardless of work schedules, family responsibilities, and deployments. eArmyU enables enlisted soldiers to complete degree requirements "anytime, anyplace they can take their laptop." More information on eArmyU can be found at www.eArmyU.com.

7-99.   EArmyU provides soldiers 100 % tuition assistance (TA), books, fees for online courses, and, at certain installations, a technology package that may include a laptop computer and other equipment. After completing 12 semester hours of continuous enrollment, the technology package becomes the property of the soldier. Added to the existing education programs and services available, this online program helps to ensure all soldiers have the opportunity to fulfill their personal and professional educational goals while also building the critical thinking and decision-making skills required to fully transform the Army. To be eligible for participation in the eArmyU program, soldiers must be regular active duty or active guard and reserve (AGR) enlisted soldiers with at least three years remaining on their enlistment. Soldiers may extend or reenlist to meet this requirement.

## ARMY/AMERICAN COUNCIL ON EDUCATION REGISTRY TRANSCRIPT SYSTEM (AARTS)

7-100.   The Army can provide official transcripts for eligible soldiers upon request by combining a soldier's military education and job experience with descriptions and college credit recommendations developed by the American Council on Education (ACE). In addition to name and SSN, the transcript contains the following information:

- Current or highest enlisted rank.
- Military status (active or inactive).
- Additional skill identifiers (ASI) and skill qualification identifiers (SQI).
- Formal military courses.
- Military occupational specialties (MOS) held.
- Standardized test scores.
- Descriptions and credit recommendations developed by ACE.
- The website for AARTS is aarts.army.mil.

## SECTION VI – RELOCATION ASSISTANCE

7-101.   The Army's Relocation Assistance Program (RAP), available through ACS, helps you settle into your new home as quickly and easily as possible. Many programs and services are available. One of the first services offered was the lending closet program, which provided for the temporary loan of basic household equipment for families to use until their own furnishings arrived. Other services include relocation guidance or counseling, education, and outreach services.

## THE LENDING CLOSET

7-102. The lending closet program provides basic items you need upon arrival or before departure. Dishes, pots, pans, silverware, toasters, irons, and ironing boards are just a few of the items available on loan at most installations. This important service helps you and your family adjust more quickly by providing basic household needs.

7-103. The lending closet program provides basic housekeeping items on temporary loan for a varied period of time (usually thirty to sixty days) to all incoming personnel. An extension may be available if the household shipment has not arrived within the designated time period. For outgoing families, items may be borrowed after the household shipment has been picked up. However, all items need to be returned prior to departure from the installation. The following list is a sample of the items that may be available through the lending closet:

- Coffee makers.
- Highchairs.
- Irons and ironing boards.
- Miscellaneous kitchen items.
- Plates.
- Playpens.
- Pots and pans.
- Strollers.
- Utensils.

## GUIDANCE COUNSELING

7-104. Guidance counseling (through RAP) helps to ensure that soldiers and families are prepared to cope with stressors and problems they may encounter throughout all of their permanent change of station (PCS) moves. RAP tries to accomplish this by providing you with the right information at the right time, counseling people on the emotional impact of moves, and educating the public to manage and plan for military relocation.

## SPONSOR TRAINING

7-105. The US Army established the Total Army Sponsorship Program to assist soldiers, civilian employees, and family members during the relocation process. Program participants are provided with accurate and timely information and other support needed to minimize problems associated with relocating to a new duty station. The program is available to the active Army, the Army National Guard, the United States Army

Reserve, and to civilian employees whose assignment to a position within the Department of the Army requires a PCS.

## FINANCIAL ASSISTANCE

7-106. You can never be too financially ready for your move. The government ships your household goods and gives you travel funds and even a dislocation allowance, but it may not be enough to cover all your expenses. While advance pay may seem like a great solution, remember that you must pay back this advance within 12 months, and the temporary hardship of relocating may impact your family for a long time. Moving expenses you can expect include rent, advance rent, deposits, vehicle licenses and registration, car rental, transportation from the car shipping port (stateside), temporary lodging, and meals. Plan ahead!

7-107. You can find additional information at your local ACS office, the Army Community Services website at www.armycommunityservice.org, or the website of your installation or the one you are moving to. You can also find detailed information about your next duty station through the Standard Installation Topic Exchange Service (SITES) website at www.dmdc.osd.mil/sites.

## TRANSPORTATION

7-108. The Army, through your local transportation office, arranges to move your household goods and other property when you transfer to a new duty station or upon leaving the service. In some situations, you may also choose to move your property yourself in a do-it-yourself (DITY) move. But you must be proactive and plan your move with your local transportation office in a timely manner. If not, you could be paying out-of-pocket for unforeseen costs or shipment problems.

7-109. Find detailed information about transportation requirements in the Joint Federal Travel Regulations (JFTR) on the Military Traffic Management Command website at mtmc.army.mil. There you will find information dealing with any situation that you may have regarding transportation. However, the regulation is very detailed and may require you to contact your local transportation office for clarification.

7-110. Your installation transportation office (ITO) is very important to you and your family after receiving orders to move. The ITO coordinates transportation, reimbursement, or a payment in lieu of transportation. This affects members and families located in the Continental United States (CONUS) and Outside the Continental United States (OCONUS). But your active and early involvement with the assistance from your ITO is necessary to have a smooth move. Don't arrange any travel or shipment of your property before you have proper authorization—orders—or it could be costly for you.

## SECTION VII – LEGAL ISSUES

7-111. You read in Chapter 3 about the military justice system and the Uniform Code of Military Justice. In this section you'll read about legal services the Army provides to soldiers. Army Legal Assistance providers worldwide advise soldiers, family members, and other eligible clients on their legal affairs in a timely and professional manner by delivering preventive law information and resolving personal legal problems.

## READINESS

7-112. Active component soldiers ordered to deploy, or reserve and National Guard soldiers being mobilized know that the time to put personal and legal affairs in order may be relatively short. Most soldiers realize that problems may arise when you are suddenly separated from your family and, for reserve component members, your business and civilian job. Advance planning will help avoid many legal problems upon mobilization or deployment. In addition, taking care of personal legal affairs now will give you and your family peace of mind.

7-113. Begin planning by anticipating what would happen if you were required to be apart from your family at a distant location for an indefinite period of time, unable to remain in continuous communications with them. Anticipate and prevent legal problems that might arise by putting your personal, property, and financial affairs in order now so that there will be no confusion or uncertainty later. Issues such as wills, medical planning, living wills, general and special powers of attorney; property and financial affairs management; and the Soldiers' and Sailors' Civil Relief Act are very complex and difficult to deal with while deployed. Some things to do before deploying are the following:

- Check your service record to make sure the information is correct.
- Make the correct beneficiary is on your SGLI election and certificate.
- Decide whether you and your spouse need to have wills drawn up.
- Decide whether or not you want a "living will," advance medical directive, or durable medical power of attorney. These documents can authorize a person to make decisions regarding your medical care in the event you cannot make those decisions yourself.
- Decide whether or not you need to give someone a general or special power of attorney. This is a legal designation for a person to execute certain duties on your behalf while you are absent.
- Decide if you need to give someone a medical power of attorney to take action in the event your minor children (if you have any) have a medical emergency.
- Before deployment, make sure that your family members know the location of important documents such as wills, marriage and birth certificates, and insurance policies.

- Verify DEERS enrollment so family members can receive needed medical care in your absence by calling 1-800-538-9552.

- Ensure your spouse knows the location of the nearest military legal assistance office for help with any legal problems in your absence.

Soldiers of the 115th Military Police Company, Rhode Island Army National Guard, prepare to enter a building in Fallujah, Iraq, while mobilized for Operation Iraqi Freedom.

## ASSISTANCE

7-114. Your installation legal assistance center can provide a great number of services that would cost hundreds, even thousands of dollars using civilian legal offices. Army legal assistance centers provide answers and advice to even the most complex problems. Such legal assistance usually does not include in-court representation.

7-115. Some of the issues that your installation's legal assistance center may be able to help with are as follows:

- Soldiers/Sailors Civil Relief Act (SSCRA).

- Marriage/divorce issues.

- Child custody/visitation.

- Adoption or other family (as expertise is available).

- Wills.

- Advice for designating SGLI beneficiaries.

- Landlord-tenant issues.
- Consumer affairs (mortgages, warranties, etc.).
- Bankruptcy.
- Garnishment/indebtedness.
- Reemployment issues under the Uniformed Services Employment and Reemployment Act (USERRA) of 1994.
- Notarization.
- Name change (as expertise is available).
- Line of duty investigations.
- Reports of survey.
- Evaluation report disputes, including relief for cause.
- Bars to reenlistment (as available).
- Inspector General investigations.
- Hardship discharge.
- Taxes.

7-116. For more information on what your legal assistance center can do for you, contact your installation center or see the Army's legal assistance website at www.jagcnet.army.mil/legal. You can also refer to AR 27-3, *The Army Legal Assistance Program.*

## TRIAL DEFENSE

7-117. Trial Defense Services (TDS) are a separate part of the Judge Advocate General Corps (Army lawyers). They are independent of local commands and local staff judge advocate offices so they are not exposed to any possible influence on their services. The TDS provide soldiers facing court martial, Article 15, or civilian criminal charges with advice and representation in courts martial. TDS also helps soldiers facing involuntary separation proceedings under Chapters 5-13, 15 and 18 of AR 635-200, *Enlisted Personnel.* TDS may also help officers under elimination actions or who are resigning in lieu of elimination (AR 600-8-24, *Officer Transfers and Discharges*).

## SECTION VIII – AFTER THE ARMY

7-118. Some day you will leave the Army. That day may be relatively soon, at the end of your current commitment, or it may be at the completion of a long and successful career. This section describes your discharge and some of the benefits all veterans may receive as recognition of their service.

## YOUR DISCHARGE

7-119. The character of your discharge, honorable, general, other than honorable, bad conduct, or dishonorable has an affect on opportunities after your service. Don't worry—nearly every soldier who leaves the Army does so with an honorable discharge. In fact, unless a soldier has been convicted in a court martial or administratively discharged for some misconduct or a few other limited reasons, that soldier will receive an honorable discharge.

7-120. Whether you serve for 180 days or 35 years, you are a veteran. Veterans have earned every benefit the Nation and the states offer. Take advantage of them. More information is available in DA PAM 350-526, *Once A Veteran*, or on the Department of Veterans Affairs website at www.va.gov.

> *There is something different in the way [a veteran] carries himself, a sparkle to his eye, a spring to his step...which another soldier will instantly recognize.*
>
> SGT Herbert E. Smith

7-121. In the following tables you will find the eligibility of veterans with various types of discharges for various benefits from the Army or the federal government. Many states also offer benefits to veterans or retirees who reside within their state. You can find those at state veterans' department websites.

7-122. The eligibility of benefits shown here are not the sole determining factors, but only list the various types of discharge. Many states also provide various benefits influenced by the type of discharge, but look for that information on state benefits from state agencies.The legend for these tables is as follows:

- HON—Honorable Discharge
- GD—General Discharge
- OTH—Other Than Honorable Discharge
- BCD—Bad Conduct Discharge
- DD—Dishonorable Discharge
- E—Eligible.
- NE—Not Eligible.
- TBD—To be determined by Administrating Agency.
- DV—Disabled Veteran. Eligibility for these benefits depend upon specific disabilities of the veteran.
- Notes—(#)—following Table 7-6

7-123. Table 7-3 shows some of the administrative effects of the types of different discharges.

### Table 7-3. Administrative Effect of Discharge

| Army Administration | HON | GD (4) | OTH (5) | BCD | DD (6) |
|---|---|---|---|---|---|
| Payment for Accrued Leave. | E | E | NE | NE | NE |
| Death Gratuity (6 months pay). | E | E | E | NE | NE |
| Wearing of Military Uniform. | E | E | NE | NE | NE |
| Admission to Soldiers' Home (1) | E | E | NE | NE | NE |
| Burial in National Cemeteries | E | E | NE | NE | NE |
| Burial in Post Cemeteries (2) | E | E | NE | NE | NE |
| Army Board for Correction of Military Records | E | E | E | E | E |
| Army Discharge Review Board | E | E | E | NE (9) | NE |
| Transportation to Home (3) | E | E | E | E | E |
| Transportation of Dependents & Household Goods to Home | E | E | TBD (8) | TBD (8) | TBD (8) |

7-124. Table 7-4 shows some of the transitional benefits available to soldiers based on the character of their discharge.

### Table 7-4. Transitional Benefits and Discharge

| Transitional Benefits & Services (14) | HON | GD (4) | OTH (5) | BCD | DD (6) |
|---|---|---|---|---|---|
| Pre-separation Counseling | E | E | E | E | E |
| Employment Assistance | E | E | E | E | NE |
| Health Benefits | E | E | NE | NE | NE |
| Commissary & Exchange Privileges | E | E | NE | NE | NE |
| Military Family Housing | E | E | NE | NE | NE |
| Overseas Relocation Assistance | E | E | NE | NE | NE |
| Excess Leave or Permissive TDY | E | E | NE | NE | NE |
| Preference for USAR/ARNG | E | E | NE | NE | NE |
| Montgomery GI Bill (additional opportunity) | E | NE | NE | NE | NE |

7-125. Table 7-5 shows the effect the character of a soldier's discharge has on the veteran's benefits he might receive.

### Table 7-5. Veteran's Benefits and Discharge

| Department of Veterans Affairs (10) | HON | GD (4) | OTH (5) | BCD | DD (6) |
|---|---|---|---|---|---|
| Dependency and Indemnity Compensation | E | E | E | E | NE |
| Pension for Non-Service Connected Disability or Death | E | E | TBD | TBD | NE |
| Medal of Honor Roll Pension | E | E | TBD | TBD | NE |
| Veterans' Group Life Insurance (VGLI) | E | E | TBD (11) | TBD (11) | TBD (11) |
| Service-Disabled Veterans Insuarnce (S-DVI) | E | E | TBD | TBD | NE |
| Veterans' Mortgage Life Insurance (VMLI ) (DV) | E | E | TBD | TBD | NE |
| Vocational Rehabilitation (DV) | E | E | TBD | TBD | NE |
| Montgomery GI Bill | E | NE | NE | NE | NE |
| Post-Vietnam Veterans' Educational Assistance Program (VEAP) | E | E | TBD (15) | TBD (15) | NE |
| Dependents' Eduactional Assistance | E | E | TBD (15) | TBD (15) | NE |
| Survivors & Dependents Educational Assistance | E | E | E | E | NE |
| Home & other Loans | E | E | TBD | TBD | NE |
| Hospitalization & Home Care | E | E | TBD | TBD | NE |
| Medical & Dental Services | E | E | TBD | TBD | NE |
| Prosthetic Appliances (DV) | E | E | TBD | TBD | NE |
| Guide Dogs & Equipment for Blindness (DV) | E | E | TBD | TBD | NE |
| Special Housing (DV) | E | E | TBD | TBD | NE |
| Automobiles (DV) | E | E | TBD | TBD | NE |
| Funeral & Burial Expenses | E | E | TBD | TBD | NE |
| Burial Flag | E | E | TBD | TBD | NE |
| Burial in National Cemeteries | E | E | TBD | TBD | NE |
| Headstone Marker | E | E | TBD | TBD | NE |

7-126. Table 7-6 shows the effects different types of discharge have on other Federal benefits.

**Table 7-6. Other Federal Benefits and Discharge**

| Administration by Other Federal Agencies | HON | GD (4) | OTH (5) | BCD | DD (6) |
|---|---|---|---|---|---|
| Preference for Farm Loan (Dept. of Agriculture, DAg) | E | E | E | E | NE |
| Preference for Farm & other Rural Housing Loans (DAg) | E | E | E | E | NE |
| Civil Service Preference (13) (Office of Personnel Management) | E | E | NE | NE | NE |
| Civil Service Retirement Credit | E | NE | NE | NE | NE |
| Reemployment Rights (Dept. of Labor, DOL) | E | E | NE | NE | NE |
| Job Counseling & Employment Placement (DOL) | E | E | E | E | NE |
| Unemployment Compensation (DOL) | E | E | NE | NE | NE |
| Naturalization Benefits (Dept. of Justice, Immigration & Naturalization Service) | E | E | NE | NE | NE |
| Old Age, Survivors & Disability Insurance (Social Security Administration) | E | E | TBD | TBD | NE (12) |
| Job Preference, Public Works Projects (13) (Dept. of Commerce) | E | E | TBD | TBD | NE |

NOTES:

1. The veterans must have served "honestly and faithfully" for 20 years or been disabled and excludes convicted felons, deserters, mutineers, or habitual drunkards unless rehabilitated or soldier may become ineligible if that person following discharge is convicted of a felony, or is not free from drugs, alcohol, or psychiatric problems.

2. Only if an immediate relative is buried in the cemetery.

3. Only if no confinement is involved, or confinement is involved, people or release is from a US military confinement facility or a confinement facility located outside the US.

4. This discharge category includes the discharge of an officer under honorable conditions but under circumstances involving serious misconduct. See AR 600-8-24.

5. An officer who resigns for the good of the service (usually to avoid court-martial charges) will be ineligible for benefits administered by the Department of Veterans Affairs (DVA).

6. Including Commissioned and Warrant Officers who have been convicted and sentenced to dismissal as a result of General Court-Martial. See AR 600-8-24, Chapter 5.

7. Additional references include DA PAM 360-526, "Once a Veteran: Rights, Benefits and Obligations," and VA Fact Sheet IS-1, "Federal Benefits for Veterans and Dependents"

8. Determined by the Secretary of the Army on a case-by-case basis.

9. Only if a Bad Conduct Discharge was a result of conviction by a General Court-Martial.

10. Benefits from the Department of Veterans Affairs are not payable to a person discharged for the following reasons:

> (a) Conscientious objection and refusal to perform military duty, wear the uniform, or comply with lawful orders of competent military authority.
> (b) Sentence of a General Court-Martial.
> (c) Resignation by an officer for the good of the service.
> (d) Desertion.
> (e) Alien during a period of hostilities.

> A discharge for the following reasons is considered under dishonorable conditions and thereby bar veterans' benefits:
> (f) Acceptance of an Other than Honorable Discharge to avoid Court-Martial.
> (g) Mutiny or spying.
> (h) Felony offense involving moral turpitude.
> (i) Willful and persistent misconduct.
> (j) Homosexual acts involving aggravating circumstances or other.

> A discharge under dishonorable conditions from one period of service does not bar payment if there is another period of eligible service honorable in character.

11. Any person guilty of mutiny, spying, or desertion, or who, because of conscientious objection, refuses to perform service in the Armed Forces or refuses to wear the uniform shall forfeit all rights to Servicemembers' Group Life Insurance.

12. Applies to Post-1957 service only: Post-1957 service qualifies for Social Security benefits regardless of type of discharge. Pre-1957 service under conditions other than dishonorable qualifies a soldier for a military wage credit for Social Security purposes.

13. Disabled and Veteran-era veterans only: Post-Vietnam-era Veterans are those who first entered on active duty as or first became members of the Armed Forces after May 7, 1975. To be eligible, they must have served for a period of more than 180 day active duty and have other than a dishonorable discharge. The 180-day service requirement does not apply to the following:

> (a) Veterans separated from active duty because of a service-connected disability, or
> (b) Reserve and guard members who served on active duty during a period of war (such as the Persian Gulf War) or in a military operation for which a campaign or expeditionary medal is authorized.

14. Transitional benefits and services are available only to soldiers separated involuntarily, under other than adverse conditions.

15. To be determined by the Department of Veterans Affairs on a case-by-case basis.

## VETERAN'S BENEFITS

7-127. Some of the more commonly known and used benefits include the veteran's home loan guaranty, civil service and government contracting preferences, and education benefits. You must apply for your education benefits within 10 years after leaving the service. The specifics change from time to time, but you can see the current benefits in the Department of Veterans Affairs *Veteran's Benefits Handbook*, available on the Department of Veterans Affairs website. Other government websites describing benefits to veterans are the Federal Office of Personnel Management website at www.opm.gov/veterans, or the Small Business Administration at www.sba.gov.

7-128. The Department of Veterans Affairs (DVA) has a great health care system for veterans who have service-connected conditions or disabilities. When you decide to leave the service, you will go through a process before and after discharge to determine if you have any service-connected disabilities or conditions. You will have physical examinations and a board will review your service medical file and exam results to make the determination. It is in your best interest to ensure your service medical file is complete, including any civilian treatment you may have had.

7-129. The disability "rating" is expressed as a percentage. Veterans who have a disability percentage receive a payment from the Department of Veterans' Affairs that varies with the degree of disability. Retirees give up the portion of their retirement check that equals the disability payment, except for those retirees whose disability resulted from wounds or injuries in combat or training for combat. Veterans who are not retired but receive a DVA disability payment do not give up any other income to do so. Disability payments are not taxable income. Soldiers may enroll in the DVA health care system if they have a service-connected disability. Retirees also have continued access to medical and dental treatment through TRICARE.

7-130. Soldiers who receive a DVA disability "rating" are eligible for additional benefits, including vocational rehabilitation and Service-Disabled Veterans Insurance (SDVI). Soldiers who receive a DVA rating that entitles them to specially adapted housing are eligible for Veterans' Mortgage Life Insurance. Application for these insurances is made to DVA. More information can be obtained at www.insurance.va.gov. Many states also offer benefits to disabled veterans.

### TRICARE HEALTH CARE BENEFITS FOR RETIREES AND FAMILY MEMBERS

7-131. As a retiree and sponsor, you should understand that the way you and your dependents use TRICARE on active duty changes when you retire. An important first step is to keep DEERS information up-to-date to ensure eligibility isn't lost and make sure dependents get their ID cards renewed in a timely manner. Retirees remain eligible for TRICARE Prime, Standard and Extra and a few other TRICARE programs. Health benefits advisors are available at your local TRICARE Service Center (TSC) or military treatment facility (MFT) to help you decide which option is best for you. For additional information about TRICARE visit their website at www.tricare.osd.mil or your local TRICARE Service Center.

## TRICARE Prime

7-132. Retirees and their family members are encouraged, but not required, to enroll in TRICARE Prime. TRICARE Prime offers less out-of-pocket costs than any other TRICARE option. Retired soldiers pay an annual enrollment fee of $230 for an individual or $460 for a family, and minimal co-pays apply for care in the TRICARE network. Although Prime offers a "point-of-service" option for care received outside of the TRICARE Prime network, receiving care from a nonparticipating provider is not encouraged.

7-133. TRICARE Prime enrollees receive most of their care from military providers or from civilian providers who belong to the TRICARE Prime network. Enrollees are assigned a primary care manager (PCM) who manages their care and provides referrals for specialty care. All referrals for specialty care must be arranged by the PCM to avoid point-of-service charges.

> *Our soldiers deserve and expect quality health care, for themselves and their family members—in retirement, as well as during their time of active service.*
>
> General John M. Keane

## TRICARE Standard

7-134. TRICARE-eligible beneficiaries who elect not to enroll in TRICARE Prime may enroll in TRICARE Standard. Beneficiaries may see any TRICARE authorized provider they choose, and the government will share the cost with the beneficiaries after deductibles.

## TRICARE Extra

7-135. TRICARE-eligible beneficiaries who elect not to enroll in TRICARE Prime may enroll in TRICARE Extra. Beneficiaries may see any TRICARE authorized provider they choose, and the government will share the cost with the beneficiaries after deductibles. TRICARE Extra is a preferred provider option (PPO) in which beneficiaries choose a doctor, hospital, or other medical provider within the TRICARE provider network.

## TRICARE Overseas

7-136. Retirees and their families who live overseas can't enroll in TRICARE Prime, but they can use TRICARE Standard. TRICARE Prime enrollees have access to both military medical facilities and to networks of local civilian providers established by the commanders of military medical facilities. Wherever possible or available, most of their care will be provided by their primary care manager. Regional TSCs will provide TRICARE Prime beneficiaries with the necessary authorizations for specialty care when referred by their primary care manager.

7-137. Overseas TRICARE Prime enrollees won't need pre-authorization for urgent or emergency care when receiving care in CONUS. Overseas TRICARE Prime enrollees traveling in CONUS will have the same priority for available appointments at MTFs as TRICARE Prime enrollees who live near these facilities.

### TRICARE for Life and TRICARE Plus

7-138. TRICARE for Life (TFL) provides expanded medical coverage for Medicare-eligible retirees, including retired guard members and reservists; Medicare-eligible family members and widow/widowers; and certain former spouses if they were eligible for TRICARE before age 65.

7-139. Some MTFs will have the capacity to offer a primary care affiliation program called TRICARE Plus. Enrolled beneficiaries have priority access to care at MTFs; however, beneficiaries who choose to use TRICARE Extra, TRICARE Standard or TRICARE for Life may also continue to receive care in an MTF as capacity exists.

### TRICARE Retiree Dental Program

7-140. The TRICARE Retiree Dental Program (TRDP) is a unique, comprehensive dental benefits program available to Uniformed Services retirees and their family members. Retirees no longer receive routine dental treatment at military facilities. Under TRDP the retiree and family will continue to receive dental treatment through participating dentists.

7-141. The eligibility requirements for enrollment in the TRDP were set forth in the law that established the program. Eligibility must be verified before enrollment in the TRDP can be completed. Applicants may be required to submit additional information if it is needed by Delta to verify eligibility. To enroll an individual must be one of the following:

- A retired soldier entitled to retired pay, including RC retirees who will begin drawing retired pay at age 60.
- A current spouse of an enrolled retired soldier.
- An enrolled soldier's eligible child up to age 21 (or to age 23 for a full-time student, or older if he or she becomes disabled before losing eligibility)
- An un-remarried surviving spouse or eligible child of a deceased soldier who died on retired status.
- An un-remarried surviving spouse or eligible child of a deceased soldier who died on while active duty and whose family members are not or are no longer eligible for dental benefits under the active duty family member dental plan (or the TriCare Dental Program effective February 2000).
- A family member of a non-enrolled soldier who meets certain criteria.

7-142. Under most circumstances, the retiree must enroll in order for a spouse or other eligible family member to enroll. However, the spouse and/or eligible child of a non-enrolled member may join the TRDP with documented proof that the non-enrolled member is—

- Eligible to receive ongoing, comprehensive dental care from the Department of Veterans Affairs.
- Enrolled in a dental plan that is available to the member as a result of civilian employment and that dental plan is not available to his family members.
- Prevented from being able to obtain benefits under the Enhanced TRICARE Retiree Dental Program due to a current and enduring medical or dental condition.

7-143. Those who are not eligible for this program are—

- Former spouses of eligible members.
- Remarried surviving spouses of deceased members.
- Family members of non-enrolled retirees who do not meet one of the three special circumstances noted above.

7-144. As with TRICARE medical coverage, retirees or family members who visit a dentist who is not part of the TRDP system will also be responsible for paying the difference between the enhanced program allowed amount and the dentist's normal charge. For complete up-to-date information visit the TRDP website at www.ddpdelta.org.

## Appendix A

# Selected Combat Tasks

Every soldier, regardless of rank, branch or MOS must be proficient in certain individual combat tasks. This appendix provides 11 of these tasks. These tasks are vitally important for every soldier on the battlefield to know. You can find these and other individual tasks in *The Soldier's Manual of Common Tasks* or your MOS-specific soldier's manual.

For more information on common tasks, see STP 21-1-SMCT, *The Soldier's Manual of Common Tasks*.

A-1. Every soldier, regardless of rank, position, and MOS must be able to shoot, move, communicate, and survive in order to contribute to the team and survive in combat. This appendix includes selected combat tasks that support these basic soldier skills. Common tasks can, of course, also be found in the *Soldiers Manual of Common Tasks*. You should master these basic selected combat tasks as well as other task that your unit may deem necessary.

A-2. **SHOOT**. Shoot means more than simply squeezing off rounds. It means being able to place effective fire on the enemy with your individual weapon. It is going out in combat and doing what is required of you and with consistency.

A-3. **MOVE**. When in combat, you can expect to encounter times that you might have to maneuver in or outside the perimeter, in cover of darkness, and over, through and around obstacles. This also can include reacting to indirect fire or direct fire when mounted. Your unit's ability to move depends on your movement skills and those of your fellow soldiers. These actions require certain skills to ensure your safety and the safety of comrades (high crawl, low crawl and rush). Fire and move techniques. Moving with maneuver units.

A-4. **COMMUNICATE.** Provide information to those who need it. There are several means of communications; digital, radio, visual, wire, sound, and messenger. The information must be transmitted and received and understood. You must know how to communicate with your leaders and fellow soldiers. You must be able to tell:

- What you see.
- What you are doing.
- What you have done.
- What you are going to do.
- What you need.

A-5. **SURVIVE.** Action taken to stay alive in the field with limited resources. Survival requires knowledge of how to take care of yourself. While thinking of survival you can not rule out security. You must do everything possible for the security and protection of yourself and your unit. Here is a list of some basic things:

- Be awake and alert.
- Keep your weapon and equipment in good operating condition.
- Move around only when necessary.
- Use lights only when necessary.
- Look and listen for enemy activity in your sector.
- Use challenge and a password.
- Use obstacle to prevent direct access in and out of perimeter.
- Employ intrusion devices on the edge of perimeter and mark them.
- Ensure that fighting position provide cover and concealment while allowing maximum fields of fire. Improve position as time permits.

A-6. Listed on the following pages are selected combat tasks or actions that are necessary and applicable for all soldiers in order to survive in battlefield conditions. You can find the tasks, conditions, standards, performance steps and measures here and in STP 21-1-SMCT, *Soldier's Manual of Common Tasks.*

## SECTION I – SHOOT, MOVE, AND COMMUNICATE

## ENGAGE TARGETS WITH AN M16A1 OR M16A2 RIFLE

**For more information see FM 3-22.9, *M16A1 and M16A2 Rifle Marksmanship*.**

**Conditions:** Given an M16A1 or M16A2 rifle, magazines, ammunition, individual combat equipment, and stationary or moving targets (personnel or equipment) at engageable ranges.

**Standards:** Detected and determined range to targets. Fired the M16A1 or M16A2 rifle, engaged targets in assigned sector of fire. Applied correct marksmanship fundamentals and target engagement techniques so that each target was hit or suppressed. Hit 60 percent or more of the targets in assigned sector of fire.

### Performance Steps

1. Assume an appropriate firing position based on the situation. The firing position should protect you from enemy fire and observation, yet allow you to place effective fire on targets in your sector of fire.

a. Foxhole. Advantages: best when available. Disadvantages: no overhead cover.

b. Prone. Advantages: steady, easy to assume, low silhouette, and easily adapted to use of cover and support. Disadvantages: effectiveness can be limited by terrain and vegetation irregularities.

c. Prone supported. Advantages: steadier than prone, other advantages the same as prone. Disadvantages: same as prone.

d. Kneeling. Advantages: used when firing from behind something; used on ground that is level or gently sloping upward. Disadvantage: exposed to small-arms fire.

e. Kneeling supported. Advantages: steadier than kneeling; other advantages the same as kneeling. Disadvantages: exposed to small- arms fire.

f. Standing. Advantages: used in assault to surprise targets or when other positions are not appropriate. Disadvantages: exposed to small-arms fire.

2. Identify targets in your designated sector of fire.

3. Determine range to a target.

a. You can use your M16A1 or M16A2 rifle sights to estimate range to targets(s). Viewed through the front sight, a man-sized target appears:

(1) Twice the width as the front sight post at about 90 meters.

(2) The same width as the front sight post at about 175 meters.

(3) Half the width of the front sight post at about 350 meters.

4. Load and fire on targets using appropriate engagement techniques.

    a. Load the weapon.

    b. Use the appropriate aiming technique.

        (1) Engage a stationary target using reference points or sighting points.

        (2) Engage a target moving towards you as you would a stationary target.

        (3) Engage a target moving laterally, using the single lead technique, by placing the trailing edge of the front sight post at the center of the target. This method causes the lead to increase automatically as the range increases.

        (4) Engage multiple targets by first firing at the one presenting the greatest danger (usually the closest) and then rapidly proceeding to next target.

    c. Use the quick-fire technique when there is no time to properly aim. Use this technique on targets within 30 meters of your location. (This technique is most effective in urban terrain or heavy bush.)

        (1) Use the standing position.

        (2) Use the raised stockwell. Looking two or three inches above the sights, on a plane that is level with the barrel.

        (3) Look at the target, NOT at the sights.

    d. Fire on the targets until they are destroyed or until you receive an order to cease fire.

**Evaluation Preparation:**

SETUP: On a live-fire range, provide sufficient quantities of equipment and ammunition to support the number of soldiers tested. Have each soldier use his own rifle and magazine.

BRIEF SOLDIER: Tell soldier that he is to detect and engage targets in his sector and, when asked, state the range to the target.

**Performance Measures (1-4)**　　　　　　　　　　**GO**　　　**NO GO**

1. Assumed an appropriate firing position based on the situation.

                                      \_\_\_\_\_　　\_\_\_\_\_

2. Identified targets in your designated sector of fire.

                                        \_\_\_\_\_　　\_\_\_\_\_

**Performance Measures (cont'd)**　　　　　**GO**　　**NO GO**

3. Determined range to a target.　　　　　＿＿＿＿　＿＿＿＿

4. Loaded and fired on targets using appropriate engagement techniques. Hit 60 percent or more of the targets in your assigned sector.

＿＿＿＿　＿＿＿＿

**Evaluation Guidance:** Score the soldier GO if all performance measures are passed. Score the soldier NO-GO if any performance measure is failed. If the soldier scores NO-GO, show the soldier what was done wrong and how to do it correctly.

**References**

**Required**　　　　　　**Related**

　　　　　　　　　　　FM 3-21.75 (21-75)
　　　　　　　　　　　FM 3-22.9 (23-9)
　　　　　　　　　　　TM 9-1005-319-10

## MOVE OVER, THROUGH, OR AROUND OBSTACLES (EXCEPT MINEFIELDS)

**071-326-0503**

**Conditions:** Given individual weapon, load carrying equipment (LCE), one smoke grenade, wood or grass mats or chicken wire, a grappling hook, wrapping material, wire cutters (optional) and a buddy. During daylight or darkness, you are in a field location, moving over a route with natural and manmade crossings and obstacles (walls and barbed wire entanglements)

**Standards:** Approached within 100 meters of suspected enemy position over a specified route, negotiated each obstacle encountered within the time designated while retaining all over your equipment without becoming a casualty to a booby trap or early warning device.

**Performance Steps (1-6)**

1. Cover your advance using smoke when crossing an obstacle. (Task 071-325-4407)
2. Ensure your buddy is covering you, since obstacles are normally covered by either fire or observation.
3. Cross barbed wire obstacles.

> **WARNING**
>
> It is threat doctrine to attach tripwire-activated mines to barbed wire.

a. Check barbed wire for booby traps or early warning devices.

    (1) Look for booby traps or early warning devices attached to barbed wire.

    (2) Throw a grappling hook with a length of rope attached over the barbed wire.

    (3) Pull the rope to set off any booby traps or early warning devices.

b. Cross over barbed wire using wood, grass mats, or some chicken wire to protect you from the barbs

    (1) Throw the wood, mat, or chicken wire over the barbed wire.

    (2) Cross carefully because such a mat or net forms an unstable path.

c. Cross under the barbed wire.

    (1) Slide headfirst on your back under the bottom strands.

    (2) Push yourself forward with your shoulders and heels, carrying your weapon lengthwise on your body and holding the barbed wire with one hand while moving.

    (3) Let the barbed wire slide on the weapon to keep wire from catching on clothing and equipment.

d. Cut your way through the barbed wire.

    (1) Leave the top wire in place to make it less likely that the enemy will discover the gap.

    (2) Wrap cloth around the barbed wire between your hands.

    (3) Cut partly through the barbed wire.

    (4) Bend the barbed wire back and forth quietly until it separates.

    (5) Cut only the lower strands

4. Cross exposed danger areas such as roads, trails, or small streams.

a. Select a point at or near a bend in the road or stream. If possible, select a bend that has cover and concealment on both sides.

b. Crawl up to the edge of the open area.

c. Observe the other side carefully before crossing.

d. Move rapidly but quietly across the exposed area.

e. Take cover on the other side.

f. Check the area around you.

5. Cross over a wall.

a. Roll quickly over the top.

b. Do not go over standing upright.

6. Cover your buddy as he crosses the obstacle.

| **Performance Measures (1-6)** | **GO** | **NO GO** |
|---|---|---|
| 1. Covered your advance using smoke. | ____ | ____ |
| 2. Ensure your buddy was covering you. | ____ | ____ |
| 3. Crossed barbed wire obstacles. | ____ | ____ |

    a. Checked barbed wire for booby traps or early warning devices.

      (1) Looked for booby traps or early warning devices attached to the barbed wire.

      (2) Threw a grappling hook with a length of rope attached over the barbed wire.

      (3) Pulled the rope to set off any booby traps or early warning devices.

    b. Crossed over barbed wire using wood, grass mat, or some chicken wire.

      (1) Threw the wood, mat or chicken wire over the barbed wire.

      (2) Crossed carefully because such a mat or net forms an unstable path.

    c. Crossed under barbed wire.

      (1) Slide headfirst on your back under the bottom strand.

      (2) Pushed yourself forward with your shoulders and heels, carried your weapon lengthwise on your body, and held the barbed wire with one hand while moving.

      (3) Allowed the barbed wire to slide on the weapon so that the wire did not catch on clothing and equipment.

    d. Cut your way through the barbed wire.

      (1) Left the top wire in place.

      (2) Wrapped cloth around the barbed wire between your hands.

      (3) Cut partly through the barbed wire.

      (4) Bent the barbed wire quietly until it separated.

      (5) Cut only the lower strand.

4. Crossed exposed danger areas such as roads, trails, or small streams.

        ____    ____

    a. Selected a point at or near a bend in the road or stream that has cover and concealment on both sides.

    b. Crawled up to the opened area.

    c. Observed the other side before crossing.

    d. Move rapidly but quietly across the exposed area.

    e. Took cover on the other side.

    f. Checked the area around you.

| Performance Measures (cont'd): | GO | NO GO |
|---|---|---|
| 5. Crossed over a wall. | ____ | ____ |

    a. Rolled quickly over the top.

    b. Did not go over standing upright.

| | GO | NO GO |
|---|---|---|
| 6. Covered your buddy while crossing the obstacle. | ____ | ____ |

**Evaluation Guidance:** Score the soldier GO if all performance measures are passed. Scored the soldier NO-GO if any performance measure is failed. If the soldier scores a NO-GO, show the soldier what was done wrong and how to do it correctly.

**References**

**Required**         **Related**

FM 3-21.75 (21-75)

# NAVIGATE FROM ONE POINT ON THE GROUND TO ANOTHER POINT WHILE DISMOUNTED

**071-329-1006**

**Conditions:** Given a standard topographic map of the area, scale 1:50,000, a coordinate scale and protractor, a compass, and writing materials.

**Standards:** Moved on foot to designated points at a rate of 3,000 meters in an hour.

**Performance Steps (1-4)**

1. Determine your pace count.

    a. When traveling on foot, measure distance by counting paces. The average soldier uses 116 paces to travel 100 meters. Check your pace length by practicing on a known 100-meter distance, like a football field plus one end zone, which is 110 yards (about 100 meters).

    b. When traveling cross-country as in the field, you use more paces to travel 100 meters, usually about 148 instead of 116. This is because you are not traveling over level ground, and must use more paces to make up for your movement up and down hills. You should pace yourself over at least 600 meters of crisscrossing terrain to learn how many paces it takes you to travel an average 100 meters over such terrain.

c. Be sure you know how many paces it takes you to walk 100 meters on both level and crisscrossing terrain.

(1) The problem in pacing is maintaining a straight line. At night, you will tend to walk in a clockwise circle if you do not use a compass. In daylight, you should use aiming points and a compass. Also, remember to figure only the straight-line distance when you have to walk around an obstacle.

(2) Another problem is keeping count of paces taken. One way is to use pebbles. For instance, suppose you want to pace off one kilometer. (A kilometer is 1,000 meters or the distance between two of the black grid lines on your map.) Put ten pebbles in your right pocket. When you go 100 meters, move one pebble to your left pocket and start your count over. When all ten pebbles had been moved to your left pocket, you have traveled 1 kilometer. Or, you can tie knots in a string, one knot per 100 meters.

d. Sample problem: You are to move 715 meters, and your pace count for 100 meters is 116 paces.

(1) Using the pebble methods, you will need seven pebbles. This will take you 700 meters. But what about the other 15 meters?

(2) To determine how many paces it will take to go the remaining 15 meters, multiply 15 meters by your pace count. (116--15 x 116 = 1,740). Mark out the last two numbers (40). The remainder (17) is how many paces it will take to go 15 meters.

(3) So you would go 715 meters using the pebble method by pacing off 116 paces per 100 meters until all seven pebbles are used, then go an additional 17 paces to arrive at 715 meters.

2. Navigate from one point to another using terrain association.

a. This technique uses terrain or manmade features to serve as landmarks or checkpoints for maintaining direction of movement. It can be used anywhere, day or night, as long as there are distinguishable terrain features. You use terrain association when moving from the unit area to the motor pool. You walk down the road or sidewalk using intersections or buildings to steer or turn on (landmarks or checkpoints). In the field, with few roads and buildings, use terrain features for your axis and checkpoints.

b. In using association, you locate first your position on the map, then your destination or objective. It will seldom be the best way to travel. For example, look at Figure A-1 (071-329-1006-1). Assume that you are to move from point A to point B. You see that a straight line could cause you to climb several small ridges and valleys (the "X's" on Figure 071-329-1006).

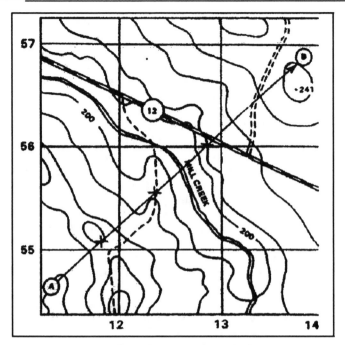

**Figure A-1. (071-329-1006-1) Straight-line route.**

c. When adjusting your route, consider the following:

(1) Tactical aspect. Avoid skylining open areas and danger areas like streams or crossings on roads and hilltops. Your tactical concern is survival. The mission is causing you to move to your objective. You need to be sure you get to that objective. Looking at Figure A-2 (071-329-1006-2), you decide for tactical reasons to cross the stream where you would not be seen from the road (C) and to cross the road in a small valley (D). You know that valleys offer better cover and concealment, so you will use them (E) (F).

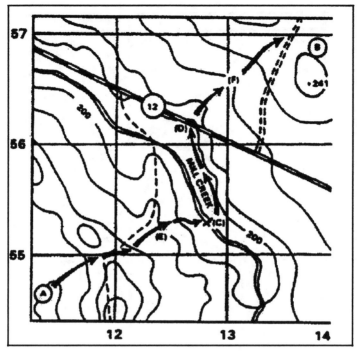

**Figure A-2 (071-329-1006-2) Adjusted route.**

(2) Ease of movement. Always pick the easiest route that the tactical situation allows. However, you achieve surprise by doing the unexpected. A difficult route increases your chance of getting lost. A difficult route may be noisy and may tire you out before you get to your objective.

(3) Boundaries. It is almost impossible to travel in a straight line, with or without a compass. Pick an axis or corridor to travel along. Pick boundaries you will be able to spot or feel. Hardtop roads, streams, high grounds, and railroads all make good boundaries. If you start to wander too far off course, you will know it.

d. You decide the route shown in Figure A-3 (071-329-1006-3) offers you easy movement. You check your axis up the valley (1); across the ridge at the saddle (2); cross the stream, turning left and keep the stream on the left, high ground on the right (4); to the third valley (5); to the saddle, then on the objective (6).

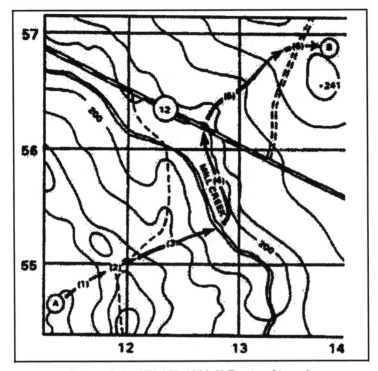

**Figure A-3. (071-329-1006-3) Route of travel.**

e. With boundaries to keep you straight, you need to know where along your corridor you are. You do this with checkpoints. The best checkpoint is a line or linear feature that you cannot miss. A linear feature across your corridor, or axis, is crossed no matter where you are in the axis. Use hardtop roads, railroads, power lines, perennial streams (solid blue lines, the dash blue lines are frequently dry), rivers, ridges, and valleys.

NOTE: DO NOT use light-duty roads and trails, there is always more on the ground than the map shows. DO NOT use wood lines, which are rarely permanent.

    g.   Referring to Figure A-4 (071-329-1006-4), pick your checkpoints.

        (1)   Saddle, use Hill 241 to line on up the right valley, and follow to –

        (2)   Stream, move along it until—

        (3)   Bend in the stream, turn right to—

        (4)   Road in the valley (the ridge crossing on the road on the 12-grid line will serve as a limiting feature), then up to—

        (5)   Far saddle, and right to your objective (B).

g. If you cannot find linear features, use an elevation change--hill or depressions, small ridge, or a valley. Look for one contour line of change during the day, two at night. Regardless of contour interval, you will spot a contour interval of change on foot.

h. Determine the distance between checkpoints. DISTANCE IS THE CAUSE OF MOST NAVIGATIONAL MISTAKES. Estimate or measure the distance from one checkpoint to another. Trust that distance.

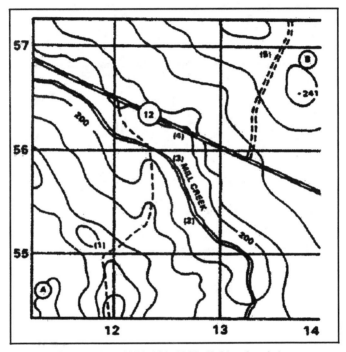

**Figure A-4. (071-329-1006-4) Checkpoints.**

i. Referring to Figure A-5 (071-329-1006-5), check your distances:
   (1) 500 meters to the saddle (1).
   (2) 800 meters to the stream (2).
   (3) 500 meters to the bend in the stream (3).
   (4) 300 meters to the road (4).
   (5) 1,000 meters to the far saddle (5).

3. Navigate from one point to another using dead reckoning.

   a. Dead reckoning is a technique of following a set route or line for a determined distance. This technique is used on flat terrain, like deserts and swamps. It can be used day or night. To use dead reckoning--

(1) Locate the start point and finish point on the map. Figure A-5 (071-329-1006-5).

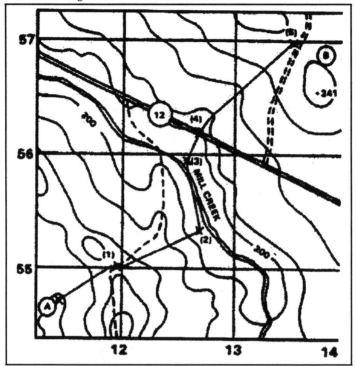

**Figure A-5. (071-329-1006-5) Distance between checkpoints.**

(2) Determine the grid azimuth from the start point to the finish point or to the first intermediate point on the map.

(3) Convert the grid azimuth taken from the map to a magnetic azimuth.

(4) Determine the distance between the start point and the finish point or any intermediate points on the map.

NOTE: If you do not know how many paces you take for each 100 meters, you should move to a 100-meter course and determine your pace count.

(5) Convert the map distance to pace count.

(6) Make a thorough map reconnaissance of the area between the start point and the finish point.

b. Before moving from the start point, shoot an azimuth on a well-defined object on the ground in the direction of travel. These objects, known as steering points, may be lone trees, buildings, rocks, or any easily identifiable point. At night, the most likely steering point will be a star. Because of the rotation of the Earth, the positions of the stars continually change. You must check your azimuth frequently. Do this only when halted. Using your compass while moving will cause you to go off-course. Your steering mark may be beyond your objective. Remember to travel the distance you determined.

c. Once you have selected a steering point, move toward it, remembering to begin your count. You should have some methods devised to keep track of the number of 100 meters you travel.

d. Upon reaching your first steering point, shoot an azimuth to another steering mark, and repeat c, until you reach the finish point.

e. If you should encounter an obstacle, you may have to detour around it. See Figure A-6 (071-329-1006-6). To do this, complete a series of 90-degree turns until the obstacle is bypassed and you are back on the original azimuth.

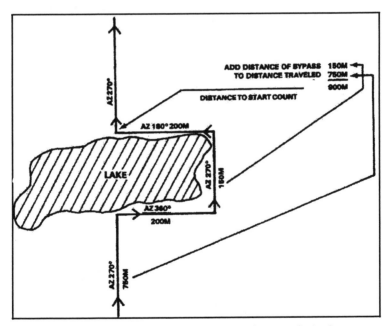

**Figure A-6. (071-329-1006-6) Bypassing an obstacle.**

(1) At the edge of the obstacle, make a note of the number of paces taken to this point.

(2) If your detour is to the right, add 90 degrees to the original azimuth.

(3) Using the new azimuth, pick a steering mark and move toward it, making sure you begin a new pace count. Move on this azimuth until reaching the end of the obstacle.

(4) Stop and make a note of the number of paces taken, again as in (2) above, add or subtract 90 degrees from the azimuth just read, and move to the far side of the obstacle.

(5) Upon reaching the far side, stop the count and make note of the number of paces taken; add this pace count to the pace count noted in (1).

(6) At this time, again add or subtract 90 degrees from the azimuth used. Using this new azimuth, move the same number of paces taken on the first leg of the offset or detour.

(7) Place the compass on your original azimuth, pick up the pace count you ended with when you cleared the obstacle, and proceed to your finish point.

f. Bypassing the same obstacle at night calls for special considerations:

(1) To make a 90-degree turn, hold the compass as you would to determine a Magnetic Azimuth.

(2) Turn until the center of the luminous letter "E" is under the luminous line (do not change the setting of the luminous line).

NOTE: If you turn to the right, "E" is under the luminous line. If you turn to the left, "W" is under the line.

(3) Proceed in the direction until you have outflanked the obstacle.

(4) Turn until the north arrow is under the luminous line and proceed parallel to your original course until you have bypassed the obstacle.

(5) Turn until the "W" is under the luminous line and move back the same distance you originally moved.

(6) Finally, turn until the north arrow is under the luminous line and proceed on your original course.

(7) You must do the pace count the same as you do for bypassing the obstacle during daylight.

g. After reaching the finish point, conduct a detailed terrain analysis to confirm your location.

4. Navigate from one point to another by combining terrain association with dead reckoning.

a. Frequently, you must consider the advantage and disadvantage of both navigation techniques.

(1) Terrain association is fast and easy, and it allows for mistakes. It also is subject to map accuracy and can only be used with recognizable terrain features.

(2) Dead reckoning is accurate and works on flat terrain that lacks terrain features; however, all work must be precise, and the technique takes time.

b. There may be times when you combine both techniques. For instance, in the desert, you may need to use dead reckoning to arrive at or near a road, or a ridge, then use terrain association to follow that feature to an objective.

## Evaluation Preparation:

SETUP: Select an area with varying terrain and vegetation that is large enough to have two points, 1,000 to 2,000 meters apart. Ensure each point is on or near an identifiable terrain feature and marked on the ground with a sign containing a letter or number. Place dummy signs not less than 100 meters but not more than 200 meters to the right and left of the correct point. Clearly mark correct points on the map. Prepare a sheet of paper giving the azimuth and distance for each leg of the course to be covered. Have pencils available for the tested soldier.

BRIEF SOLDIER:

1. Terrain Association.

    a.   Give the soldier the map and tell him to identify the best route to take between the two points that have been plotted on the map (1,000 to 2,000 meters apart).

NOTE: The best route must have been determined by an SME before the test.

b. Give the soldier the map and tell him he must move from point A on the map to point B (1,000 to 2,000 meters apart) using terrain association (no compass is used). Tell the soldier he has _____ (standards in minutes and/or hours) to complete the course.

2. Dead Reckoning. Give the soldier the sheet of paper with the azimuth and the distance for each leg of the course (three to five points, 200 to 500 meters apart), and the compass; no map will be used. Tell the soldier to move over the course shown by the azimuth and the distance on the paper. Tell the soldier to record the letter or number at the end of each leg of the course. Tell the soldier he has _____ (standards in minutes and/or hours) to complete the course.

NOTE: Time standards are based on the average time it takes two SMEs to complete the course plus 50 percent. For example, if the SMEs time is one hour and thirty minutes. SME time(1 hour) + 50 percent (30 minutes) = course test time of one hour and 30 minutes.

Tell the soldier he has 10 minutes to study the map and determine a course. At the end of this time, he will move to the start point and begins the test. Time starts when soldier leaves the start point and ends when he crosses the finish point.

| Performance Measures | GO | NO GO |
|---|---|---|
| 1. Terrain association. | ____ | ____ |

    a. Identified the best route within 10 minutes and explained reason for picking that route.

    b. Wrote down the correct letter or number at the end of each leg of the course.

| | | |
|---|---|---|
| 2. Dead reckoning. | ____ | ____ |

    a. Wrote down the correct letter or number of each leg of the course.

    b. Arrived at correct destination within the specified time.

**Evaluation Guidance:** Score the soldier GO if all performance measures are passed. Score the soldier NO-GO if any performance measure is failed. If the soldier scores NO-GO, show the soldier what was done wrong and how to do it correctly.

## References

| Required | Related |
|---|---|
| FM 3-25.26 (21-26) | |
| STP 21-1-SMCT | |

# PERFORM VOICE COMMUNICATIONS
## 113-571-1022

**Conditions:** Given one operational radio set (warmed up and set to the net frequency) for each net member; a call sign information card (5 inches x 8 inches) consisting of net member duty position (S-1, S-2), net call sign (letter-number-letter), suffix list (net control station [NCS] - 46, S-1 - 39, S-2 - 13), and a message to be transmitted.

**Situation:** The net is considered to be secure and authentication is not required.

**NOTE:** This task may have as many net members as there is equipment available. Each net member must have a different suffix and message to transmit.

**Standards:** Enter a radio net, send a message, and left a radio net using the proper call signs, call sign sequence, prowords, and phonetic alphabet and numerals with 100 percent accuracy.

### Performance Steps

1. Enter the net.
   a. Determine the abbreviated call sign and answering sequence for your duty position.
   b. Respond to the NCS issuing a net call.
   c. Answer in alphanumeric sequence.

NOTE: At this time, the NCS acknowledges and the net is open.

2. Send a message.
   a. Listen to make sure the net is clear. Do not interrupt any ongoing communications.
   b. Call the NCS and tell the operator the priority of the message you have for his station.
   c. Receive a response from the NCS that he or she is ready to receive.
   d. Send your message using the correct prowords and pronunciation of letters and numbers.
   e. Get a receipt for the message.
3. Leave the net in alphanumeric sequence.
   a. You receive a call from the NCS who issues a close down order.
   b. Answer in alphanumeric sequence.

NOTE: The NCS acknowledges and the net is closed. Note: The following call signs are used in this task as an example: Net call sign - E3E, NCS - E46, S-1 - E39, S-2 - E13.

### Evaluation Preparation:

SETUP: Position operational radio sets in different rooms or tents or at least 70 feet apart outside. Obtain call signs, suffixes, and a radio frequency through the normal command chain. Select a message 15-25 words containing some number groups such as map coordinates and times. Print the call signs for the sender and the receiver, along with the message to be sent, on 5 x 8 cards. Perform a communications check to ensure operation of the radios. Have an assistant who is proficient in radio operation man the NCS. Provide the assistant with the call signs. If the soldier has not demonstrated sufficient progress to complete the task within 5 minutes, give him a NO-GO. This time limit is an administrative requirement, not a doctrinal one; so if the soldier has almost completed the task correctly, you may decide to allow him to finish.

BRIEF SOLDIER: Give the soldier the card containing the message and call signs. Tell him the radio is ready for operation, the net is considered to be secure and authentication is not required, and to send the message to the NCS and get a receipt. Tell the soldier, if sufficient progress in completing the task within 5 minutes has not been demonstrated, he or she will receive a NO-GO for the task.

| Performance Measures | GO | NO GO |
|---|---|---|
| 1. Entered the net in alphanumeric sequence. | _____ | _____ |
| 2. Sent a message of 15 to 25 words using the correct prowords and phonetic alphabet and numerals. | _____ | _____ |
| 3. Left the net in alphanumeric sequence. | _____ | _____ |

**Evaluation Guidance:** Score the soldier GO if all performance measures are passed. Score the soldier NO-GO if any performance measure is failed. If the soldier scores NO-GO, show the soldier what was done wrong and how to do it correctly.

**References**

**Required**                    **Related**

**SECTION II – SURVIVE**

# EVALUATE A CASUALTY

## 081-831-1000

**Conditions:** You have a casualty who has signs and/or symptoms of an injury.

**Standards:** Evaluated the casualty following the correct sequence. All injuries and/or conditions were identified. The casualty was immobilized if a neck or back injury is suspected.

**Performance Steps**

NOTE: When evaluating and/or treating a casualty, seek medical aid as soon as possible. Do not stop treatment, but, if the situation allows, send another person to find medical aid.

---

**WARNING**

If there are signs of chemical or biological agent poisoning, immediately mask the casualty. If it is not nerve agent poisoning, decontaminate exposed skin and gross contamination (large wet or oily spots) of the clothing or overgarments. If nerve agent poisoning, administer the antidote before decontamination (see task, Perform First Aid for Nerve Agent Injury, task number 081-831-1044.)

---

**WARNING**

If a broken neck or back is suspected, do not move the casualty unless to save his life.

---

1.  Check for responsiveness.
    a.  Ask in a loud, but calm voice, "Are you okay?"
    b.  Gently shake or tap the casualty on the shoulder.
    c.  Watch for a response. If the casualty does not respond, go to step 2.
    d.  If the casualty is conscious, ask where he feels different than usual or where it hurts. Go to step 3. If the casualty is conscious but is choking and cannot talk, stop the evaluation and begin treatment. (See Task 081-831-1003.)

2.   Check for breathing.

a. Look for rise and fall of the casualty's chest.

b. Listen for breathing by placing your ear about one inch above the casualty's mouth and nose.

c. Feel for breathing by placing your hand or cheek about 1 inch above the casualty's mouth and nose. If the casualty is not breathing, stop the evaluation and begin treatment. (See Task, 081-831-1042.)

NOTE: Checking for pulse during mouth-to-mouth resuscitation, as necessary.

3. Check for bleeding.

---

**WARNING**

In a chemically contaminated area, do not expose the wound(s).

---

a. Look for spurts of blood or blood-soaked clothes.

b. Look for entry and exit wounds.

c. If bleeding is present, stop the evaluation and begin treatment as appropriate

(1) Arm or leg wound. (See Task 081-831-1032.)

(2) Partial or complete amputation. (See Task 081-831-1032.)

(3) Open head wound. (See Task 081-831-1033.)

(4) Open abdominal wound. (See Task 081-831-1025.)

(5) Open chest wound. (See Task 081-831-1026.)

4. Check for shock.

a. Look for any of the following signs and/or symptoms:

(1) Sweaty but cool skin (clammy skin).

(2) Paleness of skin.

(3) Restlessness or nervousness.

(4) Thirst.

(5) Loss of blood (bleeding).

(6) Confusion.

(7) Faster than normal breathing rate.

(8) Blotchy or bluish skin, especially around the mouth.

(9) Nausea and/or vomiting.

b. If signs or symptoms of shock are present, stop the evaluation and begin treatment. (See Task 081-831-1005.)

---

> ### WARNING
>
> Leg fractures must be splinted before elevating the legs for shock (See Task 081-831-1034.)

5. Check for fractures.

    a. Look for the following signs and symptoms of a back or neck injury:

        (1) Pain or tenderness of the neck or back area.

        (2) Cuts or bruises in the neck and back area.

        (3) Inability of the casualty to move (paralysis or numbness).

            (a) Ask about the ability to move (paralysis).

            (b) Touch the casualty's arms and legs; ask whether he or she can feel your hand (numbness).

        (4) Unusual body or limb position.

> ### WARNING
>
> Unless there is immediate life-threatening danger, do not move a casualty who has a suspected back or neck injury.

    b. Immobilize any casualty suspected of having a neck or back injury by doing the following:

        (1) Tell the casualty not to move.

        (2) If a back injury is suspected, place padding under the natural arch of the casualty's back.

        (3) If a neck injury is suspected, place a roll of cloth under the casualty's neck and put boots (filled with dirt, sand, etc.) or rocks on both sides of the head.

    c. Check the casualty's arms and legs for open or closed fractures.

        (1) Check for open fractures.

            (a) Look for bleeding.

            (b) Look for bone sticking through the skin.

        (2) Check for closed fractures.

            (a) Look for swelling.

            (b) Look for discoloration.

            (c) Look for deformity.

            (d) Look for unusual body position.

    d. If a fracture to an arm or leg is suspected, stop the evaluation and begin treatment. (See Task 081-831-1034.)

6. Check for burns.

> a. Look carefully for reddened, blistered, or charred skin. Also check for singed clothes.

> b. If burns are found, stop the evaluation and begin treatment. (See Task 081-831-1007.)

7. Check for head injury.

> a. Look for the following signs and symptoms:
>> (1) Unequal pupils.
>> (2) Fluid from the ear(s), nose, mouth, or injury site.
>> (3) Slurred speech.
>> (4) Confusion.
>> (5) Sleepiness.
>> (6) Loss of memory or consciousness.
>> (7) Staggering in walking.
>> (8) Headache.
>> (9) Dizziness.
>> (10) Vomiting.
>> (11) Paralysis.
>> (12) Convulsions or twitches.

> b. If a head injury is suspected, continue to watch for signs that would require performance of mouth-to-mouth resuscitation (See Task 081-831-1042), treatment for shock (See Task 081-831-1005), or control of bleeding (See Task 081-831-1033.)

8. Seek medical aid. Seek medical assistance as soon as possible, but you must not interrupt treatment. If possible send another person to find medical aid.

**Evaluation Preparation:**

SETUP: Prepare a "casualty" for the soldier to evaluate by simulating one or more wounds or conditions. Simulate the wounds using a war wounds moulage set, casualty simulation kit, or other available materials. You can coach a "conscious casualty" to show signs of such conditions as shock or head injury and to respond to the soldier's questions about location of pain or other symptoms of injury. However, you will have to cue the soldier during evaluation of an "unconscious casualty" as to whether the casualty is breathing and describe the signs or conditions, such as shock, as the soldier is making the checks.

BRIEF SOLDIER: Tell the soldier to do, in order, all necessary steps to evaluate the casualty and identify all wounds and/or conditions. Tell the soldier to tell you what first aid action (give mouth-to-mouth resuscitation, bandage the wound, etc.) he or she would take but that no first aid is to be performed unless a neck or back injury is found.

| Performance Measures (1-10) | GO | NO GO |
|---|---|---|
| 1. Checked for responsiveness. | ____ | ____ |
| 2. Checked for breathing, if necessary. | ____ | ____ |
| 3. Checked for bleeding. | ____ | ____ |
| 4. Checked for shock. | ____ | ____ |
| 5. Checked for fractures and immobilized neck or back injuries, if found. | ____ | ____ |
| 6. Checked for burns. | ____ | ____ |
| 7. Checked for a head injury. | ____ | ____ |
| 8. Sought medical aid. | ____ | ____ |
| 9. Performed all necessary steps in sequence. | ____ | ____ |
| 10. Identified all wounds and/or conditions. | ____ | ____ |

**Evaluation Guidance:** Score the soldier GO if all steps are passed. Score the soldier NO GO if any step is failed. If the soldier scores NO GO, show what was done wrong and how to do it correctly.

### References

**Required**                    **Related**

FM 4-25.11 (21-11)

# PERFORM FIRST AID FOR NERVE AGENT INJURY

## 081-831-1044

**Conditions:** You and your unit have come under a chemical attack. You are wearing protective overgarments and/or mask, or they are immediately available. There are casualties with nerve agent injuries. Necessary materials and equipment: chemical protective gloves, overgarments, overboots, protective mask and hood, mask carrier, and nerve agent antidote autoinjectors. The casualty has three sets of MARK 1 nerve agent antidote autoinjectors or three ATNAAs and one convulsant antidote for nerve agents (CANA) autoinjector.

**Standards:** Administered correctly the antidote to self or administered three sets of MARK 1 nerve agent antidote autoinjectors or three ATNAAs followed by the CANA to a buddy following the correct sequence.

**Performance Steps (1-14)**

NOTE: The Antidote Treatment, Nerve Agent, Autoinjector (ATNAA) system is a nerve agent antidote device that will be used by the Armed Forces. A single ATNAA delivers both the atropine and 2 Pam Cl. The ATNAA will replace the MARK I when supplies are exhausted. Procedures for administering ATNAA will be contained in FM 4-25.11 (FM 21-11) and FM 8-285.

NOTE: When performing first aid on a casualty, seek medical aid as soon as possible. Do not stop the first aid; if the situation allows, send another person to find medical aid.

1.  Identify mild signs and symptoms of nerve agent poisoning.
    a.  Unexplained runny nose.
    b.  Unexplained sudden headache.
    c.  Excessive flow of saliva (drooling).
    d.  Tightness of the chest causing breathing difficulties.
    e.  Difficulty seeing (blurred vision).
    f.  Muscular twitching around area of exposed or contaminated skin.
    g.  Stomach cramps.
    h.  Nausea.

NOTE: For the above signs and symptoms first aid is considered to be self-aid.

2.  React to the chemical hazard.
    a.  Put on your protective mask.

NOTE: Seek overhead cover or use a poncho to provide cover, mission permitting. Do not put on additional protective clothing at this time. Give yourself the nerve agent antidote first. Then, decontaminate exposed skin areas and put on remaining protective clothing.

    b.  Give the alarm.

3.  Administer nerve agent antidote to self (self-aid), if necessary.
    a.  MARK I.
        (1) Prepare to administer one atropine injection.
            (a) Remove one set of MARK I from your protective mask carrier, from the pocket of the MOPP suit, or from another location as specified by your unit SOP.
            (b) With one hand, hold the set of injectors by the plastic clip with the big injector on top.

(c) With the other hand, check the injection site in order to avoid buttons and objects in pockets where injecting. For injections into the thigh, grasp the trouser cargo pocket and pull forward, clearing possible obstructions from the site.

(d) Grasp the small injector without covering or holding the needle (green) end, and pull it out of the clip with a smooth motion.

(e) Form a fist around the autoinjector with the needle end (green) extending beyond the little finger end of the fist. Be careful not to inject yourself in the hand.

**NOTE**: If the injection is accidentally given in the hand, another small injector must be obtained and the injection given in the proper site.

(f) Place the needle end of the injector against the outer thigh muscle. For injections into the thigh, grasp the trouser cargo pocket and pull forward, clearing possible obstructions from the site.

**NOTE**: The injection can be given in any part of the lateral thigh muscle from about a hand's width above the knee to a hand's width below the hip joint.

**NOTE**: Very thin soldiers should give the injection in the upper outer part of the buttocks.

---

**CAUTION**

When injecting antidote in the buttocks, be very careful to inject only into the upper, outer quarter of the buttocks to avoid hitting the major nerve that crosses the buttocks. Hitting the nerve may cause paralysis.

---

(2) Administer the atropine injection.

(a) Push the injector into the muscle with firm, even pressure until it functions.

**NOTE**: A jabbing motion is not necessary to trigger the activating mechanism.

(b) Hold the injector firmly in place for at least 10 seconds.

(c) Remove the injector from your muscle and carefully place this used injector between two fingers of the hand holding the plastic clip.

(3) Prepare to administer one 2 PAM Cl injection.

(a) Pull the large injector out of the clip and form a fist around the autoinjector with the needle end extending beyond the little finger.

(b) Place the needle (black) end of the injector against the injection site.

(4) Administer the 2 Pam Cl injection.

(a) Push the injector into the muscle with firm, even pressure until it functions.

(b) Hold the injector firmly in place for at least 10 seconds.

b. ATNAA.

(1) Prepare to administer one ATNAA.

(a) Remove one ATNAA from your protective mask carrier, from the pocket of the MOPP suit, or from another location as specified by your unit SOP.

(b) Remove the autoinjector from the pouch.

(c) With your dominant hand, hold the ATNAA in your closed fist with the green needle end extending beyond the little finger in front of you at eye level.

(d) With your nondominant hand, grasp the safety (gray) cap with the thumb and first two fingers.

---

**CAUTION**

Do not cover or hold the needle end with your hand, thumb, or fingers. You may accidentally inject yourself.

---

(e) Pull the safety cap off the bottom of the injector with a smooth motion and drop it to the ground.

(f) With the nondominant hand, check the injection site in order to avoid buttons and objects in pockets where injecting. For injections into the thigh, grasp the trouser cargo pocket and pull forward, clearing possible obstructions from the site.

(g) Hold the ATNAA in your closed fist with the green needle end pointing out by your little finger.

(h) Place the needle end of the injector against the outer thigh muscle.

NOTE: Very thin soldiers should give the injection in the upper outer part of the buttocks.

---

**CAUTION**

When injecting antidote in the buttocks, be very careful to inject only into the upper, outer quarter of the buttocks to avoid hitting the major nerve that crosses the buttocks. Hitting the nerve may cause paralysis.

---

NOTE: The injection can be given in any part of the lateral thigh muscle from about a hand's width above the knee to a hand's width below the hip joint.

      (2) Administer the injection.

        (a) Push the injector into the muscle with firm, even pressure until it functions.

NOTE: A jabbing motion is not necessary to trigger the activating mechanism.

        (b) Hold the injector firmly in place for at least 10 seconds.

        (c) Remove the injector from your muscle.

4.   Secure the used injectors.

    a.   Drop the plastic clip (MARK I) without dropping the used injectors.

    b.   Use a hard surface to bend each needle to form a hook without tearing protective gloves or clothing.

    c.   Push the needle of each used injector (one at a time) through one of the pocket flaps of the protective overgarment.

5.   Decontaminate skin if necessary.

NOTE: Information on this step is provided in Task 031-503-1013.

6.   Put on remaining protective clothing.

NOTE: Information on this step is covered in Task 031-503-1015.

---

| **WARNING** |
|---|
| If, within 5 to 10 minutes after administering the first set of injections, your heart begins beating rapidly and your mouth becomes very dry; do not administer another set of injections. |

7.   Seek buddy-aid or medical aid.

NOTE: After you have given yourself the first set of MARK I injections or one ATNAA, you most likely will not need additional antidote if you are ambulatory and know who and where you are. If needed, additional injections will be given only by a buddy, a combat lifesaver, or medical personnel.

8.   Identify severe signs and symptoms of nerve agent poisoning.

    a.   Strange and confused behavior.

b. Gurgling sounds made when breathing.

c. Severely pinpointed pupils.

d. Red eyes with tearing.

e. Vomiting.

f. Severe muscular twitching.

g. Loss of bladder and/or bowel control.

h. Convulsions.

i. Unconsciousness or stoppage of breathing.

NOTE: If the casualty is exhibiting severe symptoms, assistance (buddy-aid) is required by the individual to complete first aid treatment.

9. Mask the casualty if necessary.

---

### WARNING

Do not kneel at any time while providing aid to the casualty. Contact with the ground could force the chemical into or through the protective clothing.

---

NOTE: Reposition the casualty on his back if necessary to mask the individual.

a. Place the mask on the casualty.

b. If the casualty can follow directions, have him clear the mask.

c. Check for a complete mask seal by covering the inlet valves of the mask.

d. Pull the protective hood over the head, neck, and shoulders of the casualty.

e. Position the casualty on the right side, similar to a swimmer position, with head slanted down so that the casualty will not roll back over.

10. Administer first aid to a nerve agent casualty (buddy-aid).

   a. MARK I.

      (1) Prepare to administer one atropine injection.

         (a) Position yourself near the casualty's thigh.

         (b) Remove all three sets of autoinjectors and the single CANA autoinjector from the casualty's mask carrier, BDU pocket, or from another location as specified by your unit SOP. Place the autoinjectors and CANA on the casualty's side. DO NOT place the unused devices on the ground.

         (c) With one hand, hold the set of injectors by the plastic clip with the big injector on top.

(d) With the other hand, check the injection site to avoid buttons and objects in pockets. For injections into the thigh, grasp the trouser cargo pocket and pull forward (toward you), clearing possible obstructions from the site.

(e) Grasp the small injector and pull it out of the clip with a smooth motion.

(f) Hold the injector in your closed fist with the green needle end pointing out by your little finger without covering the needle end.

(g) Place the needle end of the injector against the casualty's outer (lateral) thigh muscle.

NOTE: The injection can be given in any part of the lateral thigh muscle from about a hand's width above the knee to a hand's width below the hip joint.

NOTE: Very thin soldiers should be given the injections in the upper outer part of the buttocks.

> **WARNING**
>
> When injecting antidote in the buttocks, be very careful to inject only into the upper, outer quarter of the buttocks to avoid hitting the major nerve that crosses the buttocks. Hitting the nerve may cause paralysis.

(2) Administer the atropine injection.

(a) Push the injector into the muscle with firm, even pressure until it functions.

(b) Hold the injector in place for at least 10 seconds.

(c) Remove the injector from the muscle and carefully place the used injector between two fingers of the hand holding the clip.

(3) Prepare to administer one 2 PAM Cl injection.

(a) Pull the large injector out of the clip and hold the injector in your closed fist with the black needle end pointing out by your little finger without covering the needle end.

(b) Place the needle (black) end of the injector against the injection site.

(4) Administer the 2 Pam Cl injection.

(a) Push the injector into the muscle with firm, even pressure until it functions.

(b) Hold the injector in place for at least 10 seconds.

(c) Drop the clip without dropping injectors.

(d) Lay the used injectors on the casualty's side.

NOTE: Repeat steps 10a through 10d until the casualty has received a total (including self-administered) of three sets of antidote injections.

    b. ATNAA

        (1) Prepare to administer one ATNAA.

            (a) Obtain three or all of the remaining ATNAAs and one CANA from the casualty's protective mask carrier, from the pocket of the MOPP suit, or from another location as specified by your unit SOP.

            (b) Remove one ATNAA from the pouch.

            (c) With your dominant hand, hold the ATNAA in your closed fist with the green needle and pointing out by your little finger in front of you at eye level.

            (d) With your nondominant hand, grasp the safety (gray) cap with the thumb and first two fingers.

---

**CAUTION**

Do not cover or hold the needle end with your hand, thumb, or fingers. You may accidentally inject yourself.

---

            (e) Pull the safety cap off the bottom of the injector with a smooth motion and drop it to the ground.

            (f) With the nondominant hand, check the injection site in order to avoid buttons and objects in pockets where injecting. For injections into the thigh, grasp the trouser cargo pocket and pull forward, clearing possible obstructions from the site.

            (g) Hold the ATNAA in your closed fist.

            (h) Place the needle end of the injector against the outer thigh muscle.

NOTE: The injection can be given in any part of the lateral thigh muscle from about a hand's width above the knee to a hand's width below the hip joint.

NOTE: Very thin soldiers should give the injection in the upper outer part of the buttocks.

---

**CAUTION**

When injecting antidote in the buttocks, be very careful to inject only into the upper, outer quarter of the buttocks to avoid hitting the major nerve that crosses the buttocks. Hitting the nerve may cause paralysis.

---

        (2) Administer the injection.

(a) Push the injector into the muscle with firm, even pressure until it functions.

NOTE: A jabbing motion is not necessary to trigger the activating mechanism.

(b) Hold the injector firmly in place for at least 10 seconds.

(c) Remove the injector from the muscle.

(d) Place the used injector on the casualty's side.

(3) Repeat the procedure for a total of three ATNAAs.

11. Administer the anticonvulsant, CANA.

a. Prepare to administer the CANA injection.

(1) Tear open the protective plastic packet and remove the injector.

(2) With your dominant hand, hold the injector in your closed fist with the black needle end pointing out by your little finger.

(3) With the other hand, pull the safety cap off the injector base to arm the injector.

---

**CAUTION**

Do not touch the black (needle) end. You could accidentally inject yourself.

---

(4) Place the black end of the injector against the casualty's injection site.

b. Administer the CANA injection.

(1) Push the injector into the muscle with firm, even pressure until it functions.

(2) Hold the injector in place for at least 10 seconds.

12. Secure the used injectors.

a. Using a hard surface bend each needle to form a hook without tearing protective gloves or clothing.

b. Push the needle of each used injector (one at a time) through one of the pocket flaps of the casualty's protective overgarment.

13. Decontaminate the casualty's skin if necessary.

NOTE: This information is covered in Task 031-503-1013.

14. Seek medical aid.

**Evaluation Preparation:**

SETUP: You must use nerve agent antidote injection training aids to train and evaluate this task. Actual autoinjectors will not be used. For self-aid, have the soldier dress in MOPP level 2. Have the soldier wear a mask carrier containing a mask and the training nerve agent autoinjectors. For buddy-aid, have the soldier being tested and the casualty dress in MOPP level 2. Have the casualty lie on the ground wearing the mask carrier containing a mask and the training nerve agent autoinjectors.

BRIEF SOLDIER: For step 1, tell the soldier to state, in any order the mild symptoms of nerve agent poisoning. The soldier must state seven of the eight symptoms to be scored GO. Then, tell the soldier that he or she has mild symptoms and to take appropriate action. After the soldier completes step 4, ask what should be done next. Then ask what he or she should do after putting on all protective clothing. Score steps 5 through 7 based upon the soldier's responses. For step 8, tell the soldier to state, in any order, the severe symptoms of nerve agent poisoning. The soldier must state eight of the nine symptoms to be scored GO. Tell the soldier to treat the casualty for nerve agent poisoning. After the soldier completes step 11, ask what else he or she should do. Score steps 12 and 13 based upon the soldier's responses.

| Performance Measures (1-14) | GO | NO GO |
|---|---|---|
| 1. Identified mild signs of nerve agent poisoning. | ___ | ___ |
| 2. Reacted to the chemical hazard. | ___ | ___ |
| 3. Correctly administered the nerve agent antidote to self. | ___ | ___ |
| 4. Secured the used injectors. | ___ | ___ |
| 5. Decontaminated skin if necessary. | ___ | ___ |
| 6. Donned remaining protective clothing. | ___ | ___ |
| 7. Sought help (buddy-aid). | ___ | ___ |
| 8. Identified severe signs of nerve agent poisoning. | ___ | ___ |
| 9. Masked the casualty. | ___ | ___ |
| 10. Correctly administered nerve agent antidote to the casualty. | ___ | ___ |
| 11. Secured the used injectors. | ___ | ___ |
| 12. Decontaminated the casualty's skin if necessary. | ___ | ___ |
| 13. Sought medical aid. | ___ | ___ |
| 14. Performed steps 1 through 12 in the correct sequence. | ___ | ___ |

**Evaluation Guidance:** Score the soldier GO if all the steps are passed. Score the soldier NO GO if any of the steps are failed. If the soldier scores NO GO, show what was done wrong and how to do it correctly.

**References**

**Required**

**Related**

DVC 08-36

DVC 08-37

FM 4-25.11 (21-11)

FM 4-02.285 (8-285)

# REACT TO CHEMICAL OR BIOLOGICAL HAZARD/ATTACK

**031-503-1019**

**Conditions:** You are given mission-oriented protection posture (MOPP) gear, a protective mask, individual decontaminating kits, and a tactical environment in which chemical and biological (CB) weapons have been or may be used by the enemy. You are in MOPP 1, and one or more of the following automatic masking criteria happens:

1.  A chemical alarm sounds.
2.  A positive reading is obtained on detector paper.
3.  Individuals exhibit symptoms of CB agent poisoning.
4.  You observe a contamination marker.
5.  Your supervisor tells you to mask.
6.  You see personnel wearing protective masks.
7.  You observe other signs of a possible CB attack.

**Standards:** React to a chemical or biological hazard attack or attack without becoming a casualty. Identify chemical contamination markers with 100 percent accuracy, and notify supervisor. Start steps to decontaminate yourself within 1 minute of finding chemical contamination. Decontaminate your individual equipment after you have completely decontaminated yourself.

**Performance Steps**

1.  Identify the CB hazard automatic masking criteria.
    a.  Don your protective mask when there is a high probability of a chemical attack, when--
        (1)  A chemical alarm sounds.
        (2)  A positive reading is obtained on detector paper.
        (3)  Individuals exhibit symptoms of CB agent poisoning.
        (4)  You observe a contamination marker.
        (5)  Your supervisor tells you to mask.
        (6)  You see personnel wearing protective masks.
        (7)  You observe other signs of a possible CB attack.

    b.   Respond to the commander's policy of automatic masking.

**NOTE**: Commanders at all levels may establish a modified policy when chemical weapons have been employed by designating additional events as automatic masking criteria.

2.   Protect yourself from CB contamination using your assigned protective mask without fastening the hood.

**NOTE**: The mask gives immediate protection against inhalation of agent vapors. Do not fasten the hood. Go to the next step immediately.

3.   Give the alarm.
    a.   Yell "Gas."
    b.   Give the appropriate hand-and-arm signal.

4.   Take cover to reduce exposure, using whatever means is readily available.

5.   Decontaminate exposed skin using the individual decontaminating kit, as necessary.

6.   Assume MOPP 4. Cover all your skin (your head and shoulders are already protected by the mask and the overgarment).
    a.   Put on the gloves with liners.
    b.   Zip and fasten the overgarment jacket.
    c.   Secure the hood, and then secure the overgarment to increase protection.
    d.   Put on the overboots.
Note. Combat boots provide protection but should be covered because they absorb chemicals. It takes a long time to put on the overboots, so put them on last in an emergency.

7.   Decontaminate personal equipment using the individual decontaminating kit as necessary.

8.   Notify your supervisor of any CB hazard markers or indicators.

9.   Continue the mission.

**NOTE**: After assuming MOPP 4 and performing all the tasks according to the unit standing operating procedure (SOP), perform the following actions:

(1) Use all means of CB detection to check your surrounding area for the presence of contamination.

(2) Contact your higher headquarters (HQ) if no contamination is found or if you determine the attack was non-CB.

(3) Await further guidance. (The higher HQ contacts all adjacent/attached units to check the status of CB contamination in their areas. If all units report the absence of contamination, the information is reported up the chain of command.)

(4) Annotate the above actions on your duty log (Department of the Army [DA] Form 1594).

### Evaluation Preparation:

SETUP: A good time to evaluate this task is during a field exercise when a variety of CB hazards can be simulated. Select a site with adequate cover, and ensure that soldiers are in MOPP 1.

BRIEF SOLDIER: Tell the soldier that there will be an encounter with simulated CB contamination and/or a CB alarm will be given. The task is to recognize the hazard and/or alarm and to take appropriate action to protect himself and warn other soldiers by giving the appropriate alarm.

### Performance Measures (1-9)                     GO      NO GO

1. Identified the CB hazard automatic masking criteria.

     ____    ____

2. Protected himself from CB contamination using his assigned protective mask without fastening the hood.                    ____    ____

3. Gave the alarm.                                   ____    ____

4. Took cover to reduce exposure, using whatever means was readily available.                                       ____    ____

5. Decontaminated exposed skin using the individual decontaminating kit as necessary.                                   ____    ____

6. Assumed MOPP 4. Covered all his skin.            ____    ____

7. Decontaminated personal equipment using the individual decontaminating kit as necessary.                    ____    ____

8. Notified the supervisor of any CB hazard markers or indicators.

     ____    ____

9. Continued the mission.                            ____    ____

**Evaluation Guidance:** Score the soldier GO if all steps are passed (P). Score the soldier NO-GO if any step is failed (F). If the soldier fails any step, show him how to do it correctly.

**References**

**Required**

FM 3-11.4 (3-4)

TM 3-4230-229-10

TM 3-4230-235-10

**Related**

FM 3-11.5 (3-5)

---

# DECONTAMINATE YOURSELF AND INDIVIDUAL EQUIPMENT USING CHEMICAL DECONTAMINATING KITS

**031-503-1013**

**Conditions:** You are at mission-oriented protection posture (MOPP) 2 given the assigned protective mask, protective gloves, a full canteen of water, a poncho, load-bearing equipment (LBE), assigned decontaminating kit(s) and applicable technical manuals (TMs). Your skin is contaminated or has been exposed to chemical agents, or you have passed through a chemically contaminated area.

**Standards:** Decontaminate yourself and your individual equipment using chemical decontaminating kits. Start the steps to decontaminate and eyes within 1 minute after you found they were contaminated. Decontaminate all exposed skin and your eyes as necessary before chemical agent symptoms occur. Decontaminate all personal equipment for liquid contamination after decontaminating your skin, face, and eyes.

**Performance Steps**

1. Assume MOPP 3.

---

**CAUTION**

The M291 Decontaminating Kit is for external use only. Keep decontaminating powder out of your eyes, cuts, and wounds. The decontaminating powder may slightly irritate your skin or eyes. Use water to wash the toxic agent out of your eyes, cuts, or wounds.

---

**WARNING**

Death or injury may result if you breathe toxic agents while decontaminating your face. If you need to breathe before you finish, reseal your mask, clear it, check it, get your breath, and then resume the decontaminating procedure.

---

---

> **CAUTION**
>
> After decontamination with water, cover exposed cuts or wounds with appropriate first aid wrap or bandages before handling the decontaminating package.

2.  Decontaminate your skin using the M291 decontaminating kit according to TM 3-4230-229 10. Go to step 3 after skin decontamination is complete.

> **CAUTION**
>
> Keep the decontaminating powder out of your eyes, cuts, and wounds. Do not handle or hold leaking packets above your head, touch or rub your eyes with anything that has been in contact with the decontaminating powder, or touch your lips or the inside of your mouth with anything that has been in contact with the decontaminating powder.

> **CAUTION**
>
> Do not attempt to decontaminate a loaded weapon. Always unload, clear, and place weapons on safe before starting decontaminating procedures.

> **CAUTION**
>
> Immediate decontaminating techniques remove only the liquid hazard. Certain items may still present a vapor hazard. See your supervisor for unmasking procedures.

    a.  Decontaminate your hands, your face, and the inside of your mask.

    b.  Assume MOPP 4.

    c.  Remove the decontaminating powder with soap and water when operational conditions permit.

3.  Decontaminate your individual equipment using the M295 decontaminating kit according to TM 3-4230-235-10.

    a.  Use the first mitt to decontaminate your gloves, the exposed areas of your mask and hood, your weapon, and your helmet.

    b.  Use the second mitt to decontaminate your LBE and accessories, your mask carrier, your overboots and your gloves again.

    c.  Remove the decontaminating powder when operational conditions permit.

4.  Dispose of hazardous waste materials.

a. Dispose of uncontaminated hazardous waste materials.

(1) Dispose of expended or unserviceable materials according to federal, state, and local laws; military regulations and publications; host nation laws (if more restrictive than United States [US] laws); and local standing operating procedures (SOPs).

(2) Place used decontaminating materials in a sealed plastic bag, and label it with the contents (as a minimum). Give the bag to your supervisor.

b. Dispose of contaminated hazardous waste materials. Inform your supervisor of the status of contaminated hazardous waste.

**Evaluation Preparation:**

SETUP: A good time to evaluate this task is while in a field environment. Gather materials for disposal of hazardous waste according to federal, state, and local rules and regulations.

BRIEF SOLDIER: Tell the soldier what body parts and equipment are contaminated.

| **Performance Measures (1-4)** | **GO** | **NO GO** |
|---|---|---|
| 1. Assumed MOPP 3. | ___ | ___ |
| 2. Decontaminated his skin using the M291 decontaminating kit. | ___ | ___ |
| 3. Decontaminated his individual equipment using the M295 decontaminating kit. | ___ | ___ |
| 4. Disposed of hazardous waste materials. Complied with all federal, state, and local laws and regulations. | ___ | ___ |

**Evaluation Guidance:** Score the soldier GO if all steps are passed (P). Score the soldier NO-GO if any step is failed (F). If the soldier fails any step, show him how to do it correctly.

**References**

| **Required** | **Related** |
|---|---|
| FM 3-11.5 (3-5) | FM 3-11.4 (3-4) |
| TM 3-4230-229-10 | |
| TM 3-4230-235-10 | |

# REACT TO INDIRECT FIRE WHILE DISMOUNTED
## 071-326-0510

**Conditions:** You are a member (without leadership responsibilities) of a squad or team. You are either in a defensive position or moving on foot. You hear incoming rounds, shells exploding or passing overhead, or someone shouting "incoming."

**Standards:** Reacted to each situation by shouting "Incoming!" followed the leader's directions if available. Took or maintained cover.

### Performance Steps (1-4)

1.  Shout "incoming!" in a loud, easily recognizable voice.

2.  Look to your leader for additional instructions.

3.  Remain in your defensive position (if appropriate), make no unnecessary movements that could alert the enemy to your location.

4.  Take cover outside of the impact area (if you are in an exposed position or moving), keep your body low if the leader is not in sight.

### Evaluation Preparation:

SETUP: Take the soldiers on a simulated march or field exercise.

BRIEF SOLDIERS: Tell the soldiers they must react to indirect fire on the move and when in a fixed position when they receive the command of "Incoming."

| Performance Measures | GO | NO GO |
| --- | --- | --- |
| 1. Shouted "incoming" in a loud, easily recognizable voice. | | |
| 2. Looked to the leader for additional instructions. | ___ | ___ |
| 3. Remained in defensive position (if appropriate), made no unnecessary movements that could alert the enemy to their location. | ___ | ___ |
| 4. Took cover outside of the impact area (if they were in exposed position or moving), kept their body low if the leader was not in sight. | ___ | ___ |

**Evaluation Guidance:** Score the soldier GO if all performance measures are passed. Score the soldier NO-GO if any performance measure is failed. If the soldier scores NO-GO, show the soldier what was done wrong and how to do it correctly.

**References**

**Required**                    **Related**

FM 3-21.75 (21-75)

---

# REACT TO DIRECT FIRE WHILE MOUNTED

## 071-410-0002

**Conditions:** In a combat environment, given tracked vehicle and a requirement to react to direct fire.

**Standards:** The vehicle has returned fire and taken appropriate action after analysis of the situation based on an order received from the chain of command.

**Performance Steps**

NOTE: If the vehicle is in formation, it moves IAW company tactical SOP. If not, it should use evasive action as appropriate to avoid threat fire while performing Step 2.

1. Direct return fire to destroy or suppress threat fire.

NOTE: If threat is destroyed, continue the present mission.

2. Direct the driver to a hull down position.

NOTE: Direct dismount, if appropriate, to establish a base of fire.

3. Analyze the situation.

4. Give a situation report.

5. Take defensive or offensive action based on orders from chain-of-command.

**Evaluation Preparation:**

SETUP: At the test site, provide a tracked vehicle all equipment and materials listed in the task condition statement. Use only blank ammunition for training. Take the soldiers on a simulated march.

BRIEF SOLDIER: Tell the soldiers to simulate direct fire while mounted in a tracked vehicle.

**Performance Measures (1-5)**                    **GO**      **NO GO**

1.  Directed return fire to destroy or suppress threat fire.


2.  Directed the driver to a hull-down position.      ____      ____
3.  Analyzed the situation.                            ____      ____
4.  Gave a situation report.                           ____      ____
5.  Took defensive or offensive action based on orders from the chain-of-command.

                                                       ____      ____


**Evaluation Guidance:** Score the soldier GO if all performance measures are passed. Score the soldier NO-GO if any performance measure is failed. If the soldier scores NO-GO, show the soldier what was done wrong and how to do it correctly.

**References**

**Required**        **Related**
                    FM 3-21.7 (7-7)
                    FM 3-21.71 (7-7J)

====================================================

# SELECT TEMPORARY FIGHTING POSITIONS
**071-326-0513**

**Conditions:** You must select a temporary fighting position when in an overwatch position, after initial movement into a tentative defensive position, at a halt during movement, or upon receiving direct fire.

**Standards:** Selected a firing position that protected you from enemy observation and fire, and allowed you to place effective fire on enemy positions without exposing most of your head and body.

**Performance Steps (1-5)**

1.  Choose a position that takes advantage of available cover and concealment. See Figure A-7 (071-326-0513-1).

NOTE: Cover gives protection from bullets, fragments of exploding rounds, flame, nuclear effects, and biological and chemical agents. Cover can also conceal you from enemy observation. Cover can be natural or man-made. Concealment is anything that hides you from enemy observation. Concealment DOES NOT protect you from enemy fire. DO NOT think that you are protected from the enemy's fire just because you are concealed. Concealment, like cover, can also be natural or man-made.

**Figure A-7. (071-326-0513-1) Temporary fighting positions.**

2.  Choose a position that allows you to observe and fire around the side of an object while concealing most of your head and body.

3.  Choose a position that allows you to stay low when observing and firing, whenever possible.

NOTE: This position allows you to aim better and take advantage of concealing vegetation.

4.  Choose a position with a background that does not silhouette you against the surrounding environment.

NOTE: A position like this reduces your chances being detected.

5.  Follow your leader's directions after your initial selection of a temporary battlefield position.

NOTE: Your leader may reposition you to gain better coverage of the area.

**Evaluation Preparation:**

SETUP: Evaluate this task during a march or a simulated march in an area with varying degrees of cover and concealment. Have the soldier in full battle gear.

BRIEF SOLDIER: Tell soldier that the enemy has been reported in the area and may be encountered at any time. At preselected points during the march, at a rest halt, after ordering the soldier to take an overwatch position, or after ordering the soldier to take a tentative defensive position, have the soldier select a temporary fighting position.

**Performance Measures**                                    **GO        NO GO**

1. Chose a position that took advantage of available cover and concealment.

\_\_\_\_\_   \_\_\_\_\_

2. Chose a position that allowed for observation and fire around the side of an object while concealing most of your head and body.

\_\_\_\_\_   \_\_\_\_\_

3. Chose a position that allowed you to stay low when observing and firing, whenever possible.

\_\_\_\_\_   \_\_\_\_\_

4. Chose a position with a background that did not silhouette you against the surrounding environment.

\_\_\_\_\_   \_\_\_\_\_

5. Followed leader's directions after initial selection of a temporary battlefield position.

\_\_\_\_\_   \_\_\_\_\_

**Evaluation Guidance:** Score the soldier GO if all performance measures are passed. Score the soldier NO-GO if any performance measure is failed. If the soldier scores NO-GO, show the soldier what was done wrong and how to do it correctly.

**References**

**Required**                **Related**

FM 3-21.75 (21-75)

# Army Programs

Soldiers sometimes need help beyond what the chain-of-command or NCO support channel can provide directly. In those cases, soldiers may not be able to fully concentrate on their duties if they or their families are working through financial, substance abuse, or other problems. The Army has therefore built agencies and programs to assist soldiers and their families. Some are recreational in nature, others are assistance programs, and still others are important tools for maintaining discipline, morale, or soldier well-being. The Army also has an extensive education program that includes tuition assistance for attending college level courses. All this shows that the Army takes care of its own. In this appendix you'll find a description of many of these programs.

# MORALE, WELFARE, RECREATION (MWR) AND FAMILY PROGRAMS

B-1.   Morale, Welfare, and Recreation (MWR) is a name that covers many different programs. Though we usually think of MWR as the bowling alley or unit fund money, this term applies to Army Community Service, youth services, family programs, and outdoor recreation programs. Do you like to fish, work out, travel, play sports, act in plays, or coach? Or do your like relaxing, watching the big game on TV, hanging out with friends and eating hot pizza? Or maybe you're a golfer, bowler, swimmer, racquetball player, skier or snowboarder. Most importantly, you want your family taken care of when you're deployed. You want your children to have fun, yet be safe and supervised. Lastly, you want to be heard if you have issues or concerns about your life in the Army.

B-2.   The US Army Community and Family Support Center, Headquarters, Department of the Army agency, delivers more than 200 Morale, Welfare and Recreation (MWR), and family programs through a worldwide 37,000-member workforce, including those stationed in the Balkans and the Middle East to serve deployed troops. Commanders regard MWR as a readiness multiplier that keeps soldiers physically fit, fosters healthy families, reduces stress, builds skills and self-confidence, and creates esprit de corps. The MWR philosophy is that soldier's and their families are entitled to the same quality of life as the Americans they pledge to defend.

B-3.   Child and youth services (CYS) programs reduce the conflict between mission and parental responsibilities. Basic CYS programs are child development centers, family child care home systems, before and after-school programs, school liaison and school transition services, youth sports and fitness programs and partnerships with Boys & Girls Clubs and 4-H Clubs. Services are provided year-round and include full-day, part day, after school, hourly, special needs, seasonal, supervised programs and care options. Congress and the White House recognize the military childcare system as a "model for the Nation."

B-4.   Individual and team sports for men and women include basketball, soccer, volleyball, rugby, softball, and martial arts. At gymnasiums, certified instructors conduct aerobics for cardiovascular fitness and supervise strength training with weights. Recreation centers offer a variety of social activities, games (table tennis, billiards), classes, and meeting space. Army libraries provide books, magazines, electronic information resources, and professional reference services for academics and recreation reading. Army libraries send book kits to remote and isolated sites as well as to deployed soldiers.

B-5.   Outdoor recreations (OR) opportunities vary by geographic location, climate, and demand. They range from high-challenge activities such as ropes courses, mountain climbing, and rappelling to extreme sports such as snowboarding, para gliding, and windsurfing. Many installations have forests, parks, rivers, and lakes that invite fishing, hunting, hiking, camping, and boating. Need equipment? Rent it from Outdoor Recreation.

B-6.    Arts and crafts centers are outlets for creativity and are money-savers. Trained staff members ensure safe use of tools and equipment. At automotive craft shops, you can change your car's oil or change a motor. The centers offer tools, bays, classes, and assistance available for nominal fees. Outlets for creative expression in the performing arts include music and theater events such as Battle of the Bands, one-act play festivals, the US Army Soldier Show, community theater, entertainment contests and chart topping celebrity performers who stage concert at installations.

B-7.    Sports bars, casual dining restaurants, fast food outlets, and community clubs offer ethnic and traditional foods as well as nightlife on post. Military members enjoy significant discounts at many major amusement parks, resorts, and attractions. For more information, visit www.offdutytravel.com. The Army operates four Armed Forces recreation centers: Disney .World (Orlando, Fla.), Garmisch/Chiemsee (Bavaria, Germany), Waikiki Beach (Hale Koa Hotel, Honolulu, Hawaii), and Dragon Hill Lodge (Seoul, Korea).

B-8.    Expect to pay fees and charges for MWR and family programs; profits are reinvested locally in MWR programs. A percentage of profits from the Army and Air Force Exchange Service (AAFES) are used to fund MWR programs. When you shop at AAFES and patronize MWR, you help sustain these programs for the future. MWR programs are for all soldiers and families: active duty, reserve components and retirees, married and single, living on post or off. For additional information, visit the MWR website at www.armymwr.com.

## SOLDIER ASSISTANCE

### ARMY COMMUNITY SERVICE (ACS)

B-9.    Army Community Service (ACS) programs offers real-life solutions for soldiers and their families. Your ACS equips people with the skills and education they need to face the challenges of military life today and tomorrow. Think of ACS when deploying or relocating, needing information and referrals, needing financial assistance, employment services, or for crisis and family assistance. The following are some of the ACS programs that may exist at Army installations worldwide:

- Deployment and mobilization support.

- Assistance with family readiness groups.

- Relocation readiness.

  - Group training for pre/post moves.

  - Cross-cultural training for bicultural families.

  - SITES (Standard Installation Topic Exchange Service).

  - Guidance counseling before, during, and after the move.

- Outreach to waiting families.
- Lending closet.
- Sponsorship training.
- Financial Readiness.
  - Army Emergency Relief.
  - Education and financial planning, Consumer Affairs and Financial Assistance Program (CAFAP).
  - Confidential budget counseling and debt management assistance.
  - Emergency food voucher.
  - Consumer information and advocacy.
- Family Advocacy Program.
  - Stress and anger management classes.
  - Victim advocacy.
  - Emergency placement care.
  - Family violence prevention briefings.
- Exceptional Family Member Program (EFMP).
- Installation Volunteer Program.
- Army Family Action Plan.
- Army Family Team Building (AFTB).
- Employment Services.

B-10. ACS facilitates a commander's ability to provide comprehensive, coordinated, and responsive services that support the readiness of soldiers, civilian employees, and their families. For more information on Army Community Service programs see the ACS homepage at www.armycommunityservice.org.

## EQUAL OPPORTUNITY PROGRAM IN THE ARMY

B-11. The Equal Opportunity (EO) program formulates, directs, and sustains a comprehensive effort to maximize human potential and to ensure fair treatment for all persons based solely on merit, fitness, and capability in support of readiness. EO philosophy is based on fairness, justice, and equity. Commanders are responsible for sustaining a positive EO climate within their units. Specifically, the goals of the EO program are to—

- Provide EO for military personnel and family members, both on and off post and within the limits of the laws of localities, states, and host nations.
- Create and sustain effective units by eliminating discriminatory behaviors or practices that undermine teamwork, mutual respect, loyalty, and shared sacrifice of the men and women of the US Army.

- Additionally, in many circumstances, Department of the Army (DA) civilians may use the Equal Employment Opportunity complaint system. Army Regulation 690-600, *Equal Opportunity Employment Discrimination Complaints*, provides further guidance.

B-12. The Army provides equal opportunity and fair treatment for military personnel, family members, and DA civilians without regard to race, color, sex, religion, or national origin and provide an environment free of unlawful discrimination and offensive behavior. This policy applies both on and off post, during duty and non-duty hours, and applies to working, living, and recreational environments (including both on and off post housing).

B-13. Soldiers will not be accessed, classified, trained, assigned, promoted, or otherwise managed on the basis of race, color, religion, gender, or national origin. The assignment and utilization of female soldiers is partially governed by federal law. AR 600-13, *Army Policy for the Assignment of Female Soldiers*, prescribes policies, procedures, responsibilities, and the position coding system for female soldiers.

B-14. Rating and reviewing officials will evaluate each member's commitment to elimination of unlawful discrimination and/or sexual harassment and document significant deviations from that commitment in evaluation reports. Substantiated formal complaints require a "Does not support EO" on the NCOER or the OER. This documentation includes administering appropriate administrative, disciplinary, or legal action(s) to correct inappropriate behavior.

B-15. Equal Opportunity references include the following:

- AR 600-20, *Army Command Policy*, Chapters 4, 5, 6 and Appendix E.

- Department of the Army Affirmative Action Plan (DA Pam 600-26).

- The Army's Consideration of Others Handbook.

## EQUAL EMPLOYMENT OPPORTUNITY

B-16. The Equal Employment Opportunity (EEO) Program has similar goals as the EO Program but is designed to assist and protect the civilians supporting the Army and Department of Defense, under Title VII of the Civil Rights Act of 1964. It ensures equal opportunity in all aspects of employment for Army civilian employees and applicants for employment. Employment policies and practices in DA will be free from unlawful discrimination based on race, color, religion, sex, age, national origin, or handicap. The basic principle of equal employment opportunity underlies all aspects of the civilian personnel management program in the Army. The program allows civilian employees who believe they are victims of discrimination to make complaints through several avenues.

B-17. It is DA policy to provide equal employment opportunity to all soldiers and DA civilians under applicable EEO laws and regulations. These laws and regulations include Title VII of the Civil Rights Act of 1964, the Age Discrimination in Employment Act, the Rehabilitation Act, and AR 690-600. These laws and regulations prohibit discrimination in employment based on race, color, religion, sex, national origin, age, disability, or reprisal and promote the realization of equal opportunity. The EEO office manages the complaint-processing program and advises the commander on EEO matters.

B-18. Mediation may be a means to address conflicts, disputes, complaints, grievances, or other problems in the workplace. Mediation is best described as assisted negotiations between two parties with neutral mediators facilitating the process. It is a private process whereby the parties are empowered to resolve their own issues. For additional information read AR 690-12, *Equal Employment Opportunity and Affirmative Action*, and AR 690-600 or visit your installation EEO office.

## ARMY SUBSTANCE ABUSE PROGRAM

B-19. The Army Substance Abuse Program (ASAP) provides assistance to active duty soldiers, DACs, family members, and retirees. The ASAP goal is to strengthen the overall fitness and effectiveness of Army personnel and enhance the combat readiness of soldiers. Command involvement throughout the identification, referral, screening and elevation process is critical. Details are in AR 600-85, *Army Substance Abuse Program*.

B-20. Soldiers who fail to participate as directed by the commander or do not succeed in rehabilitation are subject to administrative separation. Soldiers will reenroll except as determined by the clinical director in consultation with the unit commander. Commanders will, without exception, separate all soldiers who are identified as drug abusers. Commanders must refer for evaluation all soldiers who they suspect of having a problem with drugs or alcohol. This includes knowledge of any convictions for Driving While Intoxicated (DWI).

B-21. The ASAP primary care manager (PCM) will conduct an initial screening evaluation interview with referred soldiers to recommend one or more of the following:

- Referral to Army Drug and Alcohol Prevention Training (ADAPT).
- Referral to ADAPT and enrollment in the out-patient program.
- Referral to the ASAP outpatient program and to the Community Mental Health Clinic.
- Referral to an in-patient or partial program if the commander and clinical director agree to in-patient or partial program placement.
- Counseling by the unit commander.

B-22. The commander's involvement is critical in the rehabilitation process. The commander must ensure that enrolled soldiers are attending sessions, getting random biochemical testing and breathalyzers, and participating in the program. The objectives of rehabilitation and treatment are to return the soldier to full duty as soon as possible or identify for separation those who cannot be rehabilitated. For more information, see AR 600-85 and the Army Center for Substance Abuse Programs website at acsap.army.mil.

## ARMY CAREER AND ALUMNI PROGRAM – TRANSITION ASSISTANCE

B-23.  The Army Career and Alumni Program (ACAP) assists military personnel, Department of Defense (DOD) civilians affected by reduction in force (RIF), and their family members with the employment search process by providing the highest quality guidance, training, resources, and support during their career transition from federal service. Family members and veterans of all branches of the armed services can utilize ACAP services. The program aids individuals and their family by identifying transitioning needs and providing assistance in meeting those needs. The ACAP job assistance personnel provide access to a national and local job resource database and career counseling.

B-24.  Soldiers preparing for retirement may begin pre-separation counseling up to 24 months prior to retirement and all other soldiers may begin pre-separation counseling up to 12 months prior to separation. Through ACAP, the Army takes care of its own. Some of the specific services include assistance in resume writing, interview techniques, job search skills, listing of job opportunities with federal, state, and local governments, and civilian agencies. The ACAP on-line is a program that provides transition and job assistance information, job listings, and links to related sites. For additional information, visit and your local installation ACAP center, the ACAP website at www.acap.army.mil, or refer to DA PAM 635-4, *Preseparation Guide.*

## ARMY EMERGENCY RELIEF

B-25.  Army Emergency Relief (AER) is a private nonprofit organization incorporated in 1942 by the Secretary of War and the Army Chief of Staff. Although AER is a private corporation, it is, in effect, the US Army's own emergency financial assistance organization. AER is dedicated to "Helping the Army Take Care of Its Own" and providing emergency financial assistance to the following persons:

- Soldiers on extended active duty and their dependents.
- Reserve component soldiers (ARNG and US Army Reserve) serving under Title 10, US Code, on continuous active duty for more than 30 days and their dependents.
- Soldiers retired from active duty and their dependents.
- Surviving spouses and orphans of eligible soldiers who died while on active duty or after they retired.

B-26.  AER can provide emergency financial assistance for the following: rent, utilities, food, emergency travel, emergency privately owned vehicle (POV) repair, non-receipt of pay, funeral expenses, emergency medical or dental expenses, clothing after fire or other disasters. Unless unusual circumstances exist, AER cannot assist with the following: ordinary leave or vacations, fines or legal expenses, debt payments, home purchases or improvements, purchase, rental or lease of a vehicle, funds to cover bad checks, and marriage or divorce. AER assistance is normally in the form of a loan. AER never charges interest on any loan. Sometimes the assistance is available as a grant or combination loan and grant.

B-27. The AER provides emergency financial assistance to soldiers and their dependents. However, as a secondary mission it provides monetary assistance for undergraduate education of dependent children of soldiers (active duty, retired or deceased) and spouses of active duty soldiers in certain overseas locations.

B-28. Active duty soldiers who wish to request AER assistance may obtain the appropriate application form (DA 1103) through their unit and must obtain their commander's recommendation. Unaccompanied family members, surviving spouses or orphans, retirees, and others not assigned to or under control of your installation may obtain the necessary forms at any local AER office. All applicants must provide their military ID card and substantiating documents (i.e., car repair estimate, rental contract, etc.).

B-29. Soldiers and their dependents can also receive assistance at any Navy-Marine Corps Relief Society, Air Force Aid Society, or Coast Guard Mutual Assistance office. If they are not near a military installation, soldiers and their dependents can receive assistance through their local chapter of the American Red Cross. For more information visit your local AER office, the AER website at www.aerhq.org, or refer to AR 930-4, *Army Emergency Relief*.

## TOTAL ARMY SPONSORSHIP PROGRAM

B-30. The Total Army Sponsorship Program provides the structure and foundation for units to welcome and help prepare soldiers, civilian employees, and family members for their new duty station in advance of their actual arrival. This program is available to soldiers in the active Army, Army National Guard, Army Reserve, and civilian employees assigned to positions within the Department of the Army. The sponsor is the key to helping the new soldier, civilian employee, and family get comfortably settled as quickly as possible, thereby putting his mind at rest so he can concentrate on his new duties as soon as possible.

B-31. The unit will appoint a sponsor within 10 calendar days after the organization receives DA Form 5434 or DA Form 5434-E unless the incoming soldier or civilian employee declines. If no sponsor is desired, the unit will send a welcome letter from the battalion or activity commander (for officers); command sergeant major (for enlisted soldiers); or commander or activity director (for civilian employees). The unit will not provide additional sponsorship action until arrival. Upon arrival, the unit will assign a sponsor to the incoming soldier or civilian employee. The assigned sponsor will be of equal or higher grade than the incoming soldier or civilian employee when practical. The sponsor will also be of the same sex, marital status, and military career field or occupational series as the incoming soldier or civilian employee when feasible. The sponsor will be familiar with the unit or activity and community.

B-32. The sponsor will normally not be the person being replaced by the incoming soldier or civilian employee, or within 60 days of permanent change of station (PCS). For more information on Army sponsorship, see AR 600-8-8, *The Total Army Sponsorship Program*, your local Army Community Service office, and your unit sponsorship program proponent.

# FAMILY ASSISTANCE

## ARMY FAMILY ACTION PLAN

B-33.  The Army Family Action Plan (AFAP) is input (concerning family issues) from the people of the Army to Army leadership. The Army's leaders have recognized that to have a quality Army, you must be satisfied with the Army way of life. AFAP is a process that lets soldiers and families say what's working, what isn't, and what they think will fix it. It alerts commanders and Army leaders to areas of concern that need their attention, and also gives them the opportunity to quickly put plans into place to begin resolving the issues. AFAP also—

- Gives commanders a gauge to validate concerns and measure satisfaction.
- Enhances Army's corporate image.
- Helps retain the best and brightest.
- Results in legislation, policies, programs, and services that strengthen readiness and retention.
- Safeguards well-being.

B-34.  Since you are in the Army, you can become an AFAP participant—

- If you are a commander, you can support a strong AFAP program in your community and you can draw on the real-time quality of life information AFAP provides.
- If you are a soldier (active or reserve), retiree, civilian, or family member you can be part of the AFAP program in the following ways:
  - Be a delegate and share your good ideas.
  - Volunteer to help with a conference, assist with the program, or be a member of the local AFAP Advisory Committee.
  - Become familiar with current AFAP issues, tell people what's happening, and get them energized to promote Army well being through the AFAP process.

B-35.  AFAP starts with local AFAP forums, active Army, reserve component soldiers, retirees, surviving spouses, DA civilians, family members, and tenant organizations identifying issues they believe are important to maintain a good standard of living. Commanders resolve local issues at the installation level and update participants quarterly at in process reviews (IPR) which are open to the public. Commanders may forward more difficult issues requiring higher level involvement to higher commands, including Headquarters, Department of the Army (HQDA) AFAP. Delegates come from throughout the Army to address the top issues and propose solutions. The General Officer Steering Committee (GOSC) reviews the progress of AFAP issues on a semiannual basis and is the final deciding authority.

## ARMY FAMILY TEAM BUILDING

B-36.   Army Family Team Building (AFTB) is a volunteer-led organization with a central tenet: provide training and knowledge to spouses and family members to support the total Army effort. Strong families are the pillar of support behind strong soldiers and AFTB's mission is to educate and train all of American's Army in knowledge, skills, and behaviors designed to prepare our Army families to move successfully into the future. AFTB's vision statement says it all: "Empowering families for the 21st century." The organization is about providing proactive, forward-thinking support for today's families and ensuring the strength of tomorrow's Army. Army Family Team Building has three separate tracks: soldiers (active and reserve), DA civilians, and family members.

## FAMILY READINESS PROGRAMS

B-37.   The mission of family readiness programs is to foster total Army family readiness, as mission accomplishment is directly linked to soldiers' confidence when their families are safe and capable of carrying on during their absence. A wide variety of resources are available to assist soldiers and spouses. You can access most of these programs through Army Knowledge Online (AKO) or your unit NCO support channel. Some of these programs are as follows:

- Married Army Couples Program.
- Unit family readiness groups.
- Family care plans.
- Information and referral programs.
- Budget counseling.
- Counseling and counseling referrals.
- Child and spouse abuse treatment and prevention.
- Employment assistance.
- Exceptional Family Member Program (EFMP).

## FAMILY ADVOCACY PROGRAM

B-38.   The Department of the Army recognizes the importance of families in retention and unit readiness. The Family Advocacy Program (FAP) uses a coordinated community approach to support soldiers and families in an attempt to prevent family violence. The key element of the FAP is prevention through the education of families about the short and long term effects of family violence. Prevention of and intervention in family violence are a community responsibility. Various agencies within the community work together to ensure an effective and comprehensive program. For soldiers and family members involved in family violence, early referral reduces risk, establishes safety limits, and provides treatment for victims and offenders affected or involved in abuse. The FAP provides training and support to units and individuals in the following areas:

- Family violence.
- Intervention and treatment.
- Emotional support and counseling.
- Emergency financial assistance.
- Parenting education.
- Relationship support.
- Child care issues.
- Victim advocacy.
- Transitional compensation.

B-39. For additional information contact your installation Family Advocacy Program Manager or refer to AR 608-18, *The Army Family Advocacy Program*.

## FAMILY READINESS GROUPS

B-40. The Family Readiness Groups (FRGs) purpose is to encourage self-reliance among members by providing information, referral assistance, and mutual support. FRGs achieve readiness by providing an atmosphere and an agenda of activities, which builds cohesiveness among unit members. FRGs serves as the conduit between the command and family members. There is no rank in the family readiness groups and that is the key to its success. All soldiers and family members are members of the FRG. Common goals of FRGs include:

- Welcoming service and family members into the unit.
- Developing relationships that enable effective communication.
- Fostering a sense of belonging to the team in all family members.
- Creating forums for family members to develop friendships and support each other.
- Establishing communication networks.
- Providing and participating in formal FRG professional development training.

B-41. Every unit manages its family readiness group differently, depending on the personality of leaders, the number of families involved, available resources, etc. The core of the family readiness group is the unit. All FRGs throughout the Army share the same purpose: to support Army families.

## EXCEPTIONAL FAMILY MEMBER PROGRAM

B-42. The Exceptional Family Member Program (EFMP) is a mandatory enrollment program for those family members who require special medical or educational services. The program provides comprehensive services consisting of medically related issues. It is also an educational and social support service that enhances the readiness and quality of life for families with special needs. An exceptional family member is a family member with a physical, emotional, developmental, or intellectual disability that requires special treatment, therapy, education, training, or counseling.

B-43. Special needs can range from learning disabilities to medical conditions such as asthma, seizure activity and/or mental health conditions. The program ensures medical and educational needs are accessible and appropriate to accommodate these individuals' needs. For additional information, visit your ACS center and local EFMP office at your installation.

# EDUCATION

## ARMY CONTINUING EDUCATION

B-44. The Army Continuing Education System (ACES) promotes lifelong learning and sharpens the competitive edge of the Army now and for the Future Force. It instills the organizational value of education within the active Army, Army Reserve and Army National Guard. ACES is committed to excellence in service, innovation, and deployability. Through Army education centers worldwide, ACES provides educational programs and services to support the professional and personal development of soldiers, adult family members, and DA civilians.

B-45. ACES programs and services help to improve the combat readiness of America's Army by expanding soldier skills, knowledge, and aptitudes to produce confident, competent leaders. The programs support leader development and soldier career progression by building job-related critical thinking and decision-making skills required for warfighting, sensitive peacekeeping operations, and success on the digitized battlefield. Education programs and services support the enlistment, retention, and transition of soldiers.

> *The advancement and diffusion of knowledge is the only guardian of true liberty.*
>
> **James Madison**

B-46. Army education centers offer a wide variety of programs (certificate, associate, bachelor's, and master's degrees) through US vocational-technical schools, colleges, and universities. Professional education counselors assist soldiers to develop education goals and educational plans to achieve them in a cost-effective, timely manner. For additional information visit your installation education center or the ACES website at www.armyeducation.army.mil. Army continuing education policy and guidance are found in Army Regulation (AR) 621-5, *Army Continuing Education System*. Related publications include AR 621-202, *Army Education Incentives and Entitlements,* and AR 611-5, *Army Personnel Selection and Classification*.

## GREEN TO GOLD PROGRAM

B-47.   The Green to Gold Program seeks talented young enlisted soldiers who want to earn a commission as an Army officer. Quality enlisted soldiers with leadership potential, who have served at least two years on active duty, are allowed to voluntary request discharge from active duty to enroll in the Army Reserve Officer Training Corps (ROTC).

B-48.   Enlisted soldiers who meet the prerequisites can either apply for a 2, 3, or 4-year scholarship or can participate in the Green to Gold Program (without applying for or earning a scholarship). Soldiers who participate in this program are discharged from active duty under the provisions of Chapter 16-2, Army Regulation 635-200. Cadets who entered the ROTC through the Green to Gold program, whether under a scholarship or not, may use their Montgomery GI Bill (MGIB) benefits and receive a tax-free stipend.

B-49.   Local Army ROTC cadre give periodic briefings on the Green to Gold Program at Army installations. You may also receive information at the ROTC detachment on a walk-in basis. Basic qualifications for Green to Gold are as follows (some waivers are possible):

- Have served on active duty for two years.
- Attain a general technical (GT) score of 110 or higher.
- Recommended by your company commander and the first field grade officer in the chain-of-command.
- Have neither UCMJ, civil convictions, nor have any such actions pending.
- Have no more than three dependents and are not a single parent.
- Pass a physical examination in accordance with (IAW) AR 40-501, *Standards of Medical Fitness.*
- Meet height and weight standards IAW AR 600-9, *Army Weight Control Program.*
- Pass the Army physical fitness test (APFT) with a minimum of 60 points in each event.
- Eligible to reenlist.
- Accepted for admission by a college or university that offers ROTC.
- Receive a Letter of Acceptance into the ROTC program from the Professor of Military Science (PMS) at the institution you will attend.

B-50.   Scholarship requirements for the Green to Gold Program are the following (no waivers):

- Complete your degree and Military Science requirements by your 25th birthday as of 30 June of the year you're commissioned. You can add one year to the 25 year limit for each year of active duty up to four years (i.e. maximum age for a scholarship is 29 regardless of time on active duty).

- Have a 2.5 grade point average (GPA) on all college work completed.
- Have a minimum American College Test (ACT) assessment score of 19 or Scholastic Assessment Test (SAT) score of 920 for a 3 and 4 year scholarship.

B-51.    To participate in the Green to Gold Program without a scholarship you must be accepted as an academic junior and have an approved academic worksheet (Cadet Command Form 104-R) that shows you will complete the program in two years.

B-52.    You may enroll in Army ROTC the same time you enroll in college. Army ROTC is available at more than 800 colleges and universities. For more information visit your nearest ROTC representative or the Army ROTC website at www.armyrotc.com.

## UNITED STATES MILITARY ACADEMY PREPARATORY SCHOOL (USMAPS)

B-53.    Each year about 200 enlisted soldiers are offered admission to the US Military Academy or the Preparatory School at Fort Monmouth, New Jersey. Although some soldiers are offered direct admission to West Point, most attend the Prep School first. All applications are made directly to West Point. Soldiers not directly admitted to West Point will be automatically considered for admission to the Prep School.

B-54.    In addition to having a sincere interest in attending West Point and becoming an Army officer, applicants must be—

- US citizens.
- Unmarried with no legal obligation to support dependents.
- Under 23 years of age prior to 1 July of the year entering USMA (under 22 prior to 1 July of the year entering the Prep School).
- A high school graduate or have a General Education Development (GED) certificate.
- Of high moral character.

B-55.    Soldiers who meet the basic eligibility requirements, have achieved SAT scores greater than 1000 or ACT composite score of 20 or higher and achieved average grades or better in their high school curriculum are especially encouraged to apply. Soldiers must obtain an endorsement from their company or lowest-level unit commander. While this endorsement constitutes a nomination, soldiers are also strongly encouraged to obtain additional nominations from their congressional nomination sources.

## FUNDED LEGAL EDUCATION PROGRAM (FLEP)

B-56.    The Office of the Judge Advocate General (OTJAG) annually accepts applications for the Army's Funded Legal Education Program (FLEP). Under this program, the Army sends active duty commissioned officers to law school at government expense if funding permits. Selected officers remain on active duty while attending law school and have an active duty service obligation (ADSO) upon completion.

B-57. Details are in Chapter 14, AR 27-1. This program is open to commissioned officers in the rank of second lieutenant through captain. Applicants must have at least two but not more than six years of total active Federal service at the time legal training begins. Eligibility is governed by Title 10 of the US Code and is non-waivable. Your local Staff Judge Advocate has further information.

### ARMY MEDICAL DEPARTMENT (AMEDD) ENLISTED COMMISSIONING PROGRAM (AECP)

B-58. The AECP allows active duty enlisted soldiers to obtain a scholarship to attend college in a full-time student status while still receiving full pay and benefits in their current grade. Application to the AECP is open to all active duty army enlisted soldiers, regardless of MOS, who are able to gain acceptance as a full time student to an accredited nursing program with an academic and clinical curriculum in English; and graduate within 24 calendar months. Soldier applicants must have a minimum of 3 years and maximum of 10 years of active component enlisted military service at the time of commission. Time in service waivers will be approved or disapproved by PERSCOM on a case by case basis. Applicants must extend or re-enlist to have at least 36 months of time remaining on active duty after graduating from the Bachelor of Science in Nursing (BSN) program, based on projected date of graduation.

B-59. Upon earning their BSN degree and successfully completing the National Council for Licensure Examination-RN (NCLEX-RN), these soldiers are commissioned second lieutenants in the Army Nurse Corps (active component). Selected soldiers will have an ADSO after commissioning. For more information contact your local Army Education Center or Army Medical Treatment Facility (MTF) Education Department. You may also see the AECP website at http://www.usarec.army.mil/AECP/.

## OTHER ASSISTANCE FOR THE SOLDIER AND FAMILY

### BETTER OPPORTUNITIES FOR SINGLE SOLDIERS (BOSS)

B-60. Better Opportunities for Single Soldiers (BOSS) is a program that helps commanders address the well-being and morale issues of the single and unaccompanied soldiers in their units. It is one of more than 200 Army morale, welfare, and recreation programs delivered by the US Army Community and Family Support Center, a headquarters Department of the Army agency.

B-61. Established in 1989 as a balance to the emphasis on increased family-oriented programming, installation BOSS programs are governed by Army Regulation 215-1, Morale, Welfare and Recreation Activities and Nonappropriated Fund Instrumentalities, and Department of the Army Circular 608-01-01, Better Opportunities for Single Soldiers Program. Designed to provide a "voice" for single soldiers, BOSS has three key components: well-being, community service, and recreation/leisure activities.

B-62. BOSS has programs at 48 installations in the continental US and 47 installations outside the US. Each installation has an MWR advisor for BOSS programs, who is in the Directorate of Community [and Family] Activities (DCA or DCFA). An elected committee or council of soldier representatives from installation units operate the BOSS program; the command sergeant major approves the committee members who serve for one year. Upon being elected or appointed, BOSS representatives are placed on additional duty orders and are expected to be at all BOSS meetings when the unit mission does not dictate otherwise.

B-63. Committee members coordinate single soldier activities and events that fall within two key components of the program: community service and recreation/ leisure activities. They also gather input on well-being issues, input which is worked to resolution at the lowest command level. Empowered with this responsibility, single soldiers feel more respected and bonded into the "Army of One." Likewise soldiers see that their voice counts and they are heard on issues that affect their well-being.

B-64. BOSS representatives must brief their chain-of-command before any program is implemented at the installation. With the aid of the MWR advisor, the soldier representative plans and executes events in tandem with the mission of the command. BOSS works in conjunction with other MWR programs such as entertainment, recreation centers, or outdoor recreation activities. BOSS soldiers assume a lead role in planning special BOSS events that meet the needs and desires of the single soldiers on that installation. BOSS councils have sponsored events such as soldier talent competitions, concerts, dances, and trips.

B-65. BOSS further encourages and assists single soldiers in identifying and participating in community service and volunteer opportunities. BOSS representatives contribute to their communities by serving in post organizations and on various councils, such as the Army and Air Force Exchange Service (AAFES), dining facilities, health promotion, MWR, barracks, Defense Commissary Agency, and Army Family Action Plan.

B-66. BOSS members plan and execute community service projects with national programs such as Big Brothers and Big Sisters, Habitat for Humanity, Adopt-a-Highway and Special Olympics. BOSS representatives coordinate partnerships with recruiters to take delayed entry program recruits on tours of an installation. They have also initiated programs, such as BOSS Against Drunk Drivers (BADD) and Adopt-a-Soldier, that address commanders' concerns about soldier isolation during holiday periods. BOSS soldiers also support installation programs by volunteering with Child and Youth Services. By partnering with the Army Community Service Installation Volunteer Coordinator, BOSS ensures all soldier volunteer hours are documented, giving soldiers valuable experience for future referrals.

## AMERICAN RED CROSS

B-67. Today's American Red Cross service to the Armed Forces is keeping pace with the changing military through its network of 900 local chapters and 109 offices located on military installations worldwide. Both active duty and community-based military can count on the Red Cross to provide emergency communication services around-the-clock, 365 days a year, keeping the service member and his/her family in touch across the miles.

B-68.   Although we are most familiar with the Red Cross messages when there is a family emergency, the Red Cross also provides access to financial assistance through the military aid societies, counseling, information and referral, and veteran's assistance. While not a part of the Department of Defense, Red Cross staff members deploy along side the military to such areas as Afghanistan, Kosovo, Saudi Arabia, and Kuwait working and living amongst the troops to ensure they receive vital Red Cross services.

B-69.   The Red Cross often conducts blood drives and offers a full menu of disaster and health and safety training courses. These activities are available to service members and their families at Red Cross chapters and on military installations. For additional information on Red Cross programs and services, go to www.redcross.org and click on AFES (Armed Forces Emergency Services) or call the toll free number 1-877-272-7337.

## CASUALTY ASSISTANCE PROGRAM

B-70.   The casualty assistance program provides assistance to the primary next-of-kin (PNOK) of deceased soldiers and retirees. The Army may provide casualty assistance to the PNOK of all deceased soldiers in the following categories—

- Active Duty military.
- USAR/ARNG enroute to/from/participating in Active Duty Training.
- Soldiers in AWOL status.
- Army retirees.
- Soldiers separated from the Army less than 120 days.

B-71.   The main objectives of casualty assistance are the following:

- Assist the PNOK during the period immediately following a casualty.
- Eliminate delay in settling claims and paying survivor benefits.
- Assist the PNOK in other personnel-related affairs.

B-72.   The Army has established Casualty Assistance Commands (CAC) at most major installations where the PNOK of deceased soldiers can get help. Department of the Army policy concerning casualty assistance is that the CAC will appoint a Casualty Assistance Officer (CAO) when a soldier is reported as deceased or missing. PNOK of retirees must request a CAO. While casualty assistance is provided to the PNOK, advice and guidance may be provided to other next of kin (NOK) if warranted by the situation, but a CAO need not be appointed.

B-73.   The CAO and CAC helps families cope with the loss of their soldier. Primarily the CAO (or CAC if a CAO has not been appointed) helps the PNOK in understanding the entitlements for a military funeral, applying for the various benefits due to the beneficiaries of the deceased and providing other assistance in regards to military benefits.

B-74. Notification of the PNOK and secondary next of kin (SNOK) occurs as promptly as possible and in a timely, professional, dignified and understanding manner. In death and missing cases, a uniformed service representative personally conducts the notification and confirms it by written communication. Soldiers who perform the notification will always be in Class A uniform. Only officers, warrant officers and senior noncommissioned officers in grade sergeant first class through command sergeant major will perform the notification. In other than death and missing cases or in the case of retirees or separated soldiers, notification is normally by telephone.

> *There's no more effective way of creating bitter enemies of the Army than by falling to do everything we can possibly do in a time of bereavement, nor is there a more effective way of making friends for the Army than by showing we are personally interested in every casualty which occurs.*
>
> **General of the Army George C. Marshall**

B-75. More information is available in AR 600-8-1, *Army Casualty Operations/Assistance/Insurance*, DA Pam 608-4, *A Guide for Survivors of Deceased Army Members*, DA Pam 600-5, *Handbook for Retiring Soldiers and Their Families*, or contact your local casualty area command for assistance. You may also visit the PERSCOM web site at www.perscom.army.mil for detailed information on the casualty assistance program.

## Appendix C

# Ceremonies

Ceremonies represent the pride, discipline, and teamwork of the Army and, in particular, the units that are part of those ceremonies. They are important in developing and maintaining unit pride, building esprit de corps, and preserving tradition. In some cases, funerals for example, military ceremonies are the only contact and impression of the Army that the public gets. In this appendix you will find examples for a change of command, change of responsibility, military funerals and memorial ceremony. You can also find here some other common ceremonies and where to find examples of them.

For more information on ceremonies, see FM 3-21.5, *Drill and Ceremonies*. The change of command is in Chapter 10. Military funerals are in Chapter 14.

C-1.     The examples in this appendix are not the only way to conduct these ceremonies or even the best way. They are suggested ways so your unit spends less time and energy "reinventing the wheel." Many units already have standard ways to conduct these ceremonies and don't need this appendix; that is outstanding. The important thing is to conduct them in a professional, military manner. You may not be responsible for making the ceremony happen, but these examples are available to save time and assist in standardization.

C-2.     A ceremony that isn't widely known is called the "Change of Responsibility" ceremony, shown in Section II. This is used when a First Sergeant or CSM change positions. Although many units don't use it, it is included here for those organizations that desire to do so. The passing of the NCO sword is symbolically powerful—like the passing of the colors in a change of command. The ceremony helps to reinforce NCO authority in the Army and highlights the support NCOs provide to the chain of command.

## SECTION I – CHANGE OF COMMAND

C-3. The change of command ceremony is described in FM 3-21.5, Chapter 10. The example shown in this appendix is tailored to a company level change of command. For ease in distinguishing a preparatory command from a command of execution, the commands of execution appear in **BOLD CAP** letters and preparatory commands appear in ***Bold Italic*** letters. Reference to positions and movements appear in *Italics*.

## COMPANY-LEVEL* CHANGE OF COMMAND CEREMONY

Note: Company is in formation at *Parade Rest* with platoon leaders in charge of their platoons and XO/COT in charge of the company. The 1SG and PSGs are to the rear of the formation.

Narrator: "Ladies and Gentlemen, the ceremony will begin in one minute, please be seated."

Action: The Outgoing and Incoming Commanders *move* to the ready line. When the Outgoing and Incoming Commander are in their positions, the COT starts the ceremony.

COT: *Faces about* and commands, "***Company***, **ATTENTION**" and "***Present***, **ARMS**." The COT executes an *about face* and *salutes* the Outgoing Commander. Upon return of his salute, the COT does an *about face*, commands "**Order, ARMS**" and "**Parade, REST**," does an *about face*, and assumes the position of *parade rest*.

Narrator: "Good Morning and welcome to the Change of Command Ceremony for (unit name). Today, CPT (Outgoing Commander's name) will relinquish Command of (unit name) to CPT (Incoming Commander's name)."

Narrator: "SPC (name) is presenting a bouquet of red roses to Mrs. (Outgoing Commander's spouse) for her devotion, dedication and tireless efforts to the soldiers and families of (unit name)."

Narrator: "SPC (name) is presenting Mr. (Incoming Commander's spouse) a bouquet of yellow flowers from the soldiers of (unit name) to welcome him to the company."

Narrator: (Reads Outgoing and Incoming Commanders' biographies and Unit History)

COT: At the completion of the unit history, executes an *about face* and commands, "***Company***, **ATTENTION**" and "***Present***, **ARMS**."

Narrator: "Ladies and gentlemen, please rise for the playing of the National Anthem and remain standing for the invocation."

COT: On the last note of the National Anthem the COT drops his salute, executes an *about face* and commands "*Order,* **ARMS**" and "*Parade,* **REST**." The COT executes an *about face* and assumes the position of *parade rest.*

Chaplain: Gives invocation.

Narrator: "Please be seated."

Narrator: "The (battalion name) Battalion Commander, Lieutenant Colonel (name), will now oversee the transfer of the guidon."

Action: The Battalion Commander** *moves* to the ready line.

COT: When the Battalion Commander is in position, the COT does an *about face* and commands "*Company,* **ATTENTION**" and "*Present,* **ARMS**".

COT: Does and *about face* and goes to the position of *present arms.*

COT: After salutes are exchanged, the COT does an *about face* and commands "*Order,* **ARMS**," then does another *about face.*

COT: In a low voice commands "*Guidon... Post.*"

Guidon Bearer: On the command of "Guidon" the unit guidon bearer assumes the position of *attention,* and the command "Post" the guidon bearer takes two steps *forward* executing a *right flank* as in marching, takes two steps, *halts* and executes *a left face.*

COT: In a low voice commands, "**MARCH.**"

Guidon Bearer: The guidon bearer takes three additional steps *forward.*

Action: When the guidon bearer has halted, the command group and First Sergeant *move* to a designated position in front of the unit guidon.

Narrator: "The transfer of the company guidon is significant in many ways; the history, traditions and accomplishments of (unit name) are embodied in it. With the transfer, the unit's legacy is passed as a building block for future performance and achievement. Historically, the flag or colors of a unit served as the point around which the soldiers of the organization rallied as they moved forward into battle. The colors have traditionally been at the side of the commander and were carried forward even when the commander fell in combat. All others may perish, but the colors live on. The guidon is an extension of the unit colors, to the company level. With the transfer of the guidon here today goes the transfer of responsibility for the accomplishment of the (unit name) mission and the welfare of the troops."

Narrator: "The senior NCO of the organization is traditionally responsible for maintenance and care of the Colors and so the First Sergeant passes the unit guidon to the Outgoing Commander, CPT (name), signifying the unit's appreciation for his leadership and guidance. CPT (Outgoing Commander's name) passes the company guidon to the Battalion Commander signifying the relinquishing of his command and gratitude for the opportunity to lead soldiers. LTC (name) then passes the guidon to the Incoming Commander, CPT (name), entrusting her with the responsibility and care of the unit. CPT (Incoming Commander's name) passes the guidon back to the First Sergeant, signifying her trust and confidence in the leaders and soldiers of the organization."

Action: The Outgoing Commander positions himself four steps in front of his guidon; the senior commander is directly to his left. The old and new commanders then take one step forward and execute *facing* movements so that they are *facing* each other. The First Sergeant takes the guidon from the guidon bearer (with his right hand above his left hand), and *faces about*. The narrator reads the assumption-of-command order.

Narrator: "In accordance with AR 600-20, Paragraph 3-4, the undersigned assumes command of the (unit name and location) effective (date). Signed, (Incoming Commander's signature block), commanding."

Action: Upon completion of the reading, the First Sergeant *steps forward* and *presents* the guidon to the Outgoing Commander (1), who grasps the guidon with the left hand above his right hand. The Outgoing Commander *passes* the guidon to the senior commander (2), who grasps the guidon with his right hand above his left hand and, in turn, *passes* the guidon to the Incoming Commander (3), who grasps the guidon with her left hand above her right hand. The Incoming commander *passes* the guidon to the First Sergeant (4) who grasps it with his right hand above his left hand, *faces about* and *returns* the guidon to the guidon bearer. This procedure (1-4) allows the guidon to be over the heart of the Incoming and Outgoing commanders. As the First Sergeant *faces about,* both commanders then execute *facing* movements back to their original direction *facing* the guidon.

Action: After the First Sergeant has returned the guidon to the Guidon Bearer, the Battalion Commander, Incoming Commander, and Outgoing Commander *face about*. The guidon bearer also *faces about*. The First Sergeant commands "*Forward,* MARCH" and the commanders march back to the ready line, the Outgoing and Incoming Commanders *exchange* positions. (Incoming commander *crosses* in front of Outgoing). The First Sergeant and guidon bearer *return* to their posts.

COT: After the command group is in position the COT does an *about face* and commands "*Parade,* REST" then does and about face and assumes the position of parade rest.

**Narrator**: "Ladies and gentlemen, the commander of the (higher unit name), Lieutenant Colonel (name)."

Battalion Commander: Battalion (senior) Commander remarks.

**Narrator**: "Captain (Outgoing Commander)."

Outgoing Commander: Outgoing Commander remarks.

**Narrator**: "The Commander of (unit name), Captain (Incoming Commander)."

Incoming Commander: Incoming Commander remarks.

Action: After remarks are complete the Incoming Commander returns to position.

COT: Executes an *about face* and commands "*Company*, ATTENTION" and *faces about*.

**Narrator**: "Ladies and Gentlemen, please stand for the playing of the (branch/unit song) and the Army Song." ***

Incoming Commander: At the completion of the Army Song, the Incoming Commander *moves* forward to assume command of the unit from the COT. After salutes are exchanged, the Incoming Commander waits until the COT is in position, executes an *about face*, and renders a hand *salute* to the Battalion Commander and reports **"Sir, this concludes the ceremony."**

Battalion Commander: **"Take charge of your company."**

Action: Salutes exchanged.

**Narrator**: "This concludes the (unit name) change of command ceremony. Please join us for refreshments in the (location), bldg xxxx."

* While the unit name "Company" is used, substitute as needed for Battery, Troop or Detachment.

** While the unit name "battalion" is used, substitute as needed for the appropriate higher unit commander.

*** See inside back cover for the words to the Army Song.

## SECTION II – CHANGE OF RESPONSIBILITY

For ease in distinguishing a preparatory command from a command of execution, the commands of execution appear in BOLD CAP letters and preparatory commands appear in *Bold Italic* letters. Reference to positions and movements appear in *Italics*.

## COMPANY-LEVEL* CHANGE OF RESPONSIBILITY CEREMONY

Note: The colors are present, located so that the company is facing them when the National Anthem is played. The guidon bearer has the NCO sword on his belt.

Note: The Senior Platoon Sergeant (Senior Platoon Sergeant) controls the company during the ceremony in place of the First Sergeant, similar to a Commander of Troops (COT) in a change of command or review. Platoons, under control of their platoon sergeants march to the final line five minutes before the start of the ceremony. When the platoon reaches the final line the platoon sergeant commands "*Mark Time*, MARCH" and "*Platoon*, HALT."

Senior Platoon Sergeant (Senior Platoon Sergeant): With platoons in position, the Senior Platoon Sergeant commands "*At close interval, dress right*, DRESS."

Platoon Sergeants: Platoon Sergeant *moves* to the left or right flank of the platoon, *aligns* the platoon, *returns* to the original position and commands "*Ready*, FRONT."

Senior Platoon Sergeant: When all Platoon Sergeants are in position, and the platoons are at the position of *Attention*, the Senior Platoon Sergeant commands "*Parade*, REST" and executes an *about face*.

**Narrator:** "Ladies and Gentlemen, the ceremony will begin in one minute, please be seated."

Action: The Outgoing and Incoming First Sergeants *move* to the ready line, the Company Commander and the Senior Platoon Sergeant are standing off to the side. When the Outgoing and Incoming First Sergeant are in position, the Senior Platoon Sergeant starts the ceremony.

Senior Platoon Sergeant: Executes an *about face* and commands, "*Company*, ATTENTION" and "*Present*, ARMS." Then the Senior Platoon Sergeant executes an *about face* and *salutes* the Outgoing First Sergeant. Upon return of his salute, the Senior Platoon Sergeant does an *about face*, commands "*Order* ARMS," and "*Parade*, REST," does an *about face* and assumes the position of *parade rest*.

<u>Narrator</u>: "Good Morning and welcome to the Change of Responsibility Ceremony for (unit name). Today, First Sergeant (Outgoing First Sergeant's name) will turn over the duties of First Sergeant of (unit name) to First Sergeant (Incoming First Sergeant's name)."

<u>Narrator</u>: "SPC (name, often an outstanding soldier such as the soldier of the month) is presenting a bouquet of red roses to (Outgoing First Sergeant's spouse) for her devotion, dedication and tireless efforts to the soldiers and families of (unit name)."

<u>Narrator</u>: "SPC (name) is presenting (Incoming First Sergeant's spouse) a bouquet of yellow flowers from the Officers and soldiers of (unit name) to welcome her to the company."

<u>Narrator</u>: (Reads Outgoing and Incoming First Sergeants' biographies and Unit History).

Senior Platoon Sergeant: At the completion of the unit history, executes an *about face* and commands, "*Company*, ATTENTION" and "*Present*, ARMS."

<u>Narrator</u>: "Ladies and gentlemen, please rise for the playing of the National Anthem and remain standing for the invocation."

Senior Platoon Sergeant: On the last note of the National Anthem the Senior Platoon Sergeant drops his salute, executes an *about face* and commands "*Order*, ARMS" and "*Parade*, REST." The Senior Platoon Sergeant executes an *about face* and assumes the position of *parade rest*.

<u>Narrator</u>: "Please be seated." After the audience is seated, "The (company name) Company Commander, CPT (name), will now oversee the transfer of responsibility."

Action: The Company Commander and Senior Platoon Sergeant *move* to the ready line.

Senior Platoon Sergeant: When the Company Commander and Senior Platoon Sergeant are in position, the Senior Platoon Sergeant does an *about face* and commands "*Company*, ATTENTION" and "*Present*, ARMS."

Senior Platoon Sergeant: Does and *about face* and goes to the position of *present arms*.

Senior Platoon Sergeant: After salutes are exchanged, the Senior Platoon Sergeant does and *about face* and commands "*Order*, ARMS," then does another about face.

Senior Platoon Sergeant: In a low voice commands "*Guidon... Post*."

Guidon Bearer: On the command of "Guidon" the unit guidon bearer assumes the position of *attention*, and on the command "Post" the guidon bearer takes two steps *forward* executing a right flank as in marching, takes two steps, *halts* and executes a *left face*.

Senior Platoon Sergeant: In a low voice commands, "**MARCH.**"

Guidon Bearer: The guidon bearer takes three additional steps *forward*.

Action: When the guidon bearer has halted, the command group and Senior Platoon Sergeant *move* to a designated position in front of the unit guidon.

Narrator: At this time CPT (name) joins First Sergeant (outgoing First Sergeant) and First Sergeant (incoming First Sergeant) for the passing of the noncommissioned officers sword. The War Department in 1840 adopted the unique noncommissioned officers sword. It is a completely functional weapon, not intended for display, but rather for hard and dedicated use. While no longer part of the Army's inventory, American sergeants wore it for over seventy years, during which occurred the Mexican-American War, the Civil War, and the Spanish-American war. The passing of the sword signifies the relinquishing of responsibility and authority from the outgoing to the incoming First Sergeant. First sergeants may come and go, but the sword remains razor sharp.

Narrator: "SFC (name), the Senior Platoon Sergeant, retrieves the sword from SPC (name) the guidon bearer. The guidon bearer, entrusted with the symbol of the unit, today also holds the First Sergeant's sword, symbol of the authority of the NCO. SFC (name) passes the sword to First Sergeant (Outgoing First Sergeant) in final deference to his authority and leadership. First Sergeant (Outgoing First Sergeant) passes the sword to the Company Commander signifying the relinquishing of his duties and gratitude for the opportunity to care for (unit) Company's fine soldiers. The Company Commander passes the sword to First Sergeant (incoming First Sergeant), delegating authority and entrusting him with the responsibility and care of the unit. The new First Sergeant passes the sword back to SFC (name) and the guidon bearer, symbolizing his dedication to the soldiers of (name) Company and the continuity of the NCO support channel."

Action: When the Narrator begins reading the previous paragraph, the Outgoing First Sergeant *positions* himself four steps in front of his guidon; the company commander is directly to his left. The old and new First Sergeants then take one step *forward* and execute *facing* movements so that they face each other. The Senior Platoon Sergeant *secures* the sword with scabbard from the guidon bearer's pistol belt (with his right hand above his left hand), and *faces about*. The Senior Platoon Sergeant *draws* the sword from the scabbard slightly (about 2 inches), steps forward and *presents* the sword to the Outgoing First Sergeant (1), who grasps the sword with the left hand above his right hand. The Outgoing First Sergeant *passes* the sword to the Company Commander (2), who grasps the sword with his right hand above his left hand and, in turn, *passes* the sword to the new First Sergeant (3), who grasps the sword with his left hand above his right hand. The Incoming First Sergeant *replaces* the sword completely in the scabbard and *passes* it to the Senior Platoon Sergeant (4) who grasps it with his right hand above his left hand, *faces about* and *reattaches* the sword on the guidon bearer's pistol belt. This procedure (1-4) allows the hilt of the sword to be over the heart of the Incoming and Outgoing First Sergeants. As the Senior Platoon Sergeant *faces about,* both First Sergeants then execute *facing* movements back to their original direction facing the guidon.

Action: The Senior Platoon Sergeant and the reviewing party *face about* and return to their post. The Senior Platoon Sergeant commands "*Forward,* **MARCH**" and the command group *marches* back to the ready line, the Outgoing and Incoming First Sergeants exchange positions. (Incoming First Sergeant crosses in front of Outgoing). The First Sergeant steps off to the left as in marching, and *marches* around the platoon to a position behind and centered on the formation. The guidon bearer executes an *about face* and returns to his position.

Senior Platoon Sergeant: After the command group is in position the Senior Platoon Sergeant does an *about face* and commands "*Parade,* **REST**" then does and *about face* and assumes the position of *parade rest.*

<u>Narrator</u>: "**Ladies and gentlemen, the commander of (company name), CPT (name).**"

Company Commander: Company Commander remarks.

<u>Narrator</u>: "**First Sergeant** (Outgoing First Sergeant)."

Outgoing First Sergeant: Outgoing First Sergeant remarks.

<u>Narrator</u>: "**The First Sergeant of (company name) First Sergeant (Incoming First Sergeant).**"

Incoming First Sergeant: Incoming First Sergeant remarks.

Action: After remarks are complete the Incoming First Sergeant *returns* to position.

Senior Platoon Sergeant: Executes an *about face* and commands "*Company,* **ATTENTION**" and *faces about.*

<u>Narrator</u>: "**Ladies and Gentlemen, please stand for the playing of the (branch/unit song) and the Army Song.**" **\*\***

Incoming First Sergeant: At the completion of the Army Song, the Incoming First Sergeant moves *forward* to assume command of the unit from the Senior Platoon Sergeant. After salutes are exchanged, the Incoming First Sergeant waits until the Senior Platoon Sergeant is in position, executes an *about face*, and renders a hand *salute* to the Company Commander and reports "**Sir, this concludes the ceremony.**"

Company Commander: "**Take charge of the company.**"

Action: Salutes exchanged.

<u>Narrator</u>: "**This concludes the (unit name) Change of Responsibility ceremony. Please join us for refreshments in (location), bldg xxxx.**"

\* While the unit name "Company" is used, substitute as needed for Battery, Troop or Detachment.

\*\* See inside back cover for the words to the Army Song

## SECTION III – MEMORIAL CEREMONY

C-4. Memorial ceremonies are patriotic tributes to deceased soldiers. These ceremonies are command-oriented so attendance is often mandatory. The ceremony is a military function that is not normally conducted in a chapel. The content of the ceremony may vary depending on the desires of the commander.

C-5. In most cases, the unit prepares a program that may include a biographical summary of the deceased soldier with mention of awards and decorations. The following elements are commonly part of a memorial ceremony:

- Prelude (often suitable music).
- Posting of the Colors.
- National Anthem.
- Invocation.
- Memorial Tribute (e.g., remarks by unit commander or a friend of the deceased).
- Scripture Reading.
- Hymn or other special music.
- Meditation (quiet moment for attendees to reflect).
- Benediction.
- Last Roll Call. This is a final tribute paid by soldiers to their fallen comrade. It has its origin in the accountability roll call conducted by the unit First Sergeant following combat. Although sometimes painful to listen through, the Last Roll is called with the conviction held by soldiers that all unit members will be accounted for, and none will ever be forgotten.
- Firing of rifle volleys.
- Taps.

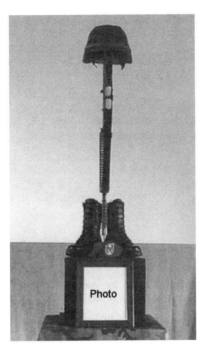

**Figure C-1. Fallen Soldier Display**

C-6.   Most units prepare a visible reminder of the deceased soldier similar
to that depicted in Figure C-1. The helmet and identification tags signify
the fallen soldier. The inverted rifle with bayonet signals a time for prayer,
a break in the action to pay tribute to our comrade. The combat boots
represent the final march of the last battle. The beret (in the case of
soldiers from airborne units) reminds us that the soldier has taken part in
his final jump.

## SECTION IV – MILITARY FUNERALS

C-7. Rendering military funeral honors is our Nation's final tribute to those who have made personal sacrifices in the service of our country. Performing duties as part of a funeral detail is a privilege. It a distinct means of honoring fellow soldiers who have served before us or who have given their lives in defense of our Nation.

C-8. Since the January 2000 National Defense Act, military funeral honors are authorized for all active duty soldiers, military retirees, and honorably discharged veterans by their parent service. For active duty soldiers and military retirees, honors include firing of rifle volleys, uniformed soldiers as pallbearers, folding and presentation of the flag to the next-of-kin, and playing of "Taps" by a bugler or a high quality recording. For deceased veterans of the Armed Forces, honors rendered may be by a two-person team to fold and present the flag and a high quality recording of "Taps."

> *The effect of having the Honor Guard perform their solemn duties with care and precision shows how much we care for our comrades in arms, as well as for the communities and families they represent.*
>
> MG Robert Ivany

C-9. Army installations, reserve component units, and ROTC detachments often support funerals of veterans by providing soldiers to conduct the military honors for those funerals. Field Manual 3-21.5, Chapter 14 provides a description of how to conduct a military graveside service. That description shows how to do the service with 14 or more soldiers. In this section you can find how to conduct the service with 8 or fewer soldiers. In any case, if you are a member of a funeral detail, remember this: you are taking part in a service for a deceased veteran and there are people present who will take comfort in your professional attitude and performance.

C-10. Many Army installations already have detailed instructions for conducting military honors at a funeral. This section may be helpful to soldiers who do not have access to such specific instructions. For every military funeral, the OIC should contact the funeral director as early as possible to determine if there will be any variations. At the completion of the service, the OIC should again contact the funeral director to conduct an informal after action review. Finally, when the detail returns to home station, the OIC should AAR the service with the tasking authority.

C-11. For ease in distinguishing a preparatory command from a command of execution, the commands of execution appear in **BOLD CAP** letters and preparatory commands appear in ***Bold Italic*** letters. Reference to positions and movements appear in *Italics*.

# 8 SOLDIER FUNERAL DETAIL

## COMPOSITION OF DETAIL

C-12. The 8 man funeral detail normally consists of an OIC or NCOIC (depending on the rank of the deceased veteran), an NCOIC of the firing party, a five or six soldier firing party (who also act as pallbearers) and a bugler, if available. For this description there is an OIC of the funeral detail and an NCOIC of the firing party/pallbearers.

## DETAIL, WEAPONS ARE IN PLACE

C-13. Weapons are pre-stacked in an appropriate position, in plain view, and a good distance from the gravesite. The firing party, acting as pallbearers, is pre-positioned along the roadside; awaiting the arrival of the hearse. The OIC is located where the hearse will stop.

## RECEIVING THE CASKET

C-14. As the hearse approaches, the NCOIC orders the detail to "*ATTENTION*" and "*Present,* ARMS." Once the hearse has passed the detail, the NCOIC calls the detail to "*Order,* ARMS" and "*Parade,* REST." The OIC comes to *attention* and *present arms* as the hearse approaches his position. The OIC terminates his salute when the hearse comes to a halt.

C-15. After the vehicle has come to a halt, the driver gets out and opens the rear door. The driver prepares the casket for movement to the gravesite by removing the stock. The driver pulls the casket to the rear of the hearse. The OIC, with a nod of his head, signals the NCOIC to move the pallbearers to the end of the hearse, three on each side, to remove the casket. The NCOIC marches the pallbearers into place, then orders "*Mark time,* MARCH;" "*Detail,* HALT" and "*Center,* FACE." After the pallbearers are facing inward, the individuals closest to the casket will grasp the handrails and pull the casket from the hearse. Each pallbearer, in turn, grasps a casket handle as it reaches him. The OIC will render a hand *salute* while the casket is being removed.

### Moving the Casket

C-16. On the NCOIC's command of "*Ready,* FACE," the pallbearers will execute the appropriate facing movements so that they are all facing the feet of the casket. The NCOIC orders the detail to "*Forward,* MARCH." Led by the OIC, the pallbearers incline to the proper direction to *move* to the gravesite, ensuring the casket is level and feet first. Once the casket is over the gravesite, the NCOIC commands "*Mark Time,* MARCH," and "*Detail,* HALT." Once at the head of the gravesite, the OIC will come to render a hand salute until the casket is placed on the lowering device. To maintain uniformity the pallbearer NCOIC will command "*Center,* FACE." When pallbearers are facing center, the casket is set on the lowering device. After the casket is set down, the pallbearers come to attention and the OIC will drop his hand salute.

## MOVING TO THE WEAPONS

C-17. On the command "*Ready*, FACE," by the pallbearer NCOIC, the pallbearers all face toward the head of the casket. The next command is "*Forward*, MARCH." The pallbearers move from the gravesite to the location of the weapons. Just prior to reaching the stacked arms, the firing party NCOIC, and formerly the pallbearer NCOIC, gives "*Mark Time*, MARCH" and "*Detail*, HALT." The firing party NCOIC assumes their position and gives a "*File from the Left, Forward*, MARCH." On the command "*March*" the firing party performs the proper movements to form a single file to the rear of the weapons. When the firing party are to the rear of the stacked arms, the NCOIC gives "*Mark Time*, MARCH" and "*Detail* HALT," and the appropriate facing movement to face the rifles.

### Retrieving the Weapons and Conclusion of Religious Services

C-18. The next command given is "*Take*, ARMS." On the command of execution, the stack man secures the first two weapons. The left and right soldiers receive the weapons from the stack man. The left and right soldiers then pass the weapons to the outside soldiers. The stack man grasps his center weapon. The left and right soldiers step toward the stack and remove their weapons, returning to the position of *Attention*. Once the left and right soldiers retrieve their weapons, the stack man secures his weapon and comes to the position of *Attention*. Once all of the firing party is at *Order Arms*, the firing party NCOIC gives them "*Parade*, REST." The firing party will remain at *Parade Rest* until the end of the religious services. Once the religious services are over, the Chaplain steps away from the casket. The OIC steps to the head of the casket and renders a hand salute. This is the signal for the firing party NCOIC to command the firing party "ATTENTION."

### Firing of Honors

C-19. After bringing the firing party to *Attention*, the NCOIC gives the command of "*Ready*." At the command of *Ready*, each rifleman executes *Port Arms*, faces *Half Right*, and moves his right foot to the right ten inches. Each rifleman then chambers a round, places his weapon on Fire, and resumes *Port Arms*. When the firing party has completed the movements, the firing party NCOIC gives the command "*Aim*." On the command of *Aim*, the detail shoulders their weapons with the muzzles of the weapons at a 45-degree angle from the horizontal. When the NCOIC commands "FIRE," the detail fires and returns to *Port Arms*. On the subsequent commands of "*Ready*," each rifleman pulls and returns the charging handle of his weapon. After the third round is fired each rifleman resumes *Port Arms*, and the firing party NCOIC commands "CEASE FIRE." Each rifleman places his weapon on Safe, resumes the position of *Order Arms*, and faces *Half Left*. The firing party NCOIC then commands "*Present*, ARMS" for the playing of "Taps". The bugler plays "Taps." If a bugler is not available, one soldier is positioned to turn on the high quality recording (and is not part of the firing party).

## STACKING ARMS

C-20. After "Taps", the NCOIC brings the firing party to "*Order,* ARMS," and then commands "*Stack,* ARMS." On the command of execution, *Arms,* the stack man grasps the barrel of his rifle and places his rifle directly in front of him. At the same time, the left and right soldiers grasp the barrels of their respective rifles, step toward the center and insert the muzzles through the sling loop of the stack man's weapon. Both soldiers swing the butts of their rifles out and then down to the ground ensuring the stack is steady. The two outside weapons are then passed to the stack man, who adds them to the stack.

## RETURNING TO GRAVESITE OR SHELTER

C-21. After *Stack Arms* is complete, the NCOIC moves the firing party two steps backward and gives the appropriate facing movement to have the firing party move back to the gravesite. From this position, the NCOIC will form the firing party in two columns by giving the command "*Column of Two to the Right,* MARCH." Once in *Column of Two* formation, the NCOIC takes the last position, and gives "*Forward,* MARCH." The firing party marches to the gravesite along either side of the casket. Once at the gravesite the NCOIC gives "*Mark Time,* MARCH," and "*Detail,* HALT." The NCOIC gives "*Center,* FACE," to ensure that all of the pallbearers are facing the casket.

## FOLDING THE FLAG

C-22. After the pallbearers have faced the casket, they use their peripheral vision to take their cues from the NCOIC. As a unit, the pallbearers reach down and secure the flag. Once flag is secured, the detail folds flag. The flag is first folded with the lower stripe area over the blue field. It is then folded so that the folded edge meets the open edge. The triangular fold is started at the striped end and is continued until only the blue field remains. The flag margin is then tucked in and the flag is ready for presentation.

## PRESENTING THE FLAG.

C-23. After the flag has been folded, it is passed down to the soldier closest to the right side of the OIC. This soldier executes a *Half Left* as the OIC executes a *Half Right* and the flag is then passed to the OIC at, chest level. After the pallbearer has passed the flag, he salutes the flag for three seconds then executes *Order Arms*. The soldier executes a *Half Right* as the OIC executes a *Half Left* and resumes their original position. At this time the pallbearers will leave the gravesite. The NCOIC commands "*Outward,* FACE," (pallbearers face towards the head of the casket) and "*Forward,* MARCH." Once the detail is out of the area, the OIC will present the flag to the next of kin or Chaplain, it next of kin is not available. The OIC recites the following passage:

*"Ma'am (sir), this flag is presented on behalf of a grateful nation and the United States Army as a token of appreciation for your loved one's honorable and faithful service."*

C-24. At the conclusion of the remarks and presentation, the OIC will render a hand salute and hold the salute for three seconds then assumes *Order, Arms.* OIC then executes marching movement and marches back towards the direction of the pallbearers.

### CONCLUDING THE CEREMONY

C-25. The firing party returns to the location of the stacked arms in the same manner as before. When commanded to "*Take*, ARMS," the party retrieves the rifles in the same manner as before. After retrieving the weapons, the NCOIC marches the detail away from the funeral site to clear and inspect the weapons. The firing party will police all of the brass after the service is over and the next of kin have left the area. The OIC is not required to escort the next of kin back to his/her vehicle.

## 2 SOLDIER FUNERAL DETAIL

### RECEIVING THE CASKET

C-26. The OIC is located where the hearse will stop. The NCO is to the left of the OIC. As the hearse approaches, the OIC brings himself and the NCO to "ATTENTION" and "*Present*, ARMS." The OIC gives the command of "*Order*, ARMS," after the hearse has come to a halt. The funeral director is responsible for removing the casket from the hearse and placing it on the lowering device at the gravesite. When the casket is being removed from the hearse, the OIC commands "*Present*, ARMS." Once the casket has cleared the peripheral vision of the OIC, then the OIC commands "*Order*, ARMS," and "*Parade*, REST."

### CONCLUSION OF RELIGIOUS SERVICES

C-27. Once the religious services are over, the Chaplain steps away from the casket. The OIC commands "ATTENTION." The OIC commands "*Ready*, FACE," and the OIC and NCO face in the direction of the casket. OIC then commands "*Forward*, MARCH," The OIC *marches* to the head of the casket, and *faces* the head of the casket, while the NCO marches to the foot of the casket facing the OIC. If a bugler is not available, the NCO moves to the device that will play the high quality recording of "Taps."

### FOLDING THE FLAG

C-28. The OIC gives the command to the NCO to secure flag. Once the flag is secure the bugler will play "Taps" and both the OIC and NCO execute *Present, Arms.* When "Taps" is complete, both the OIC and NCO execute *Order, Arms.* The OIC gives the command to side step march (just far enough to preclude the flag from touching the casket). Once the OIC and NCO have cleared the casket the OIC nods to begin folding the flag. NOTE: If a bugler is not available, once the casket is on the lowering device, the

NCOIC will march to the recording device and wait for the Chaplain to conclude religious services. He will play "Taps" after the OIC is positioned at the head of the casket. When "Taps" is complete, the NCOIC will march to the foot of the casket and then assist in folding the flag.

C-29. The flag is first folded with the lower stripe area over the blue field. It is then folded so that the folded edge meets the open edge. The triangular fold is started at the striped end and is continued until only the blue field remains. While folding the flag the NCO moves towards the OIC. The flag margin is then tucked in by the OIC and the NCO presents the flag to the OIC. Once the NCO presents the flag to the OIC, the NCO renders the hand salute and holds the salute for three seconds then executes Order, Arms. The OIC is ready for presenting the flag to the next of kin.

### PRESENTING THE FLAG

C-30. After the flag has been folded and passed to the OIC, the OIC then moves in the direction of the next of kin and presents the flag to the next of kin while the NCO marches away from the gravesite. The OIC will present the flag to the Chaplain if the next of kin is not available. The OIC recites the following passage:

> *"Ma'am (sir), this flag is presented on behalf of a grateful nation and the United States Army as a token of appreciation for your loved one's honorable and faithful service."*

C-31. At the conclusion of the passage and the flag presentation, the OIC will render a hand salute and hold the salute for three seconds then assumes Order, Arms. OIC then executes a marching movement and marches away from the gravesite.

### CONCLUDING THE CEREMONY

C-32. The OIC is not required to escort the next of kin back to his/her vehicle.

## NOTES

C-33. The meaning of the word gravesite also includes a committal shelter. The meaning of the word casket also includes a receptacle containing the cremated remains of the deceased. On windy days, the flag should already be anchored to the casket by the funeral director. If the flag is not secured, the detail will fold the flag immediately after placing the casket on the lowering device, then hand the flag to the OIC.

## OTHER CEREMONIES

C-34. **NCO Induction Ceremony** – See FM 7-22.7, *The Army Noncommissioned Officer Guide*, 23 Dec 2002, Appendix F.

C-35. **Retirement Ceremony** – Most installations conduct retirement ceremonies, see your installation DPTMS for details.

C-36. **Farewell Ceremony (for deploying units)** – Most installations conduct ceremonies to "send off" deploying units, see your installation DPTMS for details.

C-37. **Welcome Home Ceremony (for returning units)** – Most installations conduct ceremonies to welcome units back from deployments. These ceremonies often include participation from the civilian community around the installation. See your installation DPTMS for details.

## Appendix D

# Internet Resources

D-1. The Internet is a remarkable conduit to a vast storehouse of knowledge. Through the Internet, soldiers can, for example, find out how where the housing office is at Fort Carson, study for a Soldier of the Month Board, or "chat" with other maintenance soldiers in the Republic of Korea. The potential is obvious: soldiers can access and share knowledge, lessons learned and other important information in moments.

D-2. Some helpful websites are categorized as the following: General, Leadership, Assistance, Personnel, Training, History, News and Unit sites. Site addresses on the Internet often change without warning, but you can link to most of these sites through the Army Homepage or Army Knowledge Online.

## GENERAL

Army Knowledge Online – www.us.army.mil
> *Get your Army-wide email account here.*

US Army homepage – www.army.mil
> *The Army Homepage links to nearly every other official Army site.*

Army National Guard homepage – www.arng.army.mil

Army Reserve homepage – www.army.mil/usar

Reimer Digital Library — www.adtdl.army.mil
> *The Digital Library has electronic versions of most FMs, TCs, and other training documents for online viewing or download.*

US Army Publishing Agency – www.usapa.army.mil
> *Find ARs, DAPAMs and other Army administrative publications.*

Army Values – www.dtic.mil/armylink/graphics/values.html

Army Vision – www.army.mil/vision

Army Transformation – www.lewis.army.mil/transformation

Worldwide Locator – www.erec.army.mil
> *Find active and reserve soldiers around the world.*

## LEADERSHIP

The Army Leadership homepage – www.leadership.army.mil

The Army Counseling homepage – www.counseling.army.mil

US Army Sergeants Major Academy – usasma.bliss.army.mil
> *Find information on NCO matters, The NCO Journal Online and information on NCO Academies.*

## ASSISTANCE

Army and Air Force Exchange Service – www.aafes.com

Army Career and Alumni Program – www.acap.army.mil

Army Emergency Relief – www.aerhq.org

Education – www.armyeducation.army.mil

Employer Support of the Guard and Reserve – www.esgr.org
Delta Dental – www.deltadental.com
GI Bill – www.gibill.va.gov
Health Promotion and Wellness – www.hooah4health.com
Mobilization – www.defenselink.mil/ra/mobil
Morale, Welfare and Recreation – www.armymwr.com
Tricare – www.tricare.osd.mil

## PERSONNEL

Assignments – https://www.hrc.army.mil
Career Management (AC) – https://www.hrc.army.mil
Career Management (RC) – https://www.2xcitizen.usar.army.mil
Department of Veterans Affairs – www.va.gov
Enlisted Records and Evaluation Center – www.erec.army.mil
Official Military personnel File (OMPF) – https://ompf.hoffman.army.mil
NCOER – https://www.hrc.army.mil/select/ncoer.htm
Pay Chart – www.dfas.mil/money/milpay/pay
Pay Issues – https://mypay.dfas.mil/mypay.asp
Promotions (AC) – https://www.hrc.army.mil/select/Promo.htm
Promotions (RC) – https://www.2xcitizen.usar.army.mil/soldierservices
Retirement Services – www.armyg1.army.mil

## TRAINING

NCO Academies – https://www.hrc.army.mil/epncoes/ncoalink.htm
Battle Command Training Program – bctp.leavenworth.army.mil
Combat Maneuver Training Center – www.cmtc.7atc.army.mil
Joint Readiness Training Center – www.jrtc-polk.army.mil
National Training Center – www.irwin.army.mil
Center for Army Lessons Learned – call.army.mil

## HISTORY

Army Center for Military History – www.army.mil/cmh-pg
Medal of Honor Society – www.cmohs.org
Military History Institute – carlisle-www.army.mil/usamhi

## NEWS

Army News – www.dtic.mil/armylink
Army Newswatch – www.army.mil/newswatch.htm
Soldiers Radio and TV – www.army.mil/videos
Defense News – www.defenselink.mil
Early Bird News – ebird.dtic.mil

## UNIT SITES

US Army Training and Doctrine Command – www.tradoc.army.mil
US Army Forces Command – www.forscom.army.mil
US Army Pacific Command – www.usarpac.army.mil
US Army Southern Command – www.usarso.army.mil
US Army, Europe – www.hqusareur.army.mil

Eighth US Army – 8tharmy.korea.army.mil
US Army Special Operations Command – www.soc.mil
US Army Combined Arms Command – www.leavenworth.army.mil
US Army Combined Arms Support Command – www.cascom.army.mil
US Army Forces Central Command – www.arcent.army.mil
US Army Medical Command (MEDCOM) – www.armymedicine.army.mil
US Army Corps of Engineers – www.usace.army.mil
Military Traffic Management Command – www.mtmc.army.mil
I Corps – www.lewis.army.mil
III Corps – pao.hood.army.mil
V Corps – www.vcorps.army.mil
XVIII Airborne Corps – www.bragg.army.mil/18abn/default.htm

You can find most unit websites through the Army Homepage or Army
Knowledge Online (AKO).

# Professional Reading

E-1. Professional development, particularly self-development, requires reading. In addition to TMs, FMs, regulations or training circulars, it is worthwhile to read about our profession from the perspective of the many great soldiers who came before us.

E-2. In June 2000, US Army Chief of Staff General Eric K. Shinseki released a reading list to help soldiers further develop confidence, military knowledge, habits of reflection, and intellectual growth, whether they are officers, NCOs, or junior enlisted soldiers. The books on this list are designed to provoke critical thinking concerning the profession of soldiering and the unique role of our Army. There are works here that address issues and challenges relevant to each of us, from private to general. This list includes books that examine the past and those that consider the future. These readings deepen our understanding of the Army's values and traditions, the human face of battle, and the future's potential to transform the profession of arms in the 21st Century.

## BOOKS APPROPRIATE FOR JUNIOR ENLISTED SOLDIERS AND JUNIOR NCOS

E-3. *Band of Brothers: E Company, 506th Regiment, 101st Airborne from Normandy to Hitler's Eagle's Nest.* Stephen E. Ambrose, Touchstone Books, New York, 1993. During World War II, Easy Company was a world-class rifle company. Its soldiers fought on D-Day, in Arnhem, Bastogne and the Bulge; they spearheaded the Rhine offensive, took possession of Adolf Hitler's Eagle's Nest in Berchtesgaden, sustaining 150 percent casualties along the way. *Band of Brothers* is an absorbing account of some of E Company's most critical moments, providing insight into the lives of regular soldiers and their commanders. The book is based on interviews with survivors and soldiers' journals and letters.

E-4. *The Long Gray Line.* Rick Atkinson, Owl Books, New York, 1999. *The Long Gray Line* follows the 1966 West Point class through its 25-year journey from graduation to Vietnam into the difficulties of the peace that followed. The Class lived during an extraordinary time in US history, and Rick Atkinson speaks poignantly for a generation of people, such as Douglas MacArthur and William Westmoreland, who dealt with that era's turmoil, tragedy and disillusionment.

E-5. *The Greatest Generation.* Tom Brokaw, Random House, New York, 1998. Tom Brokaw tells the story of what he proclaims "the greatest generation" through individual stories of people who came of age during the Great Depression and World War II. These people were united by the common values of duty, honor, economy, courage, service, love of family and country and, most of all, responsibility for themselves. Brokaw introduces people who persevered through the Depression, then war, then went on to create the United States as we now know it.

E-6. *This Kind of War: The Classic Korean War History.* T. R. Fehrenbach, Brassey's, Dulles, VA, 2000. This book is a classic study in the consequences an army faces when it enters a war unprepared. Fehrenbach examines the challenges of maintaining a professional military force at odds with the society it is intended to defend. With the authority of personal experience, Fehrenbach describes battles and soldiers' hardships during the Korean War, foretelling with eerie accuracy some of the problems the US would face in Vietnam. In a human, realistic, concise manner, Fehrenback provides timeless insight about the US volunteer military.

E-7. *America's First Battles: 1776-1965.* Charles E. Heller and William A. Stofft, University Press of Kansas, Lawrence, 1986. The eleven essays in this book focus on the US Army's transition from the parade field to the battlefield during every war in which it has fought. Through careful analysis of organization, training and doctrine, each essay details strengths and weaknesses evidenced by the outcome of each war's first significant engagement. *America's First Battles* gives a novel, intellectually challenging view of how the United States has prepared for war, developed tactics and conducted operations.

E-8. *A Concise History of the US Army: 225 Years of Service.* David W. Hogan Jr., Center of Military History, US Army, Washington, DC, 2000. In this pamphlet David W. Hogan Jr., traces the US Army's proud 225-year history during the rise of the United States as a nation, detailing the Army's important contributions throughout US history.

E-9. *The Face of Battle.* John Keegan, Viking Press, New York, 1995. John Keegan, a senior instructor at Sandhurst, the British Military Academy, tries to answer the question: "What is it like to be in battle?" He examines the battles of Agincourt in 1415, Waterloo in 1815 and the Somme in 1916, comparing and contrasting various battlefield aspects, from hand-to-hand combat to the long-distance, impersonal destruction of faceless men in the industrial age.

E-10. *We Were Soldiers Once...and Young: Ia Drang - The Battle That Changed the War in Vietnam.* Lieutenant General (LTG) Harold G. Moore and Joeseph L. Galloway, Harper Perennial, New York, 1992. This book is a detailed account of the 1965 Ia Drang Valley Battle that marked the beginning of the massive ground war in Vietnam. As a lieutenant colonel, Harold G. Moore was the battalion commander who led the fight; Joseph L. Galloway was the journalist who accompanied Moore. From their experiences and first-hand accounts, including those of North Vietnamese commanders, they produced this chronicle of the 1st Battalion, 7th Cavalry. The book is a vivid portrait of sacrifice, perseverance and courage.

E-11. *Once An Eagle.* Anton Myrer, Harper Collins, New York, 2000. This gripping novel portrays the life of one special soldier, Sam Damon, and his adversary Courtney Massengale. Damon is the consummate professional soldier, decorated in both world wars, who puts duty, honor, and soldiers above self-interest. Massengale, the ultimate political animal, disdains the average grunt while advancing his career by making inroads into Washington's powerful elite. *Once An Eagle* is more than a chronicle of US warfare in the 20th century; it is a study in character and the values the US Army continues to cherish: courage, nobility, honesty and selflessness.

E-12. *The Killer Angels.* Michael Shaara, Ballantine Books, New York, 1974. The four days of the Battle of Gettysburg were the four bloodiest, most courageous days in the Nation's history. Michael Shaara recreates the battle in stunning detail. But the true brilliance of this historical novel is its insight into what the war meant. Two armies fought for two dreams: one for freedom, the other for a way of life. This book reveals the compassion of the men who led the Civil War armies, making their decisions understandable and even more admirable in the face of the confusion and panic they endured during battle.

## BOOKS APPROPRIATE FOR COMPANY GRADE OFFICERS, WO1-CW3, AND COMPANY CADRE NCOS

E-13. *Citizen Soldiers.* Stephen Ambrose, Simon & Schuster, New York, 1997. A broad look at the American campaign on the Western Front in WW II. The author considers every level of war, from strategy discussions of generals, to the tactics employed by junior officers, and the life of the combat soldier "on the ground." The dominant theme is that the "citizen soldiers" were called from peaceful pursuits of civilian life and matched against the fanaticism of the Third Reich, successfully. Readers gain an appreciation of the magnitude of the victory in Europe as soldiers exercise the utmost in leadership, courage, and innovation. The story is told mainly through a series of vignettes outlining the experiences of junior officers and NCOs. The book should serve any leader well as he or she prepares for the realities of warfare in a democratic society.

E-14. *The War To End All Wars: The American Military Experience in World War I.* Edward M. Coffman, Oxford University Press, New York, 1968. The War To End All Wars is the classic account of the American military experience in World War I. Coffman conducted extensive research in diaries and personal papers as well as official records and then filled out the written record with interviews of survivors, including General of the Armies Douglas MacArthur, General Charles L. Bolte, Lt. Gen. Charles D. Herron, Lt. Gen. Ernest N. Huebner, and Maj. Gen. Hanson E. Ely. By using these sources, Coffman sought to convey the human dimensions of the conflict as well as the grand strategy and the tactics of the Western Front. Coffman covers mobilization, the rudimentary training in the United States, the Navy's role in convoying the troops overseas, the organization and training of the American Expeditionary Forces in France, the American role in the air war, logistics, ground combat culminating in the Meuse-Argonne campaign, and demobilization. Coffman is particularly effective in discussing operations at the division and corps levels.

E-15. *Soldier and the State*. Samuel P. Huntington, Belknap Press of Harvard University Press, Cambridge, MA, 1957. The author traces the concept of the military professional through the two World Wars. More important, he provides the first thorough analysis of the nature and scope of professional officership. This book contains enough professional fodder to provide inquiring cadets and young officers with an image of what they might be as military professionals. A close reading of the book reveals a staggering challenge to the will and intellect of the aspirant. A classic in the basic tenets required of the professional officer in American society.

E-16. *Embattled Courage: The Experience of Combat in the American Civil War*. Gerald F. Linderman, The Free Press, A Division of Macmillan, New York, 1987. Combat studies tend to express themselves in two forms: as narrative accounts of wars, campaigns, and battles; or as accounts of individual soldiers, or groups of soldiers, in combat. Linderman's Embattled Courage, an example of the latter, examines the beliefs and behavior of volunteers from both Union and Confederate sides who sallied forth in 1861 to defeat their enemy. Based as it is on exciting and graphic excerpts from journals and letters of combat soldiers, Embattled Courage brims with authenticity and authority. As such, it offers much to the professional soldier. For those officers and enlisted personnel who have been in combat the book establishes a larger historical context which may help to better understand and digest their own experiences. For those who have not, but who may well do so in the future, Linderman has created a framework which may permit them to grasp, to a degree, the harsh realities, physical as well as psychological, of combat. To the degree which they can know these "harsh realities" through reading and study, they will adapt more quickly and perform more efficiently to a combat environment.

E-17. *Company Commander*. Charles B. MacDonald, Burford Books, Springfield, NJ, 1999. Original edition, 1947. Company Commander is Charles MacDonald's memoir of his experiences in World War II. Placed in command in September 1944 of Company I, 23d Infantry at the age of twenty-one, MacDonald, who had never been in battle, quickly underwent a harsh baptism of fire. He commanded his company until the end of the war, leading his men throughout the Battle of the Bulge, an unforgiving test of his and his company's mettle. MacDonald knew that he was responsible for other men's lives and that any mistake by him could mean someone's death. Written shortly after the war, the book communicates a keen sense of what it was like for an inexperienced officer to be thrown into a leadership role in combat, the personal skills it took to survive, and the intangibles that held small units together in the face of danger and deprivation. This book is less about tactics and weapons than what it takes on the personal and psychological level to fight and survive and be a company commander.

E-18. *Men Against Fire: The Problem of Battle Command in Future War*. S.L.A. Marshall. Reprint, Gloucester, Massachusetts: Peter Smith, 1978. Originally published by Infantry Journal Press, 1947. An examination of the infantry commander's problems in motivating soldiers in combat. Through a series of interviews with soldiers, the author describes how men can be conditioned to act as a cohesive unit under the stress of battle. Marshall raises many fundamental questions, still germane today, about why soldiers fail to fire their weapons in battle and how the lack of moral leadership can destroy the effectiveness of fighting organizations.

E-19. *For the Common Defense, A Military History of the United States of America.* Alan R. Millett, and Peter Maslowski. The Free Press, New York, 1984. For the Common Defense is one of the leading textbooks of American military history. The volume examines the American military experience from colonial times up to the fall of Saigon in 1975. Although the book describes the nation's major wars and military operations, its true focus is the evolution of American military policy. For the Common Defense puts narrower historical studies into a broader historical and intellectual context. It is vital that soldiers be acquainted with these broader themes if they are to understand the American military experience.

E-20. *Certain Victory.* Robert H. Scales, Jr., U.S. Army Command and General Staff College Press, Reprint, Fort Leavenworth, Kansas, 1994. A history of the US Army in the Gulf War (and related support activities) produced by the Army's Desert Storm Special Study Group, which was commissioned by Chief of Staff General Gordon H. Sullivan and directed by Brigadier General Robert H. Scales, Jr. The book provides one of the best summaries of how the professional of the 1980s differed from the drug-riddled and racially divided Army of the 1970s. Additionally, it shows the value of state-of-the-art weaponry and what a well-trained and equipped professional force can accomplish. The book also does an excellent job of outlining how the Army planned to transition the force and lessons learned from Desert Storm to the Army of the future. A careful and informed reading of Certain Victory will provide the reader with a view of the US Army that by 1990 knew a lot about ground combat. It was also an Army that realized you needed good people, well trained, with quality weapons and equipment to be successful on the modern battlefield. A must read for the officer wanting to understand where his Army is tending.

E-21. *George C. Marshall: Soldier-Statesman of the American Century.* Mark A. Stoler, Twayne Publishers, Boston, 1989. This fast-moving account summarizes the life and career of the foremost American soldier-diplomat of the twentieth century. He was born in a small town of an isolationist nation but took leading roles in an industrialized world power. He was trained as a nineteenth century citizen-soldier but commissioned in a twentieth century army of empire. Finally, he was the first soldier to receive the Nobel Peace Prize. In filling a series of high-level positions--Army chief of staff, special envoy to China, secretary of state and of defense--Marshall consistently acted as the dispassionate pragmatist, carefully weighing pluses and minuses to the ultimate benefit of his country. Repeatedly, Marshall mastered the nuances of congressional appropriations, coalition diplomacy, and fast-changing foreign policies as the Cold War overtook the wartime alliance, all the while retaining a fine sense of the limits of military power as well as an appreciation of the linkage between economic, military, and political issues. Marshall never let his ego get in the way of a job to be done, never confused his personal interests with those of his country.

E-22. Buffalo Soldiers *(Black Saber Chronicles)*. Tom Willard, Forge Press, New York, 1996. The stories of black cavalrymen fighting along side their white counterparts against the Plains Indians. Told through the eyes of Samuel Sharps, a young man saved from slavery, who will go on to become a sergeant major. This is the story of the all black unit nicknamed the "Buffalo Soldiers" by the Indians they fought. The book provides the reader with an appreciation of the hardships of war and frontier life and an important social commentary related to the Buffalo Soldiers as free men.

## OTHER BOOKS OF MILITARY INTEREST

E-23. *Platoon Leader.* James R. McDonough, Presidio Press, Novato, CA, 1985. This book is the story of one young lieutenant's growth during the year he fought in Vietnam. It is the story of the hard choices that a leader will have to face in combat. The author's main thesis is that war is a constant struggle between responsibilities of a leader and the desire to abandon your sense of humanity when faced with the gruesome reality of war. This book is a must for any professional soldier's reading list. The lessons that can be derived are as appropriate for the professional NCO as for the professional officer.

E-24. *Small Unit Leadership: A Commonsense Approach.* COL Dandridge M. Malone, Presidio Press, Novato, CA, 1983. Malone wrote this book in a way that most soldiers, especially leaders, can understand. It has real life stories from Vietnam. Everything is tied into the five-paragraph field order. His method is very much influenced by the behavioral science.

E-25. *The Red Badge of Courage: An Episode of the American Civil War.* Stephen Crane, W. W. Norton, New York, 1982. This book was the first unromanticized novel about the Civil War. Its heroes are not heroic soldiers, but civilians under arms, enduring the test of battle in wonder of fear. Crane describes his central character, Henry Fleming, as a youth whose mind is in the "tumult of agony and despair." This novel exposes the imagination and modern view of the ambiguities of the American character. The Red Badge of Courage has emerged as a bitter statement against the physical and psychological horrors of war.

E-26. *From Shield to Storm: High-Tech Weapons, Military Strategy, and Coalition Warfare in The Persian Gulf.* James F. Dunnigan, William Morrow, New York, 1992. Dunnigan explores the interests, motives, and miscalculations of both sides in Operation Desert Shield/Storm. He details how the immense operations that brought coalition forces into the desert were planned and executed, explains why the UN coalition's victory remains uncertain, and why what passes for peace in the Middle East will be only slightly less contentious than combat.

E-27. *None Died in Vain: The Saga of the American Civil War.* Robert Leckie, Harper Collins, New York, 1990. Based on solid scholarship and a lifetime of reading, and enhanced by the authors insight as a leading historian and his compelling narrative gift, *None Died in Vain* is crowded with in-depth profiles of fascinating and important Americans from North and South-soldiers and political leaders, heroes, and rogues. It covers grand strategy, politics, economics, and above all, the war's great battles from the siege and fall of Fort Sumter, the Union defeat at First Bull Run to the siege and fall of Petersburg, and Lee's moving surrender at Appomattox.

E-28. *A Moral Victory.* Sidney Axinn, Temple University Press, Philadelphia, 1989. Should a soldier ever disobey a direct military order? Are there restrictions on how we fight a war? What is meant by "military honor," and does it really affect the contemporary soldier? Is human dignity possible under battlefield conditions? Sidney Axinn considers these basic ethical questions within the context of the law of warfare and answers "yes" to each of these questions. In this study of the conduct of war, he examines actions that are honorable or dishonorable and provides the first full-length treatment of the military conventions from a philosophical point of view.

E-29. *To Hell and Back: The Audie Murphy Story.* Audie Murphy, Owl Books, New York, Reprint edition, 2002. America's most-decorated GI recounts his experiences in the foxholes and dugouts of World War II. It is a first hand story of the men who had only their friends and their weapons between them and the enemy. Told in simple and vital language, it is a human record that novelists, reporters, and generals haven't been able to touch. Joining his outfit in Africa, Murphy fought through campaigns in Sicily, Italy, France, and Germany. He emerged from the war as America's most decorated soldier.

E-30. *Brave Decisions: Moral Courage from the Revolutionary War to Desert Storm.* COL Harry J. Maihafer, Brassey's, Washington, DC, 1995. This book contains 15 stories of how American soldiers made brave and difficult decisions when faced with the choice of a courageous and ethical path or a safe, easier alternative. Included are Daniel Morgan at the Battle of Cowpens; Jackson at Chancellorsville; Pershing at Abbeville; and William F. Dean in Korea.

E-31. *The Story of the Noncommissioned Officer Corps: The Backbone Of The Army.* Arnold G. Fisch, Jr., Center of Military History, Washington, DC, 1989. Published during the 1989 Year of the NCO, this is the first major history of the US Army Noncommissioned Officer Corps. This book provides an overall history of the Corps including vignettes and stories of actual NCOs as well as selected documents related to the history and development of the Corps.

E-32. The United States Constitution. The Constitution is the document that our Nation is founded on, and is what every soldier promises to support and defend. The delegates to the Constitutional Convention wrote it in plain language in the late summer of 1787. It became effective 21 June 1788 when New Hampshire ratified it, the ninth state to do so. It describes the framework of the United States government, specifies powers granted to the government, and lists some of the individual rights of Americans. In

addition to the basic document are 27 amendments, including the Bill of Rights.

**Appendix F**

# Arms and Services of the Army

The Army's branches are broken down into three main categories: combat arms (CA), combat support (CS) and combat service support (CSS). There are various differences between the enlisted, officer, and warrant officer personnel management systems. This appendix highlights some of those differences.

You can find more information about the Army's occupational classification system in the following publications:
- AR 611-1, Military Occupational Classification Structure Development and Implementation.
- DA Pam 600-25, US Army Noncommissioned Officer Professional Development Guide.
- DA Pam 611-21, Military Occupational Classification and Structure.

## THE ENLISTED PERSONNEL MANAGEMENT SYSTEM AND CAREER MANAGEMENT

F-1. The management of enlisted soldiers, who represent the majority of the force, drives personnel readiness in all components of the Army. The Enlisted Personnel Management System (EPMS) is the total process that supports personnel readiness and the soldier's professional development and personal welfare. An eight-step life cycle process, EPMS includes structure, acquisition, individual training and education, distribution, deployment, sustainment, professional development, and separation.

- **Structure** is the basis underlying the personnel and all other Army functional areas. The Force Structure Allowance (FSA) restricts the total number of people (officers, enlisted and civilians) budgeted by the US Congress, and defines skills and grades.

- **Acquisition** (Accession) is the procuring of people to fill the Army's end strength requirements. Accessions include the recruitment of initial entry soldiers, reentry of prior service soldiers, and in-service recruiting of soldiers who leave the regular Army and enlist in the Army National Guard (ARNG) and the Army Reserve.

- **Individual training and education** is the identification of training criteria by career field, including required education and skills by rank and Military Occupational Specialty (MOS).

- **Distribution** is the allocation, assignment, and reassignment of individual soldiers, and, in some cases, small units throughout the Army. Distribution is based on priorities established by the senior Army leadership and the theater Commanders-in-Chief (CINCs).

- **Deployment** is the projection or movement of units and individuals to locations throughout the world based on Army requirements. While deployments normally mean deploying entire units, the Army does identify individuals and small cells of non-unit individuals to deploy on specific missions.

- **Sustainment** is the retention of soldiers within their component. This life cycle area involves functions such as reenlistment and the functions involved in the health and welfare of soldiers including pay, health care, morale and welfare services, promotions, and quality of life activities (family services and support).

- **Professional development** is the continuing education and training of individual soldiers to ensure the Army continues to train competent and capable leaders. These development functions include institutional training, self-development programs, and operational assignments that help soldiers develop their skills and knowledge.

- **Separation** is the discharge of soldiers from military control as a result of retirement, voluntary separation at the end of a term of service, or involuntary separation.

F-2.    The purpose of EPMS is to—

- Shape the enlisted force through developing and managing the inventory in accordance with Army needs.

- Distribute enlisted soldiers worldwide based on available inventory, Army requirements and priorities established by HQDA to meet the unit readiness needs of field commanders.

- Develop a professional enlisted force through programs that govern the training, career development, assignment, and the utilization of soldiers.

- Support the Army's personnel life cycle functions of acquisition, individual training, and education and distribution.

- Retain quality soldiers to maintain proper strength levels in all components of the Army force.

F-3.    Many factors continuously influence the environment in which EPMS operates. Policy comes from the Executive Branch, which acts through Department of Defense (DOD) and the Secretary of the Army. Policies are the guidelines used to access, train, professionally develop, promote, assign, and separate the enlisted force.

F-4. The annual defense budget has a major impact on the career development of enlisted soldiers. Funding limitations and allocations imposed by Congress affect the entire spectrum of enlisted personnel management, which includes force structure allowance of the enlisted force, accessions, strength management, promotion rates and pin-on-time, schooling, education programs, and permanent change of station (PCS) timing. The defense budget reflects the will of Congress to meet the perceived military threat as well as global and national economic challenges.

F-5. Each personnel proponent, generally a school commandant, has designed a career management field (CMF) based on Army requirements and supervises the development of the enlisted force within that CMF. Personnel proponents project future requirements for their CMFs and sustain or modify elements of force structure and inventory to meet future needs. Personnel proponents prescribe the requirements under the three pillars of leader development (institution training, operational assignments, and self-development) to attain qualification standards in each rank required by the enlisted force.

F-6. The Army and EPMS respond to individual needs of soldiers as well as to mission and requirements of the force. The enlisted force comes from American society. The force represents a reflection of that society and will span five decades of age groups. Career expectations, job satisfaction, discipline, leader abilities, educational abilities, and importance of family and cultural values vary widely among enlisted soldiers.

F-7. Besides the obvious advancement science and technology made in the Army's war fighting equipment, the quantum leap in information and decision-making demands of modern doctrine and warfare call for broader technological competence within most enlisted career fields. Complex and lethal weapons, joint and combined organizations, and global political and economic connectivity require the utmost competence in the enlisted force. NCOs receive progressive and sequential education, training, and experience through institutional training, operational assignments, and self-development to meet this requirement.

## THE COMPONENTS OF EPMS

F-8. The EPMS is an evolutionary system that balances the needs of the Army with the development requirements of the enlisted force. Modified by the environment, as well as force structure and leader development principles, the EPMS remains flexible and responds to proponents, commanders, and individuals to meet emerging needs. Three subsystems make up EPMS.

F-9. Strength management involves accessing, promoting, distributing, retaining, and transitioning soldiers to meet force structure requirements. These are complex activities, with soldiers in all MOSs continually moving through the personnel life cycle. Army force structure will continue to change as the Army's needs change, and enlisted strength requires active management to meet those needs defined by future force structure.

F-10. Evaluators are necessary for development feedback and are important tools for selection boards to identify NCOs with the most promising potential. The Army enlisted structure is similar to a pyramid, where the top contains fewer NCOs in relation to the wider base. Advancement to more responsible positions is based on assessments of performance and potential. The tools used to evaluate an individual's performance and potential are the Noncommissioned Officer Evaluation Report (NCOER) and the academic evaluation report (AER). Promotion, selection for school, retention in service, and career development opportunities, to include assignments, are strongly influenced by the information contained in NCOERs and AERs.

F-11. Career development requires that each personnel proponent determine the best mix of institutional training, self-development, and operational assignments needed for sustained development by soldiers at all ranks in each MOS. The development of the professional and technical skills of enlisted soldiers to meet the needs of the Army is accomplished through activities identified on proponent-designed professional development models (PDM) for each MOS. These PDMs combine the assignments, required schooling, and self-development goals that define branch-qualified soldiers in each rank by MOS. The models are based on Army requirements, indicating the numbers and types of enlisted soldiers to be accessed, retained, promoted, trained, and assigned. Career branches develop each soldier's career by using these templates while balancing Army requirements with policies for enlisted management.

F-12. The size of the enlisted force inventory is limited by the factors affecting EPMS. As requirements change over time, EPMS realigns the strength and professional development goals of each CMF to meet new challenges. As the strength and professional goals of the CMF change, soldiers may require additional training, or retraining, to be qualified in the realigned CMF.

## PROFESSIONAL DEVELOPMENT

F-13. The CMF is the center of EPMS and is necessary to meet changing requirements within the enlisted force. In simple terms, enlisted soldiers can complete their careers in a variety of assignments centered on their CMF developmental goals, such as TDA versus TOE units. One of the major objectives of EPMS is to professionally develop enlisted soldiers in their primary military occupational specialty (PMOS) and CMF through the combined efforts of the soldier, the proponent, the field commander, and the career branch managers of the Enlisted Personnel Management Division (EPMD). These combined efforts help the Army execute a total enlisted solder development program and this program includes the following:

- Development of skills and knowledge in soldiers' MOS through training and experience as they advance in rank and time in service. At each level, soldiers learn the necessary skills and demonstrate the potential for advancement to the next higher rank, culminating their career by serving at the senior NCO ranks of the Army.

- Professional development of enlisted soldiers including resident and nonresident instruction, on-the-job training, and self-development.

- EPMD assignment managers that use the proponent-designed leader development templates and professional development models in determining assignments to meet Army needs while enhancing a soldier's career development. Assignments may vary between troop and staff assignments.

- Unit commanders, senior NCOs, and career professional development NCOs at US Army Personnel Command (PERSCOM), State Area Commands or Regional Support Commands, that provide career development counseling and mentoring.

F-14. Enlisted soldiers may decide sometime during their career to change their MOS. Changing a PMOS is a major career decision and should be discussed thoroughly with unit leaders and managers of both MOS career branches involved so that soldiers make informed decisions. There may be a time or a need for enlisted soldiers to request a PMOS change, but the later in their career that they change their PMOS, the more difficult it is to compete for promotions and duty assignments. Enlisted soldiers may decide to change a PMOS for many reasons. They may have gained experience more compatible with another MOS, such as an infantryman gaining extensive experience as a maintenance NCO in an infantry battalion. They may not be able to meet their career aspirations within their current MOS.

F-15. Army Reserve and ARNG soldiers may consider changing their PMOS based on the availability of positions within their unit or geographical area or by changes in their unit's mission. You should fully understand all issues before making this major career decision. More information regarding MOS qualifications and prerequisites can be found on the PERSCOM website.

F-16. Soldiers, commanders, proponents, and EPMD all play an important part in the career development of enlisted soldiers and the enlisted force as a whole. Individual soldiers are ultimately their own best career managers. While Army requirements dictate the final outcome of all career development actions, including assignments, in most cases the enlisted soldier can participate in such decisions. Participation in the career development process is possible when enlisted soldiers reenlist or volunteer for training and education programs, complete assignment preferences, apply for entry into special programs such as drill sergeant, and recruiter, and plan long-range career goals.

F-17. Evaluation reports provide NCOs formal recognition for performance of duty, measurement of professional values and personal traits and, along with the performance-counseling checklist, are the basis for performance counseling by rating officials. Senior/subordinate communication is necessary to maintain high professional standards and is key to an effective evaluation system. The performance evaluation recorded on the NCOER is for a specific rating period only. It focuses on comparing the NCO's performance with duty position requirements, extra duties, and rater standards. The potential evaluation contained on the NCOER is used to assess the rated NCO's potential to meet increasing responsibilities in future assignments. The NCOER should include recommendations for schooling, promotion, and abilities to perform at her levels of responsibility.

F-18. Performance counseling provides the rater an opportunity to assess and assist a subordinate. If a rater identifies an area needing improvement, the rater is also tasked as the ratee's primary trainer to present and implement a training plan to bring the subordinate up to the standard. The NCO Evaluation Reporting System provides a natural stimulus for continuous two-way communication to ensure rated NCOs are aware of the specific nature of their duties. This includes changing mission requirements or focus and provides the NCO with the opportunity to participate in the counseling process. The rater uses the counseling sessions to give direction and to develop subordinates, to obtain information about the status and process of the organization and to systematically plan for accomplishing the mission. The senior/subordinate counseling session also facilitates communicating career development information, advice, and guidance to the rated NCO. This enables the NCO to take advantage of the rater's experience when making career decisions.

## THE ENLISTED CLASSIFICATION SYSTEM

F-19. The classification of positions for enlisted skills and enlisted personnel is based on qualifications. Also used are special qualification identifiers (SQI) and additional skill identifiers (ASI). The classification system impacts enlisted accessions, training, classification, evaluation, distribution, deployment, sustainment, and professional development. The classification system provides—

- Visible and logical career patterns for progression to successively higher level positions of responsibility and rank.
- Standard grade-skill level relationships.
- Self-sustainment through new accessions or selected lateral entry from other CMFs.
- Consolidations of MOS at higher ranks as practical.

### ENLISTED MILITARY OCCUPATIONAL SYSTEM

F-20. The CMF identifies a group of related MOSs that is basically self-renewing and managed in terms of both manpower and personnel considerations. The CMF is used in the development, counseling, and management of enlisted personnel. Characteristics of CMF are:

- The CMF provides a visible and logical progression from entry into the training base to retirement at the rank of CSM.
- The MOSs are so related that soldiers serving in one specialty potentially have the abilities and assignment in most or all of the other specialists in that field.

- The career content is supported by annual first-term accessions to replenish the losses from the career force of the field.

F-21. Table F-1 shows the Army's enlisted CMFs and where they fall into combat arms, combat support, and combat service support branches.

**Table F-1. Career Management Fields of the Army's Enlisted Soldiers**

| Combat Arms | Combat Support | Combat Service Support |
|---|---|---|
| 11 – Infantry | 21 – Engineer | 27 – Paralegal |
| 13 – Field Artillery | 25 – Communications & Information | 35 – Electronic Maintenance & |
| 14 – Air Defense | Systems Operations | Calibrations (del 0609) |
| Artillery | 31 – Signal Operations (del 0509) | 38 – Civil Affairs (RC) |
| 15 – Aviation | 31 – Military Police | 42 – Adjutant General |
| 18 – Special Forces | 33 – Electronic Warfare/Intercept | 44 – Financial Management |
| 19 – Armor | System Maintenance | 46 – Public Affairs |
| 21 – Engineer | 37 – Psychological Ops | 55 – Ammunition (del 0509) |
| | 74 – Chemical | 56 – Religious Support |
| | 88 – Transportation | 63 – Mechanical Maintenance |
| | 96 – Military Intelligence | 68 – Medical (add 0604) |
| | 98 – Signals Intelligence /Electronic | 71 – Administration (del 0509) |
| | Warfare Ops | 77 – Petroleum & Water |
| | | 79 – Recruitment & |
| | | Reenlistment |
| | | 89 – Ammunition |
| | | 91 – Medical (del 0709) |
| | | 92 – Supply & Services |
| | | 94 – Electronic Maintenance & |
| | | Calibrations |
| | | 97 – Bands (del 0409) |

F-22. Department of the Army Pamphlet 611-21, Part III, provides a career progression figure for each CMF that groups the MOS to reflect the routes for progression within and between the MOS. It also provides approved MOS substitution options and unique MOS qualifications (e.g. classification or training) where applicable. The MOS identifies a group of duty positions that requires closely related skills. A soldier qualified in one duty position in an MOS may, with adequate on-the-job training (OJT), perform in any of the other positions that are at the same level of complexity or difficulty. The MOS broadly identifies types of skill without regard to levels of skill.

## MILITARY OCCUPATIONAL SPECIALTY CODE

F-23. The military occupational specialty code (MOSC) provides more specific occupational identity than the MOS and is used to—

- Classify enlisted soldiers.

- Classify enlisted positions in requirement and authorization documents.

- Provide detailed occupational identity in records, orders, reports, management systems, and databases.

- A basis for training, evaluation, promotion, and other related management subsystems development.

# THE OFFICER CLASSIFICATION SYSTEM

F-24. The classification of positions requiring officer skills and personnel is based on qualifications. Skill identification (SI) codes are used to identify officer positions and personnel. The classification system supports the officer identifiers in DA Pam 611-21, Part I (includes the branches, functional areas (FAs), area of concentration (AOCs), reporting classifications, skills, and language identifiers and their related codes). The classification system is used to classify positions in requirements and authorization documents. Table F-2 shows the officer areas of concentration by branches in relation to combat arms, combat support, and combat service support.

Table F-2. Branches of the Army's Officers.

| Combat Arms | Combat Support | Combat Service Support |
|---|---|---|
| 11 – Infantry<br>13 – Field Artillery<br>14 – Air Defense<br>    Artillery<br>15 – Aviation<br>18 – Special Forces<br>19 – Armor<br>21 – Corps of Engineers | 25 – Signal Corps<br>31 – Military Police<br>35 – Military<br>    Intelligence<br>74 – Chemical | 38 – Civil Affairs (RC)<br>42 – Adjutant General Corps<br>44 – Finance Corps<br>67 – Medical Service Corps<br>88 – Transportation Corps<br>89 – Ammunition<br>91 – Ordnance<br>92 – Quartermaster Corps<br><br>**Special Branches:**<br>27 – Judge Advocate<br>    General's Corps<br>56 – Chaplain<br>60, 61, 62 – Medical Corps<br>63 – Dental Corps<br>64 – Veterinary Corps<br>65 – Army Medical Specialist<br>    Corps<br>66 – Army Nurse Corps |

F-25. Table F-3 shows other officer areas of concentration by functional area (FA).

### Table F-3. Area of Concentration by Functional Area.

| FA – AOC |
|---|
| 24 – Systems Engineering |
| 30 – Information Operations |
| 34 – Strategic Intelligence |
| 37 – Psychological Operations (add 0604) |
| 38 – Civil Affairs |
| 39 – Psycholgical Operations & Civil Affairs (del 0709) |
| 40 – Space Operations |
| 43 – Human Resource Management |
| 45 – Comptroller |
| 46 – Public Affairs |
| 47 – US Military Academy Stabilized Faculty |
| 48 – Foreign Area Officer |
| 49 – Operations Research/Systems Analysis (ORSA) |
| 50 – Force Development |
| 51 – Research, Development & Acquisition |
| 52 – Nuclear Research & Operations |
| 53 – Systems Automation Officer |
| 57 – Simulations Operations |
| 59 – Strategic Plans & Policy |
| 70 – Health Services |
| 71 – Laboratory Sciences |
| 72 – Preventive Medicine Sciences |
| 73 – Behavioral Sciences |
| 90 – Logistics |

## WARRANT OFFICER CLASSIFICATION SYSTEM

F-26. The classification system provides the policy for the warrant officer identifiers in DA Pam 611-21, Part II (includes the branches, AOC, MOS, SQI, and ASI used to classify positions in requirements and authorization documents). These data elements and their codes are combined as needed to describe position requirements according to the position classification structure. Positions are classified in Chapter 3 of DA Pam 611-1. Warrant officers are classified by the designation of branch, AOC, MOS skills and language identifiers as explained in DA Pam 611-21, Part II.

F-27. The principles of warrant officer management are for use in determining whether certain officer level positions, per appropriate regulations, should be designated for warrant officer incumbency. Such positions are those that predominately involve the direct supervision of performance of technical operations, administration, supply, and maintenance activities.

F-28. The warrant officer MOS system is an orderly structuring of codes authorized for the occupational classification of warrant officer positions and personnel. DA Pam 611-21 prescribes procedures and criteria for award of MOS to warrant officers. The MOS system is designed to support the

Army's recognized requirement for warrant officers as a necessary and distinct category of officer by—

- Establishing occupational standards for appointment, selection, training, and career development.
- Providing a basis to facilitate distribution and assignment.

F-29. Providing a framework to meet the demands imposed by technology requiring new occupations, commensurate with the concepts of warrant officer utilization.

F-30. Table F-4 shows the warrant officer branches within the combat arms, combat support, and combat service support branches. Warrant officers are classified by MOS, for example, Field Artillery Targeting Technicians are 131A. The first two digits of the MOS correspond to the warrant officer branch 13, for field artillery.

**Table F-4. Branches of the Army's Warrant Officers.**

| Combat Arms | Combat Support | Combat Service Support |
|---|---|---|
| 13 – Field Artillery<br>14 – Air Defense<br>   Artillery<br>15 – Aviation<br>18 – Special Forces | 21 – Corps of<br>   Engineers<br>25 – Signal Corps<br>31 – Military Police<br>35 – Military<br>   Intelligence | 27 – Judge Advocate<br>   General's Corps<br>42 – Adjutant General's Corps<br>60 – Medical Corps<br>64 – Veterinary Corps<br>67 – Medical Service Corps<br>88 – Transportation Corps<br>89 – Ammunition<br>91 – Ordnance<br>92 – Quartermaster Corps<br>94 – Electronic Maintenance |

F-31. Your branch works hard to ensure that you are informed with updates to your personnel management system and career management. The Army changes, combines, and adds various MOSs to reflect their needs in the branch areas of combat arms (CA), combat support (CS) and combat service support (CSS). All of the branches are equally important and depend on each other to successfully accomplish the peacetime and wartime mission. For additional information, visit PERSCOM Online, DA Pam 600-25, DA Pam 611-21, and AR 611-1. Be proud of your branch, your unit and your fellow soldiers.

# Source Notes

These are the sources quoted or paraphrased in this field manual, listed by page number. Where material appears in a paragraph, both the page and paragraph number is shown. **Boldface** indicates vignette titles. Unless otherwise indicated, vignettes about Medal of Honor recipients are based on the respective Medal of Honor citations.

Cover    US Army photo by Cleveland A. McKnight.

## Chapter 1—The Individual Soldier's Role in the Army

1-2.      Quotation by SMA Glen E. Morrell: "The Army as an Institution," *Sergeants' Business* (Mar-Apr 1987) 4.

1-3.      Quotation by General Douglas MacArthur: farewell speech given to the Corps of Cadets at West Point (USMA, 12 May 1962) US Military Academy Association of Graduates [Online] www.aog.usma.edu.

1-5.      Creed of the 272d Chemical Company, Massachusetts Army National Guard: 1SG Joseph P. Conlon, 272nd Chemical Company Drill Newsletter (Reading, MA, 2 May 2003).

1-6.      A soldier provides security: US Army photo by SGT Craig Zentkovich.

1-8.      Quotation by PV2 Jeremiah Arnold: Phil Tegtmeier, "NCOs deployed to SW Asia learn about being leaders," *The NCO Journal* (Spring 2002) 13.

1-10.     Quotation by Dr. Martin Luther King, Jr., Speech at the Great March on Detroit (Detroit, MI, 23 Jun 1963).

1-12.     Quotation by SSG David Santos: 1LT Jacqueline Guthrie, "Soldier Skills, Soldier Values," Soldiers Online (May 2000) [Online] www.army.mil/soldiers.

1-13.     **Private First Class Silvestre Santana Herrera in France:**    C. Douglas Sterner, "Silvestre Herrerra, Medal of Honor, WWII," Home of Heroes website, www.homeofheroes.com.

1-14.     Quotation by PFC Trent James David: Kate Walsh, "Another Veteran's Day at War," *The Public Spirit* (7 Nov 2002) [Online] www.ayerpublicspirit.com.

1-15.     Quotation by CSM Michael T. Hall: email message to the author.

1-16.   An NCO inspects his soldiers prior to assuming guard duty: photo courtesy of 340th Military Police Company, US Army Reserve, Jamaica, NY.

1-17.   Quotation by GEN George S. Patton, Jr.: George S. Patton, Jr., Third US Army Letter of Instruction No. 2, 3 Apr 1944, *War as I Knew It* (New York: Bantam Books, 1980) 377.

1-18.   Quotation by SGT Jack F. Holden: "The Role of the NCO in Our Changing Army." *Infantry* (Jul-Sep 1959) 62.

1-19.   Quotation by SMA William G. Bainbridge in *Top Sergeant: The Life and Times of SMA William G. Bainbridge* (New York: Fawcett-Columbine, 1995) 163.

1-20.   "The one question..." in *Manual for Noncommissioned Officers and Privates of Infantry of the Army of the United States* (Washington, DC: Government Printing Office, 1917) 149-150.

1-21.   **The Deployment** is based on an actual incident.

1-23.   Figure 1-1, Army Leadership Framework, image of "To Relieve Bastogne": Don Stivers, 1990, Don Stivers Publishing.

1-24.   Quotation by Napoleon Bonaparte: quoted by BG Fletcher M. Lamkin in "Academic Limits, the Teaching of PL 300, Military Leadership," US Military Academy Association of Graduates website (Sep-Oct 1998) [Online] www.aog.usma.edu.

1-25.   **A Better Way**: Quotation by Major (US Army, Ret.) Dale E. Wilson, Ph.D., "Patton, Eisenhower, and American Armor in the First World War," in Steven Weingartner, ed., *A Weekend With The Great War* (Wheaton, IL: The Cantigny First Division Foundation and White Mane Publishing Company, Inc., 1995/1996), 159-175.

1-27.   Convoy operations brief during Operation Iraqi Freedom: US Army photo by SGT Kyran V. Adams.

1-29.   **Ethical Dilemma—Checkpoint** is based on an actual incident.

1-30.   Figure 1-4, Ethical Reasoning Process: Chaplain (MAJ) Jeffrey L. Zust, "Ethics 102: The Ethical Land Navigation Model," *The NCO Journal* (Jan 2003) 27- 28.

1-31.   **Ethical Dilemma—Checkpoint (continued)** is based on an actual incident.

1-32.   **Ethical Dilemma—Guard Duty** is based on an actual incident.

1-33.   An NCO decides his team's next move along the Administrative Boundary Line in Kosovo: US Army photo by SGT Nathaniel Nelson.

1-33.   "When [a corporal] first receives...": BG August V. Kautz, *Customs of Service for Non-Commissioned Officers and Soldiers* (Philadelphia: J. B. Lippincott and Co., 1865) 104.

1-34.    Quotation by SGT Kerensa Hardy: "Remembering the basics makes for good leadership," *The Signal Online* (25 Oct 02) [Online] www.gordon.army.mil.

## Chapter 2—The Army and the Nation

2-2.     2-1. Section I, except where cited: Dr. David W. Hogan, Jr., *225 Years of Service, The US Army 1775-2000*, (Washington, DC: Center of Military History, 2000).

2-3.     **Crispus Attucks in the Boston Massacre**: "The Boston Massacre," Library of Congress' America's Library [Online] www.americaslibrary.gov.

2-4.     2-7. "shot heard 'round the world": Ralph Waldo Emerson, "Concord Hymn," sung at the ceremony marking the completion of the Concord Monument in Massachusetts, 4 Jul 1837.

2-4.     2-8. "Resolution of the Continental Congress in the Journals of Congress": Thursday, 15 Jun 1775, Center of Military History (CMH).

2-4.     "... The Whites of Their Eyes": National Guard Heritage Series [Online] www.ngb.army.mil/gallery/heritage (hereafter cited as NG Heritage).

2-5.     2-9- 2-11. Nathan Hale: Mary J. Ortner, Ph.D., "Captain Nathan Hale (1755-1776)," 2001, Connecticut Society of the Sons of the American Revolution [Online] www.ctssar.org.

2-5.     Quotation by Thomas Paine: *The American Crisis I* (Philadelphia, 1776).

2-6.     **The Marquis de Lafayette—Patron of Liberty**: Robert K. Wright, Jr., *The Continental Army* (CMH, 1983).

2-7.     Quotation by Colonel John Laurens: *Army Correspondence of Colonel John Laurens*, AmericanRevolution.org [Online] www.americanrevolution.org.

2-7.     Von Steuben Instructs Soldiers at Valley Forge, 1778: Edwin A. Abbey, "The Camp of the American Army at Valley Forge," photo courtesy of Pennsylvania Capitol Preservation Committee.

2-8.     2-20. Battle of Cowpens: *Historical Statements Concerning the Battle of Kings Mountain and the Battle of the Cowpens, South Carolina* (Washington, DC: Army War College, 1928); and "The Battle of Cowpens," NG Heritage.

2-9.     2-23. Legend has it that as British soldiers marched out of Yorktown, their bands played "The World Turned Upside Down," a tune known to British and American soldiers with varying lyrics.

2-10.    "The Road to Fallen Timbers": DA Poster 21-38, Center of Military History Art Collection (hereafter cited as CMH Art).

2-12.    2-35. Sergeant Patrick Gass' experiences: Elliott Coves, *History of the Expedition Under the Command of Lewis and Clark* (New York: Lithotype Printing Co., 1893) 104.

2-12.    2-38- 2-41. Battle of New Orleans: William A. Stofft et al, *American Military History* (CMH, 1989) (hereafter cited as *American Military History*) 145.

2-13.    2-43- 2-45. General Winfield Scott's Infantry Tactics: Ted Ballard, *Staff Ride Guide, Battle Of Ball's Bluff* (CMH, 2001) 56; and from *American Military History*, 155.

2-14.    2-48- 2-51. The Alamo: Stephen Hardin, "The Battle of the Alamo," Handbook of Texas Online, www.tsha.utexas.edu/handbook/online. Used with permission.

2-18.    **Antietam and Emancipation**: "Battlefield Information," National Park Service [Online] www.nps.gov/anti.

2-19.    **The First Medal of Honor Recipient**: Don Rivers, "William Pittenger, Medal of Honor Recipient," *Village News* (13 Aug 1998) Fallbrook Historical Society.

2-20.    **The 1st Minnesota at Gettysburg**: "July 2, 1863—'A most terrible day...' the bloodiest day of the battle," National Park Service [Online] www.nps.gov/gett.

2-21.    President Abraham Lincoln's letter to Mrs. Lydia Bixby: National Park Service [Online] www.nps.gov/liho/souvenir.htm.

2-22.    "The Surrender. General Lee meets General Grant at Appomattox": Keith Rocco, photo courtesy of the Appomattox Court House National Historical Park.

2-23.    **The 7th Cavalry at the Little Bighorn**: Dr. William G. Robertson et al, *Atlas of the Sioux Wars* (Fort Leavenworth, KS: Combat Studies Institute, 2003).

2-24.    "The Rough Riders": Mort Kunstler, courtesy of NG Heritage.

2-25.    **Private Augustus Walley in Cuba**: "Augustus Walley," 9th Memorial Cavalry [Online] www.9thcavalry.com; and the MOH citation for Private August Walley.

2-25.    2-82. Early Air Service history: "Evolution of the Department of the Air Force," Air Force History Support Office [Online] www.airforcehistory.hq.af.mil.

2-26.    2-83. Villa's raid on Columbus, New Mexico: Annual Report of the Secretary of War for the Fiscal Year, 1916, Vol. 1 (Washington, DC: War Department, 1916) 7–8.

2-27.    Quotation by Lieutenant Colonel Charles E. Stanton: speech at the grave of the Marquis de Lafayette (Paris, 4 Jul 1917).

2-28.    **Harlem Hellfighters**: Bob Rosenburgh, "WWI 'Harlem Hellfighter' nominated for medal," Army News Service (7 Feb 2001).

2-28.  2-91- 2-93. 3d Infantry Division and 28th Infantry Division in WWI:
"Rock of the Marne," CMH Art; and "Men of Iron," NG Heritage.

2-29.  **Sergeant Edward Greene at the Marne**: "Quartermaster Cooks—
History of Dedication," *Quartermaster Professional Bulletin*
(Summer 2002) [Online] www.quartermaster.army.mil.

2-30.  **Corporal Harold W. Roberts at Montrebeau Woods**: "Californians
and the Military, Corporal Harold W. Roberts, Medal Of Honor
Recipient," California Military Museum [Online]
www.militarymuseum.org.

2-31.  **The Unknown Soldier**: "This Week in Quartermaster History, 11-
17 November," US Army Quartermaster Corps Historian [Online]
www.qmmuseum.lee.army.mil.

2-33.  **Transformation in the 1920s**: Dr. Williamson Murray, "The Army's
Advanced Strategic Art Program," *Parameters* (Winter 2000-2001)
35.

2-33.  2-105. "The war to end all wars"is the title of a book by Edward M.
Coffman (New York: Oxford University Press, 1968).

2-35.  2-110. President Franklin D. Roosevelt coined the phrase "Arsenal
of Democracy" in his Fireside Chat radio address on national
security and the common cause (29 Dec 1940).

2-36.  Quotation by President Franklin D. Roosevelt: *The Army and You*
(Washington, DC: War Department, 1942) 7.

2-36.  Quotation by Ernie Pyle: *Brave Men* (New York: Henry Holt & Co.,
1944. Reprinted by Greenwood Press, 1974) 380.

2-37.  "Tip of the Avalanche": NG Heritage.

2-38.  2-120. US casualties on D-Day: Gordon A. Harrison, *Cross-Channel
Attack* (Washington, DC: Office of the Chief of Military History,
1951).

2-38.  **A Company, 116th Infantry on D-Day**: Stephen E. Ambrose, *D-
Day, June 6 1944: The Climactic Battle of World War II* (New
York: Touchstone Books, 1994) 328.

2-39.  **Krinkelt-Rocherath during the Battle of the Bulge**: Charles B.
MacDonald, *A Time for Trumpets: The Untold Story of the Battle
of the Bulge* (New York: Bantam Books, 1985) 386; and from the
MOH citation for Tech/4 Truman Kimbro.

2-40.  A squad leader of the 25th Infantry Division: US Army Signal
Corps photograph, Center of Military History Photograph
Collection (hereafter cited as CMH Photographs).

2-42.  2-129. Casualty estimates for an invasion of Japan: D.M.
Giangreco, "Casualty Projections for the US Invasions of Japan,
1945-1946: Planning And Policy Implications," *Journal of Military
History* (July 1997) 543.

2-42.    7th Infantry Division Band: photo from National Archives and Records Administration, John B. Wilson, *Maneuver and Firepower: The Evolution of Divisions and Separate Brigades* (CMH, 1998) 211.

2-43.    Constabulary unit equipment: US Army photo, William E. Stacy, *US Army Border Operations in Germany, 1945-1983* (Headquarters, US Army Europe and 7th Army, 1984) 21.

2-44.    **Task Force Smith**: Spencer Tucker, "Fact Sheet, Task Force Smith," United States of America Korean War Commemoration [Online] korea50.army.mil.

2-45.    Artillery Gun Crew: US Army Signal Corps photo, CMH photographs.

2-46.    **Chaplain Emil J. Kapaun in Korea**: Rodger R. Venzke, *The United States Army Chaplaincy 1945-1975* (Washington, DC: Office of the Chief of the Chaplains, 1977).

2-48.    **Landing Zone (LZ) X-Ray in the Ia Drang Valley**: LTG Harold Moore and Joe Galloway, *We Were Soldiers Once... And Young*, (New York: Random House, 1992).

2-49.    2-146- 2-148. Information on the Tet Offensive: "Named Campaigns–Vietnam," CMH [Online] www.army.mil/cmh-pg/reference/vncmp.htm.

2-50.    Quotation by President Ronald Reagan: transcript of "Vietnam: A Television History—Roots of a War (1945-1953)," Public Broadcasting System [Online] www.pbs.org.

2-51.    Soldier of 725th Ordnance Company: US Army photo by PFC Joshua Hutcheson.

2-53.    On the move during Operation Desert Storm: US Army photo.

2-54.    **Task Force Ranger**: MAJ Clifford E. Day, "Critical Analysis on the Defeat of Task Force Ranger," (Maxwell Air Force Base, AL: Air Command and Staff College, Mar 1997).

2-56.    Soldiers of 101st Airborne Division at Kandahar: US Army photo by SSG Alberto Betancourt.

2-57.    Soldiers from the 3rd Infantry Division: DOD photo by SGT Igor Paustovski, U.S.Army.

2-62.    Quotation by GEN Peter J. Schoomaker: quoted by CSM Michael Hall in an email message to the author.

2-63.    A Stryker Infantry Carrier Vehicle squad: US Army photo by CPT Timothy Beninato.

2-63     Quotation by SMA Jack L. Tilley in "A Talk with Sergeant Major of the Army Jack Tilley," *NCO Journal* (Winter 00-01) 15.

2-64.    Section III, except where indicated: Ben's Guide to the US Government [Online] bensguide.gpo.gov.

2-66.    "The liberties and heritage...": *The Noncom's Guide* (Chicago: The Military Service Publishing Company, 1957) 52.

2-73.    Quotation by then Secretary of the Army Thomas E. White: speech at the 124th NGAUS General Conference, 8 Sep 2002.

2-74.    Figure 2-4. Make up of The Army of One: data as of Oct 2001.

## Chapter 3—Duties, Responsibilities, and Authority of the Soldier

3-3.    Quotation by 1SG Isaac Guest: "Portrait of a First Sergeant," *Soldiers* (Aug 1979) 34.

3-6.    Quotation by Admiral Hyman G. Rickover: "History of the Navy Nuclear Power Program," Lesson 4 Instructor Guide (NS 402 Submarine Capstone Course, US Naval Academy) 2.

3-8.    Quotation by Colonel Louis de Maud'Huy: *Maneuver Theory* (Paris: Berger-Levrault, 1912) 13. Translation courtesy of former soldier John P. Geraci, Jr.

3-13.    **Making an On-the-Spot Correction** is based on an actual incident.

3-15.    Quotation by General of the Army Douglas MacArthur: Annual Report of the Chief of Staff, 1933, *The Greenhill Dictionary of Military Quotations*, edited by Peter G. Tsouras (London: Greenhill Books and Mechanicsburg,PA: Stackpole Books, 2000) (hereafter cited as Tsouras) 486.

3-21.    Quotation by SGT Henry Giles: *The G.I. Journal of Sergeant Giles*, edited by Janice Holt Giles (Boston: Houghton Mifflin, 1965) 4.

3-30.    Quotation by Senator Patrick Leahy, Chairman, Senate Judiciary Committee: "DOJ Oversight: Preserving Our Freedoms While Defending Against Terrorism," 6 Dec 2001.

3-31.    Quotation by GEN Colin L. Powell and CSM Robert F. Beach: "The Strength of the NCO Corps Is a National Strategic Asset," *Army* (Oct 1989) 48.

3-38.    Quotation by Stephen H. Ambrose: *Citizen Soldiers* (New York: Touchstone Books, 1998) 485.

3-39.    **Platoon Sergeant and Enlisted Soldier Relationship** is based on an actual incident.

3-40.    **Officer-Enlisted Gambling** is an example only.

## Chapter 4—Customs, Courtesies, and Traditions

4-1.    "Often, it is these customs...": R. Prasannan, "Colonial Hangover," *The Week* (28 Jan 2001) [Online] www.the-week.com

4-3.    **The Salute** vignette is based on an actual incident.

4-6.    **Parade Rest** vignette is based on an actual incident.

4-6.    Quotation by SMA Jack L. Tilley: SSG Marcia Triggs, "SMA Talks Pay, Education, War," Army News Service (23 Oct 2002).

4-9.    4-30. History of bugle calls: Rudi Williams, "Air Force Sergeant Traces Bugle's History," American Forces Press Service (8 Nov 2000).

4-13.    4-45. Quotation by General Maxwell D. Taylor: 101$^{st}$ Airborne Division's Eagle Values Education Program (May 2000) 32.

4-18.    "Each step of the ladder...": *The Noncom's Guide* (Chicago: Military Service Publishing Co., 1962) 40-41.

4-19.    Quotation by MSG Frank K. Nicolas: "Noncommissioned Officer," *Infantry* (Jan 1958) 78.

4-19.    4-53- 4-57. Janice E. McKenney, *Reflagging in the Army* (CMH, 1997) 3.

## Chapter 5—Training

5-2    Quotation by John F. Kennedy: President Kennedy's Inaugural Address, 20 Jan 1961.

5-2    Quotation by T. E. Lawrence: Tsouras, 232.

5-4    Quotation by Thucydides: Tsouras, 482.

5-5.    **The Best Machinegunner in the 101$^{st}$**: MG Russel L. Honoré, and MAJ Robert P. Cerjan, "Warrior Ethos, the Soul of an Infantryman," *News from the Front*, Center for Army Lessons Learned (CALL) (January-February 2002) (hereafter cited as Honoré), 7.

5-6.    "Gunners that can't...": *The Battalion Commander's Handbook 1991* (US Army War College) 50.

5-6.    Quotation by SMA Morrell: "As the SMA Sees It," *Army Trainer* (Fall 1984) 21, 24.

5-7.    Quotation by SMA Julius W. Gates: "From the SMA," *NCO Call* (May-Jun 1990) inside front cover.

5-12.    Quotation by Paul (Bear) Bryant: *Great Quotes from Great Leaders*, compiled by Peggy Anderson (Lombard, IL: Celebrating Excellence Publishing, 1995) 120.

5-13.    Hot Wash—An AAR at the Combat Maneuver Training Center: MSG Sieger Hartgers, "Hotwash," (CMH Art, 1995).

5-13.    "AARs are one of...": *Lessons Learned*, CALL (Oct 1989) 11.

5-18.    Building an individual fighting position: US Army photo by SPC Jacob Boyer.

5-23.    Quotation by BG James E. Simmons, Director of Army Safety: quated by LTC Mark Robinson in Risk Management presentation.

5-26. A military police soldier inspects a vehicle: photo by Denny Cox, *Sound Off,* Ft. Meade, MD, (4 Oct 2001).

5-28. **Khobar** is based on the author's experience at Khobar Towers in 1996.

5-30. **Rules of Engagement:** Honoré, 6.

## Chapter 6—Developmental Counseling and Professional Development

6-5. **Informal "Footlocker" Counseling** is based on an actual incident.

6-6. **Promotion Counseling** is based on an actual incident.

6-8. Quotation by GEN Peter J. Schoomaker: Eli Cohen and Noel Tichy "Operation-Leadership," *Fast Company* (Sep 1999) 278.

6-12. Quotation by MAJ Don T. Riley: "Serve Your Soldiers to Win," *Military Review* (Nov 1986) 12.

6-13. Quotation by MSG Frank K. Nicolas: "Noncommissioned Officer," *Infantry* (Jan 1958) 79.

6-20. Quotation by SPC Luis Feliciano: Brian MacQuarrie, "Reconnaissance Unit Ready to Scout Out Trouble," *Boston Globe* (18 Mar 2003) 27.

6-21. Reenlistment in Kandahar: US Army photo by SPC David Marck.

6-21. Quotation by Carl von Clausewitz: *On War,* edited by Michael Howard and Peter Paret (Princeton, NJ: Princeton University Press, 1976) 95.

## Chapter 7—Benefits of Service

7-15. **Medical Bills** is based on an actual incident.

7-19 7-74. Description of retirement systems: "Soldiers must Choose Retirement Option by March 1," Army News Service (12 Feb 2002).

7-28. Soldiers of 115th Military Police Company: US Army photo by SPC Robert Liddy.

7-30. Quotation by SGT Herbert E. Smith: "They Get Their Men," *US Army Recruiting News* (1 Sep 1928) 6.

7-36. Quotation by General John M. Keane: "On Health Care," Testimony before the Subcommittee on Personnel, Committee on Armed Services (2 Mar 2000).

## Appendix B—Army Programs

B-18. Quotation by General of the Army George C. Marshall: Tsouras, 69.

## Appendix C—Ceremonies

C-13.    Quotation by MG Robert Ivany: "Command Reflections—Values at Work," US Army War College (29 May 2003) [Online] www.carlisle.army.mil.

# Glossary

The glossary lists acronyms and abbreviations used in this manual. Army Regulation 310-50, *Authorized Abbreviations, Brevity Codes, and Acronyms* lists additional abbreviations and brevity codes.

| | |
|---|---|
| 1SG | First Sergeant |
| AAR | after-action review |
| AC | active component |
| ACES | Army Continuing Education System |
| ACAP | Army Career and Alumni Program |
| ACCP | Army Correspondence Course Program |
| ACS | Army Community Service |
| ACT | American College Test |
| ADT | active duty for training |
| AECP | Army Medical Department (AMEDD) Enlisted Commissioning Program |
| AEF | American Expeditionary Force |
| AER | Army Emergency Relief |
| AFAP | Army Family Action Plan |
| AIT | advanced individual training |
| AFTB | Army Family Team Building |
| AKO | Army Knowledge Online |
| AG | Adjutant General |
| AG | Army green |
| AGR | active guard and reserve |
| APFT | Army Physical Fitness Test |
| ANCOC | Advanced Noncommissioned Officers Course |
| AOC | area of concentration |
| AR | Army Regulation |
| ARCENT | Army Forces, Central Command |
| ARCOM | Army Commendation Medal |
| ARNG | Army National Guard |
| ARTEP | Army Training and Evaluation Program |
| ASAP | Army Substance Abuse Program |
| ASI | additional skill identifier |
| AT | annual training |
| AT | antiterrorism |
| ATNAA | antidote treatment, nerve agent, autoinjector |
| ATRRS | Army Training and Requirements Resource System |
| AWOL | absent without leave |
| BAH | basic allowance for housing |
| BARS | BNCOC Automated Reservation System |
| BAS | basic allowance for subsistence |
| BCT | basic combat training |
| BCT | Brigade Combat Team |
| BCTP | Battle Command Training Program |

| | |
|---|---|
| BDU | battle dress uniform |
| BEAR | Bonus Extension and Reenlistment |
| BNCOC | Basic Noncommissioned Officers Course |
| BOSS | Better Opportunities for Single Soldiers |
| BSB | base support battalion |
| BSC | Battle Staff Course |
| CA | combat arms |
| CAC | Combined Arms Center |
| CAFAP | Consumer Affairs and Financial Assistance Program |
| CALL | Center for Army Lessons Learned |
| CANA | convulsive antidote for nerve agent autoinjector |
| CCF | Communist Chinese Forces (Korean War) |
| CFNCO | command financial noncommissioned officer |
| CLEP | College Level Examination Program |
| CMF | Career Management Field |
| CMH | Center of Military History |
| COA | course of action |
| COL | Colonel |
| CONUS | continental United States |
| CPL | Corporal |
| CQ | charge of quarters |
| CS | combat support |
| CSM | Command Sergeant Major |
| CSMC | Command Sergeant Major Course |
| CSS | combat service support |
| CTA | common table of allowances |
| CTC | combat training center |
| CTT | Common Task Test |
| CW2 | Chief Warrant Officer 2 |
| DA | Department of the Army |
| DAC | Department of the Army civilian |
| DANTES | Defense Activity for Non-Traditional Education Support |
| DA PAM | Department of the Army Pamphlet |
| D-Day | execution date of any military operation |
| DEERS | Defense Enrollment Eligibility Reporting System |
| DEP | Delayed Entry Program |
| DFAS | Defense Finance and Accounting Service |
| DOD | Department of Defense |
| DOR | date of rank |
| DTP | Delayed Training Program |
| DUSTWUN | duty status-whereabouts unknown |
| DVA | Department of Veterans' Affairs |
| DWI | Driving while intoxicated |
| EEO | equal employment opportunity |
| EFMP | Exceptional Family Member Program |
| EO | equal opportunity |
| EPMS | Enlisted Personnel Management System |
| ETO | European Theater of Operations (World War II) |

| | |
|---|---|
| FAP | Family Advocacy Program |
| FPCON | force protection condition |
| FLEP | Funded Legal Education Program |
| FM | Field Manual |
| FMEAP | Family Member Employment Assistance Program |
| FORSCOM | Forces Command |
| FRAGO | fragmentary order |
| FRG | Family Readiness Group |
| FSC | First Sergeant Course |
| FTX | field training exercise |
| GEN | General |
| HMMWV | High Mobility Medium Wheeled Vehicle |
| HQDA | Headquarters, Department of the Army |
| IAW | in accordance with |
| ID | identification |
| IET | initial entry training |
| IMA | individual mobilization augmentee |
| IPFU | improved physical fitness uniform |
| IRR | Individual Ready Reserve |
| JER | Joint Ethics Regulation |
| JTR | Joint Travel Regulation |
| KIA | killed in action |
| LDP | Leader Development Program |
| LTG | Lieutenant General |
| LZ | landing zone |
| MACOM | Major Army Command |
| MCM | Manual for Courts Martial |
| MEDEVAC | medical evacuation |
| METL | mission essential task list |
| METT-TC | mission, enemy, terrain, troops, time and civilian considerations |
| MGIB | Montgomery GI Bill |
| MIA | missing in action |
| MILES | Multiple Integrated Laser Engagement System |
| MILPER | military personnel |
| MKT | mobile kitchen trailer |
| MOH | Medal of Honor |
| MOOTW | military operations other than war |
| MOS | military occupational specialty |
| MOSC | military occupational specialty code |
| MSG | Master Sergeant |
| MTOE | modification table of organization and equipment |
| MTF | military treatment facility |
| MTP | Mission Training Plan |
| MWR | Moral, Welfare, and Recreation |
| NATO | North Atlantic Treaty Organization |
| NBC | nuclear, biological, chemical |
| NCO | noncommissioned officer |

| | |
|---|---|
| NCOA | Noncommissioned Officer Academy |
| NCODP | Noncommissioned Officer Development Program |
| NCOER | Noncommissioned Officer Evaluation Report |
| NCOERS | Noncommissioned Officer Evaluation Reporting System |
| NCOES | Noncommissioned Officer Education System |
| NCOIC | noncommissioned officer in-charge |
| NCOPD | Noncommissioned Officer Professional Development |
| NG | National Guard |
| NKPA | North Korean People's Army |
| NMC | non-mission capable |
| NTC | National Training Center |
| OC | observer controller |
| OCOKA | observation, concealment, obstacles, key terrain, avenues of approach |
| OCONUS | outside the continental United States |
| ODCSOPS | Office of the Deputy Chief of Operations |
| ODSCPER | Office of the Deputy Chief of Staff Personnel |
| OHA | overseas housing allowance |
| OIC | officer in charge |
| OMPF | official military personnel file |
| OPFOR | opposing forces |
| OPLAN | operations plan |
| OPORD | operations order |
| OTH | other than honorable |
| P | needs practice in the task |
| (P) | promotable |
| PCC | pre-combat checks |
| PCI | pre-combat inspections |
| PCS | permanent change of station |
| PDF | Panamanian Defense Force |
| PDM | Professional Development Model |
| PERSCOM | Personnel Command |
| PFC | Private First Class |
| PIR | Parachute Infantry Regiment |
| PLDC | Primary Leadership Development Course |
| PLT | platoon |
| PMCS | Preventive Maintenance Checks and Services |
| PMOS | Primary Military Occupational Specialty |
| POV | privately owned vehicle |
| POW | prisoner of war |
| PRC | People's Republic of China |
| PSG | platoon sergeant |
| PT | physical training |
| PZ | pickup zone |
| QOL | quality of life |
| RAP | Relocation Assistance Program |
| RC | reserve component |
| REFORGER | Return of Forces to Germany |

| | |
|---|---|
| Ret. | retired |
| ROE | rules of engagement |
| ROK | Republic of Korea |
| ROTC | Reserve Officers Training Corps |
| RSOI | reception, staging, onward movement, and integration |
| RUF | rules on the use of force |
| SALT | size, activity, location, and time |
| SALUTE | size, activity, location, unit, time, and equipment |
| SAT | Scholastic Assessment Test |
| SATS | Standard Army Training System |
| SBP | Survivor Benefit Plan |
| SBCT | Stryker Brigade Combat Team |
| SFC | Sergeant First Class |
| SGLI | Servicemembers' Group Life Insurance |
| SGM | Sergeant Major |
| SGT | Sergeant |
| SMA | Sergeant Major of the Army |
| SMC | Sergeants Major Course |
| SMCT | Soldier's Manual of Common Tasks |
| SNA | Somali National Alliance |
| SOP | standing operating procedure |
| SPC | Specialist |
| SP/5 | Specialist 5$^{th}$ Class (E5) |
| SQI | skill qualification identifier |
| SRB | selective reenlistment bonus |
| SSG | Staff Sergeant |
| STARC | State Area Reserve Command |
| STP | Soldier Training Publication |
| STT | Sergeant's Time Training |
| STX | situational training exercise |
| T | trained in the task |
| TA | Tuition Assistance |
| TABE | Test of Adult Basic Education |
| TADSS | training aids, devices, simulators, and simulations |
| TAO | Transition Assistance Office |
| TAPES | Total Army Performance Evaluation System |
| TDY | temporary duty |
| Tech/4 | Technical Sergeant, 4$^{th}$ Class |
| T&EO | training and evaluation outline |
| TDP | TRICARE Dental Program |
| TF | task force |
| TIG | time in grade |
| TIOH | The Institute of Heraldry |
| TIS | time in service |
| TLP | troop leading procedures |
| TM | Technical Manual |
| TOE | table of organization and equipment |
| TOW | Tube Launched, Optically Tracked, Wire-Guided Missile |

| | |
|---|---|
| TPU | troop program unit |
| TRADOC | Training and Doctrine Command |
| TRICARE | Department of Defense regionally managed health care program |
| TRP | target reference point |
| TSC | TRICARE Service Center |
| TTP | tactics, techniques, and procedures |
| TUSA | Third United States Army |
| U | untrained in the task |
| UCMJ | Uniform Code of Military Justice |
| UN | United Nations |
| US | United States |
| USAAC | United States Army Air Corps |
| USAAF | United States Army Air Force |
| USAF | United States Air Force |
| USAR | United States Army Reserve |
| USASMA | United States Army Sergeants Major Academy |
| USC | United States Code |
| USMC | United States Marine Corps |
| USN | United States Navy |
| VA | Veterans' Administartion |
| VIP | very important person |
| WARNORD | warning order |
| WIA | wounded in action |
| WMD | weapons of mass destruction |
| WO1 | Warrant Officer 1 |
| WWI | World War 1 |
| WWII | World War 2 |

# Bibliography

These publications are sources for additional information on the topics in this Field Manual. The bibliography lists field manuals by new number followed by old number. Most Army administrative publications are available online at the Army Publishing Directorate website (www.usapa.army.mil). Most Army doctrinal publications are available online at the Reimer Digital Library website (www.adtdl.army.mil).

## Army Regulations (AR)

AR 27-1. *Judge Advocate Legal Services*. 30 Sep 1996.

AR 27-10. *Military Justice*. 6 Sep 2002.

AR 135-18. *The Active Guard and Reserve (AGR) Program*. 19 Jun 2003.

AR 140-111. *US Army Reserve Reenlistment Program*. 24 Jan 2003.

AR 140-158. *Enlisted Personnel Classification, Promotion, and Reduction (RC)*. 17 Dec 1997.

AR 210-50. *Housing Management*. 26 Feb 1999.

AR 310-25. *Dictionary of United States Army Terms*. 21 May 1986.

AR 350-1. *Army Training and Education*. 9 Apr 2003.

AR 385-10. *Army Safety Program*. 29 Feb 2000.

AR 525-13. *Antiterrorism*. 4 Jan 2002.

AR 600-8-1. *Army Casualty Operations/Assistance/Insurance*. 20 October 1994.

AR 600-8-8. *The Total Army Sponsorship Program*. 3 Apr 2002.

AR 600-8-10. *Leaves and Passes*. 1 Jul 1994.

AR 600-8-14. *Identification Cards for Members of the Uniformed Services, Their Eligible Family Members, and Other Eligible Personnel*. 20 Dec 2002.

AR 600-8-19. *Enlisted Promotions and Reductions*. 2 May 2003.

AR 600-8-22. *Military Awards*. 25 Feb 1995.

AR 600-8-29. *Officer Promotions*. 30 Nov 1994.

AR 600-9. *The Army Weight Control Program*. 10 June 1987.

AR 600-20. *Army Command Policy*. 13 May 2002.

AR 600-25. *Salutes, Honors, and Visits of Courtesy*. 1 Sep 1983.

AR 600-29. *Fund-Raising Within the Department of the Army*. 1 Jun 2001.

AR 600-85. *Army Substance Abuse Program (ASAP)*. 1 Oct 2001.

AR 600-89. *General Douglas MacArthur Leadership Award Program*. 16 May 2003.

AR 600-100. *Army Leadership*. 17 Sep 1993.

AR 608-75. *Exceptional Family Member Program*. 15 Oct 2002.

AR 614-200. *Enlisted Assignments and Utilization Management*. 30 Apr 2003.

AR 635-200. *Enlisted Personnel*. 26 Jan 1996.

AR 690-600. *Equal Employment Opportunity Discrimination Complaints*. 18 Sep 1989.

AR 690-950. *Career Management*. 18 Aug 1988.

## Department of the Army Pamphlets (DA Pam)

DA Pam 10-1. *Organization of the US Army*. 14 Jun 1994.

DA Pam 55-2. *It's Your Move*. 1 Jan 1994.

DA Pam 350-58. *Leader Development of America's Army*. 13 Oct 1994.

DA Pam 350-59. *Army Correspondence Course Program Catalog*. 1 Oct 2002.

DA Pam 385-1. *Small Unit Safety Officer/NCO Guide*. 29 Nov 2001.

DA Pam 600-3. *Commissioned Officer Development and Career Management*. 1 Oct 1998.

DA Pam 600-15. *Extremist Activities*. 1 Jun 2000.

DA Pam 600-25. *US Army Noncommissioned Officer Professional Development Guide*. 15 Oct 2002

DA Pam 600-35. *Relationships Between Soldiers of Different Ranks*. 21 Feb 2000.

DA Pam 690-400. *Total Army Performance Evaluation System (TAPES)*. 16 Aug 1998.

## Field Manuals (FM)

FM 1 (100-1). *The Army*. 14 Jun 1994.

FM 1-02 (101-5-1). *Operational Terms and Graphics*. 30 Sep 1997.

FM 1-04.10 (27-10). *The Law of Land Warfare*. 15 Jul 1976.

FM 1-04.14 (27-14). *Legal Guide for Soldiers*. 16 Apr 1991.

FM 3-0 (100-5). *Operations*. 14 Jun 2001.

FM 3-05.70 (21-31). *Survival*. 5 Jan 1992.

FM 3-07.2 (100-35). *Force Protection*.Initial Draft.

FM 3-19.30 (19-30). *Physical Security*. 8 Jan 2001.

FM 3-22.20 (21-20). *Physical Fitness Training*. 30 Sep 1992. Change 1, 1 Oct 1998.

FM 3-21.18 (21-18). *Foot Marches*. 1 Jun 1990.

FM 3-21.5 (22-5). *Drill and Ceremonies*. 7 Jul 2003.

FM 3-21.6 (22-6). *Guard Duty*. 17 Sep 1971. Change 1, 15 Jan 1975.

FM 3-21.75 (21-75). *Combat Skills of the Soldier*. 3 Aug 1984.

FM 3-22.9 (23-9). *Rifle Marksmanship, M16A1, M16A2/3, M16A4 and M4 Carbine*. 24 Apr 2003.

FM 3-25.26 (21-26). *Map Reading and Land Navigation*. 20 Jul 2001.

FM 3-25.150 (21-150). *Combatives*. 18 Jan 2002.

FM 3-97.11 (90-11). *Cold Weather Operations*. 12 Apr 1968.

FM 4-02.22 (22-51). *Leader's Manual for Combat Stress Control.* 29 Sep 1994.

FM 4-25.10 (21-10). *Field Hygiene and Sanitation.* 21 Jun 2000.

FM 4-25.11 (21-11). *First Aid.* 23 Dec 2002.

FM 5-0 (101-5). *Staff Organization and Operations.* 31 May 1997.

FM 5-19 (100-14). *Risk Management.* 23 Apr 1998.

FM 6-22 (22-100). *Army Leadership.* 31 Aug 1999.

FM 6-22.5. *Combat Stress.* 23 Jun 2000.

FM 7-0 (25-100). *Training the Force.* 22 Oct 2002.

FM 7-1 (25-101). *Battle Focused Training.* 6 Jun 2003.

FM 7-15. *Army Universal Task List (AUTL).* TBP.

FM 7-22.7. *The Army Noncommissioned Officer Guide.* 23 Dec 2002.

## Soldier Training Publications (STP)

STP 21-1-SMCT. *Soldier's Manual of Common Tasks, Skill Level 1.* 1 Apr 2003.

STP 21-24-SMCT. *Soldiers Manual of Common Tasks, Skill Levels 2-4.* 1 Apr 2003.

## Training Circulars (TC)

TC 21-3. *Soldier's Handbook for Individual Operations and Survival in Cold-Weather Areas.* 17 Mar 1986.

TC 21-7. *Personal Financial Readiness and Deployment Handbook.* 17 Nov 1997.

TC 25-20. *A Leader's Guide to After-Action Reviews.* 30 Sep 1993.

TC 90-1. *Training in Urban Operations.* 1 Apr 2002.

## US Army Training and Doctrine Command Publications

TRADOC Reg 351-10. *Institutional Leader Educational Training.* 1 May 1995.

## Miscellaneous Government Publications

MCM. *Manual for Courts Martial United States.* 2002.

## Internet Websites

US Army Publishing Agency, http://www.usapa.army.mil.

Army Doctrine and Training Digital Library, http://www.adtdl.army.mil.

# Index

Entries are listed with paragraph number unless otherwise indicated.

By order of the Secretary of the Army:

**PETER J. SCHOOMAKER**
*General, United States Army*
*Chief of Staff*

Official:

*Joel B. Hudson*

**JOEL B. HUDSON**
*Administrative Assistant to the*
*Secretary of the Army*
0400508

DISTRIBUTION:

*Active Army, Army National Guard, and US Army Reserve*: To be distributed in accordance with the initial distribution number 115908, requirements for FM 7-21.13.

# The Army Song

**Intro:**    March along, sing our song, with the Army of the free
Count the brave, count the true, who have fought to victory
We're the Army and proud of our name
We're the Army and proudly proclaim

**Verse:**    **First to fight for the right,**
**And to build the Nation's might,**
**And The Army Goes Rolling Along**
**Proud of all we have done,**
**Fighting till the battle's won,**
**And the Army Goes Rolling Along.**

**Refrain:**    **Then it's Hi! Hi! Hey!**
**The Army's on its way.**
**Count off the cadence loud and strong (TWO! THREE!)**
**For where e'er we go,**
**You will always know**
**That The Army Goes Rolling Along.**

**Verse:**    Valley Forge, Custer's ranks,
San Juan Hill and Patton's tanks,
And the Army went rolling along
Minute men, from the start,
Always fighting from the heart,
And the Army keeps rolling along.
(refrain)

**Verse:**    Men in rags, men who froze,
Still that Army met its foes,
And the Army went rolling along.
Faith in God, then we're right,
And we'll fight with all our might,
As the Army keeps rolling along.
(refrain)

The official Army song, "The Army Goes Rolling Along," was formally dedicated by the Secretary of the Army on Veterans Day, 11 November 1956, and officially announced on 12 December 1957. In addition to standing while the National Anthem is played, Army personnel stand at attention whenever the official song is played. Although there is no Department of the Army directive in this regard, all soldiers can encourage the tribute to the Army by standing at attention when the band plays "The Army Goes Rolling Along."

# The Soldiers Creed

**I am an American Soldier.**

**I am a Warrior and a member of a team. I serve the people of the United States and live the Army Values.**

**I will always place the mission first.**

**I will never accept defeat.**

**I will never quit.**

**I will never leave a fallen comrade.**

**I am disciplined, physically and mentally tough, trained and proficient in my warrior tasks and drills. I always maintain my arms, my equipment and myself.**

**I am an expert and I am a professional.**

**I stand ready to deploy, engage, and destroy the enemies of the United States of America in close combat.**

**I am a guardian of freedom and the American way of life.**

**I am an American Soldier.**

PIN: 081082-000

# DATE DUE

| | | | |
|---|---|---|---|
| | | | |
| | | | |
| | | | |
| | | | |
| | | | |
| | | | |
| | | | |
| | | | |
| | | | |
| | | | |
| | | | |
| | | | |
| | | | |
| | | | |
| | | | |
| | | | |
| | | | |
| | | | |
| | | | |
| | | | |

Demco, Inc. 38-293